Biochemistry; a Study of the Origin, Reactions, and Equilibria of Living Matter

BIOCHEMISTRY

BIOCHEMISTRY

A STUDY OF THE ORIGIN, REACTIONS,
AND EQUILIBRIA OF LIVING MATTER

BY

BENJAMIN MOORE

M.A., D.Sc., F.R.S.

WHITLEY PROFESSOR OF BIOCHEMISTRY, UNIVERSITY OF OXFORD

LONDON

EDWARD ARNOLD

1921

PREFACE

THIS book deals intensively with certain of the properties of living matter.

It is not meant to be a general textbook on the subject, but to give some prospect of the origin and reactions and balances of living matter.

Textbooks by the score already exist describing the details of the anatomy, so to speak, of living matter, but few treatises deal in a fundamental manner with the physiology, or work, of live things.

In all chemistry, and, indeed, in all biology, there exist these two sides, the structural and the functional, the anatomical and the physiological

The two aspects cannot by any means be divorced, for structure and function go hand in hand, and variations in structure precede and are impelled by variations in function. So evolution of the more complex from the more simple proceeded since first life appeared in the world.

It is, however, possible to decide for a school which branch it intends to study; and since the majority of schools in this country have chosen the anatomical side, to restore somewhat the balance, the school of Biochemistry at Oxford will choose the functional side.

The book is somewhat composite in character, but it is hoped that it will gain rather than lose interest on that account.

The two opening chapters were written before the experiments detailed in the six following chapters were carried out.

They have here been recorded as originally written, and the thoughts expressed in them led to the succeeding experiments, thus there are placed on record the evolution and progress of a research

The experiments are described almost verbatim from the Proceedings of the Royal Society, and my thanks are due to the Royal Society for permission to reprint.

This procedure has caused some repetition, but this may not be found tiresome; and as the book is intended for students

v

of Honours Schools and researchers, it may be of some living and historic interest to show how research bred in the mind, originated, and developed.

It is a pleasant duty to record my indebtedness to my colleague Mr. Edward Whitley and to many others who have so ably collaborated in these inquiries

The remaining chapters are re-edited from my contributions to "Recent Advances in Physiology" and "Further Advances in Physiology," edited by Dr. Leonard Hill, F.R.S , the former of which is now out of print.

BENJAMIN MOORE

LABORATORY OF BIOCHEMISTRY,
 THE UNIVERSITY,
  OXFORD
   January 14, 1921.

CONTENTS

BIOCHEMISTRY

CHAPTER I

BIOTIC STRUCTURE AND BIOTIC ENERGY

BIOCHEMISTRY may be defined as the study of the chemical substances produced by *biotic* energy—that is, the energy of life—in the bodies of living plants and animals, and the further study of the energy processes by which such substances are elaborated and used subsequently to their production for carrying on the life of the cell.

While it may be true that the living cell and its energy exchanges are rigorously subject to physical and chemical laws, it is also true that such structures as obtain in living matter are nowhere in nature found reduplicated save in living matter, and this peculiarly constructed living matter is inhabited by a type of energy bound to living matter, and not producible in its absence.

This type of energy, the machine or transformer which produces it, and the chemical substances manufactured in the course of the operations, form together the field for the study of biochemistry.

Our knowledge of the subject is still in its infancy, and much remains to be discovered, so that any presentation must be fragmentary; yet in spite of this the wealth of detail in known parts of the subject is already so great that a selection becomes necessary to illustrate a general review of the subject.

The mystery which surrounds the processes of life, like the mist on mountain-tops, leaves room for speculation and imagination, and enhances the charm and beauty of a present-day study of this young and vigorous branch of modern science

Viewed from the physico-chemical point of view, the living cell is a peculiarly constructed energy machine or energy transformer, through which a continual flux of energy ceaselessly goes on, and the whole life of the cell is an expression of variations and alternations in the rates of flow of energy, and of changes in the equilibria or balances between various types of energy.

Like all other energy discharges, life as a whole is phasic or oscillatory in character. In the organic world the phases or

1

alternations are usually much slower than those commonly dealt with in the world of inorganic physics and chemistry As long as life lasts there is no complete cessation in the flow of energy; but always in all living things there are alternating periods of activity and repose, of waking and sleeping, of action and reaction, of freshness and of fatigue.

These slower and more prolonged periods of oscillation are characteristic of life. In the inorganic world, either the phases are infinitely shorter, as in the various forms of radiant energy, or, on the other hand, the phases in some instances may be of so vast duration that we never see the swing of the pendulum, and are prone to come to the conclusion, probably quite erroneously, that the process must run irreversibly in one direction for ever. For example, the physicist supposes that all forms of energy in the Universe are moving in one direction—namely, into heat energy— and towards an equal distribution of heat potential—that is, temperature—throughout the entire space. Now, if we judge by analogy, this can only represent a movement of the energy flux in one direction, an oscillation which is so long in its duration as to appear infinite to us mortals. When all the temperatures have become equal, then may come the reversal, and all the energy move- ments, slowly at first, but ever quickening, may move in the opposite direction, and then there would be a new type of life in the Universe regulated by conditions now unknown to us.

Returning to the peculiar energy discharges of that singular energy transformer called a living cell, it may be pointed out that, in its varying phases of activity and rest, the machine is always in equilibrium, although, to maintain this, it may be working from time to time at a faster or slower rate. The index of equilibrium is set higher or lower, but there always is an index or equilibrium point. Also, there are maximum and minimum points; there is a rate above which the machine cannot be driven without breakdown, and also, unlike inorganic transformers, there is a rate below which it cannot work without such alterations in the living machine as lead to disruption and death

In the complex, co-ordinated animal there is protection against overdriving or underdriving by a most elaborate system of defences, especially in those tissues responsible for the fundamental processes of respiration and circulation of the blood If either the heart stopped beating, so that fresh blood did not reach the tissue cells, or the lungs stopped working so that the blood sent round by the heart contained no oxygen when it arrived at the tissues, then, the necessary oxygen to oxidise the chemical substances and set energy free from them for the work of the cell not being forthcoming, the operations of the cell must abruptly come to a close.

Such a catastrophe is averted by the minute chemical and colloidal structure of the master cells of cardiac and nervous tissues which regulate these fundamental vital processes. The colloidal matter of these cells is so constituted chemically that they are made oscillating or rhythmic in their discharges, and hence cannot become fatigued or overdriven. The two rhythms of respiration and heart-beat bear normally the ratio in their frequency of one to four or one to five—that is to say, there are four to five heart-beats to each respiration. And as the two processes possess the combined and complementary function of sending round an adequate supply of sufficiently oxygenated blood to the tissues this ratio is usually well maintained and the two rates go up or down together. It has been shown by Haldane and Priestley that the rate of working of these two fundamental systems is dependent upon a very simple chemical circumstance—viz., the amount of the chief gaseous product of combustion which is for the moment present in the lung spaces. If the amount of carbon dioxide in the air spaces of the lungs rises then the rates of heart-beat and respiration increase so as to get rid of it, and if the amount falls below normal the heart-beat and breathing become slower and more quiescent. This is the fundamental, primary thing which explains many different secondary causes in the way of varying tissue activity leading invariably through carbon-dioxide variations to varied rates of working of the blood and air pumps.

When we trace back the chemical bearings of this regulation, we see that variation in amount of carbon dioxide in the air of the lungs means variation in the amount dissolved in the blood, and this again variation in the osmotic pressure of carbon dioxide in the nerve cells and heart cells. But it is now well known, as was first clearly shown by A. D. Waller for nerve and muscle, that the first effect upon *all* living cells, and hence on both the nerve cell and its processes and the heart cells, of *slight* excess of carbon dioxide is to stimulate to increased activity. Later, if the increased amount of carbon dioxide be pushed further the effect is gradually to still all cellular activity. This, for example, is precisely what happens in suffocation : after a period of violent struggling, with exaggerated attempts to breathe and rapid hammering of the heart, there comes sleep, lethargy, and death.

Within physiological limits there is a delicate chemical equipoise of these fundamental processes of circulation and respiration. And this is but an example of a general labile balance of colloids favourable to chemical reaction which everywhere obtains in those substances which constitute living matter. The oxygen balance is only a particular case of that which holds also for nutrient materials in general and for the thousand and one products of the living cell's own activity or that of neighbouring cells.

We may conveniently turn aside here to deal with a very general aspect of the life of certain tissues which has excited in the past endless work and wonder amongst physiologists—namely, that it is impossible to induce fatigue in those processes of nerve cells which we call nerve fibres.

It is obvious from what has been written above that fatigue of a complete character, lasting even for two or three minutes in the case of the cardiac muscle or of those nerve cells and processes which govern the respiratory movements, would inevitably lead to death. The chance of this is obviated by means of the colloidal properties of those proteins which build up the cardiac muscle and nerve cells. The structure of these substances is so arranged that they possess a definite rhythm or reactivity of their own, which can only be interfered with to a certain degree, but cannot be entirely obliterated by outside interference or stimulation After each period of chemical activity in heart muscle or respiratory nerve cell there is an interval called the " refractory period," during which no amount of stimulation will cause a fresh discharge of energy in the shape of a muscular contraction in the one case or a nervous impulse down to the respiratory muscles in the other case. During each period of rest there is a slow return to the initial condition in labile balance of the colloids of the protoplasm. It is not until this return or rearrangement is completed that another discharge followed by another rearrangement can occur. .

The details of the chemistry of the discharge and subsequent return to initial positions following it are at present unknown to us, but we do know experimentally enough of the primary factors involved to show that the above is a substantially correct representation of what occurs in each cycle. For example, the effects of variations in osmotic pressure of carbon dioxide within the cell above described show that this substance is one of the important factors in the above discharge and rearrangement, the speed of which varies with the carbon-dioxide pressure. But whether the carbon dioxide accumulates in combination with the proteins during the discharge, and then has to be disentangled and given off during the pause, or, conversely, whether carbon dioxide accumulates, attaching itself to the colloidal proteins during the pause, and then is suddenly and explosively thrown off during the discharge, is somewhat difficult to determine. The fact, however, that slightly increased pressure of carbon dioxide hastens the rhythm of explosion and recovery, while diminished pressure slows the rhythm, would seem to indicate that irritation is heaped up to discharging point as carbon dioxide accumulates in union with protein, and that at the explosion carbon dioxide is set free.

Again, the presence in sufficient concentration of certain inorganic ions, such as those of potassium, calcium and phosphates, is absolutely essential to the regular discharge of the cardiac cycle, with due alternations of the two phases of rest and activity.

It can be shown experimentally, by varying the osmotic pressure of each of the above ions in the circulating fluid supplied to an isolated and perfused heart, that characteristic variations occur in each case in the rate and force of the heart-beat, and in the form of the time relations of contraction and relaxation as shown by the shape of the curve of the heart-beat.

These effects were first worked out experimentally by Sidney Ringer, and have now been shown to be of widespread application for all types of cells possessing, as nearly all cells do, the tendency towards a rhythmic discharge.

A mechanical analogy may illustrate the vibrating equilibrium of these poised chemical factors in the living cell. Let us consider the mechanical system composed of the mainspring of a watch and its train of wheels leading to the oscillating balance wheel and its hair-spring, and compare this with the beating of the mammalian heart. The balance wheel with its tiny hair-spring may represent the cardiac muscle, and the mechanical pressure giving energy from the mainspring represents the nutritive supply of chemical energy sent in for the heart-beat by the blood plasma and oxygen. Now the rate of vibration in the watch is regulated by the weight or inertia of the balance wheel and the reaction of the hair-spring. Two similar factors regulate the heart-beat—viz , the nature of the colloidal combinations intrinsically present in the heart protoplasm, and the osmotic pressure of the products of chemical reaction occurring in each discharge Just as tightening or slackening the hair-spring will quicken or slow the beat of the watch, so increasing or diminishing carbon-dioxide pressure will quicken or slow the heart-beat. Again, more permanent chemical combinations such as those of products of fatigue, anæsthetics, or cardiac drugs with heart proteins, will alter heart rhythm in a way more comparable to change in weight of the balance wheel. In both cases it is to be specially observed that the mechanism is only capable of bearing interference from outside within well-defined limits. Thus, pursuing our mechanical analogy a little farther, it may be pointed out that if we pull the hair-spring a little too tight, instead of causing the watch to tick faster and faster we only succeed in stopping it altogether, and contrariwise, by giving greater and greater length of slacker spring, we again simply cause stoppage. So also in the case of the heart, stimulants or sedatives carried beyond certain limits interrupt the most delicately balanced oscillating equipoise.

This law of a working interval with a minimum and maximum not very widely apart runs through the whole realm of organic nature, both animal and vegetable, and always it is found that excess is as poisonous and deadly as defect of any essential constituent in the interaction.

Great wealth and great poverty are as dangerous to the living cell as to the body politic of a civilised community, and the cell, and the animal composed of cells, lives best and healthiest when it is possessed of neither poverty nor riches, but endowed with a comfortable competence for which it yields its due meed of labour.

This great law is seen in operation in the case of the process of oxidation to choose the most general biochemical example seen in all living protoplasm from the unicellular organism up to man. Absence of oxygen, or oxygen starvation, kills ; but excess is no less fatal : breathing is only possible between well-marked limits, and health and well-being between much narrower limits still Excess of oxygen as truly asphyxiates as does its defect. Also, in the great converse process of organic nature proceeding upon such a gigantic scale all over the green earth, in the building up from inorganic carbon dioxide by means of the sun's energy of the total food of the world, this law is seen in operation. That same carbon dioxide, which is essential to the very existence of the green plant, becomes, at a somewhat higher concentration, a deadly poison to it.

What is the chemical significance of this great fundamental law of balanced concentrations ?

Simply this, that the colloids forming the active centres or mechanisms of living matter, in order to carry out their operations and exchanges, must exist in a delicately balanced mobile equilibrium with the substances upon which they are operating. When such substances become present in too high concentration, the unions with the colloid under the influence of the pressure become too firmly and tightly held ; and conversely if the osmotic pressure, or concentration in solution, is too low, the colloids can no longer keep hold of them in sufficient amount, and they are lost by diffusing out into the surrounding fluids. Between these two limits only lies the working viable range.

In such a delicately balanced system of crystalloid and colloid in labile union with one another, it is obvious that very slight interference by imported energy from outside will, or may, induce profound alterations, and the discharge of energy within the cell under such conditions may be incomparably greater than the inducing energy which may act as a crystal added to a supercooled solution or a spark or detonator applied to an explosive.

It is in such a way that nerve impulses act, and hormones, enzymes, and cell-excitants generally induce their effects, so as to set in more violent motion a system which is balanced, or at rest, or, contrariwise, to still it from activity into repose.

Fatigue is a natural example of the retarding influence of the accumulation of the waste products of activity, and this fatigue may either be slowly recovered from or the waste products as they accumulate may give rise to an explosive discharge of activity in which they are removed, and the phase of activity replaces that of momentary fatigue.

This more momentary fatigue leads to rhythmic activity, while the more permanent fatigue leads to the many times slower rhythm which we ordinarily speak of as fatigue and recuperation.

The underlying chemical factor differentiating the two forms of rhythmic activity is the structure of the colloidal molecules or aggregates at play in the different forms of tissue, and it is the presence of the more rapid rhythm in cardiac muscle and nerve fibre which renders these tissues infatigable, or indefatigable, in the ordinary sense of the word; while skeletal muscle lacking, under normal conditions, the more rapid rhythm can be fatigued

Between each beat the cardiac muscle passes rapidly through its period of fatigue and recuperation   After each contraction its structure is so changed that it is completely fatigued and so cannot again be stimulated and kept at chemical work till this phase passes over, then there follows another cycle of exactly similar form.   But each charge and discharge is complete in itself, and there can be no accumulation of waste products   Skeletal muscle, on the other hand, loses its waste products more slowly and does not at once become saturated with them , a slight accumulation does not cause it to become inactive and relax, and it can have a second stimulus, causing a second or continued contraction to be imposed upon the first. This leads to continued chemical activity and a continued accumulation of waste products similar to what is termed in therapeutics the cumulative effect of a drug.   The final result is stoppage of activity, and that more prolonged period of inaction or diminished activity ensues which we call fatigue of voluntary muscle.

It is curious that it does not appear to have occurred to those who have experimented upon the infatigability of nerve fibres, that this physiologically essential property is due to the nerve fibre possessing a rhythm which is very rapid, so that nerve fibre is never continuously active, but merely transmits short waves of activity with incomparably longer periods of repose between them in which there is a phase of fatigue and recuperation, just as in the case above described of cardiac muscle

It does not by any means follow that because what is commonly called a tetanising current, from its effects upon muscle, is being applied to a nerve, the nerve processes are thereby being tetanised or thrown into continuous activity.   The muscle attached may be in continuous activity, and yet the material of the nerve may be enjoying its regular periods of rest and recuperation between each stimulus just like a beating heart, and, for this reason, like the heart, be incapable of ordinary fatigue.   Consideration of the known results of experimental work upon the nerve impulse due to a single stimulus shows that this is the true state of affairs   The electrical variation which we may take as a true index of the duration of the chemical activity of the nerve fibre has been shown to pass over any given cross-section of the nerve in an almost infinitesimal part of a second, in something like $\frac{1}{10000}$ second.   Now suppose the nerve is being stimulated in the usual manner from an ordinary induction machine giving 100 interruptions a minute, then there will be 100 nerve impulses passing in each minute, and the period of activity belonging to each being approximately $\frac{1}{10000}$ second, it follows that the nerve tissue is active for $\frac{100}{10000}$ of its time, and resting or recuperating for $\frac{9900}{10000}$ of its time. That is to say, for 1 per cent. of working time there is 99 per cent. of resting time. Why, under such conditions, should the nerve become fatigued even if it be stimulated for hours ?

The effects of increasing the rapidity of the exciting discharges also show that the above is the true explanation of the enigma of the infatigability of nerve. As the rate of stimulation is made greater and greater, the strength of the individual stimuli must be enormously increased in order to get the threshold effect of commencing response in the attached muscle. Further, as the limit of 10,000 stimuli per second is reached, the nerve material ceases to respond to the excitation, and becomes quiescent even to maximal stimuli. It is for this reason that Tesla could show that with a smooth, rapidly alternating current even of high voltage lamps can be lit up with people's bodies forming part of the circuit, without the subjects of experiment being even conscious directly of the passage of the current through their bodies. Here the rate of oscillation is above the sympathetic point for the oscillation of the crystallo-colloids which form the protoplasm of the tissue, and hence they no longer excite it, any more than the ultra-violet rays affect the crystallo-colloids of the retinal cells. Every living physiological machine or cell possesses its distinctive colloids, and hence its specific rate of oscillatory activity.

The views and experiments of Macdonald in regard to the causation of the nervous impulse are here of great interest. This observer has shown that during activity of nervous tissues there is a detachment of certain crystalloids from the active portion of tissue which continues only so long as activity lasts, and in the period of resting is followed by recombination. Macdonald refers to the well-known effects of electrolytes in altering state of aggregation, etc., and bases his views of nervous activity upon such recurring combination and dissociation between the active chemical components of the tissue.

Similar effects in regard to variation in distribution of electrolytes accompanying variations in tissue activity have been experimentally obtained by A. B. Macallum.

The necessity of electrolytes for the possession of osmotic energy by colloids has been shown by the writer, and by Roaf and Adamson and others, and it appears as if the trend of modern work upon the chemistry of colloids was moving towards the view that the attached crystalloid governs the activity of the colloid, and that the two together constituting the crystallo-colloid make a working pair possessing phasic alterations in association and dissociation, with accompanying varying activities and affinities which lie deep at the base of the peculiar energy discharges of living matter.

The phasic properties and peculiar energy content of colloids are drawn attention to by that pioneer and master-worker on colloids, Thomas Graham, in his classical papers published in 1864 in the Transactions and Proceedings of the Royal Society, which may be said to have laid the foundation of the study of colloids.

Even at that early date Graham had realised the importance to the physiologist of the study of the properties of colloids which, as he says, form the active part of all living cells. He draws special attention to the important deductions to be drawn from his replacement of water in the colloidal form of silicic acid by organic bodies, and states, in 1864, that fat might be carried in the tissues in invisible, apparently soluble form in union with the colloidal proteins. Just now this constitutes one of the lines of modern research, and Graham's chance shot is being verified in a wonderful and remarkable manner.

Graham also draws attention to the striking similarity of the action of slight amounts of alkali in dissolving gelatinised or pectised colloids, such as colloidal silicic acid, and that of ferments upon coagulated proteins, and actually calls this process of solution "peptisation" on account of this resemblance The colloid after solution still remains in colloidal condition, as shown by the fact that the necessary amount of alkali to give a clear peptised solution is only a small fraction of that which would be required to yield a mono-molecular solution of crystalloidal silicate Here the colloid evidently passes into solution because of some kind of molecular union with the crystalloid. And each solution aggregate in the peptised solution probably consists of one active crystalloidal molecule surrounded by and attached by molecular union to several colloidal molecules.

The fact that colloidal molecules in solution possess a peculiar energy of their own was also appreciated by Graham, who remarks :

" Their peculiar physical aggregation with the chemical indifference referred to appears to be required in substances that can intervene in the organic processes of life. The plastic elements of the animal body are found in this class. As gelatin appears to be its type, it is proposed to designate substances of the class as *colloids*, and to speak of their peculiar form of aggregation as the *colloidal condition of matter*. Opposed to the colloidal is the crystalloidal condition. Substances affecting the latter form will be classed as crystalloids. The distinction is no doubt one of intimate molecular constitution.

" Although chemically inert in the ordinary sense, colloids possess a compensating activity of their own, arising out of their physical properties. While the rigidity of the crystalline structure shuts out external impressions, the softness of the gelatinous colloid partakes of fluidity, and enables the colloid to become a medium for liquid diffusion, like water itself.

" Another and eminently characteristic quality of colloids is their mutability. Their existence is a continued metastasis. A colloid may be compared in this respect to water, while existing liquid at a temperature under its usual freezing-point, or to a supersaturated saline solution. Fluid colloids appear to have always a pectous modification, and they often pass under the slightest influences from the first into the second condition.

" The colloidal is, in fact, a dynamical state of matter, the crystalloidal being the statical condition. The colloid possesses Energia. It may be looked upon as the probable primary source of the force appearing in the phenomena of vitality. To the gradual manner in which colloidal changes take place (for they always demand time as an element) may the characteristic protraction of chemico-organic changes also be referred."

The importance of these slow energy changes in colloids referred to in these words by Graham about fifty years ago, and the capability of their alteration in direction and travelling in new directions on account of small changes in the crystalloidal environment, so giving rise to phasic variations in the energy processes of the living cell, are only now receiving somewhat tardily that attention and further study which they so richly deserve. Many of the hidden wonders of cell life undoubtedly are clustered around the relationship of colloid and crystalloid. Variations in minute detail of colloidal arrangement in itself and in relationship to dissolved pabulum in the shape of organic and inorganic crystalloids lie at the root of the varying activities of the cells, and of all physiological and pathological changes.

We may now pass briefly in review some important instances of these slower variations in colloidal condition which give rise to phasic or intermittent discharges of energy as outlined above.

In the first instance, it may be pointed out that these changes in character of colloidal solution requiring considerable intervals of time for their evolution are not confined to colloids forming part of living cells, although there they reach their acme of complication combined with delicacy of balance and a perfect cosmos of co-ordination. For Graham has shown that the possession of energy and slow change are characteristic of inorganic colloids, and recently Moore and Roaf have shown that organic colloids such as gelatine solutions possess a kind of *hysteresis*, as a result of which they only respond slowly to changes in external energy conditions, so that a change may go on for days before coming to rest.

For example, heating a 10 per cent. solution of gelatine up to 70° to 80° C. for a short time causes a partial splitting up of the solution aggregates, accompanied by a considerable rise in osmotic pressure, as directly recorded in the osmometer. If, now, the solution be allowed to cool to a little above its gealing-point, say to 40°C., then, instead of the osmometric pressure dropping back in an hour or two, as it would from a mere temperature change by means of compensating diffusion of water, it is found experimentally that the pressure requires two or three days to drop to its original value, but does finally attain this with lapse of time, after which the above cycle may be repeated [1]

This type of phenomenon, varying in quantitative amount with the type of colloid or of living protoplasm affected, appears to give an indication for explaining the phasic activity found with varying speeds in different types of cell, and giving rise to their peculiar periods of charging and discharging, of activity and rest, of fatigue and recuperation

If we take once more the heart-beat as our example, we observe immediately after each beat the refractory period, followed by a period of colloidal rearrangement, in which the irritability or tendency to reversed change gradually heaps up to a point at which the

---

[1] The author just now has discovered a similar rhythm, or hysteresis, in the blood proteins, but in a reversed direction. Heated serum agglutinates, as shown by fall in osmotic pressure, and then in a few hours reverses.

colloid becomes amenable to a stimulus thrown in from without, or, passing this, to a point at which without any outside stimulus it becomes sufficiently charged with chemical products to show spontaneous irritability and discharge automatically. Here we observe at each beat a sudden chemical reversal followed by a slow period of recovery on the part of the colloid, just as in the heated gelatine solution there is a disruption at the higher temperature followed on cooling by a slow return to the original condition of combination.

A similar sequence of phenomena occurs in nearly all forms of living matter, and the periodicity can be altered, diminished, or made more evident by stimuli from without of physical, chemical, or physiological nature, or by altering in varying ways the crystalloidal ions in union with the protein. Take, for example, the induction of rhythmic activity in skeletal muscle, demonstrated by Biederman and by Sidney Ringer as a result of artificial ionic variation, and its quiescence by dipping in solutions containing the antagonistic ions.

But apart from external stimulation, phasic activity in some degree or other is inherent in the crystallo-colloids of all living matter. We see it demonstrated in the unstriated muscle of all parts of the body—viz., alimentary canal, bladder, uterus, spleen, arterial walls, everywhere in fact—and with varying rhythm in varying situations according to development and requisite physiological function. It is seen also in the rhythmical discharges of the central nervous system, we have noted its presence already in the regulation of respiration, and further characteristic examples are seen in Cheyne-Stokes breathing, in the Traube-Hering curves, and as demonstrated by Schäfer in every discharge of a voluntary character from the motor cells of the cord out to the skeletal muscles, showing here a rhythm of ten to twelve cycles per second.

The same periodicity is observable, but with much slower periods, in the case of all the secreting glands ; there is in each case a period of resting and accumulation of material, followed by a period of discharge. Exhaustion follows efficient discharge, and a period of refractoriness to stimulation supervenes before another discharge can occur.

The gland discharge may also be precipitated by stimulation from without at certain points in the cycle, but in the absence of the external and usual stimulus the potential of the cell tending towards discharge gradually rises with accumulation and corresponding increased pressure of the chemical substances formed, and finally a point is reached at which, without external aid, the discharge commences spontaneously.

A most interesting and beautiful example of such a rhythm dependent upon external stimulation under normal conditions, but capable of heaping up and becoming automatic in the absence of the usual stimulus or its delayed appearance beyond the accustomed time, is found in the case of the phosphorescent organisms so abundant in our seas, especially in the autumn months.

It might be supposed at first thought that these organisms are not observed to emit light during the day because of the presence of daylight, and that if taken into a dark room they would be found to be phosphorescent just as brilliantly as at night. This is, however, not the case; not a spark can be elicited from them even by vigorous agitation so long as there is daylight in the outer world. But if one stands by, and watches in the dark room as twilight is falling outside, although the organisms have not been exposed to light all day, one observes the little lamps light up and flash out one by one like coruscating diamonds in the darkness, till the whole dish becomes studded with flashing and disappearing lights, a glorious sight in the darkness and stillness. Nor is any agitation of the water required to call forth sparkling, although the already rhythmically lighting up organisms are, as is well known, stimulated to greatly increased activity by such mechanical disturbance. Still, without any disturbance whatever the organisms continue at regular intervals to emit bright flashes which slowly fade away and disappear until a new flash at the same spot once more appears, somewhat resembling a revolving light seen some distance off at sea. The appearances are such as would follow the expression from a minute gland duct of small drops of a phosphorescent secretion at regular intervals.

At daybreak the series of changes are the reverse of those witnessed at dusk; if the dish containing the phosphorescent organisms be observed from about an hour before sunrise, it will be seen that at first the organisms are still flashing out brilliantly, but about half an hour before sunrise the number of flashes begins rapidly to diminish, and at sunrise there are hardly any showing. For another half-hour or so flashes can still be evoked by violent mechanical agitation of the water, but later no amount of agitation will call forth a single flash.

The most remarkable fact, in addition to this well-marked rhythm of activity and repose, is that it continues apparently until the death of the tiny organisms, although the organisms are kept in complete darkness throughout the entire period of the captivity. The number of flashing points diminishes nightly, at first very rapidly, as the organisms are devoured for food by other creatures or perish from various causes, but I have succeeded in observing the recurrence of flashing at nightfall for twelve successive nights, at the end of which period of captivity nearly all the organisms had succumbed.

Similar diurnal rhythmic change has been observed for shorter periods in plant leaves, which alter their orientation in light and darkness when the plants have been kept in continuous darkness.

In the above instances we have examples of phasic activity timed to a regularly recurring stimulus, but see that in the absence of that stimulus there is something latent in the nature of the balanced chemical activities of the colloids and crystalloids which leads to phasic discharge and recuperation. For example, the phosphorescence is in all probability due to a phosphorescent secretion from a gland. This gland has been timed by its development and environment so as to load itself up to discharging-point during the day, and to be fired off as the light recedes in the evening. The colloidal constituents of the gland and their associated crystalloids possess such a chemical constitution and physical aggregation that they run their reaction of building up or synthesising the secretion at such a rate, that the secreting cell after the lapse of the hours of daylight will be charged up to a certain osmotic pressure with the phosphorescent secretion, either free in the cell or loosely united to the producing colloids. Now this concentration is the potential factor of the energy tending to force a discharge, and just as a Leyden jar will discharge as the electrical potential passes a certain maximum point and spark over, so the cell contents disrupt. The phosphorescent material if bound to colloid is set free and then discharged, or if already free is discharged from the cell, and in this way osmotic pressure is lowered and the cell's discharging power is for the time spent, so leading to the opposite phase of rest and recuperation.

The typical histological changes accompanying the periodic charging and discharging of the digestive glands are further examples of alternating rhythm. During rest chemical changes occur, having as their outward histological expression increase in volume of the cells, the obscuration of the cell outlines and nuclei, and the appearance of discrete granules packing the cells ; when this has proceeded to a certain extent the gland commences to discharge, either because of an adequate stimulus by nerve impulse reflexly reaching it, or by hormone in the circulation arising from some other physiological chemical process preceding it in order of time, or in absence of these usual causes by a slightly higher charge leading to spontaneous discharge, and the chemical processes are reversed in the metabolism of the colloids.   The same effects are seen even more typically in the case of the mammary glands during lactation.

The whole of the physiological and chemical processes of reproduction in the mammalia, as well as in other lower animal classes, illustrate the phasic activity of living matter in a most striking fashion.   In the lower mammalia, there are the seasonal periods of sexual activity during which in ordered sequence the whole reproductive system passes into excitement in its different parts, showing the pre-œstral period, then the active mental and other excitement of the œstrus, followed in turn by the post-œstral period.   In the human being, there is the monthly variation in the sexual activities affecting ovaries and mammary glands, and then the uterus in menstruation refreshing the uterine mucous membrane, followed by the period of sexual desire, and this again by the period of sexual quiescence completing the cycle.

If fertilisation occurs, there is during gestation the modified disturbance at each monthly interval during gestation, culminating normally at the tenth monthly cycle with the expulsion of the matured fœtus.

Similar phasic variations connected with the reproductive processes are seen throughout the whole animal world, and even become more striking the lower the organism is placed in the scale. Witness the sexual metamorphoses in the insecta, and the developmental history of echinodermata and mollusca.   Also in protozoa there are the alternations of sexual and asexual cycles determined apparently by alterations in chemical constitution, and capable of induction by variations in the environment

In the vegetable world there are the same phasic variations in the activities of the cells accompanying the alternations of the seasons, which have as their basis alterations in chemical equilibrium induced by varying external stimuli of physical and chemical nature.

The sequences in the series of ocean plankton dawning forth with the season's changes also wonderfully illustrate the cyclic activities of all living things.

Again, the whole history of the evolution of the complex animal from the two parent cells in sexual reproduction is a study in varying cyclic activity. The colloidal matter in the fertilised cell is endowed with peculiar energy properties as a result of which the potential or intensity factor of its energy rises to such a level that there becomes induced an alteration in the discharges of energy.

To prevent further rise in the potential or pressure factor as the total energy goes on increasing the capacity factor must be increased. This accommodation is made by the cell dividing into two daughter cells, under the influence of the high potential factor of the biotic energy. In each of the daughter cells the potential factor has now fallen, but, accompanying growth, the potential again rises, and the process of cell division at a certain point must be repeated, so giving rise to four cells. In the complicated interplay between this peculiar energy form characteristic of living cells and the crystallo-colloidal aggregates composing the cell structure, there are provided those potential variations which give rise to the different alterations in structure and function of the living matter as the animal body is fashioned out.

The causation of the marvellous changes by which an organisation so complex as that of a human being arises from the conjugation of two minute cells is at present hidden from our knowledge, and even the details of the colloidal chemistry of the simplest form of cell division. Yet we can safely say that there are two primary essential things—first, a very specific colloidal structure differing in its first details from the germ cell of the most nearly allied species of animal; secondly, this colloidal mass must be in meta-stable equilibrium, and its component parts not at rest, but possessed of a type of energy which we may term biotic energy to show that it is typical of such living structure, and possesses its own set of characteristics. This biotic energy receives, as the organism grows, additions by transformation into it of chemical energy derived from the nutrition, and possesses potential and capacity factors like other forms of energy.

One form of structure, arrangement, and subdivision of the living

2

matter of any given organism cannot pass into another in the long chain of metamorphoses occurring in development, without the accompaniment of energy changes and the energy content of the system or organism varying. The changes in the matter and the changes in the energy are most highly specific for living matter; nothing quite similar or identical either in structure or energy properties to a living cell is seen elsewhere in nature. Some term is requisite to express this, and if we are justified in speaking of living matter or biotic matter we are equally justified in speaking of living energy or biotic energy.

The living matter is composed of well-known chemical elements —carbon, hydrogen, oxygen, nitrogen, etc.—but these are built up in matter possessing life, into aggregates which have other additional properties than inorganic matter (using this term to include the carbon compounds not possessed of living structure). These aggregates, by virtue of their structure and arrangement and of the energy properties accompanying that structure, have come to be alive —that is, to demonstrate energy phenomena—such, for example, as cell division not seen anywhere except in living structures; the energy inhabiting the structures can be transformed to and fro into other types of energy, obeying the thermo-dynamic laws in the process, just as in the case of any other form of energy, and giving it the name biotic means simply that it is a type of energy *sui generis*, as are each of the inorganic types, and that it is typically seen in living cells.

There is no hiatus between biotic energy and other energy types, and if a sufficiently complex colloidal aggregation could be experimentally constructed, it would be possible to set it in this peculiar slow phasic vibration, and so simulate a lowly form of life. The hysteresis of gelatine solutions previously referred to is probably a first commencement of this labile metastable equilibrium, but far below any sign of life such as characterises the living cell.

Also, many cell products such as enzymes, toxins, and such bodies appear to possess properties intermediate between dead colloids and living cells, and carry outside the cell certain properties belonging to living matter.

Enzymes and similar bodies also act intracellularly, and it has even been supposed that practically all the work of the cell is done by proper combination in due concentration of a host of enzymes.

In the living cell we have, however, both chemically and biotically, one degree higher of complexity than any enzyme or cell product.

This is shown by possession of the property of self-multiplication or reproduction by cell division, which has not yet been shown to be possible in any enzyme or toxin, although this has been mooted as a possible carrier of the infection in those diseases where the microscopist speaks of an ultra-microscopic germ.

The difference between the living cell and any of its *quasi* living products is also demonstrated by the linkage of reactions occurring in the cell, and never seen in the case of enzymes or similar extra-cellular substances inducing reactions.

In spite of what is known as reversibility of enzyme action, the law holds universally that an enzyme can never use energy derived from one reaction to run another in which building up of energy occurs, while in the living cell this is done in a thousand forms in which myriads of synthesised products are built up. An enzyme always runs a downhill reaction, and when it is apparently reversed this really only means that the concentrations requisite for reversal are such that (chiefly due to osmotic pressure variations) the reversed reaction now runs downhill.

Not to trespass too far on the work of another chapter, we may put it that in the more complex organisation or colloidal structure of the cell the possibility arises that work set free in one part of the colloid aggregate may be used for running a reaction requiring energy in another portion of the colloid. For example, oxidation of carbohydrate may be running continuously with reduction in another part to form higher fatty acid and fat.

The cell is necessary for this co-ordination. If all the enzymes contained within a cell were placed there without the co-ordination that the cell structure gives them they might be compared to a horde of savages without organisation, while the same enzymes built up into the other colloidal parts of the cell become organised like a disciplined army, or a civilised community, acting in a co-ordinated or linked-up manner.

In the living cell, then, we have two primary things, structure and energy, and in every process of development, evolution, growth, and physiological activity the energy swings the structure from one phase to another, and each structural change gives rise to a corresponding adapted energy variation. To suppose that structure alone dominates the situation, and that the whole structure of the man is laid down in the germinal cells, reminds one of Loewenhoek's quaint notion that he saw the heads and faces of the future men and women in the "homunculi" which his microscope demonstrated to him for the first time.

Given a definite, labile, colloidal structure specific for each species of organism, and an initial energy charge upon this, then as each stage develops it must automatically swing on into the next.

The only experimental method whereby to penetrate as far as possible into the mysteries of these cell changes which presents itself to us at present is that of studying the effects of varying the external stimuli and environmental conditions and nutrition, and interfering artificially by physical and chemical means with the cell processes

Such general study of cell growth under artificially varied conditions will not only prove fertile in increasing our knowledge of cell division, but will yield rich fruit in application to the study of pathological processes and disease, notably in the study and elucidation of cancer and other malignant growths.

A tumour or growth, whatever may ultimately be found to be its exciting cause or causes, is essentially a number of cells escaped from the ordinary laws of growth of the organism, and it is benign or malignant according to whether it lives apart by itself and interferes with nothing else, or whether it invades and suppresses normal tissues, gets carried to other regions, and starts secondary growths or metastases, or gives out toxins and chemical products which interfere with the general physiological well-being of the entire organism.

The stimulus to the growth of abnormal tissue may be an irritating micro-organism, as in the tubercles of tuberculosis and the gummata of syphilis, or interference with nutrition by diminished or increased blood-supply, as in scar tissue and nævi, or stimulation by foreign or pathological chemical substances, as in the tophi of gout and nodules of cirrhosis, and possibly in cancer by altered composition of blood-plasma, though here we know at present nothing definite, and a micro-organism, bacterial or protozoan, is by no means yet excluded.

In many different ways energy may be thrown in from without, and the normal processes of cell division, development, and growth interfered with, and it is by experimental methods of this sort that many of the most pressing problems of biology and medical science will ultimately be solved.

CHAPTER II

LIFE AND LIGHT

Few people have probably considered or realised how entirely and absolutely dependent we are upon energy accumulated by living processes in all our human undertakings. With the exception of the energy of falling water and the work of the winds, all the energy utilised by man for all the acts of his existence, and to drive forward his manifold schemes of activity, is derived from the operations of living matter. All the electricity, all the steam power, all the power of prime movers of any type, come from living structures or from materials which have been at some period living. Without the energy of living things in actual being once upon the earth all the great industrial processes of the world would come to a standstill. Not only does the energy of living men direct these processes and give the intelligence for them, but the energy produced by living creatures, plant and animal, actually drives them onward to a successful issue.

Not only does the life of past ages supply the energy to keep us warm in winter : it supplies the clothes we wear, which in their entire material and substance are of biotic origin, and in their fabrication by weaving or other textile process were fashioned by biotic energy. The furniture of our rooms, whether of wood, metal, or textile fabric, is due entirely to biotic energy, for even in the case of metals biotic energy was essential to provide the fuel to smelt and purify the ore and fabricate the metal into the finished article. The dinner we eat was produced by the operations of living creatures ; so were the table and the cloth upon it, the plate we eat from, and the knife and fork we use in eating. The pen this is written with, the paper written upon, and the ink upon the paper are all biotic in their origin or fabrication; the book has been printed, bound, sold, and delivered by means of biotic energy, and the reader is utilising biotic energy to read it.

Truly we are dependent upon other living creatures, either contemporary with us or our predecessors in natural history, for every act we perform, and there is no form of energy so universally distributed upon the earth and so indispensable as biotic energy.

In studying this interesting form of energy and its manufactured products, the first fundamental question cropping up is the manner in which it is produced, and the energy form or forms transformed into it in order to keep up the supply as the stores are utilised and reconverted into the simple inorganic forms.

Let us get down to fundamental facts, and from these trace upwards over the many unknown lacunæ, as far as our present knowledge will allow us, to the energy transformer endowed with that property which we call life.

In any ordinary transformation of energy from one type to another three things are essential, and this is also true of those changes in which biotic energy is involved. These three things are a suitable energy transformer, such as a water-wheel, turbine, steam-engine, dynamo, or living cell; secondly, a type of matter which is to be the habitus of the energy in each case, or a reservoir for it, such as the water, or steam, or electric wire, or colloid aggregates of the cell ; and, thirdly, a source of energy in another type, such as chemical energy (in the form of coal, spirit, petrol, food, etc.), or sunlight, or other type of radiant energy.

Now, whatever secondarily may be the form of energy supplied to the cell, primarily all biotic energy is dependent upon sunlight. Coal, petroleum, spirit, organic foodstuffs, the nitrates of the soil even, all are derived from the sun's energy.

Next, in regard to the material used for the habitation of this energy, the most essential constituents are most simple in their chemical nature, and consist of carbon dioxide from the atmosphere and water taken usually from the earth, holding in solution a few simple salts, such as nitrates, phosphates, sulphates, chlorides, and silicates of ammonium, sodium, potassium, iron, calcium, manganese, magnesium, aluminium, and a few other elements in minute traces. Most abundantly taken up and manipulated in the process are the four elements—carbon, hydrogen, oxygen, and nitrogen ; small amounts only of the others are required, but they are none the less essential and indispensable.

It is a most remarkable and interesting fact that the whole life of the world, as at present constituted, is dependent upon the presence of a mere trace of carbon dioxide in the atmosphere. This carbon dioxide, which is the gas produced when carbon or charcoal

is burnt and so completely oxidised in the air, is present only to the
extent of between three and four parts in ten thousand of the air.
The living cell takes up all its materials in solution, and if we regard
the carbon dioxide as in solution in the atmosphere we gain a clear
idea of the enormous dilution at which plants take this their most
important raw material.

Since the molecular weight in grammes of any gas occupies at
atmospheric pressure and standard temperature a volume of about
22 litres, and air contains 4 litres of carbon dioxide in 10,000, it
follows that 22 litres, or the molecular weight in grammes, will be

contained in $\dfrac{22}{4} \times 10{,}000 = 55{,}000$ litres.   That is to say, the atmo-

sphere is approximately a $\frac{1}{55{,}000}$ molecular solution, and at this
exceedingly dilute strength plants take in all their supply of carbon.

The supply of carbon dioxide is taken in only by the green parts
of the plants, especially the leaves, and by these it is taken up with
the greatest avidity for it has been shown that a 7·5 per cent. solution of sodium hydrate only absorbs carbon dioxide at about five
to six times the rate of an equal surface of green plant leaf in the
sunlight.   Brown and Escombe found that the comparative rates
of absorption of strong alkali and leaf were less than double.

In the absence of light this rapid absorption abruptly ceases,
and instead there is given out an excess of carbon dioxide arising
from the oxidation processes of life going on in the living cells of
the plant.

It is only when the energy of the light at sufficient intensity
(which here corresponds to the potential or pressure factor of this
form of energy) is poured upon or into the energy machines existing
in the green cells that chemical energy begins to be formed by transformation from the energy of the light, and this process must not
by any means be confused with the output of carbon dioxide due to
respiration of the plant, which goes on continuously and all over the
plant whether it is in sunlight or in darkness.

In the leaf, in sunlight, the synthetic processes mightily out-
balance the respiratory or oxidation processes, and the result is
rapid disappearance of carbon dioxide with simultaneous appearance
of oxygen in equal or somewhat greater volume.[1]   In feeble light

[1] The reverse of what is called the animal respiratory quotient occurs
in plant syntheses, in that on the whole more oxygen is produced than carbon
dioxide taken up, the excess oxygen coming from water.   In the green leaf

or in darkness synthesis and reduction fall off, and oxidation predominates with output of carbon dioxide. To set the balance towards carbon dioxide assimilation in excess with oxygen production a considerable light intensity is requisite ; thus moonlight is insufficient, but slight oxygen production has been noticed by algæ in the twilight, and in electric light of, say, 1,000 candle-power the balance is turned at a distance of about half a metre to a metre and a half from the source of light.

Turning our attention now to the minute energy transformers by which the radiant light energy is converted into chemical energy, we find that these are contained in hundreds of thousands in the cell in the form of what are called chloroplastids or chloroplasts

The shape of these microscopic chloroplasts varies in different plants, as also their dimensions, but in all cases they consist of two kinds of material—a *colourless* material, probably consisting of protein and being bioplasmic in nature and origin, which forms a stroma or spongework, and a green-coloured material, oily as to physical character, which fills up the meshes of the stroma without mixing with it, and is particularly developed in a network of varying forms upon the surface of the plastid. The colourless part of the plastid can develop independently of the action of the light, and colourless plastids occur in plants which have been grown in the dark, and hence are etiolated or colourless These colourless plastids on being exposed to light rapidly commence to turn green in colour from development of the green-coloured oily matter, and now photo-synthesis commences After a certain amount of the green oily matter has been synthesised by the action of the light, further manufacture of it ceases, and it then acts as an agent or transformer for conversion of the radiant energy into other forms of chemical energy, such as sugars, starches, or oils, which accumulate in the cell.[1]

There is no doubt that botanical chemists have laid too much stress upon the synthesis of sugars and starches only by the plastids, as if this synthetic activity was confined to one line of synthesis. It is known that fats may appear very early in the process and be

---

the synthesis is nearly all carbohydrate synthesis, and here, as in the animal, the quotient approximates to unity; but in fat formation in other parts hydrogen in excess is laid down in the molecule and the quotient exceeds unity just as it falls below it in fat oxidation in the animal body.

Compare with succeeding chapters.

deposited instead of starch granules in the plastids. Also the plastids and the cells containing them multiply rapidly, and for this purpose utilise the solar energy given to them, there being no proof that the materials first formed must visit roots or other organs of the plant before being converted into proteins to meet this plastid production. Most of the nitrogen entering the leaf enters it in the form of inorganic salts, and is transformed into protein nitrogen in the leaf. This misconception that carbohydrate must first be formed before fats or proteins can arise is based upon no clear experimental evidence, but upon a series of ingenious but rather unsuccessful attempts to demonstrate the first steps of photo-synthesis.

The most popular idea regarding the first step is that first proposed by A. von Baeyer—viz., that formaldehyde is formed by union of carbonic acid and water under the influence of the input of light energy somewhat in this fashion:

$$CO_2 + H_2O = OC{<}^{OH}_{OH} \quad \text{(carbonic acid)}$$

$$OC{<}^{OH}_{OH} \;+\; 2H{\cdot}OH \;=\; OC{<}^{H}_{H} \;+\; 2HO{\cdot}OH$$

(carbonic acid)   (water)   = (formaldehyde) + (hydrogen peroxide)

$$2HO{\cdot}OH = 2H_2O + O_2$$

or, if written in shortest form, so as to express the net result:

$$CO_2 + H_2O = H{\cdot}CHO_2 + O_2$$

It is quite possible by juggling with the formulæ of organic chemistry to write many dozens of such equations, and to show the possibility *on paper* of the formation of hundreds of organic substances other than formaldehyde; but the real question is, Do such reactions occur in the cell?

Formaldehyde is a substance for which many delicate reactions exist capable of showing extraordinarily minute traces of aldehyde, and these reactions have been most ingeniously applied to show that minute traces of formaldehyde exist in the green leaf and in increased amount after active photo-synthesis.

The defect of all these reactions for aldehyde is, in the first place, that they are too delicate, and, in the second place, that they may be given by other aldehydes than formaldehyde, and by other organic products of cellular metabolism. Further, even admitting that the positive results of such tests after photo-synthesis may be due to formaldehyde, this does not prove that formaldehyde is the main primary product of photo-synthesis, and it may only be produced as a by-product in minute traces in secondary metabolic reactions It is in fact only in the minutest traces, the upper limit being about 0 001 per cent , that formaldehyde, which is one of the most intense of protoplasmic poisons, can be borne by living cells   Direct experiments with less than the lethal dose of formaldehyde in regard to photo-synthesis have given negative results; plants subjected in presence of light to solutions containing 0 001 per cent. of formaldehyde do not form as much starch as in its absence

Again, starch granules appearing in the cell are not always the first visible sign of photo-synthesis, although the most frequent, for in certain plants the starch granules are replaced by oil droplets. Also, when we begin with the etiolated cell, we see that chlorophyll, the green colouring matter itself, which is a very complex nitrogenous organic body, is formed under the influence of light in the plastid, and that under the influence also of light the protein matter of the plastid increases in amount

It hence becomes probable that carbohydrates, proteins, and fats, as also chlorophyll, a body of lecithide nature, are *all* formed in the plastid, and accordingly it appears likely that the carbon dioxide, water, nitrates, etc , required for the building up of all these bodies should first form an integral part of the plastid, and then, after synthetic processes in which the complicated biotic molecules of the plastid take a part, be detached as proteins, lecithides, fats, or carbohydrates [1]

Theoretically, the supposed formaldehyde production rests upon an exceedingly crude basis of organic chemistry and the experimental evidence on behalf of it, in spite of much most earnest and painstaking work, is of the flimsiest character [2] Sugars are aldehydic in character, and if we reduce the formula of a hexose to its simplest form by dividing by six it becomes CH_2O, which is the rational formula of formaldehyde; also by condensation of formaldehyde it has been shown that a mixture of hexoses containing fructose can be

[1] A considerable amount of evidence has recently been accumulated by Parkin to show that cane-sugar is one of the earliest carbohydrates to make its appearance in the green leaf

[2] See, however, succeeding experimental work detailed in Chapters III., IV , and V of this book.

obtained. All this does not demonstrate that the first action of the chloroplastid is identical in kind, and, moreover, it furnishes no light whatever on the rôle played by the plastid or the chlorophyll it contains. It merely leaves the chloroplastid out, so to speak; but in some way or other the carbon dioxide and water molecules must at some stage in the synthesis have chemical attachment to either the chlorophyll or colourless matter of the plastid, and this attachment must be of an unstable vibratile type, which can be influenced by the vibrations of the light waves. When once the carbon dioxide and water molecules become attached to the colloidal, organic complex molecules of the plastid, they become reduced by the agency of the light waves which yield energy for the detachment of the oxygen, and the conversion thereby of the newly attached groups to the big molecule, as aldehydic, carboxylic, or ketonic groups, or it may be as amidogen groups if simple nitrogenous inorganic groups are simultaneously presented. These new groups are attached very similarly to polypeptide formation, or like the process of manufacturing the long chain of the fatty acid, or like the acids of so many glucosides found in plant structures. There is no necessity experimentally or theoretically to suppose that they should always be detached from the synthesising mechanism of the plastid as free formaldehyde, nor to suppose that formaldehyde as such is formed anywhere along the line. The next process, when these have become too abundant or condensed in connection with any colloidal molecule in the plastid, will be the shedding of them off as reserve material in the form of starch granules or fatty droplets.[1] This view would bring starch production in photo-synthesis into line with known metabolic processes going on in other organs of the plant, such as roots, tubers, and seeds, where from sugar brought from leaves or elsewhere are formed starchy, fatty, or protein depots as also with the facts of animal metabolism, where ingested sugar in excess of immediate demands is stored as glycogen, or as

[1] The hexoses are always active bodies on account of the presence of the aldehydic or ketonic group; in the formation of higher carbohydrate, or of fats, these groups either disappear on account of molecular changes, or neutralise each other by interlinking, so that quite neutral bodies tend to form as the molecule becomes more complex. From this point of view it is interesting to point out that sucrose, or cane-sugar, which consists of two very active hexoses—viz., glucose and fructose—loses its active properties, and no longer acts as a reducing agent from the interlinking of the aldehydic group of the glucose with the ketonic group of the fructose.

glycerides in the fatty depots ˙of the connective tissue, or elsewhere.

If a protein molecule existing in colloidal complexity in the living cell can take up molecules of hexose, and from energy obtained from intercurrent reactions linked on at neighbouring positions of the colloidal complex can fashion these into a portion of itself first, and then turn them out into detached and growing granules of starch or of fat, as we know experimentally it can, then it does not seem improbable that the colloids of the chloroplastid can similarly attach carbon dioxide and water molecules, and by means of the light energy, causing molecular swingings or reinforcing them, in neighbouring positions on the big colloidal molecule, can detach oxygen and formaldehyde or similar groups.

This view appears to the author more probable than the view of free detached formaldehyde, for this if formed would immediately unite to protein before it could be condensed to hexoses, and of all aldehydes formaldehyde is most unlikely to be present, because it would enter into fatally stable union with the protein instead of retaining a labile easily altered form for further change under the action of the light vibrations.

Priestley, the discoverer of oxygen, first showed that green plants exposed to light produced oxgyen, and the meaning of this discovery was appreciated and further study devoted to the subject by another British philosopher, Ingenhouze,[1] who as early as 1779 pointed out that the under surface of the leaf was most concerned in the output of oxygen, that very young or very old leaves gave a diminished yield, that all plants poisoned the air during the night, and, if they were in shadow, during the day also, and that mosses also, but not fungi, produced oxygen. ˙ At a later period in these earlier days of the study of photo-synthesis much exact knowledge was added by the labours of Senebier, Saussure, and Mohl, and by Sachs, who first appreciated truly the function of the chloroplast.

The rapidity with which photo-synthesis occurs depends upon several factors such as intensity of illumination, concentration of carbon dioxide in the atmosphere of air or water surrounding the plant, and temperature of the surroundings The plant also in the orientation of its leaves, amount of opening of the stomata or minute openings leading to its air vessels which form the respiratory system, and degree of development of chlorophyll or other pigments, pos-

---

[1] " Experiments upon Vegetables " London, 1770

sesses means of adapting itself to the wide variations occurring diurnally and seasonally in these outer conditions.

The natural amount of carbon dioxide present in atmospheric air or water in equilibrium with atmospheric air appears to be the best for the growth and development of plants, although it is not by any means that at which for short periods the photo-synthesis proceeds at the most rapid pace. Results of various observers differ as to the correspondence between amount of carbon dioxide in the air or water of the environment and the rate of photo-synthesis; thus Kreusler[1] found that the rate was nearly doubled with seven times as much carbon dioxide as in ordinary air, and with 1 per cent.—*i.e.*, about thirty-five times as much as atmospheric air—there was only two and one-third times as active photo-synthesis as in air, and this formed about a maximum. Kreusler used continuous lighting with an electric arc light of 1,000 candle-power at a distance of 31-45 centimetres.

Brown and Escombe, on the other hand, using sunlight in two parallel experiments with sunflower leaves, exposed to like condition of sunshine but with varying percentages of carbon dioxide, found that up to seven or eight times the atmospheric amount of carbon dioxide the activity rose in linear proportion, so that approximately seven or eight times as much carbon dioxide disappeared when the partial pressure was correspondingly increased. This condition of affairs obtained only for shorter intervals, for the authors discovered that plants grown in an atmosphere richer in carbon dioxide than normal, put on less dry weight than in a normal atmosphere; the area of green leaf developed was smaller and the colour of a deeper green.

They repeated their work in a large-scale experiment conducted in a greenhouse, which could be closed airtight and filled with air containing known amounts of carbon dioxide in one half, the other symmetrical half containing ordinary air. Under such conditions they found that after some weeks' exposure the growth was affected in an extraordinary manner by this plenitude of carbon dioxide. The chief results were that in many cases the leaves dropped off and were replaced by smaller ones of a deeper green; the internodes became much shorter and developed more rapidly, and there was a profusion of axillary shoots, so that the plants from the artificial atmosphere, which were of about equal height with the controls

---

[1] *Landwirth, Jahrbücher*, 1885, Bd. xiv., p. 913.

grown under otherwise like conditions in ordinary air, assumed a stunted and bushy appearance Lastly, and perhaps most important of all, the reproductive system became entirely aborted, not a single flower in any case arriving at maturity.

It is thus obvious that excess of carbon dioxide possesses a most potent influence upon cell division and regulation of growth in plant cells, similar to that which has been noted as obtaining in animal cells in the previous chapter

Somewhat divergent results also exist amongst the records as to the effects of variations in *light intensity* upon speed of photo-activity. All authors agree as to the existence of an optimum intensity of illumination, but some place it at full sunlight, others at half or quarter of full insolation, finding little or no increase, or even elimination, as the light intensity is increased beyond the observed optimum. Again, in the region of intensities where admittedly increasing illumination causes increased synthesis, some authors find a direct proportionality of linear type, while others find the photo-synthesis advancing much more slowly than light intensity

Thus, Pantanelli[1] found the optimum assimilation at one-fourth of full sunlight, and a diminution at greater intensities Kreusler found, when experimenting with electric arc light, that the action was roughly proportional to the light intensity, but Brown, experimenting in sunlight, found the uptake of carbon dioxide only doubled, while the light intensity increased twelvefold Tréboux and also Pantanelli discovered that the optimum intensity of light and optimum concentration of carbon dioxide varied together, and this may account for some of the discordance between different authors —thus, with one-fourth the intensity of direct sunlight, maximum photo-synthesis corresponded to 10 per cent by volume of carbon dioxide, with full sunlight to 15 per cent. of carbon dioxide, and fourfold sunlight produced by a converging system yielded the maximum effect with 20 per cent of carbon dioxide.

It is obvious that the amount of photo-synthesis occurring at various periods of the day will vary with the intensity of the light, but when the light is artificial and kept continuous and constant, it is found that there is no habit corresponding to the natural alternating diurnal activity and rest of the chloroplasts, but the activity with equal artificial illumination is about the same in the

---

[1] For references see Czapek, " Biochemie d Pflanzen," vol 1, p 434.

day and night periods; this would indicate that the first steps at least in the synthesis are more purely chemical and out of control of the cell and the plant of which it is a part.

Serious consequences to the plant, however, occur if it is kept assimilating day and night without its normally recurring periods of darkness and rest. Thus it has been shown by Siemens and others that plants exposed continuously to electric light—such, for example, as decorative plants in winter gardens—soon fade, dropping their leaves and showing other pathological changes. The formation of green in the etiolated plant occurs with a lower intensity of light than that which just suffices to give a credit balance of photo-synthesis over respiratory production of carbon dioxide, and induce an increase in organic dried weight.

All rays of the spectrum are not supposed to be equally effective in inducing photo-synthesis. It has been suggested by Lommel, and afterwards by Timiriaseff, who threw a spectrum upon a starch-free leaf and then determined the relative amounts of starch produced under different spectral regions, that the greatest activity lies where most light is absorbed by a chlorophyll solution —viz., in the red between the B and C lines. Other optima lie under the positions corresponding to the other absorption bands of chlorophyll.[1]

By its green fluorescent action on the light, chlorophyll, more-over, possesses the property of reducing a good deal of the light of higher frequency of vibration to a colour and speed of vibration at which it produces a greater photo-synthetic effect in the plant.

The spectrum of fresh chlorophyll is very characteristic in the plant world, just as is that of hæmoglobin in the animal world, although the two spectra are entirely different from each other. These two pigments show many interesting similarities in chemical constitution. Both are lecithides in their relationships in chloroplastid and in blood-corpuscle respectively—one contains iron, the other magnesium in colloidal form in the molecule; one causes photo-synthesis accompanied by reduction, the other the complementary process of breaking down of the synthesised products

---

[1] This is the orthodox view, but recent experiments by the author and Mr. Edward Whitley have shown that all regions of the visible spectrum very effectively photo-synthesise even in regions where there exist no absorption bands of chlorophyll.

accompanied by oxidation. Both yield practically identical products in their own breaking down, at a stage of considerable degradation, after they have parted with their iron or magnesium.

These two colouring matters, the green of the higher plant and the red of the higher animal, are the two most important in all organic nature, and it is most interesting that they should show these complementary functions and possess these chemical similarities in their derived products [1]

It will have been gathered, from what has been written, that the higher plant and higher animal are complemental to each other in the natural scheme of the organic world as we see it at present in operation.

The higher plant takes up the radiant solar energy, and from inorganic materials, the most important and abundant of which are carbon dioxide, water, and nitrates, it builds up organic bodies, containing chemical energy, for its own purposes in growth, reproduction, and increase. These synthesised products yield directly or indirectly the energy for all the higher animals, in whose bodies, by up and down processes of oxidation and reduction, but on the whole with a downward trend of oxidation, the synthesised products are converted again into simple inorganic bodies, carbon dioxide, water, and very simple nitrogenous compounds Thus the great cycle of Nature is completed. Those plants which do not contain chlorophyll, and hence cannot synthesise directly from inorganic materials, are compelled like animals to live on plants or decaying vegetable matter, or upon the bodies of living or dead animals

It is tempting here to reflect upon the origin of organic life upon the earth, for the scheme of the vegetable and animal worlds which has been outlined above, while it provides for the supply of the organic material forming the food under the influence of sunlight, gives no hint as to how this cosmos came into first existence. The whole of the theories and facts of evolution also fail us when we attempt to form any picture of the first origins of the organic world, for everything in the system begins with the presence of organic matter on which the simplest organic creatures can live, or with the

---

[1] This statement again represents the orthodox knowledge of the time, but see later (Chapters III , IV , V), where research has recently shown that chlorophyll and its allies are probably only colour screens of a protective character, the real transformer lying behind them Similarly, hæmoglobin is an oxygen-carrier and not an oxidising agent

presence of highly organised plants containing chlorophyll and responsive to the sun's rays. Such a high order of development as that shown by the green plant could, however, almost certainly not have constituted the beginning of all things living, as our earth cooled down to the temperature at which bodies sufficiently complex to form the habitation of biotic energy could without rapid combustion exist upon its surface.

The view that cosmic dust from another planet or astral body first carried some biotic fragments or simple living organisms, much as the winds might carry new species to a desert island and start life there, carries us but little farther, for at a still more distant epoch we are again met with the same difficulty of how life first began from inorganic matter in that distant planet.

The myth of spontaneous generation, of the type thought of somewhat more than a generation ago by our forefathers, when Pasteur waged warfare with this crudest doctrine of the origin of living species, need only be mentioned to be dismissed, for such a kind of spontaneous generation required organic matter for the organisms to appear, and the problem we are facing now is that of how, spontaneously or otherwise, organic matter arose endowed with biotic energy in a world where there was no trace—not merely of living matter—but no vestige of dead organic matter. Such a world as that it is barely possible for us as inhabitants of this green earth, covered with teeming energetic life, to realise or postulate to ourselves.

Yet in this dead inorganic world, somewhere about the time when life, on account of temperature conditions, first became possible, living creatures promptly, in the geological sense, became present, as the record of the oldest sedimentary rocks teaches us to-day.

The degree of chemical complexity capable of existing in the materials found on the earth is definitely fixed by temperature. At a white heat (for example, at such a heat as exists in the sun's atmosphere) only such forms of matter as we term elements can remain in equilibrium, and probably many of these decompose just as radium goes on decomposing at ordinary earth atmospheric temperatures. At a somewhat lower temperature binary compounds, such as oxides, can remain stable in a condition of equilibrium with either complete or incomplete combination. Lower still in the temperature scale, saline compounds of the halogens, and of neutralised acidic and basic oxides, can stand the heat, and such bodies as the carbonates of the alkaline earths, for example, can be present in an incomplete state of combination, partially oxide and partially carbonate, in labile equilibrium with a varying partial pressure of carbon dioxide in the atmosphere.

But it is only at a very much lower temperature that compounds at all complicated in structure can exist in equilibrium, and for those compounds of many hundreds of atoms which are characteristic of life the range is narrowly limited. Thus, practically all the life of the planet would be completely destroyed at a temperature which we may place for inclusive purposes at 56° C. At a little more than 10° below this moderate limit all birds and mammalia would have disappeared, and even at 30° C the vast bulk of cold-blooded creation would have perished. Even the highly organised ferments called enzymes, which still bear half impressed upon them the properties of the living cells from whence they came, begin to suffer rapid deterioration in all cases at about 50° C , and at 60° to 70° they are rapidly destroyed

We may next note that as the temperature begins on the cooling planet to reach the limit at which sufficient complexity of chemical structure to support life becomes possible, then more and more complex chemical compounds are not only possible of existence, but begin to exist

For example, as soon as the temperature will admit of carbonate formation in equilibrium, then carbonates come into existence In other words, when equilibrium conditions admit of it, matter of its own properties tends where energy is available to take on the complex forms.

Next in order of development, inorganic colloids begin to arise on the cooling globe   Single molecules existing in solution, and capable of forming colloids with alteration in temperature, begin to form complexes or solution aggregates in which the unit of structure passes from the *atom* to the *molecule*. Now instead of single atoms uniting to form simple single molecules, we find molecules behaving as atoms, and uniting with a new order of affinities altogether to form colloidal aggregates

Accompanying these structural changes the energy types and phases inhabiting the unit of structure also vary. The rates of vibration or of phasic activity in the colloidal aggregates would be slower than in the simpler molecules of the crystalloids. All that has been described in the previous chapter from Graham's writings and elsewhere as characteristic of colloids—viz., slowness of reaction, meta-stable equilibrium, hysteresis, etc., would be present in the higher molecules now capable of existing in equilibrium with their environment.

As the complexity of structure increased, the nature of the equilibrium in the colloidal aggregates would approximate more and more to that labile, easily destroyed, but also readily constructive condition which has been described in the preceding chapter as characteristic of all living things. In this manner we can conceive that the gulf between non-living and living things can be bridged over, and there awakens in our minds the novel conception of a kind of spontaneous generation of a different order from the old. The territory of this spontaneous production of life lies not at the level of bacteria or animalculæ springing forth into life in dead organic matter, but at a level of life lying deeper than anything the microscope can reveal, and possessing a lower unit than the living cell, as we form our concept of it from the tissues of higher animals and plants.

In the future the discovery of the fact that inorganic colloids are capable of absorbing external energy forms, such as light, and so building up in complexity will yield a new outlook upon life, opening a vista of possibilities as magnificent as that which the establishment of the cell as a unit gave when there came the development of the microscope less than a century ago.

It was no fortuitous combination of chances and no cosmic dust which brought life to the bosom of our ancient mother earth in the far distant pre-Cambrian ages, but a well-regulated order of development, which comes to every mother earth in the universe in the maturity of its creation, when the conditions arrive within the suitable limits.

Given the presence of matter and energy forms under the proper conditions, life must come inevitably, just as, given the proper conditions of energy and completion of matter in the fertilised ovum, one change after another must introduce itself and give place to another, and spin along in infinite variation till the mature embryo appears, and this in turn must pass through the phases of growth, maturity, reproduction, decay, and death.

If this view be the true one, there must exist a whole world of living creatures which the microscope has never shown us, leading up to the bacteria and the protozoa. The brink of life lies not at the production of protozoa and bacteria, which are highly developed inhabitants of our world, but away down amongst the colloids, and the beginning of life was not a fortuitous event occurring millions of years ago and never again repeated, but one which in its primordial stages keeps on repeating itself all the time now in our generation; so that if all intelligent creatures were by some holocaust destroyed, up out of the depths in process of millions of years intelligent beings would once more emerge.

In this process of chemical evolution up to the stage which we at the present day regard as living, it is to be observed that as the non-living colloid becomes more and more complex, and accordingly more and more labile, it at the same time must become more and more susceptible to the influence of external stimulation by different forms of energy. This means that it must, under such conditions that it can remain in equilibrium without decomposition, become more and more a machine for uptake and utilisation of energy. The fact that the present basis of the system of living creatures in the world is light energy leads to the view that at a certain stage in the development of colloids, probably long before the appearance of chlorophyll, the colloids began to be affected by the light, and acquired the property of retaining and utilising light energy for further development of structure, or, in other words, synthesis of more complex colloids.

A second point of importance is the gradual increase in time periods arising as development progressed The simpler a chemical reaction is, as a general rule, the more instantaneous it is; with increasing complexity the time phases grow longer. This, as stated previously, Graham observed in regard to colloids, which are infinitely slower in their reactions than crystalloids.

The early stages in development up towards life would hence be rushed through rapidly, and be easily and constantly reproducible. As complexity increased so would the time grow longer for any chemical evolution. A vastly increased time interval would be necessary for the evolution of a course of events from the commencing simpler organic conditions upwards in increasing complexity, and more especially the time necessary to reach any higher stage of organisation *de novo* would be immensely increased on account of instability and tendency to break down again as different and more delicately balanced stages were passed. There would here come in the tendency of external conditions to stop the process at certain levels, and the steeper slopes of development would only be infrequently ascended until the establishment of something resembling a species, but still short of life, arose by a run over into a stable condition in one case out of many millions possible. This species of highly organised colloid could then more easily reproduce itself by inoculation into suitable material than by starting from simpler bodies *ab initio*, and would form a fresh starting-point for further development, just as at the stage of living things each new species would form a fresh point of departure. A labile equilibrium, stable and capable of reproducing itself so long as there existed examples of itself with suitable conditions of material and energetic environment, would so be set up, but would require a long period of time for redevelopment if once the type were lost.

In any search for synthesis of colloids up towards living structures we must accordingly turn to a new field, and begin searching for colloids susceptible to light or other forms of external energy, and look for evidence of building up in colloidal complexity and colloidal synthesis under input of energy.

Whatever may have been the origin of living matter in the past history of the world, we find such matter to-day in all living organisms existing as a number of exceedingly complicated colloidal structures, the origin of all of which can be traced directly or indirectly to the energy of sunshine, fashioned into chemical energy in organic colloidal bodies, the chloroplasts, formed in the green cells of plants, or plantlike organisms. These colloids always exist in intimate relationship with crystalloids, and cannot be fabricated or utilised without crystalloids.

All their energy properties are closely bound up with an unstable or labile equilibrium allowing of ready attachment or detachment of constituent groups, and the very strength and suitability of the constituents depends upon the ease with which they can be broken down. As a result of this lability and tendency to change, the constituents of living matter possess in highest degree the power both of joining with one another and of inducing what is styled by the chemist conjugation or condensation to form highly complex molecules.

CHAPTER III

SYNTHESIS BY SUNLIGHT IN RELATIONSHIP TO THE ORIGIN OF LIFE

SYNTHESIS OF FORMALDEHYDE FROM CARBON DIOXIDE AND WATER BY INORGANIC COLLOIDS ACTING AS TRANSFORMERS OF LIGHT ENERGY

It is important to emphasise the point that in considering the origin of life in a world containing inorganic matter only, the nutrition of the first living structure on such a world must be carefully borne in mind. This observation is still true whether life is to be regarded as arising *de novo* on the planet, or as being borne there from some other planet as a germ from pre-existent life. No living organism such as a bacterium or mould which did not possess the power of transforming energy and of synthesising organic from inorganic matter could exist or flourish in total absence of preformed organic matter and must inevitably perish.

A substance acting as a transformer of light energy with accompanying synthesis of organic from inorganic matter now exists in our world, in chlorophyll, the green colouring matter of plants, and also allied bodies such as the blue-green colouring matter of the Cyanophyceæ[1] possess a similar power But both these substances are exceedingly highly organised and complex, quite unsuitable by their nature to be thought of as the first stage in the evolution of organic from inorganic matter at the dawning of life in a world hitherto devoid of anything organic.

The protoplasm of the living cell also is built up of the most complex organic compounds known to us such as could scarcely arise in an entirely inorganic world as the first step from inorganic to organic matter.

The first primeval step would appear to be indicated by the union of single crystalloidal inorganic molecules to form inorganic colloids, and that these meta-stable colloids acting on inorganic carbon compounds, such as carbon dioxide, in presence of water and sunlight,

[1] The blue algæ.

38

and taking energy from the sunlight, built up at first simple organic bodies, and now these in turn reacting with one another formed more and more complex organic compounds. In any such transformation external energy is necessary, because the reacting bodies, carbon dioxide and water, are fully oxidised, and must be reduced with evolution of oxygen and uptake of energy in what is called an endothermic reaction. To this reaction, the inorganic colloid plays the part of an activator or catalyst, the solar energy being converted into chemical energy of the organic compound, so serving as a reservoir of the energy necessary for the coming living organic world.

It was first suggested by von Baeyer[1] that the initial stage in the synthesis of organic matter from inorganic by the green plant consisted in a reaction of carbon dioxide and water to produce formaldehyde and oxygen, the energy for the endothermic reaction being supplied from the energy of the light vibrations. This has been confirmed by delicate reactions, for although the change is a transitory one, the formaldehyde being condensed into other organic substances as it is formed, yet colour reactions for aldehydes are known so delicate that they will clearly indicate 1 part in 1,000,000 of aldehyde.

Any accumulation of formaldehyde would rapidly kill the living cell, and it is soon transformed into other products, but the colour tests are so delicate that its presence in traces has now been confirmed by several observers.[2]

Acting on the hypothesis outlined above, experiments with a view to testing the synthetic action of sunlight in presence of inorganic colloids were commenced in 1911, but for over a year only negative results were obtained, on account of difficulties in adjusting proper concentrations of solution, securing adequate illumination in vessels made of suitable material, and obtaining delicate enough methods for separating and identifying formaldehyde. After overcoming these experimental difficulties, and with the aid of the brighter sunshine, a large number of positive results have been obtained, and the synthesis of formaldehyde under the conditions to be described below has been shown quite unmistakably by all the usual colour reactions for formaldehyde.

It has also been shown that it is the ultra-violet rays which are

[1] *Berichte d. deut. chem. Gesellsch.*, 1870, vol. iii., p. 68.

[2] See especially Usher and Priestley, *Roy. Soc. Proc.*, 1906, B, vol. lxxvii., p. 369, where references to other papers are given.

most effective. The use of quartz flasks as containers for the colloid gives, with the same intensity of insolation, definite results in a much shorter period, and it has been found that a " Uviol " mercury arc, in a " Uviol " glass protecting vessel, immersed in an outer wider cylinder of glass so as to produce a thin layer of the colloid, through which the carbon dioxide is passed, gives quite clearly positive reactions for formaldehyde by all the colour tests, with an exposure to light of only four or five hours.

The results are obtained either with colloidal hydrated ferric oxide, or colloidal oxide of uranium, in exceedingly dilute solution. For example, in the case of uranium, 0 028 per cent. of the oxide, and, in the case of the iron, 0·113 per cent. of ferric oxide were the concentrations used

Controls carried out in the absence of light give no formaldehyde. The same point is shown by our earlier unsuccessful experiments in which the illumination was inadequate

Formaldehyde in small amounts has already been synthesised from inorganic sources in several reactions in which hydrogen in the nascent condition, or absorbed in palladium, has been present. But there is here chemical energy as such, presented by the hydrogen, and so far as we are aware there is no case known of utilisation of light energy by an inorganic catalyst which does not itself become altered in the reaction.

Thus Bach[1] obtained formaldehyde from hydrogen palladium and carbon dioxide, Fenton[2] obtained it by the action of carbon dioxide and water on metallic magnesium, and other observers have obtained it by the interaction of dilute sodium amalgam and moist carbon dioxide

The only experiment approaching more closely to our own as recorded below is one devised by Bach,[3] and later repeated with modifications by Euler[4] and by Usher and Priestley [5]

Bach passed a current of carbon dioxide through a solution of 1 5 per cent. *crystalloidal* uranium acetate, and in the presence of light obtained a precipitate of mixed oxides of uranium, which did not occur when light was excluded during the passage of the carbon

---

[1] *Comptes Rendus*, 1898, vol. cxxvi , p 79.

[2] *Journ. Chem Soc Trans.*, 1907, vol xci , p 687

[3] *Comptes Rendus.* 1893, vol. cxvi , p 1145

[4] *Berichte d deut chem Gesellsch.*, 1904, Jahrang 37, vol. ii , p. 3411.

[5] *Roy Soc. Proc.*, 1903, B, vol lxxvii., p. 369; and 1906, B, vol lxxviii., p. 322.

dioxide. He adduces no direct experimental evidence of the presence of formaldehyde in the solution, but makes the hypothesis that the carbonic acid by the action of light forms formaldehyde and per-carbonic acid. Then the per-carbonic acid decomposes and forms peroxide of uranium. Lastly, the formaldehyde attacks uranic oxide forming lower oxides recognisable by their colour in the precipitate of mixed oxide. In confirmation he shows that when peroxide of uranium and actually added formaldehyde are exposed to sunlight a reduction to lower oxide occurs with production first of a green and then a violet colour.

It will be observed, first that the crystalloidal salt of uranium employed undergoes permanent change, and secondly that there is no clear evidence of formation of formaldehyde, although our experiments recorded below show that Bach's hypothesis is probably a correct one. All the experiment actually proves, however, is that acetate of uranium in crystalloidal solution, in presence of carbon dioxide and sunlight, is decomposed, yielding a mixture of oxides of uranium. At the same time it is an important pioneer experiment in this field.

In a later experiment, Bach obtained evidence of the formation of formaldehyde by exposing to light a solution of dimethylaniline in dilute sulphuric acid through which carbon dioxide was passed. There is here, however, the objection of using an organic body as catalyst, although the reaction is interesting as a photo-synthesis.

The same objection holds as to the presence of the acetic acid anion in the uranium acetate solution used above, since this might serve as a source of formaldehyde.

A considerable increase in our knowledge was given in the papers of Usher and Priestley quoted above, in which they repeated and extended Bach's experiment.

The experiments of Bach were repeated and confirmed by these authors, both as to the production of peroxide and formaldehyde. The amount of decomposition obtained in three weeks in bright weather was extremely small, and this was ascribed to the poorness of the uranium as a catalyst, and the non-removal of the separated oxygen which remained as uranium peroxide and acted as a destructive agent upon the formaldehyde.

The authors accordingly took tubes of Jena glass, cooled them in liquid air, passed in carbon dioxide, sealed, and exposed for 24 hours, suspended outside a south window, in bright sunlight.

A precipitate appeared after 15 minutes' exposure, and in 24 hours the reaction was complete. The tubes on opening were found to contain uranium peroxide and formic acid, but no formaldehyde.

Usher and Priestley then repeated their experiments, using uranium sulphate instead of the acetate. Carbon dioxide was passed through a 2 per cent. crystalloidal uranium sulphate solution, and the solution was exposed to sunlight on a roof for nearly a fortnight. Several grammes of a precipitate of mixed oxides of uranium were obtained of a pale violet colour. The greater part was a mixture of uranous and ordinary uranic hydroxides soluble in acetic acid. The insoluble residue was a hydrate of uranium peroxide. The filtrate from all these mixed hydroxides was distilled and examined for formaldehyde. None, however, was found, though the liquid reduced Fehling's solution and silver nitrate It was subsequently found to contain formic acid, the lead salt of which was prepared and identified. The undistilled residue was then evaporated down, and when nearly solid was repeatedly extracted with dry ether in order to remove any formic acid which had not evaporated. The residual solid was extracted with absolute alcohol, and the solution on evaporation left a small quantity of a brown syrup, bitter to the taste, which reduced Fehling's solution. It could not be proven that this formed an osazone, but it closely resembled in its properties a substance called "methylenitan" obtained by Butlerow from formaldehyde and milk of lime. The body was obtained in minute amount only.

This experiment constitutes a distinct advance, since the organic substances (formic acid and the body above mentioned) were obtained by the action of light on purely inorganic substances.

The points still left against the results, from the aspect mentioned at the outset of the present chapter, are that the catalyst is an extremely rare one in nature, that it was used in high concentration in crystalloidal solution, and that it underwent changes in itself and was precipitated as the result of the reaction The fact that formic acid was obtained instead of formaldehyde, looked at from our point of view, is relatively unimportant, since both are organic bodies of increased energy content.

By the use of many times more dilute colloidal uranic hydroxide, we have been able now to obtain formaldehyde, and this without precipitation or other visible change in our catalyst. Compared with a stronger solution of crystalloidal uranium nitrate alongside, and given the same exposure and general conditions, we have been able to show that the colloidal condition is much more active in this photo-chemical reaction. In this comparative experiment the crystalloidal uranium nitrate was precipitated while no precipitation whatever occurred in the colloidal uranic hydroxide.

Passing on, we have shown that similar photo-synthesis of organic from inorganic matter easily occurs with colloidal ferric hydroxide, and by the use of the " Uviol " mercury lamp we are enabled to experiment at all times and obtain synthetic results readily in a few hours, a consideration of some importance in working in a country where sunlight is so variable, and so often unavailable for days.

The experiments with uranic hydroxide and ferric hydroxide were made concurrently in time, but for convenience we shall describe first the uranium experiments and then those with the ferric hydroxide.

Photo-Synthesis by Colloidal Uranic Hydroxide.

Method of Preparation of the Colloidal Solution.—A strong solution of uranium nitrate (approximately 10 per cent.) is taken and treated in the cold by adding a saturated solution of ammonium carbonate until the precipitate just ceases to redissolve. The solution is then filtered and dialysed in a tube of parchment paper for several days against running water. The greater part of the uranium is still in the crystalloidal state, and dialyses away at this state. Great care is required in the first step to get the proper relative amount of ammonium carbonate; also it is as well not to wait for the removal of the last traces of crystalloidal uranium, but to take the solution when it still gives a faint reaction with potassium ferrocyanide. The amount so left is, however, very minimal compared with the crystalloidal uranium solutions as used in the experiments recorded below, and nearly all the uranium at the end is present as colloidal uranic hydroxide.

This method is practically the same as that described by Graham for the preparation of colloidal ferric hydroxide and as used in the preparation of our colloidal iron solutions.

The amount of uranium in this solution was determined by evaporating a measured volume to dryness and weighing the residue, and was found to be 0·478 per cent. of Ur_2O_3.

In carrying out the photo-synthetic experiments this solution was either diluted fifteen to twenty fold with distilled water, and carbon dioxide, evolved from marble and pure hydrochloric acid and washed by water in a wash-bottle, passed through in a slow stream, or it was diluted to the same degree with distilled water previously saturated with carbon dioxide, and sealed up hermetically in glass tubes, which were then exposed to such direct sunlight as was available on the flat roof of the laboratory

It will accordingly be observed that the concentration of the colloidal uranic hydroxide in the solutions actually exposed to the light was only 0·024 to 0·035 per cent. The stock solution of the colloid had a pale lemon yellow colour, and the diluted solutions were almost colourless, showing just the merest trace of yellow colour, and the solutions throughout remained water clear. The colloidal solution is very sensitive, and is precipitated by traces of added crystalloid

The test solution for aldehyde used in our earlier experiments was Schiff's reagent, which consists of a dilute solution of fuchsin (about 1 per cent. in water) through which sulphur dioxide is passed until it is just decolorised .This reagent added in the proportion of 3 drops to 10 c c. of a dilute formaldehyde solution shows the presence of the latter by a distinct pink coloration, developing in about half an hour at a dilution of 1 in 500,000

At a later stage our observations were confirmed by the Schryver test, which was found to be the most reliable.

Schryver's test was carried out by preparing a 5 per cent solution of potassium ferricyanide and a 1 per cent. solution of phenylhydrazine hydrochloride, which was used as follows: To 10 c.c. of the solution suspected of containing formaldehyde 2 c c of the phenylhydrazine solution are added, then 1 c c of the potassium ferricyanide solution followed by 3 c c of concentrated hydrochloric acid, when a pink coloration appears If this is diluted with water it becomes colourless ; this colourless solution is shaken with ether, and the ethereal solution which is not coloured is separated off. Finally the ethereal solution is shaken up with a few cubic centimetres of concentrated hydrochloric acid, when, if formaldehyde be present, a strong pink or carmine colour appears in the hydrochloric acid layer.

All of the colour tests for formaldehyde have been obtained on many occasions.

Experiment I.—Twenty c.c. of dilute colloidal uranic hydroxide solution containing approximately 0·03 per cent. of Ur_2O_3 were placed in a test-tube on the roof, and carbon dioxide generated in a Kipp, and washed as above described, was slowly bubbled through. The day was a bright sunny one (May 26, 1913), and the experiment was continued all day. Half of the solution was taken out, and of this the greater part was distilled off from the colloid. Tested with Schiff's reagent this distillate gave a distinct pink coloration within half an hour. The remaining half of the colloidal solution was kept on the following day, which was also a bright sunny day, on the roof with carbon dioxide bubbling slowly through it ; it was then tested in the same way for aldehyde, and gave a still stronger reaction. Blanks were carried out with distilled water, and the Schiff's reagent and the contrast was most marked, the distillate from the colloid exposed to light giving a deep pink, while the distilled water control remained colourless.

Experiment II.—Thirty c.c. of the same dilute colloidal uranium solution were taken in a wide test-tube, saturated with carbon dioxide by bubbling the gas through, and then hermetically sealed. The tube was left resting on its side on the roof for two days, both of which had a good deal of bright sunshine. The contents of the tube showed no visible alteration or precipitation at the end of the period. The tube was now opened and about two-thirds of its contents were distilled off. The distillate tested with Schiff's reagent gave a marked formaldehyde reaction.

Experiment III.—A soda-water syphon with a " sparklet " apparatus for charging with CO_2 was taken, and in it were placed 500 c.c. of distilled water and 30 c.c. of the stock colloidal uranium hydroxide solution, giving accordingly a concentration of 0·035 per cent. of Ur_2O_3.

This was charged with carbon dioxide from a " sparklet " bulb, and left on the roof for thirteen days, of which seven were bright days with strong sunlight. At the end of the period a portion was withdrawn and distilled. It gave strong positive reactions for formaldehyde with both Schiff's reagent and Schryver's test.

The stock solution of colloidal uranium hydroxide diluted equally and distilled without previous exposure to light gave negative results in both tests.

Experiment IV.: Contrast of Action of Colloidal Uranium and Crystalloidal Uranium.—Two glass tubes were taken of similar dimensions; in the first were placed 20 c c. of distilled water saturated with carbon dioxide from a " sparklet " syphon, and 2 c c. of stock colloidal uranium hydroxide solution; in the other tube, 20 c c. of the water charged with carbon dioxide from the same syphon and 0 2 c.c. of 20 per cent. crystalloidal uranium nitrate solution.   At the end of the experiment, by drying and incinerating a measured volume, the percentage of uranic oxide was determined, and it was found that the colloidal solution contained 0 041 per cent., and the crystalloidal 0·08 per cent , so that the crystalloidal solution was approximately double in concentration that of the colloidal. The two tubes were hermetically sealed and placed on the roof for six days, three of which had bright sunshine, the others very cloudy and raining   The two tubes were opened, and the contents separately distilled in a similar fashion   The distillate from the crystalloid showed negative results with the Schiff's test, while the distillate from the colloid gave a most strongly marked positive reaction.

Experiment V.: Illustrating the Necessity for Strong Direct Sunlight —Two solutions, one of colloidal uranic oxide, the other crystalloidal uranium nitrate of approximately equal concentration, were taken, of each 50 c.c , in a glass tube, and washed carbon dioxide was bubbled through each in a slow stream. These were exposed on the roof for two days   Both these days were dull with practically no sunshine; there was, however, fairly bright diffuse daylight. The contents were then distilled as in the preceding experiments, but negative results were obtained in both cases.

Experiment VI.—Four similar wide glass tubes were taken, and into each was introduced 30 c.c. of distilled water charged previously with carbon dioxide, and 2 c.c. of colloidal uranic oxide solution, containing 0·478 per cent. of Ur_2O_3. Accordingly, the concentration of colloid in each case was approximately 0 03 per cent., or 3 in 10,000 parts.   The four glass tubes were then sealed up hermetically and treated as follows.

1. The first tube was exposed on the roof to such sunlight as was available for six days, in four of which there was brilliant sunshine all day.

2 The second tube was preserved for the same period in a dark cupboard in the laboratory.

3. The third tube was immersed in a wider open glass tube containing a strong alcoholic solution of chlorophyll, so as to give a

chlorophyll shade all round it, between it and the sunlight, and then the open tube was closed by a cork. This tube was then, thus sheathed, exposed to the sunlight on the roof alongside the first tube and for a similar period.

4. The fourth tube was immersed in a 5 per cent. solution of quinine sulphate in a similar manner to that described for tube No. 3, and was then exposed in like manner to Nos. 1 and 3, and for the same period.

The contents of the four tubes were distilled off in each case, and the four distillates were comparatively tested alongside one another, using the Schiff's and Mulliken's tests.

The tube kept in the dark gave completely negative results, while all three exposed to the light (Nos. 1, 3, and 4) gave positive results; the tube surrounded by chlorophyll (No. 3) was the strongest, and next was that surrounded by the quinine solution, both being more marked than the tube exposed to direct sunlight. But much more experimentation is required here. There is, however, no doubt that active rays penetrate both chlorophyll and quinine solutions, as the reactions were most distinct, and it appeared as if these solutions possibly had prevented the passage of rays with a slowing effect on the reaction.

Experiment VII.: Dilute Colloidal Uranic Oxide Solutions exposed to Light from a " Uviol " Mercury Arc in a Transparent Quartz Test-tube.—Forty c.c. of a colloidal uranic oxide solution made by diluting the stock solution fifteen-fold, and so containing 0·03 per cent. of the colloid, were placed in a tube of transparent quartz, and after saturation with washed carbon dioxide from a Kipp apparatus were exposed about $2\frac{1}{2}$ inches from a " Uviol " mercury arc for the period during three days in which the lamp was lit, probably about 12 hours in all. At the end of the period the fluid was distilled and the distillate tested by Schryver's test. It gave a strongly marked reaction, corresponding to at least 1 part in 100,000 of formaldehyde.

PHOTO-SYNTHESIS BY COLLOIDAL FERRIC HYDROXIDE.

Preparation of Colloidal Solution.—The colloidal ferric hydroxide solution was prepared after the method originally given by Graham.[1] A strong solution of ferric chloride is taken, about 20 per cent., and

[1] *Phil. Trans.*, 1861, vol. cli., p. 208.

to this a saturated solution of ammonium carbonate is added gradually with shaking so long as the precipitate first formed continues to dissolve.   The solution is then dialysed for some days, ten days or more, until the reaction for chloride becomes very faint The solution so obtained is of a deep reddish-brown colour, even in a 1 per cent solution, and if converted back into the crystalloidal form by boiling with a drop or two of acid the change is remarkable, to a pale lemon-yellow colour.   At the dilutions used in the experiments below the colour scarcely shows when reduced to the crystalloidal condition, but in the colloidal condition, even at this dilution, the solutions possess a deep sherry colour.   The dilute solution in an ordinary small test-tube absorbs the blue of the spectrum completely, as shown by a pocket spectroscope.   When examined by light transmitted from a " Uviol " mercury lamp, the solution viewed directly transmits a yellowish-green light, and at the sides, reflected from the glass surfaces, there is a deep green fluorescence, which reminds one strongly of the fluorescence of a strong solution of chlorophyll

The colloidal iron solution so prepared is readily coagulated by boiling, and is most sensitive to added crystalloids, it is thrown out by 1 part in 1000 of ammonium carbonate, and a mere trace of decinormal caustic soda throws it completely down.   It is in a delicately reactive, meta-stable condition, which reminds one forcibly, as it did Graham fifty years ago, of the proteins and the constituents of living cells.

When set up in the " Uviol " apparatus and the transmitted light observed with a spectroscope, it is seen that the bright lines of the mercury arc spectrum in the blue and violet have entirely disappeared, and the only ones now visible are those of the red, orange, and green.   An examination of the solar spectrum shows complete absorption of all higher wave-lengths than green.

There is this difference between the solar and the mercury arc light absorption, that in the former there is a continuous spectrum absorbed from green onward, while in the mercury arc spectrum the absorption is that of three sets of wave-lengths, one at the junction of green and blue, the other far over in the blue, and the third in the violet portion of the visible spectrum   We have not hitherto been able to observe the absorption of the ultra-visible rays.   The light energy from these definite wave-lengths of the spectrum seems, however, from the results recorded below, to be very effective for the particular synthesis under consideration.

In describing the synthetic results with the ferric oxide colloid, a few earlier experiments made in glass vessels with rather poor daylight illumination may be passed over, merely remarking that these led us on to the others in which unmistakable evidence of organic synthesis was obtained, and only the latter are here recorded. With sufficient illumination either with sunlight or the mercury arc spectrum, and especially when " Uviol " glass or quartz has been used, we have never failed to obtain clear evidence of synthesis.

Experiment I.—A dilute solution of colloidal ferric hydroxide containing 0·2 per cent. of Fe_2O_3, was placed in a thin blown flat-sided glass bottle, made like a wash-bottle with ground-glass stoppers. A slow current of carbon dioxide, washed by passing through a wash-bottle containing water, after evolution from marble in a Kipp apparatus, was passed through the colloidal solution during two days of fairly bright sunshine on the laboratory roof. On distillation this gave a moderately strong positive reaction to the Schiff's test.

Experiment II.—A glass soda-water syphon with a " sparklet " apparatus attached was charged with 500 c.c. of distilled water and 5 c.c. of a colloidal ferric oxide solution, and after dilution contained about 0·05 per cent. of colloidal ferric oxide. This was saturated with carbon dioxide by a sparklet bulb, and left on the roof for a period of twenty days, in which there were about thirteen days of bright sunshine. At the end of the period, 40 c.c. were withdrawn and distilled. A very distinct positive reaction for formaldehyde was obtained with Schryver's test.

Experiment III. : Exposure to Sunlight in Transparent Silica Flask.—A colloidal solution of ferric hydroxide of a concentration of 0·14 per cent., measuring 50 c.c., was placed in a silica flask through which carbon dioxide was passed, on the roof. The experiment lasted for two days, of which the first was dull, and the second almost continuous bright sunshine. On distillation this gave a most marked positive reaction with Schiff's test, indicating from the short period of exposure that the reaction probably proceeds more rapidly in silica vessels which are more transparent to the shorter wave-lengths of light.

Experiment IV. : Exposure to Mercury Arc Lamp with " Uviol " Glass Shade.—A colloidal solution of ferric hydroxide diluted 1 in 20 from a stock solution of 2·26 per cent., and hence containing 0·113 per cent of colloid, was placed in a wide 1000 c c. measuring cylinder. In this glass cylinder was immersed a wide round-bottomed tube of " Uviol " glass of somewhat smaller diameter to serve as a protector between the heated lamp to be placed in the interior and the surrounding fluid between the " Uviol " tube and the outer cylinder of glass. The mercury lamp was then set going, and inserted in the centre of the " Uviol " glass protecting tube. The mercury lamp tube, also of " Uviol " glass, has a diameter of 3 cm. approximately, the protecting tube a diameter of 5·4 cm. externally, and the outer glass cylinder an internal diameter of about 6·2 cm. The light generated at a distance of about 2 cm., after passing two thicknesses of " Uviol " glass and a layer of air of somewhat less than a centimetre, passed through a layer of the colloidal solution about 4 to 5 mm. thick and then reached the outer glass vessel   On account of the rounded bottom of the " Uviol " protecting tube there was a certain considerable volume of the solution at the bottom not so well illuminated. The total volume of colloidal solution at the bottom and in the annular space between the two tubes was approximately 300 c c.

A slow, steady stream of washed carbon dioxide was passed through the colloidal solution.

After about half an hour's running the colloidal solution became too warm and began to coagulate, so the current was switched off and the lamp allowed to cool. The whole was then immersed in a wide square-sided glass jar of about 17 litres capacity through which a stream of cold water was continuously circulated. The lamp was now relit and kept going for a period of 2 hours, making $2\frac{1}{2}$ hours of illumination in all. In this first experiment with the " Uviol " apparatus, the colloidal solution had coagulated at the end, but this did not happen in later experiments when the heat was better regulated.

The colloidal solution was removed and tested for formaldehyde in two ways   One portion was distilled as in the previously recorded experiments, and the distillate gave a most marked positive reaction with Schiff's reagent—a deep pink coloration   A second part was simply filtered off from the coagulated iron precipitate, and at once tested. It also gave a marked positive reaction both with Schiff's and Mulliken's tests.

Experiment V.—An experiment of the same type as the preceding one. A colloidal solution of 1 in 20 of the same stock solution was taken, and exposed to the mercury arc light as before—illuminated during two periods of 55 minutes and 2 hours 50 minutes respectively, making 3 hours 45 minutes in all. Part of the solution distilled off gave a distinct positive reaction with Schiff's test. Another portion coagulated by boiling, and filtered from iron, but not distilled, gave a positive reaction with gallic acid and concentrated sulphuric acid (Mulliken's test).

The experiment was continued next day, from 10.15 a.m. till 2.15 p.m.; at the end of this 4 hours' period the solution coagulated, owing to a failure in the water circulation and the temperature rising. The coagulated fluid was filtered and the filtrate tested; it gave a marked positive effect with Schiff's test and also a positive result with Mulliken's test; a trace of iron left over interfered with the Schryver test, but on distillation this also was obtained.

Experiment VI.—This was conducted similarly to the above Experiments IV. and V. for a period of 1 hour 40 minutes. Then a trace of ammonium carbonate amounting to only 1 part in 1000 was added with the view of forming hexamethylenetetramin and so concentrating the formaldehyde, but even this trace coagulated the solution.

The experiment was, however, continued for $5\frac{1}{2}$ hours additional. A small portion was acidified and distilled. The distillate gave a marked positive reaction with Schryver's test.

Experiment VII.—A dilute colloidal solution of ferric hydroxide (1 in 15) of stock solution, equivalent to 0·13 per cent. of ferric oxide, was exposed after saturation with carbon dioxide in a silica test-tube 3 inches away from the mercury arc, during the time the lamp was lit on three days, probably about 12 hours in all. A most marked reaction to all tests. The reaction quantitatively is slightly less than the uranium effect (see Experiment VII. of previous section), and throughout it appears that the uranium catalyst is somewhat more powerful than the ferric catalyst.

Conclusions.

Organic matter (aldehyde) has been synthesised from inorganic colloidal uranic and ferric hydroxides in very dilute solution. These colloids act as catalysts for light energy, converting it into chemical energy in a reduction process similar to the first stage of synthesis of organic from inorganic substances in the green plant by the agency of chlorophyll.

Such a synthesis occurring in nature probably forms the first step in the origin of life. For chlorophyll and protoplasm are substances of far too complex chemical constitution to be regarded as the first step in the evolution of the organic from the inorganic

Without the presence of organic material, when life was arising in the world, any continuance of life would, however, be impossible.

The process of evolution of simple organic substances having once begun, as now experimentally demonstrated, substances of more and more complex organic nature would arise from these with additional uptake of energy. Later, organic colloids would be formed, possessing meta-stable properties, and these would begin to show the properties possessed by living matter of balanced equilibrium, and up-and-down energy transformations following variations in environment.

There can be little question that such energy changes as are above described occur at present, and are leading always to fresh evolutions of more complex organic substances, and so towards life, and equally is it true that they must occur on any planet containing the necessary elements for the evolution of inorganic colloids and exposed to light energy under suitable conditions of environment

CHAPTER IV

THE PRESENCE OF INORGANIC IRON COMPOUNDS IN THE CHLOROPLASTS OF THE GREEN CELLS OF PLANTS, CONSIDERED IN RELATIONSHIP TO NATURAL PHOTO-SYNTHESIS AND THE ORIGIN OF LIFE

SINCE the days of de Saussure,[1] now over a century ago, the green colouring matter of the leaf, chlorophyll, has been regarded as the fundamental agent for the worldwide photo-synthesis of living matter. But it is remarkable how completely this view is based upon indirect or circumstantial evidence, and how little, if any, direct observation can be cited in its support.

Chlorophyll is known by the biochemist to be one of the most complex of substances, comparable to hæmoglobin in its molecular structure, and yielding a host of disintegration constituents themselves complicated substances of high molecular weight. Between the simple colloidal molecules of inorganic iron salts in solution or suspension and such a highly complex organic substance as chlorophyll there is a wide interval, and it was with the view of discovering some intermediate links or finding some explanation for the gap that the present experiments were commenced.

Before describing the experiments in detail it is desirable to touch upon present views as to photo-synthesis in the green cell as far as these bear upon our investigation, in order to give an appropriate setting to the new facts, and show how present knowledge regarding the absolute necessity for the presence of iron in the green leaf, which has been hitherto devoid of all explanation, led up to these experiments.

Photo-synthesis with production of oxygen only occurs in the chlorophyll-containing parts of the plant, and only in these when they are exposed to light. Also, when a plant is allowed to grow in darkness, the leaves are found to be pale yellow in colour, or chlorotic, instead of green. When a plant grown in darkness, and, as a result, possessing chlorotic leaves, is then exposed to light, the pale yellow

---

[1] "Recherches Chimiques sur la Végétation" (1804), *Ostwald's Klassiker*, Nos. 15 and 16.

colour is rapidly replaced by a green, and then photo-synthesis is readily demonstrable by the evolution of oxygen and the appearance of starch granules.

The above reasoning constitutes the whole of the evidence that chlorophyll is the primary cause in the first act of photo-synthesis. It is to be observed that the entire chain of evidence is inferential, and that in order to form a valid proof, chlorophyll would require to be the only substance present in the chloroplast, which is very far from being the case. No observer has ever obtained an appreciable and satisfactory synthesis with pure chlorophyll in solution or suspension when removed from the other constituents of the chloroplast. Certain observers have observed minute traces of formaldehyde formation with chlorophyll solutions or emulsions, but even these traces of photo-synthesis have been stoutly denied by other competent observers. In any case, the photo-synthetic effect produced is infinitesimally small compared to that observed in the intact green cell.

The most recent and careful experiments upon this subject are those performed by Usher and Priestley[1] and by Schryver.[2] Usher and Priestley found that when a chlorophyll-containing extract from green leaves was spread out as a film or emulsion on a gelatine plate, small but distinctly demonstrable amounts of formaldehyde were formed on exposure to sunlight. But in this case there is gelatine containing inorganic colloids, since an ash is obtained on combustion of the gelatine, and in the chlorophyll extract there would undoubtedly be iron salts present, because about one-fourth of the iron of green leaves comes away in the alcoholic extract.

Schryver worked with an ethereal solution of chlorophyll allowed to evaporate at room temperature on a strip of glass, and found that although such films of chlorophyll on glass produced no formaldehyde in darkness even in presence of moist carbon dioxide, a minute amount of formaldehyde was formed when the film was exposed to sunlight even in absence of carbon dioxide, and a distinct reaction when the film was exposed to sunlight in presence of moist carbon dioxide. The amount of formaldehyde formed in all such experiments is, however, very minute compared to the products of photo-synthesis under natural conditions by the complete chloroplast

[1] *Roy. Soc Proc.*, B, vol lxxvii, p 369 (1906); B, vol. lxxviii., p. 318 (1906); B, vol lxxxiv , p 101 (1911).

[2] *Roy. Soc. Proc.*, B, vol lxxxii., p. 226 (1910).

Now the chloroplast contains a great deal more than chlorophyll, and when all the chlorophyll has been removed by some such reagent as hot alcohol there remains behind a colourless body, the so-called stroma. The chloroplast after the extraction is still a solid-looking body, and to all appearances the only thing that has happened is that a thin layer of green colouring matter has been removed. There is no shrinking or shrivelling up of the chloroplast.

There is accordingly no experimental evidence that the primary agent in the photo-synthesis may not be contained in the colourless part of the chloroplast, and the chlorophyll may be evolved at a later stage in synthetic operations induced by some constituent of the colourless part. The function of the chlorophyll may be a protective one to the chloroplast when exposed to light, it may be a light screen as has been suggested by Pringsheim, or it may be concerned in condensations and polymerisations subsequent to the first act of synthesis with production of formaldehyde.

All these views and others are possible, and the function of chlorophyll in the chloroplast remains for solution, but it has not been proved that chlorophyll is the primary causative agent in the photo-synthetic process where the chief energy uptake occurs with formation of formaldehyde.

There are other pieces of experimental evidence apart from the repeated failures to obtain satisfactory synthesis with isolated chlorophyll which go to indicate that chlorophyll is not the transformer in the first link of the synthetic chain.

In the first place chlorophyll itself is a product of photo-synthesis, and therefore there must be some active photo-synthetic substance present in the chloroplast before the chlorophyll appears which indeed first produces the chlorophyll by its activity.

When a yellow etiolated leaf taken from the darkness is exposed to the light it contains no chlorophyll, but photo-synthesis, in the absence of chlorophyll, sets in, and chlorophyll itself is one of the products, not the originator or agent, of this photo-synthesis. The period from first exposure to light to the appearance of chlorophyll is too short to determine whether oxygen production and starch formation commence before chlorophyll is formed.

In the next place Engelmann,[1] by the application of his ingenious method of the oxyphile bacteria, has clearly demonstrated two

[1] *Botanische Zeitung*, 1881, p. 446, and 1887, pp. 394, 410, 418, 426, 442, 458.

important facts : first, that the chloroplast alone, even when displaced from the rest of the cell, can, in presence of light, go on synthesising and producing oxygen; and, in the second place, a still more important point in our chain of evidence—namely, that certain leaves such as those of the yellow variety of elder, which do not produce chlorophyll when exposed to light but contain yellow chromatoplasts, cause synthesis and produce oxygen   These observations as to synthesis by healthy yellow leaves have been confirmed by other observers such as Tammes, Josopait, and Kohl.[1]

The strongest piece of evidence, however, that iron salts are more fundamental to photo-synthesis and take an earlier share in it than chlorophyll, is that furnished by that process frequently occurring in green leaves known as " chlorosis."

Chlorosis is a pathological condition of green leaves of considerable practical importance in arboriculture, and the discovery of its cause is, as Molisch states, one of the most interesting and beautiful in the history of plant physiology.

It was shown in 1843 by Eusebe Gris[2] that chlorosis naturally occurring in the leaves of shrubs or trees could be entirely removed either by applying dilute solutions of iron salts to the roots, or by placing the detached chlorotic branch in a dilute solution of iron, or even by painting the chlorotic leaf with a very dilute solution of an iron salt. In some cases within 24 hours, and in nearly all cases in a period of a week to ten days, the green colouring matter developed in the leaves where none had been before.

These results have been often confirmed and have been extended by Salm Horstmar, A. Gris, and Sachs.[3] Molisch[4] has, moreover, shown in a long series of experiments with different species of plants that all green plants, *even when fully exposed to light*, become afflicted with chlorosis and fail to develop chlorophyll when they are grown in a culture fluid especially made devoid of iron   As soon

---

[1] Quoted by Czapek, " Biochemie der Pflanzen," vol. 1 , p. 447.

[2] "De l'Action des Composés Ferrugineaux sur la Végétation," 1843. See also *Comptes Rendus*, vol xix., p. 1118 (1844); vol. xxi., p 1386 (1845), vol xxiii., p. 53 (1846), and vol xxv., p 276 (1847).

[3] Salm Horstmar, "Versuche uber die Ernahrung der Pflanzen," 1856; A Gris, *Annales d Scien Nat.*, Series IV., vol vii., p. 201 (1857), Sachs, " Flora, ' 1862.

[4] Molisch, "Die Pflanzen in ihren Beziehungen zum Eisen," Jena, G. Fischer (1892) Many of the references given are quoted from this source

as the reserve store of iron always contained in the seed embryo and cotyledons has been exhausted in the primordial leaves, only chlorotic pale yellow leaves are formed. These pale yellow leaves rapidly turn green if minute quantities of an iron salt are added to the culture fluid, or even if the surface of the leaf be painted over with a dilute solution of an iron salt, as had been previously shown by Gris to be the case with pathologically chlorotic leaves. So that iron is as indispensable to the green leaf as it is to the red blood-corpuscle.

The remarkable thing in view of this failure to develop chlorophyll in absence of iron, is that chlorophyll itself is shown by all the more recent researchers to be quite free from iron.[1] Chlorosis and its cure by iron salts has accordingly remained a puzzle to plant physiologists ever since the time of the discovery of Gris.[2] The experiments to be recorded below furnish, for the first time, a rational explanation of chlorosis and its cure. The iron salts are necessary for the formation of the colourless portion of the chloroplasts; for when all the chlorophyll and other fatty bodies and pigments are removed from the chloroplast by extraction with alcohol, and the colourless chloroplastic residue is treated with the microchemical tests for inorganic iron, a positive reaction in unmistakable degree is usually given by the colourless residue of the chloroplast.

This inorganic iron in presence of sunlight must give rise to photosynthesis and production of formaldehyde, which is then carried on into sugar and starches by other constituents of the chloroplast, and it is probably here, somewhere in the later processes, that the chlorophyll finds its function. The chlorophyll itself, as shown by the facts of chlorosis, its removal by administration of iron, and the presence of iron salts in the colourless part of the chloroplast, is a product of synthesis from colourless substances or from the light yellow pigment. For the production of the chlorophyll under normal conditions, both the presence of iron and the energy of sunlight are essential.

The reason for the earlier erroneous view that the chlorophyll molecule contained iron was that a certain fraction of the iron compounds contained in the green leaf becomes extracted by the

---

[1] See Molisch, *loc. cit.*, and R. Willstätter u. A. Stoll, "Untersuchungen über Chlorophyll," Berlin, J. Springer (1913).
[2] See Czapek, "Biochemie der Pflanzen."

alcohol used in the first extraction of the leaf,[1] so that all crude chlorophyll extracts contain iron. This, however, disappears on treating the alcoholic extract with benzol, and the product of purer chlorophyll separating from the benzol fraction is iron-free. At the same time its spectrum and other physical properties prove it to be unaltered chlorophyll

Other facts which show the importance of iron compounds in the green leaf are that leaves which are not deciduous annually, such as pine needles, contain more iron in their later years, and also in leaves of annual growth the older the leaf is the more iron does it contain in its ash. Thus Boussingault found in the ash of young leaves of *Brassica* 2 per cent. of Fe_2O_3, while old leaves contained in their ash 9·64 per cent   *Lactuca sativa* had in the young leaves 2·67, and in the old leaves 6·43 per cent. of Fe_2O_3 in the ash.   Another point is the curious conservation, resembling that seen in the animal economy, of the iron of the leaf in the case of deciduous leaves. Before the leaf drops a good deal of the iron is reabsorbed and stored for future use.   This is shown by analyses of the iron of the leaves of *Fagus sylvatica* made by Rissmuller[2] in successive months   The figures quoted give quantities of Fe_2O_3 in 100 parts of dried leaves collected at the times of year stated :

		May	June	July.	Aug	Sept	Oct	Nov.
Oxide of iron	..	0·35	0·51	0 58	0 75	1·03	0·60	0·59

The gradual increase of iron content to a maximum followed by a fall as the leaves grow sere is very interesting

It has been shown by Molisch (*loc cit*) that iron is an essential constituent for the growth of all plants, whether green or otherwise, but the saprophytic and parasitic plants which contain no chlorophyll require much less iron and, as a rule, contain much less in their ash.   Our own experiments show that the histochemical reactions for iron develop much more slowly in the fungi and are much less intense in degree   These feebler reactions probably arise from organic compounds of iron slowly being decomposed in traces and setting free ionic iron.   These organic iron compounds of the fungi are concerned with some other function than photo-synthesis or chlorophyll formation; they probably take a part in nuclear struc-

---

[1] According to early observations of Boussingault (*Agronomie*, vol. v., p 128) from one-quarter to one-third of the iron is removed by the alcohol.

[2] " Ueber die Stoffwanderung in der Pflanzen," *Landw. Versuchsstationen*, 1874 (*Just's Jahresbericht*, vol ii , p 849, 1874)

tures, for many nucleins are iron-containing, and, as has been shown by Macallum, after treating with acid alcohol to unmask the iron previously present in an organic form, the chromatin of nuclei always contains iron.

The reactions for inorganic iron are shown most markedly with the more lowly organised plants such as unicellular green plants occurring alone or in lichens, or in delicate algal threads, but when proper precautions are taken they can also be clearly demonstrated in the chloroplasts of the higher plants. The reactions are particularly well shown by the chloroplasts of aquatic plants, where, as is well known, the percentage of iron in the ash is also high.

These facts are in keeping with the natural order of evolution and are also in accord with other observations. For example, many algæ (such as certain confervæ and cladophora) deposit around them a layer, yellow to rust-red in colour, consisting of mixed ferrous and ferric oxides; this is often actively secreted from waters containing only traces of iron.

A considerable number of lichens also secrete incrustations of the mixed oxides of iron to such an extent as to change their appearance to an iron oxide or ochre colour, so that they have been termed by systematic botanists " formæ oxydatæ, ochraceæ " or " iron lichens." The iron oxide forms a fine incrustation usually on the mycelium of the fungus. No association of this iron oxide with a photo-synthetic function has ever been suggested, but in view of our present knowledge of the photo-synthetic activity of iron salts some investigation in this direction is highly desirable. It is an interesting observation of Molisch, from our point of view, that these " iron lichens " flourish exclusively on the oldest primitive rock formations (" Urgestein "). They are never found upon chalk formations, but grow upon granite, gneiss, syenite, and porphyry. Molisch was unable to find inorganic iron in the other lichens, but this doubtless arose from the less delicate methods he had at his command at that time, and from the fact that the fatty bodies contained in the green cells of the algæ of the lichen had not been removed. When the lichen is extracted with alcohol and Macallum's hæmatoxylin test then applied, the algal cells rapidly stain a deep blue-black, showing the presence of inorganic iron, while the hyphæ of the fungus only take on a brownish tinge during the same time, and only give a faint positive reaction at the end of some days or weeks.

It is somewhat remarkable that the presence of iron in the chloroplast should for so long have escaped discovery. The explanation probably lies in the fact that little attention has been given to the application to the green cell of the histochemical tests for iron since the discovery by Macallum of the more delicate hæmatoxylin iron test, as also to the delicacy of the chloroplasts to the more drastic earlier method used by Molisch, and to these factors may be added the difficulty with which some of the chemical reagents for iron penetrate the green cell, and the presence in the chloroplast itself of fatty and lipoidal substances which prevent the ingress of the water-soluble stains

Macallum[1] in 1894, before his discovery of unmordaunted hæmatoxylin as a reagent for iron, and using then ammonium sulphide in glycerine as a reagent, states that bacteria gave no evidence of an inorganic iron compound, but in the cyanophyceæ the chromophilous portions of the " central substance " contain iron, and iron may be also demonstrated in the peripheral granules containing the so-called·cyanophycin At this period, Macallum was specially concerned in proving the presence of inorganic iron in the chromatin of the nucleus and was not searching for iron in the chloroplasts, so that the reference above to the presence of iron in the cyanoplasts of the cyanophyceæ is highly interesting to-day.

Molisch (loc. cit.) used long immersion in saturated potassium hydrate as a preliminary method for setting free masked iron (i.e., organic iron) in available form for after-detection by potassium ferrocyanide and hydrochloric acid, and in the later testing used very strong hydrochloric acid (10 to 20 per cent). Such drastic procedures are very dangerous, because the alkali breaks down the delicate chloroplasts, and may also itself contain iron salts in traces, also, in the second place, as pointed out by Quincke,[2] such strong acid will fairly rapidly set iron free in inorganic or ionic form from the potassium ferrocyanide reagent, and this ionic iron reacting with the remainder of the reagent will give the Prussian blue colour Molisch found more iron in the epidermis and fibro-vascular bundles of green leaves than in the green mesophyll, but, as he himself admits, " the potassium hydrate so disorganises the nucleus and chlorophyll-granules that one can conclude nothing as to the distribution of iron in the cell "

[1] Roy Soc Proc., vol lvii , p 261 (1894)
[2] Arch. f Exp Path u. Pharm , vol xxxvii., p. 183 (1896)

So far as we have been able to discover there exist no records later than the above in the literature of the subject on the occurrence of iron in the chloroplasts of the green cell, nor any information as to the form in which iron compounds are present. No investigations with the iron hæmatoxylin test of Macallum appear to have been made hitherto upon plants.

EXPERIMENTAL METHODS.

In carrying out tests for the detection of inorganic iron in the chloroplasts, and in plant tissues generally, two points must be carefully borne in mind: first, the previous preparation of the tissue and its subdivision so that the parts possibly containing iron may be penetrated by the reagents used for the detection; and secondly, that the reagents be applied carefully so that false results are not obtained. Here care must be taken with the concentration of the reagents and the relative periods of time within which positive results are obtained.

In regard to the preparation of the tissues, if sections are to be cut, care must be taken that this is done with a clean burnished knife. Control experiments show that a clean steel knife leaves no iron on the section. But, in most cases, since the question at issue is not the structural arrangement but rather whether this or that constituent contains iron, it is better to work with finely teased or broken-up tissues. For this purpose glass rods drawn out to a point were always used instead of steel needles, and also, in order to break up some of the green cells and set free the chloroplasts, a portion of the tissue in each case was still more broken up by turning upon it the blunt end of the glass rod and grinding it between this and the microscope slide on which it was being mounted.

In choosing tissues for examination, preference so far as possible is given to those where the chloroplasts are more conspicuous in size, and also in some cases, such as spirogyra, delicate filaments were chosen which could, after extraction as described below with alcohol, be mounted without breaking up.

In certain cases, such as pleurococcus, staining can readily be obtained without previous chemical preparation of the tissue, but, in the majority of cases, the lipoids present along with the chlorophyll in the chloroplast prevent the penetration of the stain, also the green colour modifies and masks the blue of the hæmatoxylin in

Macallum's test   For this reason it is well to remove the lipoids and chlorophyll, and in many cases this is by no means an easy task   In some cases standing in cold alcohol removes the chlorophyll quite effectually and leaves the tissue colourless and ready for staining; but in other cases the tissue may be left at ordinary temperatures for days in alcohol, and this may even be followed by several extractions with ether and still some of the green colour remains   After a good deal of experimentation the best extractive in these latter cases was found to be boiling alcohol.

The tissue, either partially teased with the glass points if it is bulky like the leaf of a higher plant or a piece of lichen or moss, or left intact if a delicate structure like an algal filament or pleurococcus, is placed in water in a watchglass, and then absolute alcohol is gradually added portionwise and pouring away excess of the mixture at intervals until the fluid is finally all absolute alcohol   The preparation is then boiled in the alcohol and the greenish extract poured away, and this is repeated till the green tissue becomes colourless.   The decolorised tissue is then brought back again into distilled water by gradually adding the water to the alcohol, and pouring off   Finally, it is allowed to stand a few minutes in a watchglass in water redistilled from glass, and is then ready for staining.

In addition to the unmordaunted simple aqueous solution of well-washed hæmatoxylin in $\frac{1}{2}$ per cent. concentration introduced by Macallum,[1] the older histochemical tests for iron were also utilised—namely, potassium ferrocyanide and hydrochloric acid for ferric salts, potassium ferricyanide and hydrochloric acid for ferrous salts, and ammonium hydrogen sulphide in glycerine for both   In our opinion the Macallum test surpasses all these in reliability and delicacy.   Its only fault is that it is too delicate, and the small traces of inorganic iron set free from organic compounds in the tissues on long standing cause faint but increasing staining when a preparation is left over for some days.   When a blue-black is obtained, however, within a few hours with this reagent it is a decisive proof of loosely combined, or inorganic, iron in the situation where the staining occurs.

Ammonium hydrogen sulphide when added to the tissues with an equal amount of glycerine, and the whole kept at 36° C for some hours, produces a distinct blackening as compared with the normal,

[1] *Journ Physiol.*, vol xxii , p. 92 (1897).

but the effect is not very pronounced and is only clear on comparison of treated and untreated tissue.

Potassium ferrocyanide and hydrochloric acid never gave a blue colour, but a blue colour is frequently, and very distinctly, given within a few hours by potassium ferricyanide and acid, demonstrating that the inorganic iron of the chloroplasts is present in the ferrous condition; this was typically observed in the case of spirogyra and vaucheria.

There is always some doubt, however, about using a reagent which itself contains the element sought for, and, moreover, is fairly readily broken down in presence of organic matter and acid.

The hydrochloric acid used should not exceed 0·5 per cent. in concentration, and be used in equal volume with the 1·5 per cent. ferricyanide solution so that the concentration of acid acting on the tissue is only 0·25 per cent. Then, if a blue stain is obtained with a considerable intensity within 24 hours, it may fairly certainly be attributed to ferrous iron in that particular situation. The result, however, ought always to be confirmed by the Macallum test, for solid starch or casein left for 24 hours in contact with the above reagents each gives a faint blue colour which increases as the mixture is left standing.

When a solution of hæmatoxylin in pure distilled water is mixed with a very dilute solution of an ordinary iron salt such as ferric chloride, a deep blue-black coloration is immediately produced. If, instead of an ordinary iron salt solution, a solution of highly colloidal or dialysed iron oxide be mixed with the solution of hæmatoxylin, there is obtained instead a deep chocolate-brown coloration. In the course of some hours to a day or two, this chocolate-brown is replaced by the blue-black colour obtained with ionic or crystalloidal iron salts. Similar results are usually obtained when the hæmatoxylin solution is used as a detector of iron in the tissue of plants. In certain cases, notably unicellular green plants and algal filaments, a deep blue-black is obtained within a few minutes without any previous appearance of the brown stain characteristic of colloidal iron oxide, while in many of the higher plants (mono- and dicotyledons) the green leaf at first stains a deep brown, which gradually, in a varying period of a few hours to a day or two, changes to a blue-black, just as is seen in the test-tube when colloidal iron oxide solution is mixed with the reagent. In certain cases, however, the brown colour is found to persist for weeks without change.

This deep-brown coloration is not simply due to imbibition by the tissue of unaltered hæmatoxylin, for it is far too deep for this, and, moreover, is not removed by washing with a mixture of equal parts of alcohol and ether as recommended by Macallum. It is a true staining of colloidal iron, present in those parts of the tissues where the brown occurs, and possesses just the same dark brown colour that is obtained on mixing colloidal iron oxide solution and hæmatoxylin.

In contrast with vegetable tissues, such a direct staining (either brown or blue-black) is only found in the embryonic condition in the tissues of higher animals, for the iron in the majority of such animal tissues is firmly bound organically and gives no coloration with hæmatoxylin.

It is to be remarked that this staining as a test for iron is quite different from the ordinary use of hæmatoxylin as a nuclear stain in histological technique. In the ordinary use of hæmatoxylin as a staining reagent a mordaunt is always used either preceding the hæmatoxylin—as, for example, the iron-alum mordaunt for Heidenhain's iron-hæmatoxylin method—or simultaneously as in the use of the hæmalum stain, where the mordaunt alum is mixed with the hæmatoxylin. But in Macallum's use of the stain no mordaunt whatever is used, but instead a simple aqueous solution in pure distilled water. This solution only strikes a colour where a mordaunt is naturally present in the tissue. Now with iron in colloidal form the colour struck is the deep brown mentioned above; with iron in crystalloidal form the colour struck is blue-black. Thus Macallum's method resembles Heidenhain's staining, but with the previous iron treatment naturally provided in the tissues, and the blue-black effect obtained closely resembles in many cases a Heidenhain iron-hæmatoxylin stain.

In order to use the method effectively, it is not merely necessary to avoid all minute traces of iron in the water and other fluids used, but also all traces of alkali and acid, since these interfere with the delicacy of the reaction. Alkali gives a rose-red colour with the hæmatoxylin, and acid inhibits the development of the blue-black when the amount of iron is small. In making up the stain itself, water twice distilled from glass vessels must be used as the solvent, the second distillation having been made immediately previous to use. To make the staining solution, 0·3 grm. of pure hæmatoxylin is weighed out, and washed with the twice distilled water till the crystals are colourless, and the wash-water is only pale yellow without any trace of red. The solution is then made up to 50 c.c. and kept in a Jena glass flask, for the alkali which is slowly dissolved out from ordinary glass rapidly turns the solution pink. The reagent should be pale yellow when used, in order to obtain the best effects, and does not keep in good condition for more than a few days.

After the chlorophyll and fats have been removed from the tissue by allowing it to stand in cold alcohol, or by boiling up with alcohol, the colourless tissue must be well washed with water, and the water used must, as described above, be doubly distilled from glass.

The staining process may be watched in progress, when it will be found that escaped chloroplasts from ruptured cells take on the stain first, and in many cases show a deep purple-blue within a few minutes. Within the intact cell the stain does not penetrate so rapidly, and the cell wall may show a blue staining in some cases before the contained chloroplasts, but eventually these also stain a deep blue, sometimes preceded by a dark brown. The nuclei of the green plant cells also stain a deep blue (unlike animal cell nuclei), and there is usually a much slighter diffuse blue in the remaining cytoplasm. The fibres associated with the vascular bundles also show in many cases a blue staining. This probably means that the iron salts are carried along this route to the green cells. But the early and deep staining of chloroplasts and nuclei is characteristic in the preparations.

In addition to tissues containing chloroplasts, several preparations have been made from plants not containing chlorophyll, such as yeast, moulds, and larger fungi. There is a marked contrast found here: a blue stain does not appear for some days, and then in only a comparatively feeble manner. The conidia and the conidiophores show more iron than the mycelium filaments. It is probable that this slow and feeble staining is due to organic iron compounds slowly breaking up and yielding traces of inorganic iron.

A series of ash analyses of chlorophyll-containing and chlorophyll-free plants show in all cases a much higher percentage of iron in the ash of the green plant; this furnishes presumptive evidence that iron plays an important part in photo-synthesis.

A large number of plants of different types have been examined, and the main results are given in the following account.

Amongst unicellular green plants there were examined chlorella, obtained as plankton from a green-coloured pond-water; pleuro-coccus, obtained in nearly pure condition growing on an oak fence near Oxford, and stained and examined in collaboration with Mr. Edward Whitley, several forms of diatom and several unicellular forms found in lichens.

The blue-black effect is very readily obtained with these uni-cellular green plants, often without previous removal of the chloro-phyll In the case of the lichens the contrast is marked between the green cells and the fresh hyphæ of the fungus, but dead or decaying fungal matter often gives a blue stain

The algæ observed were species of vaucheria, spirogyra, ulva, and ulothrix. The effects were often repeated in several experi-ments, both with hæmatoxylin staining and with ferricyanide and hydrochloric acid. The ferricyanide solution does not appear to penetrate well, and only some filaments in an alga like spirogyra are coloured, but the staining has been obtained within an hour or two of treatment with this reagent, and is a very beautiful effect when obtained in spirogyra. The light blue colour follows the spirals of the chlorophyll bands, and the granules are obviously more deeply blue than the rest of the bands. The deep blue-black with hæmatoxylin is more readily and uniformly obtained, coming often within a few minutes of applying the stain to the decolorised alga, and furnishing again a beautiful effect. Sometimes, however, the brown colour of colloidal iron is obtained in spirogyra.

Ulva latissima gives a very deep blue-black coloration, rendering the cells almost opaque; its ash shows a high content in iron.

Cladothrix, when growing in water containing small amounts of iron, as is well known, secretes, or excretes, a tube of iron oxide around the filaments, and is then known as an " iron bacterium " When these so-called " iron bacteria " are treated with hæmatoxylin they turn blue-black almost instantly, and if the stained specimens are examined under the microscope the interesting fact is im-mediately observable that not only the external tube, but the sub-stance of the organism itself, is stained blue-black, so settling a much disputed point The same is seen in vaucheria—an incrustation of iron-oxide particles is demonstrable in the gelatinous sheath sur-rounding the filaments, either by ferricyanide or hæmatoxylin staining, but, in addition, both reagents show inorganic iron within the filament itself

Many higher aquatic plants, such as lemna and elodea, possess such incrustations of iron oxide on their leaves when grown in water containing only traces of iron, but in such cases it is also found that the chloroplasts of the green cell itself are very rich in inorganic iron. The higher aquatic plants examined have been these two and a variety of watercress, and all three were found to give a strong positive reaction.

Ordinary lawn grass contains a high percentage of iron in the ash, and, when teased out and deprived of chlorophyll by hot alcohol, forms a very suitable object on account of the ease with which strands of fibre with attached cells separate. The staining of the chloroplasts is at first a dark brown, passing later into a blue-black. The leaves of many species of dicotyledonous plants were examined, and it was found that here the transition from dark brown to blue-black was much slower as a rule, and in some cases the staining remained permanently of a deep orange-brown to a pure dark brown colour. But in all cases the chloroplasts stained more deeply than the remainder of the cytoplasm.

The catalyst for the photo-synthesis may not in all cases be an iron salt, or oxide, but an iron salt is present and capable of operating as a catalyst in a large number of instances.

Various substances known to be present in the ash of leaves have been tested for their photo-synthetic activity in connection with the work, and it has been found that magnesium and calcium phosphates and bicarbonates are entirely ineffectual, but that marked photo-synthesis of formaldehyde is obtained with chlorides or colloidal hydrates of iron or aluminium.

Summary

1. Inorganic iron salts and iron or aluminium hydrates in colloidal solution possess the power of transforming the energy of the sunlight into chemical energy of organic compounds.

2. Inorganic iron, in crystalloidal or colloidal form, is present in the colourless part of the chloroplast of the green plant cell in many plants.

3. In the absence of iron the green colouring matter cannot develop in the leaf, although the green colouring matter itself contains no iron.

4. In the presence of sunshine, the iron-containing substance of the chloroplast develops the colouring matter, so that this itself is a

product of photo-synthesis induced by the iron-containing compound.

5. These facts afford an explanation of chlorosis, and its cure by inorganic iron salts, and demonstrate that iron is a primary essential in photo-synthesis and the production of chlorophyll.

6. The iron-containing substances of the colourless portion of the chloroplast, and the chlorophyll produced by them, then become associated in the functions of photo-synthesis as a complete mechanism for the energy transformation.

CHAPTER V

THE FORMATION OF NITRITES FROM NITRATES IN AQUEOUS SOLUTION BY THE ACTION OF SUNLIGHT, AND THE ASSIMILATION OF THE NITRITES BY GREEN LEAVES IN SUNLIGHT

THE number of chemical changes brought about by the activity of light is multitudinous, and the study of these reactions has been very intensive in recent years. In the majority of the photo-chemical reactions, the effect produced is that of hastening an exothermic reaction, and in this resembles the action of a catalyst. The substances formed have a less content of chemical energy than the mother substances, and are usually of a more simple structural type. In such cases there is no clear proof of transformation, or conversion, of light energy into chemical energy, and the light acts more as a detonator to a chemical reaction in which chemical energy is set free.

The most important case of an endothermic reaction set up by the action of light is that in which the synthesis of formaldehyde and carbohydrate is effected in the green leaf by that action of light upon water and carbon dioxide in which the light energy is converted into chemical energy and stored up.

It has been shown in previous chapters that the first step—namely, that of formaldehyde formation—in which the greatest up-building of molecules with large storage of chemical energy occurs, can be effected by certain catalysts, such as the ferric and uranium salts in colloidal solution in water, when these are supplied with light energy, and evidence has also been adduced that such inorganic catalysts are present in the chloroplasts of green cells.

If it be agreed that life at some period first arose on this or some other planet by a process of evolution from simpler constituents, it becomes of great importance to study fully the action of light upon those inorganic substances which are present in air and water, and might be presumed, from their nature and present position as nutrients of living organisms, to have been capable of being acted upon by light with inductance of endothermic chemical reactions and formation of more complex compounds of organic character.

Our knowledge of the first steps in the assimilation of both carbon and nitrogen so as to take their part in the organic compounds is still very incomplete, but that regarding nitrogen assimilation is much the more fragmentary of the two.

It is true that the living cell can by linkage of reactions utilise the energy stored up in the form of carbohydrates to induce endothermic reactions and build up fats and proteins. It has already been indicated, and the subject will again be taken up in a later chapter, that a certain amount of carbohydrates can be oxidised, and the energy so set free within the cell can be transferred to reduce another portion of carbohydrate to fat, or to reduce nitrogenous compounds and build in amino-groups to form proteins   Other examples of such linked reactions are seen in the action of certain bacteria and other unicellular organisms, such as azotobacter, the nitro-bacteria of the nodules of the leguminosæ, the philothionic organisms which derive stores of energy from the oxidation of sulphur or reduced sulphur compounds, and the iron bacteria which similarly utilise the energy obtained by oxidation of metallic iron or of ferrous compounds to build up organic carbon compounds from carbon dioxide and water. Such linked reactions require, however, the presence of a living cell containing protoplasm, possessing as its substratum organic compounds containing both carbon and nitrogen in very complex combinations. Moreover, the substrata of reduced compounds so utilised in linked reactions have demanded at earlier epochs the existence of living organisms for their reduction by the conversion of the energy of sunlight. None of these substances could have existed in a planet cooling down from a red-hot condition on account of their chemical instability at higher temperatures. So also all the bound nitrogen in vegetable and animal organisms, and their decomposition products, such as coal, guano, and nitrates, must at one time have existed as atmospheric nitrogen, for no nitrates or nitro-compounds could have withstood the earlier high temperatures. The enormous stores of compounds containing the oxides of nitrogen now used in warfare, agriculture, and industry must have been formed endothermically from atmospheric nitrogen and oxygen with uptake of energy, and whether this occurred through the electric discharge of the thunderstorm or by the agency of living organisms, the first source of the energy, just as in the cases of the organic carbon compounds, was the sun's rays. It follows that the agencies by which sunlight was utilised to form reduced compounds of carbon and nitrogen must have existed antecedently to the advent of life, for in its ultimate composition the substratum of proteins necessary to the living organism contains both types of endothermically produced radicles. It was such considerations which induced the series of experiments here recorded, which show that the energy of sunlight can be absorbed by dilute solutions of nitrates and institute an endothermic reaction in which the more reactive nitrites are formed even in absence of living organisms, and also that the green cells of plants possess the power of absorbing these nitrites.

It is well known from the thermo-chemical determinations of Faure, Thomsen, and Berthelot that in the formation of the oxides of nitrogen from their elements the acme of absorption of energy lies at the point of formation of nitric oxide (N_2O_2), and that the reaction runs endothermically towards this point, whether the starting-point be nitrous oxide (N_2O) or nitrogen pentoxide (N_2O_5). The amounts of heat involved and differences in transition from one oxide to another are shown succinctly in the following table abstracted from Mendeléeff[1] in which the numbers in the upper row represent thousands of grm. calories for a grm. molecular formation from the elements; and the lower shows in thousands of grm. calories the heats of transition from one oxide to the other:

$$\begin{array}{ccccc} N_2O & N_2O_2 & N_2O_3 & N_2O_4 & N_2O_5 \\ -21 & -43 & -22 & -5 & -1 \\ & -22 & +21 & +17 & +4 \end{array}$$

$$\longrightarrow$$

This table shows that in passage from N_2O_5 to N_2O_3 a supply of energy must be given to the reacting system amounting to $4+17=21$ thousands of grm. calories for each grm. molecule converted. The figures are for the gaseous condition, but it may be taken that they would be approximately the same for dilute solutions, and so that the amount of energy for the passage of a grm. molecule of a nitrate to a nitrite (say, from KNO_3 to KNO_2) would be about half this amount, or about 10,000 grm. calories, for 1 grm. molecule of nitrogen pentoxide yields 2 of nitrate, which is converted into 2 of

[1] Mendeléeff, "Principles of Chemistry," translated by Kemensky and Pope, vol. i., p. 287. Longmans, London, 1905.

nitrite.   These figures show clearly that the transition from nitrate to nitrite is a strongly endothermic reaction, and can only occur either by transformation of other forms of energy, such as that of light, into chemical energy, or by a linked chemical reaction with oxidation of previously formed reduced chemical substances

Not only do the nitrites contain a greater storage of chemical energy than the nitrates, the energy potential factor of the energy quantity possesses a higher value, so that the nitrites react more readily than the nitrates, and many changes occur between living organisms and nitrites which are not given directly by nitrates. The experiments recorded below show that this endothermic reaction occurs in sunlight when dilute solutions of nitrates are exposed to the direct rays of the sun, either dissolved in redistilled water or as they occur in natural waters   In addition, it has been found that green leaves immersed in water possess, in presence of sunlight, the power of absorbing the nitrites so formed in the water

In the earlier stages of the investigation the source of the nitrites obtained was not clearly understood.   The outset point was that the nitrites and nitrates found to be present in atmospheric air by many previous observers could not be satisfactorily explained on the basis of the disruptive electrical discharges of thunderstorms, because there has not been traced any definite correspondence between the amount of nitrites, and nitrates in air and rain water, and the prevalence of thunderstorms, such as must undoubtedly exist were the energy of the lightning discharge the main cause of the production of nitrites and nitrates in the air.

Rain collected in the course of these experiments when there had been no recent thunder was found to contain nearly as much nitrite (about 0 5 part per million) as rain caught in a thunderstorm, and, as has been shown by Ilosvay,[1] the morning dew contains nitrites. Also, although the amounts of nitrites and nitrates present at any given time in the air are small, the amounts abstracted by condensing aqueous vapour and falling as rain or condensing as dew on the surfaces of leaves and ground in the course of the year is enormous, and this would appear to demand some uniformly distributed and more constantly acting source of energy, such as sunlight, rather than be dependent upon fortuitous electrical discharges

These nitrites of the rain and dew form one of the chief supplies of nitrogenous nutrition for plants and animals supported by soils

---

[1] Ilosvay, *Bull Soc. Chim* [3], vol ii , p 666.

not artificially enriched with nitrogenous manure; the experiments given below, and others recorded in later chapters, show that there is also an aerial uptake of nitrites by the green leaves.

A source of much error and confusion in estimating the so-called "active" oxygen of air, rain, or dew by different observers at meteorological stations has been the use of test-papers, impregnated with starch and iodides, which were moistened and exposed to air, and indicated, by the rapidity of development of a blue colour, the degree of "active" oxygen in air. This "active" oxygen was assumed to be present mainly as ozone or hydrogen peroxide without more proof, but this liberation of iodine from iodides is accomplished quite as readily by nitrogen tri- or tetr-oxide as by ozone or hydrogen peroxide. All the more recent researches[1] indicate that ozone and hydrogen peroxide are absent from the air at the earth's surface, and the important purifying and bleaching reactions hitherto ascribed to them must now be transferred to the intermediate oxides of nitrogen. At high dilutions, such as are shown below to occur under atmospheric conditions, the odour of ozone and that of the oxides of nitrogen are indistinguishable.

The present experiments show that air, rain, and dew invariably contain a mixture of nitrites and nitrates, and that on keeping the nitrites pass over into nitrates, but by insolation this process is reversed, and nitrites are formed from nitrates.

The test used was Ilosvay's modification of the diazo-reactions discovered by Griess, yielding compounds deeply coloured even at high dilutions; one of the best of these reactions for the purpose is that in which solutions of sulphanilic acid and α-naphthylamine in acetic acid are added to the water suspected of containing nitrites. This test is given only by nitrites, and not by either ozone or hydrogen peroxide.

Ilosvay, by the use of this test, showed that the well-known reaction upon a paper impregnated with starch and potassium iodide often used to show the supposed presence of ozone in the atmosphere was really produced by nitrites, and demonstrated that at the earth's surface both ozone and hydrogen peroxide were normally absent. The same observer[2] found a strong reaction for

[1] Ilosvay, *Ann. Chem. Pharm.*, vol. cxxiv., p. 1; vol. clxxxvi., p. 2.

[2] Hayhurst and Pring, *Chem. Soc. Trans.*, vol. xcvii., Pt. I., p. 868 (1910); Pring, *Roy Soc. Proc.*, A, vol. xc., p. 204 (1910), and Strutt, *Roy. Soc. Proc.*, A, vol. xciv., p. 260 (1918).

nitrites in the morning dew on various leaves and grasses, and also adsorbed upon ignited sand and upon earth exposed wet to the atmosphere, and in water in absorption tubes through which air was drawn.

This test will clearly indicate, by the development of a pink colour, the presence of nitrites in a dilution of one in ten million. The test, when applied to the solutions exposed to sunlight, as described below, gave reactions indicating amounts of nitrite lying between two in a million and one in ten million.

These concentrations may appear at first sight infinitesimally low, but attention must be paid to the enormous areas in green leaves over the earth's surface which are exposed to the reaction. The strengths of solutions from which living organisms absorb essential constituents from their environments often belong to this order of concentration. The concentration of silicic acid in pond water, from which diatoms build up their siliceous skeletons, is of the same order of magnitude. A similar condition of affairs emerges if the assimilation of carbon compounds is considered, for all such assimilation depends on a concentration of only about 3 parts *by volume* of carbon dioxide in 10,000 of atmospheric air.

The concentration of carbon dioxide in the atmosphere of 3 parts in 10,000 by volume, small as it may appear to support all life upon the earth, looks at first sight enormous, compared to the concentrations at which silica is absorbed in plants, or to the concentrations of nitrites with which we are dealing in the present experiments; but this arises entirely from the usual conventional mode of expression of the concentration in relative gaseous volumes in the atmosphere.

If the mass of carbon dioxide dissolved in water be expressed in relationship to the mass of water, the ratio drops to the same order of magnitude as obtains in the case of other essential constituents demanded for organic life, all of which, it must be remembered, including carbon, are synthesised from solutions and not in gaseous form. Thus, the absorption coefficient of carbon dioxide between a system of air and water may be taken sufficiently accurately for these purposes as equivalent to unity, so that if an atmosphere containing 3 parts in 10,000 of carbon dioxide be brought into equilibrium with water, the aqueous solution will contain 3 volumes of gaseous carbon dioxide in 10,000 volumes of water. That is, in 10 litres of water there will be dissolved 3 c.c. of carbon dioxide. Now, since 44 grms. of carbon-dioxide gas measure at normal temperature and pressure 22,000 c.c., this means that 3 c.c. of carbon dioxide weigh approximately 6 mgrms.; 6 mgrms. of carbon dioxide in 10 litres, therefore, represents a concentration of 6 parts in 10,000,000 parts of water. It is the carbon in the carbon dioxide which is utilised in formation of the organic carbon compounds of the plant, and this stands to carbon dioxide in the relationship of 12 to 44, so that the concentration of assimilable carbon becomes reduced to about 1 part by weight in 6,000,000 parts of water.

So far as nitrogen assimilation is concerned, the amount of nitrogen required by plants is not on the average more than about 5 per cent. of the required carbon assimilation, so that other factors, such as coefficients of distribution between air and water, being taken as equal, a concentration of nitrites or nitrates in the atmosphere or cell sap about equivalent to 1 part of nitrogen in 120,000,000 parts of water ought to supply sufficient for assimilative purposes.

In a series of twenty experiments it was shown that both rain and dew invariably contain nitrites, but these slowly diminish, so that water drawn from a reservoir by a service tap gives a quite negative result when tested by the diazo-reaction for nitrites. If, however, another portion of this same sample of water be exposed, either in the open or within a transparent quartz container, to sunlight or an artificial source of light rich in short wave-lengths, in one or two hours a strong reaction is given for nitrites. In this manner, by testing water before and after exposure, the presence and relative amounts of nitrite and nitrate may be determined. Similar changes, only greatly diminished quantitatively, are obtained when the exposures are made in glass vessels, showing that it is the ultra-violet waves which are most potent. That this result is due to conversion of nitrates into nitrites, and not conversion of dissolved nitrogen and oxygen, is shown by the fact that it does not occur with distilled water holding air in solution; but if a small amount of potassium nitrate—say, 1 part by weight in 10,000 parts—be added, an intense reaction occurs on insolation. In several experiments it was shown that the presence of green leaves from different types of plants diminished the amount of nitrites present after exposure, as contrasted with control flasks alongside containing no green leaves.

It is clear from these experiments that nitrates taken up by the rootlets of plants from the soil can be converted into the more reactive nitrites in the green leaf with absorption of solar energy ; simultaneously, non-nitrogenous organic bodies are being built up in the same situation, which suggests that by interaction under the influence of light protein synthesis as well as carbohydrate may occur in the green leaf.

The presence of nitrites and nitrates in rain and dew indicates their occurrence in atmospheric air, and this was ultimately proven in a series of experiments which showed that the main portion of the oxidised nitrogen from air is found in water, after bubbling air through it, as nitrate and not as nitrite.

Great care is required in order to give a rigorous proof of this, because the condition of the absorbed substances from the air may be modified in the act of collection if light be not carefully excluded, and nitrate from the air be changed by insolation into nitrite.   This fact first emerged from a series of experiments intended to study the relative amounts of nitrite in air by day and by night, when apparently the interesting result was obtained that there was practically no nitrite in night air, but a considerable amount in day air.   Just then the effect of light in converting nitrates into nitrites was learnt, and a repetition of the experiment was made, using a blackened bottle with distilled water as absorbent   This distilled water had been twice distilled, and was so free from nitrate that it gave no Griess-Ilosvay reaction even after prolonged exposure to ultra-violet light   The result now obtained was that, whether the air were bubbled through by day or by night, only a very slight reaction for nitrites was obtained, but on now exposing to sunlight this distilled water through which air had been bubbled in darkness, whether by day or by night, a strong reaction was obtained in each case, showing that oxidised nitrogen is present always in air both by day and by night.

It is not possible to conclude that the relative amounts of nitrate and nitrite in bubbled air give an indication of the relative amounts of the two oxides of nitrogen in the air, for if the absorption be attempted in the presence of light there will be a reduction to nitrite, and if in darkness the great volume of oxygen simultaneously bubbled through may have oxidised nitrite to nitrate, so that there is a labile equilibrium between a given degree of light exposure and nitrates, nitrites, and oxygen.

Researches are called for to determine the earlier stages of nitrogen fixation from the atmosphere. The light of the sun in the upper strata of the atmosphere, where the ultra-violet has not yet been absorbed, must produce vast amounts of ozone, and these disappear as the earth's surface is approached; in so disappearing, the ozone may oxidise nitrogen and give nitrites and nitrates. Whatever their source, these nitrites are most reactive with organic substances and destructive to micro-organisms, and many of the natural bleaching, deodorising, and sterilising activities in air and water which have been hitherto ascribed to ozone and hydrogen peroxide are more probably due to nitrites.

SUMMARY.

Dilute solutions of nitrates exposed either to sunlight or to a source of light rich in light energy of short wave-length (such as light from mercury vapour arc enclosed in silica) undergo conversion of nitrate into nitrite.

There is an uptake of chemical energy in this reaction transformed from light energy as in formation of organic carbon compounds in foliage leaves; it is to be added to the relatively small number of endothermic reactions known to be induced by light.

Interposition of a layer of glass between source of light and solution of nitrate greatly slows the reaction, showing that the most effective rays are those of short length.

When green leaves are immersed in nitrate solution, comparatively little nitrite accumulates, indicating that nitrites are rapidly absorbed by the green leaf. Nitrates taken up by plants from soil would, in presence of sunlight, be changed to nitrites, which are much more reactive than nitrates. This indicates that the early stages of synthesis of nitrogenous compounds are carried out in the green leaf and aided by sunlight.

Rain water collected for a considerable time contains no nitrites, all having been oxidised to nitrates, but if exposed to bright sunlight or ultra-violet light for a few hours a strong reaction for nitrites is always obtained.

Freshly collected rain water or dew always contains a mixture of nitrites and nitrates, as shown by the nitrite test appearing without any previous treatment of the water and the great enhancement of this on exposure to strong illumination.

Air bubbled through nitrite- and nitrate-free distilled water gives a mixed reaction afterwards when the water is tested for nitrites and nitrates, showing presence of both forms of oxides of nitrogen in air.

There is no hydrogen peroxide or ozone in air at surface level. The fresh odour in open air, commonly referred to as " ozone," is probably nitrogen peroxide, which at high dilutions has the odour of ozone. The oxides of nitrogen are probably formed by the action of sunlight, rich in ultra-violet rays, in upper regions of the atmosphere upon air and aqueous vapour

Attention is drawn to the importance of these actions of light in purification of air and water, and enrichment of soils and waters by this continuous supply of matter essential to organic growth, the energy of which, like that for upbuilding of non-nitrogenous organic compounds, comes from sunlight.

CHAPTER VI

THE ACTION OF LIGHT RAYS ON ORGANIC COMPOUNDS, AND THE PHOTO-SYNTHESIS OF ORGANIC FROM INORGANIC COMPOUNDS

IN this chapter it will be shown that, in addition to salts of iron, a considerable number of other inorganic salts in dilute solution in water, and in either crystalloidal or colloidal solution, possess activity as transformers in the action of light on water and carbonic acid; next, the action of light upon formaldehyde at higher concentration will be considered to show how more complete organic compounds arise; and, finally, the action of light upon organic bodies of more complex nature still, such as carbohydrates, proteins, vegetable and animal juices and extracts, and other substances of biochemical interest will be described.

Photo-Synthesis by Inorganic Transformers.—In a previous chapter it has been mentioned that oxide of uranium in the colloidal state gives a far greater photo-synthetic effect than the crystalloidal salts, and the inference was drawn that the state of aggregation of the colloid was favourable to the reaction. Accordingly in the earlier experiments with iron compounds, colloidal ferric oxide was employed. Continued investigation of the iron compounds has, however, shown that the size of the solution aggregate may easily become too great, and that there is a certain degree of aggregation at which the catalytic action has an optimum value.

Thus, while dialysis of uranium oxide gives a condition in which the photo-synthetic effect is much greater than that obtained with an equal concentration of uranium nitrate in crystalloidal condition, dialysis of iron compounds, on the other hand, gives a condition in which less effect is obtained than with an equal concentration of ordinary ferric chloride.

It is to be remembered, however, that there is often in the case of ordinary solutions of salts of heavy metals a good deal of complex formation approaching a colloidal condition. This is shown, for example, in the case of solutions of cupric salts by the apparent lack of agreement between the molecular weights as deduced by the

79

freezing-point method and the degree of ionisation as given by conductivity determinations. It is shown in the case of ferric chloride solutions by the darkening in colour of dilute solutions on warming, approaching the colour shown by colloidal iron solutions, and persisting after the heated solution has cooled again, for prolonged periods of time. Also, if a dilute solution of ferric chloride be boiled a precipitation of a part of the iron as ferric oxide is obtained, and the precipitate remains permanent on cooling although the period of boiling is far too short to remove a corresponding amount of hydrochloric acid. All these facts demonstrate that there are ions and molecules in the ferric chloride solution of greater molecular complexity than the mono-molecular condition.

The explanation, then, of the greater effect with undialysed ferric chloride, as contrasted with colloidal ferric oxide solution, is that the mass of the complex molecule in the ordinary ferric chloride solution is that which can best take up the light vibrations and absorb the energy, whereas in the colloidal ferric oxide solution the solution aggregate has become too heavy to take up the light energy and convert it into chemical energy.

On the other hand, with the uranium salts, the optimum solution aggregate to act as a transformer for light energy lies nearer that found in the dialysed solutions than in the ordinary uranium nitrate solutions, and accordingly the former show a higher photo-synthetic activity.

Silicic acid and its salts show the same kind of effect as the uranium compounds, for dialysed silicic acid solution gives a strong photo-synthetic action, while both sodium silicate solution and undialysed silicic acid solution are inactive.

There appear, therefore, to be two factors in the production of photo-synthetic activity by a given light source—viz., (1) the specific character of the inorganic catalyst or transformer, (2) the degree of its molecular aggregation in solution.

In view of criticisms that have been made as to the necessity of inorganic catalysts in the solution, and as to the possibility of the ultra-violet rays producing the synthetic effect when passed into pure water charged with carbon dioxide, as also the view that the formaldehyde obtained might be produced from the minute traces of organic matter in the dialysed solutions and not synthetically from carbon dioxide and water, the following critical series of experiments was carried out.

1. Water alone, freshly redistilled, was saturated by a stream of carbon dioxide and then exposed in a quartz test-tube during the whole of a bright summer day on the roof to direct sunlight; alongside it in a similar quartz test-tube was exposed a 1 per cent. solution of ferric chloride also saturated with carbon dioxide, and a third test-tube filled with 1 per cent. ferric chloride saturated with carbon dioxide was kept in a dark cupboard.

Tested at the end, after distilling away from the iron salts, the distilled water tube and ferric chloride tube kept in darkness gave a negative result, while the tube of ferric chloride exposed to sunlight in presence of carbon dioxide gave a bright pink colour with Schryver's reagent corresponding to about 1 in 500,000 of formaldehyde.

2 A solution of 1 per cent. ferric chloride was made up with distilled water which had been freshly boiled and was free from carbon dioxide; this solution contained in a quartz test-tube was exposed during a whole week of bright sunshine in June on the laboratory roof. It was then distilled and tested with negative results.

These experiments clearly show that an inorganic energy transformer is necessary, and that carbon dioxide alone in aqueous solution in sunlight does not form formaldehyde; secondly, that the formaldehyde is not a decomposition product of traces of more highly organised substances, but is actually built up by the inorganic colloid absorbing the energy of the sunlight and so becoming activated and reacting on the water and carbon dioxide, transferring the energy and producing formaldehyde.

Both the elements hitherto described—viz , uranium and iron—form higher and lower oxides, and it might, therefore, be urged that the higher oxide became reduced by the energy of the sunlight to a lower oxide with greater energy content, and that this lower oxide parting with its acquired energy to the water and carbon dioxide formed the formaldehyde to which the energy of the sunlight was thus indirectly transferred. Such a view is of interest because similar changes do actually occur in certain life processes, where various types of micro-organism, such as iron organisms, sulphur organisms, and nitrogen-assimilating or carbophilous organisms carry out similar energy transformations. The so-called iron bacteria are capable in darkness, as within an iron watercistern or water-main, of utilising the energy of metallic iron or ferrous oxide, when given out in the process of oxidation to the ferric

6

condition   The organism is enabled by a linked reaction to utilise for building up from carbon dioxide and water those reduced organic substances which form its body material. Similarly, the philothionic organisms are capable of utilising the energy of sulphur, or reduced sulphur compounds, to build up organic carbon compounds, and the nitrogen-assimilating organisms fed with organic carbon compounds can link up to the endothermic reactions necessary to convert the atmospheric nitrogen into ammonium salts or nitrites, and from these build up proteins

In all cases where the energy of light is absent, however, there must evidently have been previously a light-transforming reaction at some earlier period of history, for without this the metal or lower oxides, or sulphur or sulphide, would never have been formed upon which the organism not utilising light depends for its store of energy In a world cooling down from red-heat, in presence of free oxygen in its atmosphere, all these substances would have been completely oxidised, and so the immense world deposits of pyrites and ferrous oxide and suchlike reduced substances, just like coal, shale, and petrol, must have originated from previous life processes, accompanied by energy transformations in presence of sunlight.

It is accordingly of some interest to enquire whether such transformations of sunlight into chemical energy by inorganic transformers are associated with a temporary chemical change from a higher to a lower oxide, or whether the change is a surface action in which the light energy is converted into chemical energy at the surface of the colloidal aggregate

Our experiments favour the latter view, for if the lower oxide reacted with the water and carbon dioxide to form formaldehyde, then a greater reactivity might be expected when ferrous salts were employed instead of ferric salts; this is, however, not the case, for we have found ferrous salts to be entirely inert, nor have we been able by titration with permanganate to show any formation of ferrous salts when ferric salts are exposed in aqueous solutions in presence of carbonic acid   Moreover, many of the active inorganic transformers which we have lately investigated, as recorded below, do not form higher and lower oxides under the conditions in which we have used them   It is therefore probable that the energy transformation is one induced by the energy of the light at the surface of the colloidal particle upon which probably carbon dioxide concentrates.

A number of other solutions were then tested after exposure to the rays from a quartz mercury vapour arc. In addition to the ferric salts and uranic salts, strong positive results were obtained with 1 per cent. solutions of dialysed silicic acid, and with a 1 per cent. solution of beryllium chloride; less active solutions, but distinctly positive in 1 per cent. solution, were copper chloride and sulphate, nickel chloride, palladium chloride, manganese chloride, erbium chloride. Negative results were given by ferrous sulphate and chloride, sodium silicate, an undialysed hydrochloric acid solution of silicic acid, zinc chloride, cobalt chloride, potassium chloride and chromate, barium chloride, aluminium chloride, borax, and telluric acid.

The above-named solutions were exposed in each case for a period of four to five hours in transparent quartz test-tubes, at a distance of 7 cms. from a mercury vapour arc in a quartz tube.

Action of Sunlight and of Ultra-Violet Light upon more Concentrated Solutions of Formaldehyde.—When formaldehyde is once formed by the action of sunlight from carbon dioxide and water, practically all the energy necessary for formation of carbohydrates by the condensation of formaldehyde groups has been absorbed; for although the heat of combustion of formaldehyde has never been determined, judging from analogy in similar cases, the heat of combustion of 6-grm. molecules of formaldehyde should be almost equivalent to that of 1-grm. molecule of a hexose sugar. For example, the energy of formation, or combustion, of 2-grm. molecules of any hexose is almost equivalent to that of 1-grm. molecule of a biose or disaccharide, and all sugars and starches possess almost equal stores of chemical energy in equal masses.

As will be shown in a later chapter, it is under such conditions that the typical reactions in living systems occur. When the total chemical energy of the reacting substances on either side of the equation is large, but the difference on the two sides is small, then typical reversible reactions are seen with the equilibrium point a considerable distance removed from either end-point.

This condition of affairs so characteristic of biochemical reactions is due to a labile balance between osmotic energy and chemical energy, and it is for this reason that conjugation with formation of more complex molecules is favoured by higher concentration, whereas dilute solution favours cleavage into simpler molecules. This point is of great importance in biological synthesis, and for understanding reversal of action within and without the cell, and as it is not yet sufficiently appreciated an example illustrating it may be adduced

Taking the heats of combustion as determined by Thomsen, the following equation gives the heat of reaction in the change between glucose and maltose (K=100 grm calories).

$$C_6H_{12}O_6 + C_6H_{12}O_6 \quad \rightleftarrows \quad C_{12}H_{22}O_{11} + H_2O - 33K,$$

(Glucose) + (Glucose) $\rightleftarrows$ (Maltose),

6737K   +   6737K $\rightleftarrows$ 13,507K   − 33K.

Thus the reaction is apparently a slightly endothermic one, as it runs from glucose into maltose (a rule which holds for all the similar reactions), but observe that as the reaction runs in this direction the osmotic energy of the system diminishes, for every two molecules of glucose passing out of the system are replaced by only one of maltose   Hence for every grm molecule of glucose passing into maltose a definite amount of osmotic energy is set free, which can be converted into chemical energy, and hence make an apparently endothermic reaction run without added energy from without.   The amount of osmotic energy set free by the disappearance of the molecules of a constituent varies with the pressure at which it disappears, and therefore increases with the concentration of the solution,[1] and hence it came about that the first successful experimental proof of reversibility was given by Croft Hill[2] by the use of exceedingly concentrated sugar solutions, and that all such conjugations occur in concentrated solutions.   Local concentration will have a like effect, and in living cells concentrations on surfaces and interfaces will produce such a result.

In many of the reactions of inorganic chemistry the differences in totals of chemical energy on the two sides possess a high magnitude at ordinary temperatures—as, for example, in the reaction between hydrogen, oxygen, and water.   Here the changes in osmotic energy are too insignificant to produce an appreciable effect, and so the reaction runs practically completely to one end or phase.

But in the type of reaction with which we are here dealing of conjugation or cleavage where the chemical energy change is relatively small, the osmotic change becomes a powerful factor

In the green cell of the living plant the formaldehyde can be condensed on an interface and there conjugate, although general

[1] The thermodynamic proof of this is given in a later chapter.

[2] *Journ Chem Soc*, vol lxxiii, p 634 (1898); vol lxxxiii, p. 578 (1903).

concentration in the cell is kept at a low level. If it be sought to imitate this in a solution of formaldehyde, the concentration must be increased so that the decrease of osmotic pressure may yield energy to supply that required in conjugation, or assist energy supply from without, such as light energy, to increase the potential towards chemical union.

This is what has been done in the experiments here recorded, in which a reducing substance has been obtained by subjecting comparatively concentrated formaldehyde solutions to the light of the quartz mercury-vapour lamp.

When six molecules of formaldehyde condense to form one molecule of a hexose, there is only one molecule of dissolved material contributing to keep up the osmotic pressure where there were formerly six, and a corresponding amount of osmotic energy has disappeared as such, and been utilised to yield the slightly higher content of chemical energy which the hexose possesses over that of the formaldehyde which went to form it. The energy so yielded will evidently be proportional to the osmotic pressure at which the formaldehyde molecules disappear—that is to say, to the concentration of the formaldehyde solution. The osmotic pressure represents the intensity or potential factor of the osmotic energy, and this comes into equilibrium with the intensity factor of the chemical energy, tending to disrupt hexose into formaldehyde and set energy free.

This osmotic energy supply is sufficient to yield the amount required, and hence, in this type of reaction, the light plays mainly the part of a catalyst, and not a provider of energy as in the synthesis of formaldehyde from carbon dioxide and water, or in the synthesis of nitrites from nitrates.

Hence it arises that very dilute solutions of formaldehyde do not yield hexoses under the action of light, and that dilute solutions of sugars do not condense to form disaccharides. Conversely, if dilute solutions of the higher condensations, such as disaccharides or polysaccharides, be exposed to light, they split up into simple sugars, and these invariably yield formaldehyde, as will be shown later in this chapter.

The first synthetic sugars were obtained by Butlerow,[1] by Loew,

[1] Butlerow, *Liebig's Ann.*, Bd. cxx., p. 295; O. Loew, *Berichte d. D. Chem. Gesellsch.*, Bd. xix., p. 141 (1886); Bd. xx., pp. 141 and 3039 (1887); Bd. xxi., p. 278 (1888); Fischer and Passmore, *Berichte d. D. Chem. Gesellsch.*, Bd. xxii., p. 359 (1889).

and later by Fischer and Passmore by acting upon concentrated solutions of formaldehyde or other organic substances with caustic alkalies Thus Loew used formaldehyde and milk of lime, and later freshly precipitated hydroxide of lead, Butlerow dioxymethylene and caustic potash, Fischer and Passmore acrolein bromide and baryta water.

Such powerful reagents accomplish the condensations and give origin to reducing sugars even in darkness and without need of external supply of energy. In the absence of the alkali which acts as a catalyst, the reaction towards equilibrium is held in check, or proceeds only at an infinitely slow rate, so that a concentrated solution of formaldehyde can be kept in the dark for an indefinite period without developing any reducing substances.

In nature, no such strong hydroxyl-ion concentration is found in plant tissues as that of the reagents used for synthesis of sugars *in vitro* as mentioned above; it is therefore interesting to obtain condensation with light exposure in absence of any high alkalinity.

At the time of these experiments we were unaware of any existing observations on the subject, but we have since discovered a paper by R. Pribram and A Franke,[1] in which condensation of formaldehyde and formation of reducing substances was brought about by exposure of concentrated aqueous solutions to ultra-violet light, also a paper by an Italian observer, G. Inghilleri,[2] who exposed a mixture of concentrated aqueous formaldehyde and 6 per cent of oxalic acid in sealed glass tubes in sunlight for several months, and obtained a hexose which he identified as the sugar sorbose (inactive) In both these cases, although the authors do not comment upon it, the law, stated above, of condensation in strong solutions holds.

Formaldehyde itself reduces Fehling's solution in slight degree after long boiling, though not so readily as any hexose solution.   It was therefore of importance to find, if possible, some indicator which would not be reduced by formaldehyde, but would be reduced by more strongly reducing organic substances This was found in Benedict's solution, an alkaline solution of copper sulphate in presence of sodium citrate and sodium carbonate, this is not reduced at

[1] *Berichte d D. Chem. Gesellsch.*, Bd xliv , p. 1035 (1911), and *Monatsh. f. Chem* , Bd xxxiii , p 415 (1912).

[2] *Zeitsch. f. Physiol Chem* , Bd. lxxi., p. 105 (1911), and Bd. lxxiii , p. 44 (1911).

all even on prolonged boiling with formaldehyde, but a solution of formaldehyde after exposure to ultra-violet light reduces it readily, and the same change is brought about, though much more slowly, by sunlight.

This condensation reaction with formaldehyde differs from the synthesis of formaldehyde from carbonic acid and water in that it does not require the presence of an inorganic activator. In the earlier experiments this was not known, and in these the reduction of the copper salt occurred around the colloidal silicic acid, added as an intended activator, showing the interesting fact that the sugar, or reducing substance, had been absorbed by the silica. Later experiments demonstrated, however, that the reaction proceeds with equal or greater rapidity when a solution of 4 to 5 per cent. of formaldehyde in water only is exposed in quartz tubes to ultra-violet illumination.

Experiment I.—A solution containing 5 per cent. of formaldehyde and 0·97 per cent. colloidal silicic acid was exposed at 9 cms. distance to the rays from a quartz mercury-vapour lamp for a period of six hours. At the end of the period a distinct reduction, chiefly in the precipitated silica, was obtained with Benedict's solution. A control, exactly similar, but kept in the dark, gave no reduction. A portion of control solution kept warm in darkness also gave no reduction.

Experiment II.—Two quartz tubes were exposed alongside each other for a period of eight hours at 9 cms. distance from lamp; one contained 5 per cent. formaldehyde in water only, the other 5 per cent. formaldehyde in colloidal silicic acid solution. At the end, the tube with silicic acid reduced Benedict's solution, but to a much less degree than that containing formaldehyde alone, showing that dialysed silicic acid probably acts as an anticatalyst.

Experiment III.—A sufficient concentration of the formaldehyde appears to be reached at about 5 per cent., in order to develop the maximum rapidity of formation of the reducing substance. Thus two quartz test-tubes, one containing 40 per cent. and the other 8 per cent. of formaldehyde, were exposed to the quartz mercury-vapour lamp at the same distance (9 cms.) for the same period (three hours) in each case. Both gave quite a marked reduction, at least as great in the less concentrated solution as in the highly concentrated one. This result, and that of the succeeding experiments (Experiment IV.), does not invalidate the reasoning given above, for 2 per cent. solution of formaldehyde is already a concentrated solution possessing as high a molecular concentration as a 12 per cent. solution of a hexose, and the optimum has already been reached.

Experiment IV.—In a similar experiment, four quartz flasks of 250 c.c. each were filled respectively with 0 5, 1, 2, and 4 per cent. solutions of formaldehyde, and exposed to ultra-violet light at $7\frac{1}{2}$ cms. from the lamp. As a result of the greater volume in the flasks per unit of surface, the appearance of reducing substance is slower than in the quartz test-tubes, but the 2 per cent. solution showed distinct reduction after seven hours' exposure; the stronger 4 per cent. solution and the two more dilute solutions at this time gave no reduction. Tested again after ten hours' total exposure, the $\frac{1}{2}$ per cent solution was still negative, while the 1 per cent. showed a faint reduction, the 4 per cent. somewhat more, and the 2 per cent. still gave the best reduction The $\frac{1}{2}$ per cent solution only begins to reduce after about thirty hours' exposure, when all the others are giving a copious reduction. Control flasks kept at 40° C in a thermostat showed no development of reducing power during this period

Experiment V.—The formaldehyde used in the above experiments had not recently been distilled, and contained para-formaldehyde In order to test if the simple aldehyde, or its polymer, or both, gave the reducing substance under the action of the ultra-violet light, a portion of the commercial 40 per cent. solution was distilled, and the first portion coming over, as well as the solid polymer left behind in the retort after distilling over the greater part, were separately made up in aqueous solution, and exposed to light in about 4 per cent solution. The solid was dissolved in distilled water, and the distilled aldehyde was diluted with distilled water. Both were tested with Benedict's solution before exposure, and neither gave any reduction The two solutions in two quartz test-tubes were then exposed for four hours at 8 cms. distance, and on testing a copious reduction was obtained in both cases.

Experiment VI.—This experiment was mainly designed to locate the wave-length of the light causing the condensation. Two test-tubes were taken, one made of transparent quartz, the other of ordinary soft glass, the dimensions and thicknesses of wall of the tubes were about the same, the capacity of each being about 35 c.c. Each test-tube received 25 c c. of the same 4 per cent aqueous solution of formaldehyde which had recently been distilled, and the two tubes were placed in equally favourable positions alongside each other at about 5 cms. distance from the quartz tube of a mercury-vapour lamp. At the outset the formaldehyde gave no reduction of Benedict's solution. After three hours' exposure the contents of the quartz tube gave a fair reduction of Benedict's solution, while those of the glass tube still gave a complete negative with this test solution. At the expiry of six and a half hours' exposure the contents of the quartz tube gave a copious reduction, but the contents of the glass tube had not yet developed any reducing substance. At the end of twelve hours the contents of both tubes showed reduction, those of the glass tube to about the same extent as had been obtained in the quartz tube in three hours, while the contents of the quartz tube now gave a heavy precipitate of cuprous oxide when tested by Benedict's solution.

The remainder of the contents of the quartz tube were distilled at ordinary atmospheric pressure almost to dryness, leaving a white solid residue in the distilling flask. The residue was taken up with warm water, in which it readily dissolved, and made up to the original volume. Both distillate and residue were then tested with Benedict's solution, and both were found to reduce it readily, the residue containing apparently somewhat more reducing substance than the distillate. Again, both distillate and residue reduce neutral silver nitrate solution and mercuric chloride solution. This experiment shows that the short wave-lengths are the most powerful, and that the limit lies at about the shortest wave-lengths transmissible by glass.

Experiment VII.—In a somewhat similar experiment two quartz test-tubes were taken, of the same dimensions as above, and the same concentration of formaldehyde was employed, but around one of the tubes as thin a sheet of mica as could be split off was folded so as completely to surround the quartz, and held in position by two loops of thread at top and bottom. The mica was so thin that it readily folded over the test-tube (about 3 cms. in diameter) without cracking. Yet this thin layer of mica was so effective a screen that there was not a trace of reduction after a twelve hours' exposure similar to that given above in glass; the contents of the unshielded quartz tube showed a distinct reduction after two hours' exposure.

Experiment VIII.—Only preliminary experiments have hitherto been made towards the identification of the substance or substances giving the reductions with these metallic salts. It is natural to suppose that there should be representatives of intermediate condensation products lying on the path between formaldehyde and the hexoses. Pribram and Franke, in the papers above referred to, believed they were able to identify glycolaldehyde arising from the condensation of two molecules of formaldehyde, and Inghilleri claims to have isolated the racemic sorbose by means of its osazone.

It was evident to us that we were dealing with a complex mixture, and although there is a quite distinct effect with phenyl-hydrazine in acetic acid solution, quite different from that of formaldehyde, and giving abundance of coloured precipitate, we have not yet succeeded in isolating a crystalline osazone, though we have on several occasions obtained crystals mixed with amorphous smears.

In order to prepare large quantities of material, four quartz flasks, each of about 300 c c. capacity, were completely filled with a 4 per cent. solution of formaldehyde, and exposed at a distance of about 4 inches from the lamp for several hours daily for a week The result was disappointing, on account of the slowness of action The effect appears, like many effects of light, even in clear solutions, to be all concentrated within a comparatively thin layer lying next the incident surface. Accordingly, as in these larger vessels the volume increases much more rapidly than the exposed surface, the concentration of reducing substance in the solution progresses at a correspondingly slow rate   At the end of the week there was a fair amount of reduction in all four flasks, but not more than would be obtained in a small quartz test-tube with a single day's exposure. In continuation, four quartz test-tubes, each of about 30 c c. capacity, were filled with part of the contents of one of the flasks, and exposed at 5 cms. distance for two days.   The contents were mixed and used for the following experiments:

Several attempts to obtain an osazone were made by heating with excess of phenyl-hydrazine and acetic acid. The unchanged formaldehyde interfered, and although attempts were made to overcome this by fractional precipitation, the most that could be obtained was occasionally small microscopic tufts of crystals, mixed with oily and amorphous material.

Changes due to the exposure are evidenced by the deep orange colour and orange precipitate obtained on boiling with the phenyl-hydrazine in the case of the exposed solution, while similar treatment of the unexposed formaldehyde gave only a pale yellow colour in both solution and precipitate

An attempt was made to remove the unchanged formaldehyde by forming the addition compound with aniline, but unfortunately the reducing substance also precipitated with the aniline. When added to exposed formaldehyde solution aniline causes a white precipitate as it does with unexposed formaldehyde, but the latter precipitate remains white on heating, while that given by the exposed solution turns a dark orange colour when heated. The filtrate from the aniline precipitate no longer reduces Benedict's solution, even when concentrated on the water-bath, neither does the aniline precipitate reduce. It was not possible to separate from the precipitate anything but formaldehyde and aniline.

Exposed formaldehyde solutions turn yellow when concentrated by distillation either at atmospheric or reduced pressure, and leave behind a yellow syrup with a bitter taste which strongly reduces Benedict's solution; unexposed formaldehyde solutions leave a smaller residue of white paraldehyde.

Experiment IX.—The condensing action of light is aided by slight alkalinity. Three quartz test-tubes were taken: in the first was placed a mixture of equal volumes of 4 per cent. formaldehyde solution and water, in the second and third a mixture of equal volumes of 4 per cent. formaldehyde solution and of a 1 per cent. solution of sodium carbonate (Na_2CO_3). The first and second were exposed for three hours at a distance of 3 cms., while the third was kept in darkness in an incubator at approximately the same temperature as that caused by the irradiation—viz , about 50° C. At the end of the period the unexposed solution gave no reduction with Benedict's solution, and the tube contents exposed in presence of the alkaline carbonate gave practically double the intensity of reduction of those equally diluted with water. Tested again at the end of fifteen hours the contents of the tube kept warm in darkness still gave no reduction, while the other two now gave each a heavy reduction. Even after an additional period of three days in the incubator the dilute formaldehyde and sodium carbonate solutions kept in darkness gave no reduction with Benedict's solution.

The General Formation of Formaldehyde by the Action of Light upon Organic Substances of Biochemical Origin.—The series of experiments leading to the generalisation made in this section were induced by an attempt to construct an emulsion of chlorophyll in extractives from green leaves along with colloidal ferric hydrate so as to produce an artificial system resembling that present in the chloroplast of the green plant, which might then be exposed to light and tested for production of formaldehyde. For this purpose a quantity of grass leaves was washed with water, and then extracted with absolute alcohol   The filtrate was allowed to remain at room temperature in a desiccator over sulphuric acid until the alcohol had evaporated and a green extract remained behind   This was rubbed up and shaken into an emulsion with a colloidal solution of ferric oxide   This emulsion was saturated with carbon dioxide and exposed for about four hours to the light of the quartz mercury-vapour lamp   At the end the chlorophyll had bleached, and the ferric hydrate had coagulated so that the whole could be filtered. The result was surprising as to the intensity of the formaldehyde return; when the Schryver test was applied there was at once a deep pink colour produced.   Even after a twenty-five-fold dilution a reaction was obtained of about 2 parts of formaldehyde per 1,000,000, showing an amount of about 1 part in 20,000 in the original emulsion. This result was not, however, due to the combined action of chlorophyll and colloidal ferric hydrate, for a similar intense result was obtained when an exposure was made of an emulsion of chlorophyll extract alone in distilled water and without any carbon dioxide.

It follows that the formaldehyde must have originated either from the chlorophyll or the other organic substances in the green leaves taken out by the alcohol along with the chlorophyll

Additional experiments revealed the interesting fact that practically any complex organic substance of biological origin yields formaldehyde when exposed to the action of ultra-violet light, and also—though more slowly—when exposed to sunlight. Solutions or emulsions were exposed of all the commoner sugars (such as glucose, fructose, maltose, lactose, saccharose), of glycogen, starch, glycerine, egg-albumen, milk, and various vegetable juices.   After three to four hours' exposure and subsequent filtration or distillation these all showed the presence of formaldehyde in varying amount. The more transparent solutions gave the more intense reactions, and amongst these the sugars were most rapidly disrupted by the action of the light   The action appears to be one of successive hydrolysis; thus, for example, cane sugar is first inverted, and after an hour or two gives a strong reduction with Benedict's solution. The reaction takes place also with sterilised sugar solutions, in sealed glass tubes, exposed to bright sunlight, but the speed of reaction is much less than when a quartz container is used, and the exposure must be continued for several days.

The action of sunlight and of ultra-violet light on organic substances has been studied by many observers[1] and on a vast number of substances. The production of formaldehyde in a certain number of instances has been noted by different experimenters, but no one appears hitherto to have noticed the generality of the appearance of formaldehyde when any complex substance of vegetable or animal origin is exposed to light vibrations of short wave-length. This may be due to the employment here of a more delicate reagent, and to a systematic testing for the formaldehyde in all cases.

Certain of the observers, such as C. Neumann and D. Berthelot and Gaudechon, appear to consider a catalyst as essential to the reaction, and for this purpose have used salts of uranium. The reactions of deduplication of these organic substances in dilute solutions take place, however, quite readily without a chemical catalyst. The reactions are exothermic, and the light itself acts as the catalyst.

This production of formaldehyde has several important and interesting relationships which may now be pointed out.

In the first place, it has a practical bearing on all enquiries as to the presence of formaldehyde in green leaves exposed to light, or of chlorophyll solutions, or artificial schemata of various types, exposed to light and afterwards tested for formaldehyde to elucidate the functions of the chloroplast in the green leaf. Many observers throughout the past generation have laboured at proving the presence of formaldehyde in green leaves exposed to light, but if it be true that practically any organic substance of biochemical origin exposed to light develops formaldehyde, then the presence of formaldehyde in green leaves furnishes no proof of its synthesis by sunlight from carbon dioxide and water. The same holds for all the schemata, for these always contain substances from which formaldehyde could arise. But even although no other organic substance save chlorophyll, or any mixture of pure chlorophylls, were present and yet

---

[1] The papers on the subject are too numerous to quote separately; a key to the literature will be found in the following: Ciamician and Silber, *Berichte d. D. Chem. Gesellsch.*, from 1901 onward; *Atti Real. Accad. Lincei,* from 1901; C. Neumann and Co-workers, *Biochem. Zeitsch.*, from 1908 onward; V. Henri and Co-workers, *Comptes Rendus Acad. des Sci.*, and *Comptes Rendus Soc. de Biol.*, from 1910 onwards; and D. Berthelot and Gaudechon, *Comptes Rendus Acad. des Sci.*, from 1910 onwards.

formaldehyde were formed in abundance on exposure to light, this would be of no avail as a proof of photo-synthesis of formaldehyde from the inorganic, for the same change would happen in a solution of cane sugar, and there is no proof that the chlorophyll·is not simply behaving like a legion of other organic compounds and yielding formaldehyde by its own decomposition.

It has recently been shown by Jorgensen and Kidd[1] that pure chlorophylls, exposed as a suspension in water to light in presence of oxygen, at first bleach and then yield formaldehyde. Under natural conditions in the leaf and under all conditions of exposure to light of artificial schemata, used by previous observers, there has always been present atmospheric oxygen, so that this appearance of formaldehyde from pure chlorophyll emulsions after exposure to light confirms the view expressed above.

In the second place, the general production of formaldehyde when these substances resolve themselves under the influence of light into simpler forms possesses a teleological bearing, for if in the uptake of solar energy the first storage from the inorganic be in the stage of formaldehyde, it would be very probable that in the process of unbuilding this step should be retraced.

The general production of formaldehyde by the action of light on biochemical materials may also stand related to the important lethal effects of sunlight and ultra-violet light upon micro-organisms, which is seen in the sterilising action of sunlight upon many pathogenic organisms and in the similar use of ultra-violet light installations for sterilisation purposes.

The relationship of the lethal effects to the wave-length of the light has been studied by many observers. Downes and Blunt[2] showed, at an early period, not only that both direct and diffuse sunlight inhibited the appearance and slowed the growth of organisms self-sown in Pasteur's cultivation fluid, but that this action did not appear when the cultures were preserved behind red or yellow glass screens, while blue or violet glasses allowed light to pass which possessed as much deterrent action as light through clear glass. Marshall Ward[3] was the first to invent an ingenious method of making

---

[1] *Roy. Soc. Proc.*, B, vol. lxxxix , p 342 (1916)

[2] *Roy Soc Proc* , vol xxvi , p 488 (1877); vol. xxviii , p 199 (1879)

[3] *Roy. Soc Proc.*, vol liv., p 472 (1893); other papers by Marshall Ward on this subject, *Roy Soc Proc* , vol. lii , p 393 (1892); vol. liii., pp. 26 and 164 (1893); vol lvi , p. 345 (1894).

the organisms record their own destruction, which has again been independently rediscovered by two other sets of investigators at intervals of several years. The method consisted in throwing a spectrum, obtained by directing sunlight, or the light of electric arcs in air, through a quartz spectroscope, upon an agar-agar plate sown over with the organism. A number of slots were cut out on the covering lid of a shallow plate like a Petri dish, and some of these were covered with quartz and others with thin glass strips. The spectra were directed through these on to the agar-agar culture. The remainder of the surface was protected by an opaque cover of tinfoil. After exposure for twelve hours the plate was incubated for four days, and then the results were photographed. When the glass was interposed the only area of destruction was that of the blue and violet, but when the quartz only intervened between source of light and organisms the destruction passed far on into the ultra-violet region. A quite similar method was used by Barnard and Morgan,[1] who found the lethal action in the ultra-violet so intense that the bright spectral lines in the ultra-violet were mapped out as clearly almost as on a photographic plate. These authors also determined the wave-lengths of the lethal zone of the spectrum, and found its limits to lie between 3287 and 2265Å. Quite recently the work has been independently repeated with similar results by Browning and Russ.[2]

Some of the authors quoted, especially Marshall Ward, consider the nature of the chemical reaction involved. Marshall Ward drew attention to the oxidising action of blue light upon oils, and considered it probable that the effect might be due to such an oxidation of the fat reserve and not a direct action on cell protoplasm.

It is highly interesting that the chemical reactions upon substances of biochemical origin, here described, are also produced by the same short wave-lengths as those which occasion death of organisms, as is shown by the enormous decrease in activity when the light is screened by passing through glass or mica.

Now the substances present in the bodies of the organisms are of those organic types which yield formaldehyde, as shown earlier, when exposed to the action of light vibrations of the shorter wave-lengths. It is well known that formaldehyde in high dilution is

---

[1] *Roy. Soc. Proc.*, vol. lxxii., p. 126 (1903); *Brit. Med. Journ.*, November 14, 1903.
[2] *Roy. Soc. Proc.*, B, vol. xc., p. 33 (1917).

poisonous to such living organisms, and when produced nascently by the action of sunlight, or ultra-violet light, and probably at selective concentrations on interfaces, it is quite probable that the death of the whole organism might so be induced. The action of the light would be progressive upon the living cell just as it is within quartz containers upon the more complex organic substances, and would manifest itself in a continuous hydrolysis of the more conjugated to less conjugated substances. The first effect would be upon the state of colloidal aggregation of the system, but concurrently formaldehyde and other organic compounds of simple type would be set free.

It is noteworthy that formaldehyde and other simple related substances, such as would be the first stages in the evolution of the organic from the inorganic, are all highly poisonous to the much later product in evolution—namely, the living organism. Such simple substances are formaldehyde, formic acid, oxalic acid, hydrocyanic acid, methylic and ethylic alcohols, hydrogen peroxide, and the simpler nitrites and nitriles; all these are poisonous to the highly organised and labile colloids of the bioplasm, and probably on account of that very property which makes them essential in the first stages of organic evolution—namely, their high reactivity and the ease with which they take part in additive reactions of organic substances. For this reason they must undergo change in any living cell whilst still at high dilution, or else they so interlock into the labile system of organic colloids within the cell as to clog all metabolic change. Hence it is that the energy of light, which is essential to healthy growth and the upbuilding of organic material from inorganic, supplied in a wrong fashion and not shielded in its onset, may reverse these delicate processes and cause death and degeneration of living substance, instead of being the potent agency towards building up fresh material.

The subject is one of enormous and far-reaching importance. Blue light is the most universal and potent natural purifier of our oceans and streams and our supplies of drinking-water. Light is also the agency which in spring, when the sun attains a certain altitude and less of the actinic light is absorbed by the atmosphere, penetrates the water of the ocean and lakes in sufficient intensity to stimulate the great outburst of vegetable plankton, which initiates the long sequence of swarms of animal life up to the fishes, and supports all the life of the seas. This is evident, because the spring outburst of floating plant life occurs before there has been any rise in the temperature of the sea water. The bronzing of the skin, caused by exposure to bright sunshine, and the pigmentation of human races in tropical climates, is almost certainly a protective screen against these injurious rays, and Marshall Ward has pointed out that the pigments of those micro-organisms and fungi which can flourish in light always absorb these injurious rays, and allow passage to the reds, greens, yellows, and oranges, which are not injurious. Even blue and violet pigments occurring in nature, when carefully examined spectroscopically, are found in many cases to absorb the violet and shorter waved blues.

The same is true of the colours of flowers, and even of the green colouring matters of the foliage leaves, and it may well be that the function of the chlorophyll, which usually occurs as a thin layer like a skin over the chloroplast, is to temper and screen the light for the really effective transformer lying underneath.

The absence or great diminution of the blue and ultra-violet rays in hazy or sunless weather may also be of great importance in allowing the disease organisms of the higher plants to flourish unchecked, and it is such weather in autumn which often heralds the outbreak of disease and blights.

SUMMARY.

The results recorded in this chapter may be placed under three headings: (a) Photo-synthesis by inorganic transformers; (b) action of sunlight and of ultra-violet light upon concentrated solutions of formaldehyde; (c) the general formation of formaldehyde by the action of light upon organic substances of biochemical origin.

In the first section, the reactions of a number of inorganic systems in presence of carbon dioxide and exposure to light are investigated, and it is shown that certain of these can build up formaldehyde while others are inert. The activity is shown to be related to the development of an optimum degree of colloidality, and is not due to formation of higher or lower oxides, but more probably to surface condensation on interfaces.

The second section deals with the condensation of formaldehyde to form reducing substances leading to carbohydrates, and discusses the conditions favourable for such condensations. The energetics of such a system are treated of in this section, and the effects of general or local concentration are considered. The equilibrium point in reversible reactions is shown to be dependent on concentration.

In the concluding section a general reversible reaction is described as a result of which formaldehyde arises in all intense reactions of light upon substances of biochemical origin. This reaction in presence of excess of light is an interesting reversal of the process by which all organic matter has been built up from inorganic sources.

The bearing of this process upon the germicidal action of sunlight, and the destruction of living organisms by ultra-violet light, is discussed, and it is pointed out that the simple organic products so formed are incompatible with the life processes of living organisms, and so lead to their destruction.

CHAPTER VII

STUDIES OF PHOTO-SYNTHESIS IN FRESH-WATER ALGÆ

1. THE FIXATION OF BOTH CARBON AND NITROGEN FROM THE ATMO-
   SPHERE TO FORM ORGANIC TISSUE BY THE GREEN PLANT CELL.
   2. NUTRITION AND GROWTH PRODUCED BY HIGH GASEOUS
   DILUTIONS OF SIMPLE ORGANIC COMPOUNDS, SUCH AS FORMAL-
   DEHYDE AND METHYLIC ALCOHOL.   3. NUTRITION AND GROWTH
   BY MEANS OF HIGH DILUTIONS OF CARBON DIOXIDE AND OXIDES
   OF NITROGEN WITHOUT ACCESS TO ATMOSPHERE.

THE two most primeval and most fundamental chemical processes
for living organisms are those two in which their living substance is
synthesised from inorganic sources with uptake of energy.   By one
of these carbon is built into organic compounds, starting with the
oxidised carbon dioxide of the atmosphere and utilising the energy of
sunlight.   The source of the inorganic nitrogen, which in the second
is likewise built into organic forms in the amino-acids and proteins,
is more obscure, and has in the course of 150 years led to much
disputation.   In the present and succeeding chapters evidence will
be adduced that the source of the nitrogen utilised by the plant does
not lie in the soil (although a luxury or *luxus* supply may be given
from the soil), but in the air, and that the reaction by which the
atmospheric nitrogen and oxygen are made reactive is a photo-
synthetic one, in which the energy of sunlight is absorbed and
converted into chemical form as nitrites in the green cell.

This view places these two processes of carbon and nitrogen
assimilation upon the same basis, and makes them coeval in the
process of evolution; this, as will presently be pointed out, must
have been the case, in order that any living organism could ever
have appeared upon the earth.

The importance of this question of the fixation of nitrogen has
induced much study of it and led to many polemics, and it is interesting how invariably the weight of scientific authority has been

upon the wrong side. Eminent men, supporting error unconsciously with negative experiments, have stated that the nitrogen was obtained from the soil and never by the leaves from the air, less known men, backing their statements by positive proofs, were on the other side, but the eminence and authority of their rivals was too much for them, and so it comes about that in this matter we still almost universally believe and teach " the thing that is not "

It was Priestley himself, the discoverer of the like process for carbon assimilation, who in 1771 first asserted that plants were able to absorb the nitrogen of the air, and Ingenhousz shortly after endorsed this statement. But this earlier view was contradicted, first by de Saussure, and later by Woodhouse, Senebier, and then by the eminent agricultural chemist Boussingault, in France, and the no less eminent Lawes, in England

Ville, in France, stoutly maintained that plants absorb nitrogen from the air, and his findings were confirmed by a specially appointed Committee of the Académie des Sciences. Boussingault repeated his own experiments with the utmost care and every precaution, and again obtained negative results This was later confirmed in an elaborate series of researches made by Lawes at Rothamsted; and the eminence and great authority of these two distinguished men settled the controversy in their favour for a generation.

Experiments that we have ourselves made in the course of the present investigation, as to the growth of the seeds of higher plants (mono- and di-cotyledons) in sand and water cultures, upon media free from compounds of nitrogen, have convinced us that the experimental results of these observers were correct, but their deductions profoundly erroneous. The seedlings we obtained were dwarfs, although they flowered and seeded, and they assimilated scarcely any nitrogen. This does not by any means settle the problem, it only proves that, so far as the higher plants are concerned, this is an abortive method of experimentation. If the conditions of environment are such as to make any feeble growth pathological, and if the dry weight of the plant scarcely exceeds that of the seed from which it grew, it is scarcely to be expected that there should be an increase in nitrogen. On the other hand, had the seeds grown into anything like normal plants, it would have been an unthinkable monstrosity in nature that carbon, hydrogen, and oxygen should go up without any accompanying increase in the nitrogen.

It has been shown by Jamieson,[1] in several species of higher plants, that when a minimal amount of nitrogen is supplied, these grow, increase in weight, and form far more combined nitrogen both in soil and plant than has been supplied in original soil and added media. These experiments of Jamieson's were carried out with the utmost care, attention being paid to every possible source of gain or loss of nitrogen. Moreover, they are supported by several other series of observations, such as gain of nitrogen in aquatic plants with no soil roots, growth of large trees rooted in clefts in basaltic and granitic rocks, where the total nitrogen in the soil could not afford sufficient for one annual crop of leaves, analysis for nitrogen of plants found growing in hard mortar in walls where the amount of nitrogen available, except from the atmosphere, was practically negligible.

A careful perusal of the wealth of facts published by Jamieson in the "Annual Reports of the Aberdeen Agricultural Research Association," against which there are only to be set these negative results of Boussingault and Lawes, is convincing as to the positive solution of the problem in favour of the assimilation of nitrogen from the air by the green cell. These results have been confirmed by Mameli and Pollacci[2] at Pavia; they are reinforced by the experiments described in this chapter upon Fresh-Water Algæ, and also by others to be recorded later upon Marine Algæ.

Our approach to this problem has been from a different point of view from those who have preceded us; they have been engaged in its consideration in relation to the biochemistry of the plant, or its importance in nutrition in agricultural chemistry; we have been investigating the matter from the point of view of the primeval origin of living organisms, before there was yet anything so complicated as a green cell upon the earth, and when organic compounds were first being synthesised from inorganic sources.

The minutest micrococcus visible under the microscope contains organic nitrogenous compounds in the form of proteins; it is probable that the ultra-microscopic particles, called filter-passers, which can pass through a Chamberland filter and yet can reproduce themselves in organic media, and transmit diseases, also contain

---

[1] Jamieson, "Reports Agricultural Research Association, Aberdeen," 1905-1911.

[2] Mameli and Pollacci, "Sull' Assimilazione, dell' Azoto atmosferico nei Vegetali," Pavia, *Atti. Ist. Bot.*, vol. xiv, pp. 159-257 (1911).

organic nitrogenous substances. Their very specific reactions show these ultra-microscopic germs to be highly organised systems, on the path from the inorganic to the organic. It is hence futile to seek at the level of bacteria for the origin of the organic; the first stage must have been an inorganic colloidal solution aggregate, capable of utilising sunlight and of building up on its surface or in its meshes organic substances as a forerunner for the still ultra-microscopic living cell. The powers of such a synthesising colloid in evolving more complex forms of matter would soon have been exhausted had it not been able to fix nitrogen as well as carbon from its environment. This power of nitrogen fixation, as evolution proceeded, must necessarily have been passed on to the more highly organised forms as these arose, for without such assimilative power they could not survive in a fresh world containing no ready-formed organic food.

Just as in carbon fixation, at a certain stage in evolution, a *luxus* method of fixation was evolved in the chloroplast of the green cell, which was able to work at a higher velocity and use longer wave-lengths of light than the simpler inorganic colloid which preceded it, so in the case of nitrogen the slow union of nitrogen and oxygen to form oxides of nitrogen, induced by sunlight, in inorganic systems, became replaced by more rapid transformers in the unicellular green plant; and when organic matter began to accumulate, still another *luxus* channel was opened by those bacteria and other unicellular organisms which can use the supply of energy of decaying non-nitrogenous matter to build up nitrogenous compounds, utilising atmospheric nitrogen for the purpose. Examples of such cases of *luxus* fixation are the azoto-bacter living free in the soil and the nitrogen-fixing bacteria in the tubercles of the rootlets of the leguminosæ It is obvious, however, that there existed no decaying organic matter at the first dawn of the organic, and that leguminosæ and all plants living in symbiosis with nitrogen-fixing organisms are late creations in the evolution of life

Interesting and of great practical importance as are these symbioses of a carbon-fixing organism with a nitrogen-fixing organism subsisting upon it or upon its dead products, it is logically quite clear that they cannot have formed the origination of life and are only bypaths of evolution. One of the earliest organisms must have possessed the dual function united in a single cell, or solution aggregate, of fixing both carbon and nitrogen. Approaching the subject from this aspect, we have examined the simplest unicellular algæ, and have found that they do possess this dual function.

In order to obtain as pure air as possible, the exposures and growths were made in the open air at Heron's Lodge, Heronsgate, Chorley Wood, Herts. The house is about $1\frac{1}{2}$ miles from the railway line, stands on high ground at an elevation of about 400 feet, and possesses a large lawn, in the middle of which all the experiments, except the first, were made. The air was tested daily for nitrites by starch and potassium iodide papers, and nitrites were nearly always present. At the conclusion of the experiments, the growths and waters were taken to the laboratory and analysed for content of nitrogen by the Kjeldahl method, when an unmistakable amount of fixation was found. The experiments were made in the spring and summer of 1918, in the months of April to August inclusive.

Experiment I.—Commenced April 15, finished August 5. Two clear glass flasks of Jena glass, each of 1000 c.c. capacity, were taken, and provided with ground-glass stoppers. These were almost completely filled with water from a clear stream near the house. One was filled up to the glass stopper, and then the stopper was inserted, so that the contents of the flask were completely shut off from the air. The other flask was filled so that the water stood in its neck about 4 cm. from the top; the glass stopper was not inserted, but instead a loose plug of cotton-wool was used. Over this a piece of fine muslin was placed and tied round the neck of the flask with thread; air, accordingly, had access to the contents of this flask. The glass-stoppered flask is a control to give the amount of nitrogen present at the outset plus any that can possibly be formed in absence of air.

The two flasks were placed outside on the ledge of a first-floor window, facing almost due west, so that direct sunlight was only obtained for a few hours in the afternoon. Care was taken to give equal chances to the two flasks by reversing their positions on the ledge every two or three days. Also a small beaker was inverted over the cotton-wool, to prevent contamination by rain. The flasks were not inseminated with any organism, but left to develop their crops naturally.

On May 2 a distinct green growth appeared in both flasks, slightly greater in the glass-stoppered one. On May 7 the open flask showed a distinctly greater growth than the stoppered one. In direct sunlight bubbles of gas are evolved from both, but most from

the open flask. May 14.—Growth in the stoppered flask has
stopped, no gas bubbles are given off in sunlight, but there is a brisk
effervescence in the open flask, and the growth is obviously increasing   May 20.—All growth is stopped in the closed flask, and
the growth has turned brown and flocculent.   But the growth in the
open flask is healthy and increasing, and gives off bubbles in sunlight
Frequent observations were taken till the conclusion on August 5,
but for brevity these may be omitted.   The growth in the open
flask remained green and healthy to the end   No fresh growth
started in the stoppered one, and at the end it had only a very few
brown flocculi from the initial effort, ere its small store of dissolved
carbon dioxide and nitrogen became exhausted   The contrast at
the end between the two flasks was most marked.

Frequent examination with the microscope, through the wall of
the flask, of the growing clumps of green organisms, showed the
presence of only two types of round-celled unicellular algæ.   One of
these was smaller than the other and of a brighter green, and was
identified as chlorella; the other was of about twice the diameter,
not so regularly spherical, and of a brownish-green colour   There
were no diatoms or other motile green organisms   No mycelium
or other evidence of fungi were seen, and the absence of any turbidity
at the end showed there was no appreciable development of bacteria.
Drops examined at the end showed no bacterial growths.

Blank experiments on the water used showed that it contained
about 1 mgrm per litre of amino-nitrogen, and about 0 3 mgrm.
per litre of nitrogen as nitrite and nitrate.   In addition to this
control, there is the control of the stoppered flask contents.

The contents of the two flasks were analysed on August 5.   The
water in each, slightly acidified with sulphuric acid to prevent any
loss of amino-nitrogen, was evaporated down almost to dryness;
then in each case the growth was added, destruction with sulphuric
acid followed, and the nitrogen determination was made by the
ordinary Kjeldahl process

The results were that the open flask contained 5 00 mgrms. of
nitrogen, while the stoppered flask contained only 1·95 mgrms.
A third flask of transparent silica, containing the same water, which
had been exposed during the entire period of the experiment to such
bright and direct sunlight as was available, developed no growth
whatever, probably because the cells were destroyed by the intenser
light and shorter wave-lengths   The water in this flask was

examined similarly to the two above, and yielded 1·80 mgrms. per litre. There is thus a distinct and quite unmistakable gain of 3·05 mgrms., which has no other conceivable source than the atmosphere. It may be pointed out that this weight of nitrogen roughly corresponds to about 100 mgrms. of dried algæ, or to 500 mgrms., or about ½ grm , of moist-plant. It is an increase in nitrogen, lying many times outside the limits of error of the analytical methods employed.

Experiment II.—Commenced May 31, 1918; terminated September 9, 1918. This experiment was carried out in a series of twelve screw-stoppered, fruit-preserving jars, called " Kilners," each of about 850 c.c. capacity. These jars are of pale green bottle-glass, and possess a flat flange at top, over which is placed a flat rubber band; on this is placed the glass cover, provided with a flat flange to come in apposition. An air-tight union is obtained by means of a metal screw-top working on a glass screw-thread moulded on the outside of the wide neck of the jar. It was hence possible to keep certain of the jars in connection with the atmosphere by merely covering with a tied-on cap of lawn, and in others to screw down the lids and shut off access to the atmosphere. Each jar received 200 c.c. of tap water, the supply being Rickmansworth water. This is a surface water containing a small amount of calcium salts, but otherwise a pure, good water.

Each jar was next inseminated with 2 c.c. of a dilute stirred-up suspension in water of an algal growth which had been developed by self-growth in a small muslin-covered jar on the west window. The amount of nitrogen introduced in this insemination was infinitesimal, and, in any case, its amount, as well as any trace in the 200 c.c. of tap water, can be accounted for by deducting the average small amounts of nitrogen found in Nos. 1, 3, and 4, which really serve as controls; the net increases in the others then show the favouring action on nitrogen fixation of the various procedures. After the addition of the 200 c.c. of tap water and the 2 c.c. of algal suspension in all twelve cases, each was next treated as noted in the schedule below, and afterwards they were either kept closed with glass lids screwed down, or covered with fine lawn only, and were kept in light or darkness as noted. Darkness was secured in a wooden shed close alongside. Light meant full exposure to daylight, on the middle of the grass lawn, except at midday in the hot weather, when a muslin shade was thrown over, and tin sheets placed loosely on top to protect from excessive light and heat, which are fatal to algæ.

In order to save space in tabulation the amounts of nitrogen found by the Kjeldahl determination carried out at the conclusion of the experiments are here placed opposite the description of the treatment of each jar:

No. 1.—Tap water and algæ only, glass lid screwed down, kept in light. Nitrogen=0·3 mgrm.

No. 2.—Tap water and algæ only, no glass lid, top covered by fine lawn, kept in light. Nitrogen=1·6 mgrms.

No. 3.—Tap water and algæ only, the glass lid screwed down, kept in darkness. Nitrogen=0·1 mgrm.

No. 4.—Tap water and algæ only, covered by fine lawn, kept in darkness. Nitrogen=0·3 mgrm.

No. 5.—Tap water, algæ, 2 c.c. of 5 per cent. $Na_2HPO_4,12H_2O$ (*i.e.*, 0·05 per cent. of $Na_2HPO_4,12H_2O$), lawn cover only, kept in light. Nitrogen=8·1 mgrms.

No. 6.—Tap water, algæ, 0·05 per cent. of Na_2HPO_4 screwed-down glass lid, kept in light. Nitrogen=1·0 mgrm.

No. 7.—Tap water, algæ, 0·05 per cent. of Na_2HPO_4, 0·05 per cent. of $NaNO_2$, lawn cover only, kept in light. Nitrogen= 12·3 mgrms.

No. 8.—Tap water, algæ, 0·05 per cent. of Na_2HPO_4, 0·05 per cent. of $NaNO_2$, screwed-down glass lid, kept in light. Nitrogen= 0·7 mgrm.

No. 9.—Tap water, algæ, 0·05 per cent. Na_2HPO_4, 0·05 per cent. $NaNO_2$, formaldehyde vapour at high dilution supplied from side tube as described below, glass lid screwed down, kept in light. Nitrogen=3·8 mgrms.

No. 10.—Tap water, algæ, 0·05 per cent. Na_2HPO_4, no $NaNO_2$, formaldehyde vapour, glass lid screwed down, kept in light. Nitrogen=1·0 mgrm.

No. 11.—Tap water, algæ, 0·05 per cent. Na_2HPO_4, 0·05 per cent. $NaNO_2$, dilute methylic alcohol vapour supplied from side tube, glass lid screwed down, kept in light. Nitrogen=7·4 mgrms.

No. 12.—Tap water, algæ, 0·05 per cent. Na_2HPO_4, no $NaNO_2$, dilute methylic alcohol vapour from side tube, glass lid screwed down, kept in light. Nitrogen=1·1 mgrms.

Notes on Growth.—These were taken at frequent intervals and were concordant throughout; so as to save space only two samples will be given. It may be noted that in the course of growth the experiment was demonstrated to many scientific friends, and exhibits made at meetings of societies, such as the Biochemical and Royal Microscopical Societies, and it was admitted that the differences in growth existed; this is confirmed by the nitrogen determinations now given at the conclusion of the experiment.

July 1, 1918.—No. 1, no growth; No. 2, slight green growth; Nos. 3 and 4, no growth; No. 5, growth in clumps; No. 6, one spot of growth only; No. 7, strong dark green growth all over bottom and sides, best of series; No. 8, slight growth; No. 9, slight growth, better than No. 8; No. 10, no growth; No. 11, fair growth; No. 12, no growth.

July 20, 1918.—No. 1, no growth; No. 2, fair growth, quite obvious difference between Nos. 1 and 2; Nos. 3 and 4 (in darkness), no growths; No. 5, good growth in thick discrete clumps; No. 6, only one colony, commencing to degenerate; No. 7, the best of the series. Abundant dark green growth and many gas bubbles; No. 8, fair growth, but distinctly less than in Nos. 7, 9, 11; Nos. 9 and 11, both show three or four times as much green growth as No. 8; No. 10, no growth; No. 12, very slight growth.

At the end, just before Kjeldahling, a microscopical examination was made of Nos. 5, 7, 9, 11. All these showed almost pure growths of small round single green cells (chlorella); there were no mycelia or spores or other types of non-green cells.

Commentary.—Several distinct facts are shown by this experiment, and taking the final amount of nitrogen as quantitative guide, these will now be pointed out. It is interesting in the first place to notice the increase in nitrogen which could only come from the atmosphere in those cases where no source of nitrogen was added from without, but other essential conditions of growth were more or less perfectly satisfied. It is next of importance to note the effects of limiting each essential factor in turn—namely, carbon dioxide, easily available nitrogen (nitrites), alkaline phosphate—and to note the great swing in photo-synthesis in No. 7, where all are adequately satisfied. Lastly, the important proof is clearly furnished, we believe for the first time, that carbon dioxide can be completely cut off if its place be supplied by simple organic substances, such as formaldehyde and methylic alcohol, which have hitherto been regarded as the first products of photo-synthesis in the green cell.

on purely circumstantial evidence, or upon very weak and uncertain positive experiments.

The uptake of nitrogen from the atmosphere is shown by the difference between Nos. 1 and 2 with nothing whatever added, only tap water and a slight insemination with the algæ present, the sole difference being that No. 1 is screwed up airtight, while No. 2 is open to the air, The difference in nitrogen-content, $1\cdot6 - 0\cdot3 = 1\cdot3$ mgrms., is quite unmistakable. The limiting factor to growth here is unquestionably deficiency in phosphate in the tap water, as is clearly proven by Nos. 5 and 6, where this defect is supplied. This experiment again in a still stronger way shows the absorption of nitrogen from the air.

The fillip of the phosphate in No. 6, with screwed-down lid, has caused a light commencing growth until carbon dioxide became exhausted, amounting to 1 mgrm.; but when this is contrasted with No. 5, differing only in access of air— i.e., available carbon dioxide and nitrogen—the figure runs up to $8\cdot1$ mgrms., an increase of $7\cdot1$ mgrms. Now taking this No. 5 as it stands by itself, and not contrasting it with any of the others, the proof is given that in 200 c.c. of tap water, plus 2 c.c. of 5 per cent. solution of disodium hydrogen phosphate, plus a minute insemination of chlorella, there is an abundant growth, and the absorption from the air of 7 to 8 mgrms. of nitrogen. The controls are abundant and the conclusion seems to us inevitable.

Next observe the effects of a *luxus* addition of easily available nitrogen as nitrite, as shown by No. 7. This differs from No. 5 only in the extra addition to the culture medium of 0·05 per cent. of sodium nitrite, and the crop goes up by 50 per cent. from 8·1 to 12·3 mgrms. Similarly in the effect produced by manuring with ammonium salts or nitrates, a luxury supply produces a *luxus* crop.

The small growth in No. 8 with lid screwed down shows that available phosphates and sources of nitrogen may be present, but when the supply of carbon dioxide is cut off, and no substitute supplied, no photo-synthesis can occur. This is obvious, but No. 8 is a necessary control to No. 7, where CO_2 is supplied from the air, and to Nos. 9 and 11, where the air is shut out, but a supply of excessively dilute vapours of formaldehyde and methylic alcohol respectively was obtained from these substances contained in narrow test-tubes placed slantingly in the jars before the lids were screwed down. The result demonstrates that supplied in this manner the vapours of these simple organic substances can substitute carbon dioxide quite well, there being 3·8 mgrms. of nitrogen with the formaldehyde vapour and 7·4 mgrms. with the methylic alcohol, as against 0·7 mgrm. in the control. This does not show quantitatively that methylic alcohol is better as a nutrient than formaldehyde, for with somewhat increased concentrations both vapours would kill the growing green cells, and it is a difficult problem so to regulate the concentration of each at these excessive dilutions that the maximum beneficial result is obtained. The real point is that these vapours of simple organic substances, when sufficiently dilute, act not as poisons to the green cell but as nutrients which can replace carbon dioxide.

The bearing of these results upon the fundamental hypothesis of Baeyer, that the first step in the synthesis in green cells of the organic from the inorganic is formaldehyde, is so intimate that a little more consideration appears desirable. Hitherto this hypothesis has rested mainly upon circumstantial evidence. No one has ever been able to demonstrate the presence of formaldehyde in the living cell. Various solutions of chlorophyll and emulsions of chlorophyll in water, or upon colloidal membranes, such as gelatine, have been exposed to light, and afterwards formaldehyde has been tested for by delicate chemical tests. The results have been contradictory; some observers have found formaldehyde and others have failed to detect it. But we have previously shown that practically any organic system, when exposed to light, yields formaldehyde. Hence the presence of formaldehyde under such conditions means nothing and probably comes from a reversed system, not of building up but of breaking down of organic substances. Even if formaldehyde could be shown intravitally in a living cell it might only mean excessive light exposure and breaking down of living substance and not building up. Attention may again be drawn to the fact that the lethal action of light upon bacteria and other living cells is probably due to such a reversed reaction, in which formaldehyde and other simple and poisonous organic substances are set free.

The other channel of approach experimentally to this question is more promising—namely, Can these simple organic substances act as nutrients for cells ? If formaldehyde be the primary stage in photo-synthesis by which green cells are nourished, then it ought to be possible by supplying formaldehyde when carbon dioxide is shut off to make green cells grow and flourish.

Many attempts have been made in this direction, but have all failed, or given very dubious results, because of the highly poisonous action of formaldehyde. Formaldehyde, if and when formed in a green cell, must immediately be condensed into a sugar or some other non-poisonous organic compound or the cell will perish; there is, accordingly, no demonstrable amount of formaldehyde in the cell. If now it be supposed that the cell in sunlight is always producing formaldehyde which at once is changed into something else, then in order to mimic this process experimentally a system must be invented in which formaldehyde at minute concentrations is fed in slowly, at a rate not greater than the cells of the system can assimilate it. The formaldehyde must not be added to the solution in which the cells are growing at the outset, for any quantity detectable afterwards by increase in the cells would kill them. It must be continuously and very slowly administered as a dilute vapour.

Two glass tubes of about 0·5 cm. in diameter, each about 18 cm. long, were sealed at the one end so as to make narrow test-tubes. One of these was about half filled with formol (40 per cent. formaldehyde), the other with methylic alcohol. The tube containing formol was placed slanting in bottle No. 9, the closed end resting on the bottom of the bottle, and the upper end on the inside of the neck close beneath the glass lid. The tube containing methylic alcohol was similarly placed in No. 11. Both glass lids were tightly screwed down to exclude atmospheric carbon dioxide. The nutrient solutions contained nitrite as well as phosphate. The two flasks were kept exposed to light, and after some weeks there were good growths obtained in both.

Judged from the amounts of nitrogen, there was a fixation of 3·5 mgrms. in the formaldehyde nutrition, and a fixation of 7·1 mgrms. in the methylic alcohol nutrition. To get from the nitrogen fixation to the carbon fixation these figures must be multiplied by a factor of at least 8, for the weight of carbon even in protein is treble that of the nitrogen, and there is carbon but no nitrogen in carbohydrates and fats. If this factor be applied there is a fixation of 28 mgrms. of carbon from formaldehyde (=70 mgrms. of formaldehyde) and of 56·8 mgrms. of carbon from methylic alcohol (=151 mgrms. of methylic alcohol). The bottles Nos. 10 and 12 were a similarly conducted experiment, but without available nitrates or other easily assimilable nitrogen, and this has greatly repressed the production of growth. The two amounts of nitrogen of 1·0 and 1·1 mgrm. are, however, considerably above the controls—namely, 0·1 to 0·3—so that it would appear probable that there was a slow fixation of atmospheric elemental nitrogen. (See in this connection the next experiments, Nos. 3 and 4, and the succeeding chapter on Marine Algæ.)

Experiment III.—Commenced August 9, 1918; terminated August 29, 1918. This set was likewise carried out in Kilner jars, and was designed to test whether, with exclusion of the free atmosphere, nutrition and growth could be achieved by feeding with high dilutions of carbon dioxide, and of oxides of nitrogen. The experiment was carried out as follows:

Eight Kilner jars were taken. Each of these received 100 c.c. tap water, 1 c.c. of a 1 per cent. solution of sodium chloride, 1 c.c. of a 1 per cent. solution of alkaline potassium phosphate (K_2HPO_4), and two drops of a 1 per cent. solution of ferric chloride (equivalent to 0·14 c.c.). Then to each was given a minute insemination of 1 c.c. of a dilute suspension of a unicellular green algal growth. The eight jars were set out on the lawn in the daylight on August 9, each being loosely covered by its lid, but opened daily, so as to establish growth in each case preparatory to the subsequent treatment. On August 16 growths were evident, and about equally advanced in all the jars; numerous fresh colonies had started attached to the bottoms, and in the precipitated calcium phosphate. The eight jars were now divided into four pairs. The first pair (Nos. 1 and 2) simply had their lids screwed on airtight. The second pair (Nos. 3 and 4) first had a narrow test-tube, similar to that described in Experiment II., and half filled with solid sodium bicarbonate inserted, and both then had their lids screwed on airtight. The third pair (Nos. 5 and 6), instead of the sodium bicarbonate tube, had a similar tube, containing a system designed to evolve nitrogen peroxide and other oxides of nitrogen very slowly into the air of the jar. The fourth pair (Nos. 7 and 8) each had two tubes, one containing sodium bicarbonate, and the other the nitrous system. This nitrous system was constructed thus: A few crystals of sodium nitrite were introduced into the narrow test-tube, the tube was then gently half filled with water, and on top of this there was introduced a column of about 3 cm. of 1 in 10 nitric acid.

The design of the experiment was to shut off all atmospheric supply of carbon dioxide and of nitrites, and in one pair leave the algæ destitute of both these; in the next, supply carbon dioxide and restrict nitrites, in the third, supply nitrites but restrict carbon dioxide; and in the fourth, supply both carbon dioxide and nitrites. The dissociation pressure of carbon dioxide from sodium bicarbonate lies between 1 mm and 2 mm of mercury, so it is ample to supply the needs of the algæ, also the nitrous system was so arranged as to give off the nitrous fumes at such a rate that the algæ could cope with them and utilise them, so that the nutrient medium did not become acid

Examined on August 30—*e*, fourteen days after the addition of the side-tube—it was found that Nos. 1 and 2 (no addition) and Nos 5 and 6 (nitrites only) were dead and degenerating This had occurred in about a day in Nos. 5 and 6, probably because they could not grow from lack of carbon dioxide, and so the oxide of nitrogen absorbed by their culture media accumulated and killed them. Degeneration did not occur in Nos 1 and 2 for about a week to ten days, but at the end of the fortnight they were obviously dead and degenerating

The contrast in the case of the other four jars was striking; all four had lived, increased in amount, and were flourishing at the end It was obvious that the pair which had received both carbon dioxide and oxides of nitrogen were much in advance of the other pair, which had been supplied with carbon dioxide only The latter, of course, had a supply of elemental nitrogen in the enclosed air of the jar.

The united contents of each pair of jars, when Kjeldahled, gave the following results:

	Nitrogen
Nos 1 and 2 (no additions) . . .	3·46 mgrms.
Nos 3 and 4 (sod bicarb only) .	5 40 ,,
Nos 5 and 6 (oxides of nitrogen only) . .	2·50 ,,
Nos 7 and 8 (both sod bicarb and oxides of nitrogen)	14·10 ,,

The larger weight of nitrogen found in Nos. 5 and 6, which did not grow after addition of oxides of nitrogen, as compared with the controls of the previous experiment, arises from the growth during the first week open to the atmosphere, when the growths were allowed to strike, no such period was allowed in the preceding experiment If the amount of 2·50 mgrms in this pair be taken as the control, then the amount of nitrogen fixed by jars with no additions, before succumbing to lack of carbon dioxide, is 0·96 mgrm When carbon dioxide is supplied from the sodium bicarbonate, but no oxides of nitrogen are given to the air, so that the only source for the fixation of nitrogen[1] is the elemental nitrogen of the air enclosed in the jars, this figure rises to (5·40 – 2·50) 2·90 mgrms. This result is of high importance, for it shows that, given supplies of carbon dioxide, nitrogen, and oxygen, in presence of sunshine, the cell can form its own oxides of nitrogen and build these into amino-compounds, although at a much slower rate than when oxides of nitrogen are supplied.

This is confirmed again by the experiments on marine algæ to be detailed in the succeeding chapter. In the sea water a source of carbon dioxide already exists in the bicarbonate of magnesium and calcium dissolved in it.   Hence no side-tube is necessary, and a marine alga simply shut up airtight photo-synthesises and fixes both carbon and nitrogen.   The stimulating and growth-quickening effect of traces of oxides of nitrogen, passing from the air to dissolve in the aqueous medium bathing the green cell, is shown by the great rise when these oxides are supplied, as in Nos. 7 and 8.

The amount of nitrogen here fixed is 11·60 mgrms., as compared with 2·90 when elemental nitrogen is the sole source.

Summary.

1. The primeval living organism, like the inorganic colloidal systems which were its precursors, must have possessed the power of fixing carbon and nitrogen and building these up into reduced organic compounds with uptake of energy. The source of the energy was sunlight.

2. This power is still possessed by the lowliest type of synthesising cell existing—namely, the unicellular alga.

3. A synthesising cell must have existed prior to bacteria and other fungi, since these can only exist upon organic matter, and the primeval world before the advent of life could contain no organic matter.

4. Their specific reactions show that even the ultra-microscopic filter-passing organisms are highly organised products on the path from the inorganic towards life, and it hence follows that there is a

---

[1] As we have shown previously, this air contains a trace of nitrites, but the amount in the few hundred cubic centimetres of air contained in the jar is infinitesimal and may be neglected.

long intermediate range of evolution. The first synthesising system acting upon the light was hence probably an inorganic colloidal system in solution, capable of adsorbing the simple organic substances which it synthesised. It is hence futile to search for the origin of life at the level of bacteria and torulæ.

5 As complexity increased with progressive evolution more and more rapid transformers for the capture of the energy of the sunlight came into existence. Such transformers are found in the green cell for fixation of both carbon and nitrogen The earlier transformers in the inorganic colloidal systems can only utilise light of short wave-lengths; the later transformers in the living cells are adapted to utilise longer wave-lengths, and the very short wave-lengths, which are lethal, are cut off by their colour screens of chlorophyll, etc.

6. The earliest products of photo-synthesis, such as formaldehyde and methylic alcohol, are highly poisonous to the green cell, but fed to it at sufficiently high dilution, can be used as nutrition in absence of carbon dioxide, and very marked growths have been obtained with these substances as the sole source of carbon

7. In the absence of all other sources of nitrogen save the elemental nitrogen of the atmosphere, but with abundance of carbon dioxide, the unicellular algæ can fix nitrogen, grow and form proteins.

8. The rate of fixation and growth is, however, greatly accelerated if nitrites or oxides of nitrogen are available.

9. These oxides of nitrogen can be supplied in gaseous form from the atmosphere, and pure country air normally contains such oxides of nitrogen, especially in spring and summer.

CHAPTER VIII

STUDIES OF PHOTO-SYNTHESIS IN MARINE ALGÆ

1. FIXATION OF CARBON AND NITROGEN FROM INORGANIC SOURCES
IN SEA WATER. 2. INCREASE OF ALKALINITY OF SEA WATER
AS A MEASURE OF PHOTO-SYNTHESIS.

THE results of a series of observations upon marine algæ confirm and
amplify those obtained with fresh-water algæ, which, as recorded
in the preceding chapter, show a convincing uptake of nitrogen from
the air, but on account of the change of the medium of growth from
fresh to sea water there are several important modifications in the
medium itself as well as in the growing algæ, which appear to
possess considerable importance in the annual life of the sea, and
in the inductance at certain definite periods of the year of increased
processes of cell division and reproduction of species, and possibly
may guide the development of variations in species, and the process
of evolution.   The details of seasonal variation in growth are
furnishing to us at present most interesting results, but here will
be recorded only work now completed dealing with light action
apart from seasonal variation.

There is in the case of marine plants none of that uncertainty
which obtains in the case of the higher terrestrial plants as to how
much of the nitrogen being built into organic compounds comes from
the roots.   Even in the case of such massive plants as Laminaria
and Fucus it is obvious that the roots are merely modes of attachment to the rocks, and that the whole plant is built up from the sea
water.   It is an impossibility that nitrogen could be extracted from
the hard stones to which the plants are anchored, and in the case of
the floating diatoms, and other minute green cells, which form the
phyto-plankton, floating free in the sea, it is clear that the whole
organism is formed from the sea water.   Hence the entire plant life
of the sea is produced by the action of sunlight upon the water of the
sea and its dissolved constituents.   In so far as sources of ready-
formed and easily absorbable nitrogenous compounds are concerned,
the sea water is remarkably poor, and the volumes of sea water

115

necessary to feed the algæ with nitrogen, were this the source, would be immense Thus, Gebbing[1] found the amount of nitrogen as ammonia present in sea water to be only 0 05 mgrm. per litre, and the amount as nitrite plus nitrate as 0 47 mgrm. per litre.[2] These results are confirmed by some to be given later in this chapter

This paucity of nitrogenous compounds in sea water, while it indicates that the nitrogen of the plant tissues is probably derived from the dissolved elemental nitrogen of the atmosphere, is not, however, clear proof, for the sea water, for example, contains but a trace of that silica from which the skeletons of the diatoms are derived. It might be argued that in the restless movement of the sea the volume of water which daily laved the plants was ample to compensate for the small amount of dissolved nitrogenous compounds in the water. To settle this query it is obviously necessary to grow marine algæ in a limited volume of sea water and then to determine the amount of nitrogen fixed. If this latter many times exceeds the amounts of nitrogen present as ammonia, nitrites, and nitrates in the sea water used, then clearly—for here there is no soil to obscure the issue—this fixed nitrogen must come from the dissolved nitrogen in the sea water, which in turn came from the nitrogen in the air

This has been done in the experiments recorded below, with the clearest proof that marine algæ do so fix their nitrogen.

As photo-synthesis proceeds, and the supply of carbon is drawn from the dissolved bicarbonates, the reaction of the nutrient medium becomes all the time more alkaline[3] The increased alkalinity can be used as a measure of the photo-synthetic activity, and was so employed by Moore, Prideaux, and Herdman[4] in determinations made at Port Erin during the years 1912–1915, and subsequently by Osterhout and Haas[5] It is interesting to note the

---

[1] J. Gebbing, *Centralb. f. Bacteriol.*, 2 Abth , vol xxxi.

[2] *Cf.* also Moore, Edie, Whitley, and Dakin, "The Nutrition and Metabolism of Marine Animals," *Biochem Journ.*, vol vi., p. 255 (1912); Raben, *Wissensch Meeresuntersuch* . Kiel, vol. viii (1905)

[3] See Czapek, "Bio-chemie der Pflanzen," 2nd edition, vol i , pp 518, 519, where numerous references may be found

[4] "Report on the Lancashire Sea-Fisheries Scientific Investigations for 1914," Herdman, *Trans Biological Society of Liverpool*, vol xxix , p 171 (1915).

[5] "On the Dynamics of Photo-Synthesis," *Journ of General Physiology*, vol i., p. 1 (1918)

level to which this enhanced alkalinity can attain without destroying the green cell which is producing it. Angelstein[1] found that, in solutions containing one part of bicarbonate to two of carbonate, the plants continued to give off oxygen. Osterhout and Haas determined by the titration method that the alkalinity can be increased until it reaches a level represented by $P_H=9$. Moore, Prideaux, and Herdman had previously fixed the limit at P_H less than 9·1; the last-quoted observers further point out in this earlier work that this corresponds to the point at which all the bicarbonates have been converted into carbonates, and this has again been confirmed in the present experiments.

If a sample of normal sea water be titrated with centinormal acid in the presence of a stable indicator such as " dimethyl " or " methyl orange," a figure defining the entire content of alkali present as bicarbonate is obtained. This figure scarcely ever varies with season or otherwise, and amounts to about 24 c.c. of centinormal alkali per 100 c.c. of sea water. If, now, some sea water be taken, and a green algal growth be exposed in it to bright daylight or sunshine, so as to produce as intense a degree of photo-synthesis as possible, and then the amounts of normal carbonates formed from bicarbonates, as carbon is synthesised into organic compounds, be determined by titrating the alkalinity to an indicator such as phenolphthaleïn, it will be found that the limit is just about half the preceding value—namely, 12 c.c. of centinormal alkali per 100 c.c. of sea water. This limit marks the point at which all the bicarbonates of magnesium and calcium present in the sea water have become converted into normal carbonates. If photo-synthesis passed this point, free hydrates of magnesium and calcium would commence to be present in the sea water, and there would be a correspondingly rapid increase in hydroxyl-ion concentration and fall in hydrogen-ion concentration.

It is this accumulation of alkali which limits photo-synthesis by killing the cell, for up to quite close to this " all-carbonate " point the cell flourishes and synthesises rapidly, but if kept for some time by too violent exposure to sunlight at this point, the algæ turn yellow and the growth is killed, for there is no recovery, even if removed from the strong light. The degree of alkalinity reached by the green cell before death is, however, remarkable. It is much greater than anything which can be borne by any mammalian cell,

[1] "Cohn Beiträge," vol. x. (1911).

and even by any delicate marine animal organism, such as a developing embryo plaice or a fertilised echinus egg.

The increase of hydroxyl-ion concentration and corresponding decrease in hydrogen-ion concentration are such that the water shows a full pink with phenolphthaleïn, and is more alkaline than the full strength of the decinormal " alkaline phosphate " (Na_2HPO_4) in the Sörensen phosphatic mixtures for determination of hydrogen-ion concentration. This means, expressed in the usual logarithmic notation, a concentration of less than P_H, $10^{-9.1}$.

This increase of alkalinity is about equal to that shown in 1905 by Moore, Roaf, and Whitley,[1] to promote disordered cell division, and, later, death in the dividing cells of fertilised echinus eggs. Now, when the sunshine is strong in spring and summer, in every pool upon the seashore above half-tide level, when isolated from the sea, such active photo-synthesis must proceed with development of alkalinity, and such changes must have a marked effect upon any animal forms of life in the pool. Such environmental changes, with their stimulating action upon cell division, may play a part in originating deviations and producing variations. In winter such influences would be slight, but as the spring days lengthen and the altitude of the sun increases their power augments and reaches a maximum just as reproductive processes and rapid cell division are at their height. In the experiments recorded below, in order to prevent death from alkalinity, a supply of carbon dioxide was given by blowing air from the lungs through the sea water in which those algæ were immersed which were exposed to full day or sunlight, whenever the titrations showed an approach to the lethal limit.

The main series of experiments was carried out during the period of March 28 till April 5, 1919, in two sets of twelve each of the Kilner fruit-preserving jars, each of about 800 c.c. capacity and provided with airtight, screw-down lids, as described in a previous chapter. Afterwards, for purposes of analysis, the two sets at the end were combined and preserved together. As there were two similarly treated jars in each set, the Kjeldahl determinations for nitrogen came to be made upon the contents of four jars; thus a good average was obtained.

The green seaweed utilised was *Enteromorpha compressus*, which grows abundantly in the open wooden runnels supplying the freshly pumped-up sea water to the ponds of the Fish Hatchery at the

---

[1] Moore, Roaf, and Whitley, *Roy. Soc. Proc.*, B, vol. lxxvii., p. 102 (1905).

Marine Biological Station, Port Erin. This weed is well suited to the purpose because it is easily divided and can be accurately weighed out in definite amount. A quantity of the enteromorpha was gathered and relieved of excess of sea water by pressing gently between folds of filter-paper. It was then weighed out into 0·5 grm. quantities, and one of these quantities was placed in 200 c.c. of fresh sea water in each Kilner jar. Nothing save the weed and water was added to any jar. The first dozen jars were started on the morning of March 28, and the second set on the afternoon of the same day; they were pickled together in absolute alcohol as preservative on the morning of April 5, and also the waters in which they had grown were taken away for analysis, with the results given below.

The two sets were treated identically as to exposures, and the first set may be taken as an example for both:

Nos. 1 *and* 2.—Kept with lids tightly screwed on in such day-light and sunlight as were available outdoors.

Nos. 3 *and* 4.—Ditto, but instead of tightly screwed-on lids, these were covered above only with a double layer of muslin, so that there was free access of atmosphere.

Nos. 5 *and* 6.—Exposed to diffuse light only indoors on shelf in laboratory, with lids tightly screwed on.

Nos. 7 *and* 8.—The same as to light, but open, with muslin covers only.

Nos. 9 *and* 10.—Kept in complete darkness in cupboard with lids tightly screwed on.

Nos. 11 *and* 12.—Also kept in darkness in cupboard with muslin covers only.

At intervals, as noted in the subjoined table, a quantity of 100 c.c. of sea water was taken from one jar of each type of exposure, 4 drops of 0·5 per cent. of phenolphthaleïn were added, and the water was titrated to neutrality with the results shown. Then 100 c.c. of fresh sea water were added to restore the former volume, and the jar restored to *statu quo* as to exposure. The samples of weed in each set of four jars with identical exposures did not during the experiment ever receive more than 1000 c.c. of sea water in all. Samples of fresh sea water, and of that from the jars open in sunlight, were analysed for amino-nitrogen by Kjeldahl destruction and Nesslerising at the termination of the experiment, and the amount in each case was found to be 1·3 mgrms. per litre. Also, in each case, analysis for nitrite and nitrate gave in both cases 1 in 10 million to 1 in 15 million expressed as nitrogen. It follows that the nitrogen converted by the growth in light of the algæ could not be obtained from combined nitrogen as ammonia, nitrite, or nitrate   The only other available source is dissolved nitrogen in the sea water derived from the air.

A glance at the fifth column of the table given below shows that the four jars, closed airtight but kept in sunshine, fixed nitrogen almost as rapidly as the open jars in sunshine.   This furnishes proof that the source of the nitrogen fixed is not the nitrogen peroxide, or so-called ozone, of the air, but the elemental nitrogen   This does not, of course, exclude nitrogen peroxide as a nutrient and a stimulant, experiments in the preceding chapter on fresh-water algæ have shown that dilute nitrogen peroxide can so stimulate growth   But both series of experiments agree in proving that, given an ample supply of carbon—either as carbon dioxide or as bicarbonate—and the presence of light-energy, then elemental nitrogen from the air in solution in the nutrient medium can be fixed and built up into organic compounds   At the conclusion of the series of experiments, the four samples of weed in each set of four bottles were separated from the sea water, united, pressed between filter-papers, and the moist weight taken.   As at the outset 0·5 grm was weighed out into each jar, the initial weight in each set was 2 grm.

After weighing, each set of weed was placed in a wide-mouthed glass-stoppered bottle, and preserved in a quantity of about 80 c c. of absolute alcohol.

When the analyses were started, the preliminary step in each case was to evaporate off the alcohol in a weighed capsule, add the preserved weed, and dry to constant weight; these dried weights are recorded in column 4 of the table   Then each dried weight was analysed for nitrogen by the usual Kjeldahl method, and the results are given in column 5.

Commentary on Table.—The figures given in column 2 show the alkalinity developed by the photo-synthesis.   Notice how much greater it is in full light than in diffuse light, and that in complete darkness it becomes negative because the carbon dioxide discharged in oxidative processes in darkness renders the sea water acid to phenolphthalein.   The normal sea water at this period possessed an alkalinity to this indicator represented by about 2·5 c.c. per 100 c.c.

of sea water. The alkalinity tends to rise higher in the " shut " jars in sunshine, because in the " open " jars in sunshine the atmospheric carbon dioxide can enter through the muslin and partially reneutralise the normal carbonates of magnesium and calcium formed.

TABLE.—FIXATION OF NITROGEN BY MARINE ALGÆ. EXPERIMENT OF MARCH 28-APRIL 5, 1919 (SEVEN DAYS' INTERVAL).

1.	2.		3.	4.	5.
Nature of Exposure.	Titration in c.c.'s of N/100 acid in 100 c.c. of sea water required to neutralise to phenolphthalein.		Wet weight at end. Initial weight in each case, 2 grms. in 800 c.c. sea water.	Dry weight at end in grammes.	Total nitrogen by Kjeldahl. In milligrams.
	April 2.	April 5.			
1. Sunlight, in *shut* jars, outdoors	13·3	9·7	2·57	0·476	11·3
2. Sunlight, in *open* jars, outdoors	6·7	6·7	2·38	0·457	12·4
3. Diffuse light, no direct sun, on shelf indoors. Shut jar	0·4	3·4	1·71	0·284	8·7
4. Same exposure as No. 3, but jars open	0·0	+ 1·7	1·47	0·285	8·0
5. Darkness, in cupboard. Shut jars	− 1·7	− 1·4	1·45	0·259	6·4
6. Same as 5, but jar open	− 1·2	− 0·3	1·50	0·275	6·5

It is of some interest to make a rough calculation of the quantities of fixed carbohydrate, protein, or fat that these amounts of fixed carbon dioxide, as estimated from the titrated increases of alkalinity, would account for during the period of experiment. Taking the mean of the two amounts of alkalinity upon the two days observed— viz., 13·3 and 9·7—one obtains 11·5. Deducting 2·5 c.c. for the level of normal sea water at this period of the year the result is 9·0 c.c. of centinormal alkali resulting from photo-synthesis per 100 c.c. This change occurred in 800 c.c. in each set for a period of seven days. This works out at 500 c.c. of centinormal alkali during the period. Now 1000 c.c. of normal alkali corresponds to 12 grms. of carbon fixed, and on this basis the carbon fixed is 60 mgrms. This would correspond, on the basis of 45 per cent. of carbon in carbohydrates, 60 per cent. in proteins, and 75 per cent.

in fats, to a fixation of 130 mgrms. of carbohydrate, 100 mgrms. of protein, or 80 mgrms. of fats.

Turning now to the increased moist weight during the experiment from 2 00 grms. to 2 57 grms and taking the dry weight at the end as 0·476 grm., the increase in dried weight works out at 106 mgrms (the initial dry weight being calculated as $0.476 \times \dfrac{2\ 00}{2\ 57}$ grm).

There is thus a close correspondence between the increase in weight and that which would be expected—viz , increase in dried weight found, 106 mgrms   expected increase in dried weight if all were converted into carbohydrate, 130 mgrms. , expected increase if all protein, 100 mgrms.; expected increase if all fat, 80 mgrms.

If next the increase in the nitrogen be considered, this amounts to about 3 mgrms., which corresponds to about 20 mgrms. of protein; the remaining 80 to 90 mgrms. fixed would therefore represent the carbohydrates and fats.

ADDENDUM ON NITROGEN-FIXING BACTERIA.

Our attention has been drawn to the fact that three different observers[1] have demonstrated that the surface of the ordinary large seaweeds is regularly colonised by nitrogen-fixing bacteria, and it has been stated that these bacteria have been identified with the nitrogen-fixing bacteria known in soils.

Reinke states that nitrogen bacteria were found without exception on all the marine algae of Heligoland sent to the Botanical Institute at Kiel for examination   The thoroughly washed alga was placed in a suitable nutritive medium, and there followed a heavy development of azotobacter and corresponding fixing of nitrogen from the air

In Keutner's experiments small pieces of various algæ were introduced into a culture medium, and in about ten days the fluid became turbid and a scum was formed on the surface of the water and on the pieces of seaweed   The bacteria could be identified in the slime on the algæ.   Experiments made on fresh-water plants gave the same results.   This observer definitely states that the culture flasks were kept either in a closed chest or cupboard or in a thermostat—that is to say, in the dark.

[1] Reinke, *Ber. deut bot Gesell* , vol xxii , p. 95 (1904); Keutner, *Wissen. Meeresuntersuch.*, Kiel, vol. viii , p 27 (1905), Keding, *ibid* , vol ix., p. 275

Keding's work is a continuation and development of the foregoing, and the statement that the algæ-colonising bacteria are the same as those known in soils can probably be traced to his finding that the azotobacter of the Baltic and that of the land " sich wenigstens in den in Betracht kommenden physiologischen Eigenschaften identisch verhalten." This at least is the only evidence that we are able to find for such a conclusion.

With the above results before him, Herman Fischer[1] is inclined to attribute to the action of bacteria, in the majority of instances, such cases of fixation of nitrogen by green plants as have hitherto been recorded, and holds that in every case where a claim is made to have observed such fixation a need exists for proof that the technique was perfect.

It is to be regretted that we had not the results above quoted before us when starting our series of experiments, and that in consequence no special precautions were taken to exclude nitrogen-fixing bacteria from our jars. Yet in our opinion it may be reasonably assumed that their presence did not seriously affect the results obtained, for the following reasons:

1. What we consider to be definitely proven as a result of these and former experiments above referred to is the utilisation of solar energy for the purpose of nitrogen fixation. Column 5 in the table shows a marked difference in the amount of nitrogen fixed, according as the seaweeds were exposed to sunlight, or kept in weak light, or in the dark. It appears to us to be a point of secondary importance whether that energy is so utilised by the alga itself or by an associated bacterium. If the effects observed are to be ascribed to the latter, it would be a novel experience to find a chlorophyll-less organism so functioning in relationship to light, and the proof that it could do so would be of unsurpassed interest in relation to the problem of the origin of life in a chlorophyll-less world.

2. It is to be noted that, in order to get nitrogen fixed in appreciable quantities, previous observers have found it necessary to grow their bacteria in appropriate culture media containing small quantities of glucose, mannitol, or other organic compounds, as well as the inorganic phosphates, etc. These media in due course became turbid, and bacterial scums were formed. Our experiments were carried out in pure sea water only, and, during the eight days

[1] " Das Problem der Stickstoffbindung bei Pflanzen," *Ber. deut. bot. Gesell.*, vol. xxxv., pp. 423-454 (1917).

that they lasted, there was no sign whatever of bacterial growth. The water remained perfectly clear throughout, and there was no indication of a scum on water or weed either in the jars exposed to sunlight or those kept in the dark. From this, one may legitimately conclude that the nitrogen-fixing bacteria, if present, had not multiplied to any great extent nor sufficiently to account for the results obtained.

SUMMARY.

1. Marine algæ, like fresh-water algæ, can fix elemental nitrogen from water and thus indirectly from air, in presence of sunlight, but not in darkness.

2. The store of bicarbonates of calcium and magnesium present in sea water furnishes an abundant source of carbon dioxide utilisable for carbon fixation, and as fixation proceeds the sea water becomes more alkaline. The limit of alkalinity is that at which all bicarbonates have become converted into carbonates, and at this point the potential of hydrogen-ion concentration has fallen below the value $P_H = 10^{-9.1}$.

3. In the strong sunshine of spring and summer this degree of alkalinity is sufficient to favour increased rapidity of cell division and induce abnormal and varying forms.

4. Marine algæ grown in a limited volume of water and a limited supply of air in sunlight and full daylight fix both carbon and nitrogen rapidly into organic compounds. The amount of nitrogen fixed exceeds many times the total nitrogen originally present as ammonia, nitrite, or nitrate in the water. Moreover, the small initial amounts of nitrogen present in these forms are not decreased. It follows that the only available source is the free nitrogen of the atmosphere.

CHAPTER IX

ENERGY TRANSFORMATIONS IN LIVING MATTER

REGARDED from the physical standpoint, all the acts which constitute our existence are due to transformations of energy in the world outside us and in our own bodies. It is by the medium of such energy transformations occurring in our sense organs that we are made aware of the existence of the external world, and kept informed of the changes going on in it, and it is by such transformations going on in the various living cells which constitute our bodies that energy is obtained for all those operations by which the body is nourished and enabled to adapt itself to the rest of the world around it.

The same statement is true of all organised and living matter, however high or low its degree of organisation may be. Whether the living matter belong to the vegetable or animal division, to micro-organism or man, it is alike a field for the display and reception of energy transformations, and its life manifests itself by the taking in of energy in one or more forms and the giving of it up in others.

In dealing with the physical aspect of the phenomena of living organisms, it may be well to discuss in some detail how closely such phenomena are associated with those observable in the inorganic world.

In the first place, the bodies of living organisms are built up from the same chemical elements as are found in inorganic structures. In the process of organisation the chemical constitution becomes so complex, and the physical organisation of the complex chemical molecules, whereby living matter is eventually formed, so intricate, that the organic chemist and physical chemist have hitherto not been able to follow the process, and hence we know but little regarding the constitution and structure of living matter.

Although the intermediate stages in the process cannot be followed by any means at present known to us, we can learn something by watching the ends of the process, by noting the ingesta

125

and egesta of the living matter, and studying, qualitatively and quantitatively, the energy changes displayed by living matter As a result of such observations, it is found that the two fundamental laws of the inorganic world—namely, the conservation of matter and the conservation of energy—are obeyed throughout the whole range of organised nature. Both these laws can be as well demonstrated by using a living animal, and making a debit and credit account for the matter and energy taken in and given out, as by performing a combustion experiment or causing any other transformation of energy and matter by means of non-vital matter and non-vital energy transformers. We see that this must be so when we consider that living matter is formed from the same material sources as non-living matter, and, further, that both its building up and its sources of energy for all its changes, when built up, arise from non-vital forms of energy; thus the same fundamental laws must apply to it as to the inorganic world, for otherwise no balance could exist between the two domains.

It by no means follows from this, however, that there is no difference except complexity of structure between living and non-living matter, that there is no form of energy peculiar to living matter, and that if we only knew how to apply to living plants and animals the laws pertaining to the forms of energy found in inorganic nature, we should find nothing superadded, nothing to justify such terms as *living* or *vital*. The very existence of such words as " living " and " vital " indicates the primary conception of something essentially different in nature, and it ought to be noted that it is the presence of certain peculiar energy phenomena which gives rise to the necessity for introducing such words, and not complexity of structure or development. We call things *living* because of the energy changes they exhibit, and not because they are complex chemically or physically Further, when these peculiar energy phenomena are gone, the objects are dead, and even during life they are more typically living the more markedly they chance to show the distinctive energy phenomena of life.

The rapid advances of physical chemistry within the past generation have fostered and encouraged in many minds the belief, which every day appears to grow stronger and more popular, that all the phenomena exhibited by living structures are capable of explanation by application of the laws governing non-living matter, that by processes of diffusion and osmosis through peculiarly constructed membranes, behaving somewhat differently indeed from those as yet fabricated by the art of man, but nevertheless membranes, all the complex changes and transformations affected by the cell are capable of explanation.

The evidence of experiment clearly shows, however, that the living cell is not a peculiarly constructed membrane obeying, even where it most directly seems to disobey, the physical laws of diffusion and osmosis; but is an *energy machine or transformer* by virtue of the operation of which a form of energy appears peculiar in its manifestations and phenomena to living matter, and producing adaptations and combinations in non-vital matter, which in many instances have not been imitated, and in others have only been imitated by obviously different processes, by the application of other forms of energy acting through non-vital transformers.

At the same time it may be pointed out that this in no way stultifies the application of physical chemistry to biological problems, or minimises the great service which an increased knowledge of physical chemistry has done and will do for biology.

In recent times, advances in physical chemistry, and in the knowledge of the properties of solutions, and of reactions occurring in solution, have pointed the path to advances in biological science, and it is in this direction that in the future most onward movement is to be expected.

A knowledge of physical chemistry, and more especially of the laws and phenomena of solutions, both of colloids and crystalloids, is indispensable to the modern biologist, taking that word in its widest sense, for it is here that we shall gain our closest approach, as far as can be at present seen, to the phenomena taking place in the living cell.

This follows because the cell in structure consists of colloids and crystalloids in common solution in water, and hence much may be gained by a knowledge of the laws of such a solution.

It is imperative to add, however, that this peculiar solution possesses something superadded, that this colloidal solution has a structure and organisation which differentiate it from all non-living colloids, such as starch, gelatine, or proteid in solution; impress upon it peculiar properties; and make it the scene of those typical energy transformations which we aggregate together under the term *life*.

It is unfortunate that the rebound from the bondage of the

old view of a mysterious *vital force* or *vital energy*, possessing no connection or correlation with the forms of energy exhibited by non-living transformers of energy, should have led to the equally mischievous view of the present day, that no form of energy whatever is present in living cells save such forms as are seen in the case of non-living matter

In order to avoid confusion with ancient fallacies, the use of the term " biotic energy " may be suggested for the future to represent that form of energy peculiar to living matter, and exhibited only in those energy phenomena which are confined to living matter and are indeed its intrinsic property, by which it is differentiated and known to be alive

This point of view is equally different on the one hand from the ancient one of vital force, which postulated something entirely distinct from the forms of energy of the non-living world, and on the other from the modern view that there exists in living matter no form of energy which is not *identical* with the forms of energy exhibited in non-living structures.

The conception, in brief, is that biotic energy is just as closely, and no more, related to the various forms of energy existing apart from life, as these are to one another, and that in presence of the proper and adapted energy transformer, the living cell, it is capable of being formed from or converted into various of these other forms of energy, the law of conservation of energy being obeyed in the process just as it would be if an exchange were taking place between any two or more of the inorganic forms.

We know no more or no less of the intrinsic nature of this biotic energy than we do of any of the non-vital forms, but we do know that it is confined to living matter, which acts as a transformer between it and other forms, and that the loss of this property means the death of the living matter, that the phenomena are as distinctive as those of other forms of energy, and that these phenomena are studied by the same kinds of study as are applied in other forms of energy.

It is perhaps not as commonly recognised as it ought to be that for all forms of energy the object of study of the chemist or physicist is the transformation of one form of energy into another, and the phenomena observable during such transformations

Our advances in natural science are made by studying experimentally new transformers by which hitherto unobserved forms of energy are developed, by noting as closely as possible the nature of the instrument or transformer and adapting this to its work, and by studying the effect of each form of energy so developed upon various forms of matter, and the routes or transformers by which it is dissipated into other forms of energy.

In all cases we observe that some material agency or arrangement is necessary in order that the transference from any one specific form to any other may be effected, and that this agent differs with the forms between which exchange is going on. The machine or structure through which the change is effected may be termed the *energy transformer*.

Observation teaches that bodies or substances which by their structure or arrangement are specially adapted for promoting certain energy exchanges are quite inert with regard to other exchanges.

In the case of some energy transformations the property of acting as transformer appears to be shared by all forms of matter, although in varying degree, while in other transformations the property is most specific, and associated with some special arrangement of matter. Thus, for example, all metals possess the property in varying degree of electrical conductivity, and in inverse proportion act as transformers for the conversion of electrical energy into heat energy. The specific agencies of the green plant, on the other hand, possess in high degree the power of converting light energy into chemical energy, and here act as peculiar energy transformers. Similarly, all enzymes are energy transformers, limited and specialised in range of action, for the transformation of chemical energy. Again, iron in most marked degree (and a few other metals to a less extent) is, by some special structural arrangement, specially adapted to act as a transformer in the case of magnetic energy, effecting its conversion into electrical or mechanical energy, or *vice versa*. Similarly, for radiant light and heat some bodies are transparent, and transmit these forms of energy unaltered, while others are opaque and transform the energy into other forms.

It is not necessary to go on multiplying examples, but it may be urged that in exactly similar fashion the protoplasm of the living cell of plant or animal is on account of its peculiar structure and constitution a transformer of energy, specially adapted for the intermediate conversion of chemical energy, presented in certain suitable forms, into biotic energy, and for its final conversion into other forms, such as mechanical energy and heat.

A consideration of the forms of energy recognised as different in the non-living world shows us that the only criterion of difference in type is the existence for each type of energy of a set of phenomena peculiar to it, and the production by the play of the particular form of energy of results typical of it, which cannot be produced, at any rate under like conditions of operation, by any of the other forms of energy.

It is no argument against the existence of a discrete form of energy that it is only produced from other forms of energy and passes back again into other forms. In fact, it must be so produced and so pass back, or the balance of which the law of conservation of energy is the expression would be upset. Hence the facts that vital phenomena arise from the expenditure in the cell of chemical energy, and that the phenomena are accompanied by development of heat, electricity, and other forms of energy are no arguments that such vital phenomena are not characteristic of a type of energy found only in living structures.

It is only necessary to prove that a set of energy phenomena exist in living structures which are characteristic of life, that energy effects are produced and can be demonstrated in living cells which cannot be shown apart from life, in order to prove that we here have to deal with a type of energy which does not appear in non-living matter.

We may pass, accordingly, to an enumeration of some of the peculiar energy properties of living matter upon which reliance can be placed as proving that such matter is a peculiar energy transformer in which a peculiar type of energy (biotic energy) is developed alongside of other forms which also occur in inorganic nature.

I. The mode of production of living matter is characteristic, and cannot be brought about by the action solely of inorganic forms of energy. Living matter is produced only by the action of other living matter upon the materials and forms of energy of the non-living world. In the process the matter involved is built up into substances of great chemical complexity, and it has been supposed that this is the essential portion of the process of production of a living structure; but it must be noted that even this very production of complexity of structure from simple inorganic bodies at the expense of the energy of the solar rays takes place and can only take place in a living structure itself.

The very building up of the machine or transformer in which the manifestations of biotic energy are subsequently to take place is then a cogent argument tha there we are dealing with a type of energy which is not met with elsewhere. For nowhere else in nature does a similar process appear to that of the production of living structure, and by no combination or application of the forms of energy apart from life can it be repeated or simulated.

II. The life cycle of the cell, no less than its birth or first production, yields a strong argument for the existence within it of a peculiar type of energy.

It might be argued that it was merely the complex structure of the protoplasm that was required in order that the inorganic forms of energy might be set in play; and that given this structure, osmosis and diffusion and chemical and electrical energy did the rest. But how comes it, then, that a cell perfect in structure does not remain perpetually an engine for the play of such inorganic forces, and why does not life last perpetually in the same cell in a state of equilibrium ? Why does the cell divide and reproduce itself and pass through a cycle, if it is merely a structure for the play of inorganic forms of energy ? No such phenomena of change and reproduction and death are seen anywhere in the inorganic world, nor can they be reproduced elsewhere than in living cells.

If, on the other hand, the living cell possesses, in addition to its peculiar and complex chemical and physical structure, the property of producing from the inorganic forms of energy a type of energy of its own, some means of accounting for the division and reproduction of the cell become at once apparent.

Nearly all, if not all, other known forms of energy are *phasic* or *cyclic* in character, and it is certain that biotic energy is cyclic also, as has been proven in previous chapters, the conditions of the cycle differs in different types of cell, and under different conditions of environment, and at certain stages alternations must occur as the result of variation in the biotic energy of the cell.

In other forms of energy we recognise what has been termed the potential factor. Now, if we suppose that in the living cell there is produced a type of energy peculiar to living structures, from the non-living forms of energy supplied from without by means of the cell acting as transformer, then it may be supposed that if there is any tendency to accumulation of biotic energy, the capacity factor being fixed by the size of the cell, the potential factor must increase and lead to division and reproduction. Naturally any such process must be modified by other factors playing in upon the cell, such as food, temperature, and other conditions of environment, but the process is guided and controlled by the biotic energy of the cell.

The division and reproduction of the cell, therefore, furnish energy phenomena of a type not found outside living matter.

III. Heredity, and the reproduction of like species from like, shows that there is something present not dependent merely upon structure, but that the cell possesses a type of energy which causes a retention of properties, and a capacity for communication of these onward.

By variations in the factors of such a form of energy the character of the effects is capable of alteration, much in the same way as variation in vibration period can alter the effects produced by radiant energy, or alterations in constituent groups of the chemical molecule can alter the chemical energy.

The closest histological examination reveals no essential difference between the ovum of one species of mammal and that of another, yet the cells develop into widely different species. This cannot all be due alone to the operation of inorganic forms of energy upon cell structures so similar that the microscope can show no difference in design. Nor can the unicellular ovum contain already laid down in it structurally some representation of each cell or even each tissue of the animal which is to be formed from it. It is too minute and too simple in its organisation to render such a view tenable. Nor is the chemical composition of the complete animal represented in that of the early embryo. It is evident that the course of cell division and development by which a constant species is arrived at is not attained by means of structure in the embryo, the ingress of chemical energy from without, and the action of diffusion and osmosis. But if there be added to these the presence of a distinct type of energy peculiar to living matter which controls and regulates the energy phenomena of the growing embryo, and which is attuned initially to the species of living creature to which the embryo belongs, then a more feasible basis for the explanation of the course of development of the individual becomes apparent. At each step this biotic energy will regulate the growth and division of the cells of the growing embryo. As each stage is reached, similar changes in the distribution of energy will occur as in previous generations, for the new embryo will arrive at them with the same distribution as in past generations of its store of energy, and hence the same phases in the energy phenomena will repeat themselves, except in so far as these are modified by nutrition and environment in a secondary degree.

In the process of growth, the oxidation of the food yields the necessary energy, and then this is utilised in building up fresh cellular material, in fabricating chemical substances for the use of the cells, and in producing other forms of energy. Throughout the wonderful cycle, the biotic energy retains certain intrinsic characteristics derived from the fertilised ovum, and by the impress given by these the process is directed.

IV. The fundamental properties possessed by living matter of *irritability, contractility,* and *conductivity* are all energy phenomena characteristic of life, and nowhere manifested by the operation of other forms of energy in non-living matter. While it is undoubtedly true that the exhibition of these properties in living tissue is accompanied by manifestations of other forms of energy, such as chemical change, electricity and heat, and indeed necessarily must be, since the cell obtains the energy used in the production and propagation of these changes from such non-biotic forms of energy, yet the alterations in irritability are characterised by phenomena which are not chemical, electrical, or caloric, and cannot be placed under any of the known forms of non-biotic energy.

Take, as an example, the nerve impulse travelling along a living nerve-fibre. A similar phenomenon cannot be reproduced in any non-living structure, and while it is accompanied by an electric wave which travels at the same rate, it cannot be held that the electrical energy is the nerve impulse, any more than that the chemical change or electric wave accompanying a muscle contraction wave is the contraction wave itself; or, to choose an example from energy transformation in non-living matter, that the heat in the wire and magnetic field around it are the electric current travelling along the wire. In many other manifestations of irritability than the nerve impulse it is known that increased electrical negativity is associated with increased physiological activity, and hence the most logical view certainly is that the negative wave accompanying the nerve impulse betokens a wave of increased irri-

tability propagated along the fibre.   Here we have, then, a phenomenon of biotic energy in a typical form, and can even get at one
property—namely, the rate at which the wave of biotic energy is
carried along this particular type of conductor.   In the muscle cell
a similar wave is seen traversing a different form of conductor at a
different rate.

V. The *metabolism* of the cell furnishes further proof that
energy changes in the cell are produced by the action of a type
of energy not found elsewhere than in living tissues.   The production of the living protoplasm of the cell itself has already been
alluded to as a proof of the existence of such a type of energy;
but in addition to the substance of the energy transformer itself
there are to be considered the products formed interstitially within
the cell.   Most of these are so complex that they have not yet been
synthesised by the organic chemist; but even of those that have
been synthesised, it may be remarked that all proof is wanting
that the syntheses have been carried out in identically the same
fashion and by the employment of the same forms of energy in the
case of the cell as in the chemist's laboratory.   The conditions in the
cell are widely different, and at the temperature of the cell and with
such chemical materials as are at hand in the cell no such organic
syntheses have been artificially carried out by the forms of energy
extraneous to living tissue.

Again, the regulation of the production and breaking up of
such substances, the variations in rate of action, and the regulation
of the manifold intercurrent reactions running simultaneously
within the minute compass of a single cell, even more powerfully
than the mere synthesis of the substances point to a controlling
and regulating type of energy different from anything outside living
matter.   The reversal of chemical action from period to period,
and the sudden changes in chemical activities produced by the
activity of the nervous system, have no parallel outside the realm
of living cells.

Much has been made of the fact that intracellular enzymes
have been isolated from living cells which are capable of producing
actions hitherto only observed in the presence of the cell, and it has
been surmised that all or nearly all the chemical activity of the cell
may be due to the action of a large number of such intracellular
enzymes.   It has, in fact, been supposed that if a solution could be
prepared containing the proper number of enzymes, each in appropriate concentration, the solution would act much like a cell.

Without disparaging the importance and value of such work of separation of intracellular enzymes, it may, however, be urged that there is in such a view no explanation of the phasic activity of the cell, no taking into account of the action of the living cell in co-ordinating, so to speak, the myriad activities going on within it whereby the whole process is regulated. Such a solution of enzymes compared with a living cell would be like a horde of savage warriors compared to a civilised and disciplined army of soldiers, or a mass of unicellular organisms compared to a highly differentiated mammal.

There must obviously in the cell be some type of energy controlling all this metabolic activity, and this is the rôle played by the biotic energy of the cell.

VI. The *osmotic* phenomena of the cell demand for their explanation the presence of a type of energy not found elsewhere than in living structures.

Even in the case of those cells of the body which in form look most like simple membranes, such as the air cells of the lung and the thin endothelial cells of the wall of lymphatic and blood capillaries, it has been clearly shown that the laws of diffusion and osmosis as observed in the case of inert, non-living membranes are not obeyed. These structures are not inert membranes, but living cells displaying biotic energy, taking up energy from the plasma in chemical form and using that energy by converting it into volume or osmotic energy, and effecting thereby separation of substances in solution in greater concentration; that is to say, such cells act as energy transformers, the ultimate conversion being from chemical into volume energy.

Such a change is seen in the secretion of gases both in the swimming bladder of the fish, and, according to Bohr and other observers, in the mammalian lung, where the partial pressure of the carbon dioxide separated in the alveolar air is higher than that in the blood of the pulmonary capillaries. Here the cells of the lung are acting against pressure, and, no matter what the intermediate steps may be, volume energy is increased in the process, and must be obtained from the chemical energy of the cell, the cell protoplasm acting as the energy machine or transformer.

Similar instances of gaseous secretion are seen (with the difference in these instances that the gas is retained in solution, and the increased pressure is osmotic) in the case of the secretion of saliva and of bile, where in both cases the pressure of dissolved carbon dioxide is greater in the secretion than in the venous blood flowing from the organ.   Here, just as truly as in the alveoli of the lung, volume energy is increased in the process of secretion.   In a similar manner hypertonic salt solutions are taken up from the serous cavities by the blood and lymph capillaries lining their walls against the gradient of osmotic pressure.   The absorption of isotonic effusions, whether normal or pathological, is a process which also demonstrates that the cells lining the vessels are not inert membranes comparable in action to non-living membranes, whether permeable or semi-permeable; but are living cells, capable of acting as active absorbent channels, by behaving as machines possessing the important function of the conversion of chemical into volume energy. But it is in the case of the typical secretory and excretory cells of the body that this function of the living cell of acting as an energy transformer between volume energy and chemical energy is seen developed to its highest degree.   In these cases, it is observed not only that the amount of volume energy developed is larger, but that the action is eminently selective according to the nature of the dissolved substance.

This subject will be gone into in greater detail in the chapter on secretion and excretion; we need not therefore enter more fully upon the matter here than to indicate that, in the kidney, for example, urea solution is concentrated from less than ·04 per cent. in the circulating blood up to 2 per cent. in the urine, and that in this process, no matter what may be the intermediate stages, the kidney cells develop volume energy, against the usual laws applicable to inert semipermeable membranes, just as much as a mechanical engine attached to a piston and cylinder would do in compressing a gas from a pressure of about 130 mm. of mercury and a volume of 75,000 c.c. to a pressure of about 6500 mm. of mercury and a volume of 1500 c.c., these being the volumes of the blood and urine and pressures of the ·04 and 2 per cent. solutions respectively.

In the face of this experimental evidence, surely it is time to cease regarding kidney cells as semi-permeable membranes to which the laws of osmosis apply.   The case is exactly the reverse of the semi-permeable membrane, in which the solvent passes through, tending to equalise pressures and reduce volume energy; for in the kidney cell the dissolved substance passes through at a greater rate than the solvent, increasing the difference in pressure on the two sides and developing volume energy.

It is not intended at all to represent that the phenomena described are contrary to the laws of energetics, but to make clear that the cell does not play the part of an inert membrane, that the laws of osmosis deduced from observations on inert membranes do not apply, and that there is a form of energy and type of energy transformer at work which are not to be observed elsewhere than in living cells.

The study of the properties of this particular energy transformer, and the interactions between biotic energy and the inorganic forms of energy carried out by its action, is the province of the biologist, who must approach and has been approaching the subject in the same manner as the physicist and chemist approach the study of other types of energy—that is, by acting upon the cell with other types of energy, and studying its reaction to such treatment.

Experiments on any form of energy consist in observing the interactions between it and other forms, in studying the nature of the transformer, and of the changes, if any, which occur in it.

The structure of the cell must hence be taken up from the point of view of its function; and we must study the chemical and physical composition, the effect of the several constituents upon one another, and upon the medium in which the cell lives, the nature and action of the input and output of the cell, including its secretions and how these are produced, the osmotic phenomena and the effects of changes in the surrounding medium, the characteristic accompaniments of stimulation of the cell and of conduction of stimulation from part to part, and the effects produced by cells possessing a life in common, as in the multicellular animal.

Physical chemistry affords us one of the most powerful experimental engines in conducting such inquiries for a reason which has already been touched upon—namely, that the living cell is in structure a complex solution containing both colloids and crystalloids, and that the chemical reactions occurring in the cell are reactions in solution. Accordingly, although the whole matter is profoundly affected by the fact that the cell is alive, it is evident that our knowledge of cellular activities must be based on knowledge of the properties of solutions, both of colloids and crystalloids; of reactions in solution, the velocity of such reactions and the conditions of equilibrium; of the mutual effect of crystalloids and colloids upon one another when in common solution, and of the effects of the living cell as a peculiar energy transformer upon osmosis and diffusion.

CHAPTER X

CHEMICAL TRANSFORMATIONS IN LIVING MATTER AND ITS PRODUCTS

CHEMICAL EQUILIBRIUM AND REACTION—ENZYMES AND CELLS AS CATALYSTS OR ENERGY TRANSFORMERS

THE supply of energy necessary for all the changes observable in living structures arises from chemical reactions occurring in solution. The energy exchanges occurring in any such reaction are initiated and controlled by the cell and its secretions, or the substances present in the cell, acting as energy transformers in the sense indicated in the preceding chapter. In the present chapter it is proposed to consider the conditions governing reactions in solution, and as far as possible how these are modified by the presence of the peculiar energy transformers found in the living cell itself or its products

Let us, first of all, take a general survey of the cycle of energy changes which occur in living structures as matter and energy are taken up from the inorganic world, sent through various changes in the living cell, in which many varied forms of matter are produced and different types of energy are exhibited, and finally both matter and energy are returned in other forms to the inorganic world   The matter involved in these changes is directly or indirectly taken from inorganic sources, and the energy from the light energy of the solar rays, for whether the food of an animal be of animal or vegetable nature, in the first instance it must have come from vegetable sources   In the green parts of plants, the chemical energy is first accumulated in matter which afterwards, being carried to other parts of the plant, or being used as the food of animals, furnishes the store of energy used in carrying on the reactions of all other cells

In the process of building up in the chlorophyll-bearing cell the chlorophyll, or something underying it, acts as a transformer— that is, an interaction it induced between forms of energy (in this case light energy and chemical energy) which would not occur

138

in its absence or could only occur incomparably more slowly. In this process the changes in the chlorophyll itself are so insignificant, in comparison with the amount of changes in light energy and chemical energy, that they may be left out of consideration, and we may regard the chlorophyll as a mechanism for carrying on the energy exchanges, just like a chemical catalyst or an enzyme, although the types of energy between which it works are different, as well as the limitations of its action. In the chemical modifications subsequent to the action of the chlorophyll, the various cells may be similarly regarded as catalysing agents differing somewhat in their mode of action upon the chemical materials supplied to them, and in the products formed, but agreeing in that they cause large amounts of interchange between chemical energy and other forms, without being themselves altered permanently, or proportionately to the reactions which they induce. The same is true of the enzymes formed by the action of the cells, which induce various reactions either within the cells, or after separation from them in the secretions.

Hence we may regard the processes occurring in plants and animals as energy reactions induced by the cells or their enzymes acting as energy transformers.

Excepting in the green cell in the presence of sunlight, the net result of the energy interchanges induced by the cells and their secretions is that the chemical energy produced by the absorption and disappearance of the light energy is used up and converted into other forms, such as heat, mechanical energy, osmotic energy, electrical energy, etc. The process is accompanied by absorption of oxygen, and the matter passes back again into inorganic forms identical with or closely resembling those with which the process began, and containing little or no more energy than at the start.

In the intermediate reactions of metabolism the process is not, however, purely one of oxidation; the cell, on account of its peculiar properties as an energy transformer, and probably by the production intermediately of its own peculiar type of energy, is capable of inducing synthetic processes in which chemical energy is taken up. The supply of energy for such a synthetic process is obtained from energy given out by other chemical processes running concurrently in which energy is set free.

It is in this respect that the more complex transformer which is seen in the cell differs from the simpler inorganic catalysts and the enzymes formed by cells. As a rule, the simpler enzymes are only capable of inducing reactions in which no substances are formed with larger storage of chemical energy. But the cell is able from a supply of substance, such, say, as soluble carbohydrate, to oxidise part to yield energy, and utilise this energy to build up a smaller amount of a substance, such as a fat, possessing for an equal weight a higher amount of chemical energy.

The fluids with which the cells are bathed and which permeate them may be regarded as solutions containing, in a few common forms supplied universally to all the cells, energy in a chemical form which is utilised by the cells to carry on their reactions.

Depending upon the type of the cell and the enzymes which it contains, varying reactions are induced in this common medium, so that different products are formed, and different amounts and types of energy set free.

In following out the energy exchanges it is hence necessary to consider the properties of solutions, such as the velocity of reaction and the conditions of equilibrium between the reacting substances; the forms in which energy is present and the amount of change in energy as the substances react; and how the presence of catalysts alters the energy exchanges in the solution.

The law of conservation of energy teaches that the total amount of energy must remain the same, and hence the algebraic sum of the amounts of energy changing from one form to another must be equal to zero.

Since we possess no means of stating the absolute amount of energy contained by a system in any of the varied forms in which energy manifests itself, we can only estimate the *change* of energy in any given form as the system passes from one condition to another, and to obtain the total change in the system the amount of change in each particular form of energy undergoing change must be taken into account. The amount of change in each form of energy is obtained from the product of the capacity factor of the system for any particular form of energy, and the change in the potential factor of that form of energy.

In the case of certain forms of energy the capacity and potential factors are still unknown to us, and the amount of energy taken up or given out in these forms during a change of energy from one given form to another can only be estimated by a statement of corresponding changes in other forms of energy as a result of the re-action. The two forms of energy in which such changes of energy can best be expressed are heat energy and mechanical work, or dynamical energy, and it is for this reason that energy exchanges are considered upon a thermo-dynamical basis.

Energy equilibrium or reaction is determined by the values at any given time of the potential factors of the various forms of energy, by the facilities presented in the system for potential equalisation, and by the manner in which energy is bound or related to par-ticular forms of matter in the system. In so far as any particular form of energy is free to distribute itself throughout the system that particular form of energy tends to equalise its potential all through the system, and hence the energy always passes from a point of higher to a point of lower potential. Thus in any system where redistribution is possible heat always passes from a position of higher to one of lower temperature, electricity from a higher to a lower electrical potential, a fluid or gas from a higher to a lower level of pressure, and so on for every form of energy. In any such change the velocity of equalisation is directly proportional to the difference in potential, and inversely proportional to what is termed the *resistance*. The resistance, however, means only that the equalisation is opposed by the potential factor of some other form of energy, and that this opposition has to be overcome in effecting the equalisation. If the potential factor of this opposing energy is sufficiently high the equalisation may be entirely stopped, or its speed only may be lessened so that the equalisation takes longer and proceeds with diminished intensity.

It is impossible for equalisation of potential, or change towards equalisation of potential, of any form of energy to take place without conversion of a portion of the energy so changing potential into other forms, and all physical measurements of change in potential are based upon changes of the energy into other forms.

In any condition of equilibrium of a system there is a balance between the intensity factors of the various forms of energy capable of interacting with one another, and that balance is dependent upon the facilities provided in the system for interaction between the various forms of energy. Further, in the absence of equilibrium the velocity or intensity of reaction is dependent on the same factors —namely, the values of the potential factors and the facilities for interaction.

Hence the state of equilibrium or reaction may be disturbed by addition or removal of energy so as to disturb the potential factors, or by alterations which change the ease of passage from one form to another.

It is the variation in the potential factor or intensity factor which appeals to our sense organs, and determines the results of all physiological stimulation, and it is for this reason that the potential factor and methods for measuring variations in it[1] were known to mankind long before the recognition of corresponding quantities of energy.

CHEMICAL ENERGY AND CHEMICAL EQUILIBRIUM.[2]

The energy changes which interest us most in connection with the biological chemistry of the cell are those in which chemical energy plays a part, and accordingly we pass on to the energy conditions in a solution. In order to simplify the matter we shall assume at first that there is no catalyst present, and investigate the equations governing energy changes in solution under different conditions in which energy interchanges are possible between the various forms of energy which can react in the solution. That is, we shall leave out of consideration at present the mechanisms by which the energy changes are brought about, which can alter the velocities with which the changes occur, or which, by bringing into play other forms of energy, can alter the conditions of reaction and the equilibrium point.

The three forms of energy which normally undergo alteration in value when a chemical reaction occurs in solution[3] are the chemical energy, the heat energy, and the osmotic energy. The law of conservation of energy teaches that the algebraic sum of the three alterations must be zero. Or, if C represent chemical energy,[4] H heat energy,[5] and V volume energy, for the change

---

[1] Such, for example, as the thermometer in connection with heat energy, the manometer in connection with volume energy.

[2] This chapter requires some knowledge of mathematics, but may be omitted, or taken as granted, without disturbing continuity in the reading.

[3] The same holds for gases: the investigation is the same for both conditions of matter.

[4] This does not mean heat of reaction, but the total amount of chemical energy set free or absorbed when a given amount of substance changes form.

[5] The value of H is not the heat of reaction in the usual sense of the term, but the amount of heat energy due to the change of the fixed quantity at the definite osmotic pressures obtaining at a given instant or stage in the reaction.

of any fixed quantity of matter from one chemical form to the other, we have:

$$C + H + V = 0$$

If attention be paid to change of sign any of these three quantities may be moved from one side of the equation to the other.

Hence if C represent chemical energy *disappearing* and *given out* in the other two forms we have:

$$C = H + V.$$

Let us take it that a grm. molecule of the substance changes chemical form, and that the volume of the solution in which such a change occurs is so large that no appreciable change takes place in the osmotic pressures of the two substances in solution.

Then in the above equation C is the change in chemical energy accompanying a change in chemical constitution from the first form on one side of the chemical equation to the other form on the other side of the chemical equation. As C is dependent only on the change in chemical constitution it is a constant, the value of which is determined by the sum of the values of (1) the heat (H) for the change of a grm. molecule at given concentrations (P_1 and P_2) in solution of the two substances on the two sides of the chemical equation, (2) the change in volume energy due to the conversion of a grm. molecule of the first substance at pressure P_1 into a grm. molecule of the replacing substance at pressure P_2.

The heat energy produced by the change of a grm. molecule when the first substance has a pressure P_1 and the second substance a pressure P_2 is a variable quantity dependent upon the values of P_1 and P_2.

The value of V, the change in volume energy for the change of a grm. molecule of first substance at osmotic pressure P_1 into second substance at pressure P_2, is also a variable.

When as the result of a reaction a grm. molecule of a substance comes into solution at a definite pressure, a certain fixed amount of volume energy appears dependent upon the pressure, and as a result the heat produced will be less by this amount; and similarly when a grm. molecule disappears at another different pressure, a definite amount of volume energy disappears, and by this amount the heat of reaction will increase. Accordingly the difference in these two amounts will express V, the change in volume energy in the reaction.

The difference in volume energy before and after the reaction cannot be obtained by taking the differences in the total osmotic pressures before and after the reaction, because the quantity of substance appearing is not brought during the change from the one of these pressures to the other, but from the zero of pressure to the pressure at which it is finally found in the reaction—that is, to the partial pressure of the component substance to which it belongs; and similarly the grm. molecule of substance disappearing passes from the partial pressure at which that substance happens to be present in solution to zero pressure. Hence the amount of volume energy must be obtained separately for each substance taking part in the reaction.

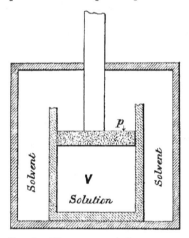

FIG. 1.—WORK DONE IN COMPRESSION OF A SOLUTION IN A SEMI-PERMEABLE CYLINDER.

This amount of energy may be obtained as follows: Suppose a definite amount of a substance to be in solution in a semipermeable cylinder fitted with a semipermeable piston, as sketched in the diagram, and surrounded by solvent. Then if the pressure on the piston be changed, just as in the case of a gas, the solution will correspondingly change in volume. The work done by the dissolved substance or *solute* is PdV, where P is the pressure and dV the small change in the volume. Or, using the gas law $PV = RT$, we have on differentiation $PdV = -VdP$, and again since $V = \dfrac{RT}{P}$, $PdV = RT\dfrac{dP}{P}$. On integrating this yields for the work done by the gas in expanding isothermally from pressure P_1 to pressure P_2 the well-known expression $W = RT \log \dfrac{P_1}{P_2}$.

This amount of work may be expressed as heat energy by giving the proper value to the constant RT, which for a grm. molecule of a substance which obeys the gas law works out to 5·8 K calories[1] at 0° C.

[1] The K (calory) is the amount of heat necessary to raise 1 grm. of water from 0° to 100° C., and is approximately equal to 100 grm. calories.

From this expression the amount of energy required to transform a solute from the minimum or zero pressure (P_0) to any given pressure (P), or *vice versa,* may be expressed as heat energy, the expression being, $\pm RT \log \dfrac{P}{P_0}$.

When a chemical reaction takes place and molecules appear and disappear as a consequence, the change in volume energy is the algebraic sum of the changes in volume energy of each kind of molecule so appearing or disappearing. When a grm. molecule of a substance appears in solution at the pressure P the volume energy increases by $RT \log \dfrac{P}{P_0}$, and conversely when a grm. molecule of a substance disappears from solution the volume energy decreases by a like amount.

This may now be applied to the energy changes taking place in different types of reaction.

1. The simplest case is that in which a grm. molecule of a substance A is formed and a grm. molecule of substance B disappears, as, for example, when a substance changes into an isomeric body, according to the equation,[1]

$$A \rightleftharpoons B.$$

To simplify matters, we shall assume that the volume of solution is so large that a grm. molecule of A can change into B without causing any appreciable differences in P_A, the pressure of A or P_B, the pressure of B.

The disappearance of A causes a diminution of volume energy given by $RT \log \dfrac{P_A}{P_0}$, and the appearance of B an increase of volume energy given by $RT \log \dfrac{P_B}{P_0}$. Therefore the net increase in volume energy is $RT \left(\log \dfrac{P_B}{P_0} - \log \dfrac{P_A}{P_0} \right)$, which is $RT \log \dfrac{P_B}{P_A}$. Accordingly we have the equation

$$C = H + V$$
$$\therefore C = H + RT \log \dfrac{P_B}{P_A}.$$
$$\therefore H = C - RT \log \dfrac{P_B}{P_A}.$$

In this equation P_B is the osmotic pressure at which B appears, and P_A the osmotic pressure at which A disappears. The value of C

---

[1] The double arrow in a chemical equation is used, instead of the sign of equality, to signify that the reaction may proceed in either direction.

is constant, being the chemical energy set free by the passage of a grm. molecule from the form A into the form B, and the variable value H expresses the heat energy set free by the reaction when a grm. molecule changes form at those particular pressures.

If we begin at the point where nearly all the substance is present in the form A, then P_B has a very low value, and consequently log $\frac{P_B}{P_A}$ has a large negative value, and this being prefixed by a negative sign, it follows that the heat of reaction[1] at this stage has a large positive value. As the reaction proceeds P_B continuously increases and log $\frac{P_B}{P_A}$ decreases in negative value; accordingly the heat of reaction diminishes. As P_B still increases and P_A diminishes, log $\frac{P_B}{P_A}$ becomes positive in sign and progressively increases in value; the heat of reaction accordingly still diminishes until, when RT log $\frac{P_B}{P_A} = C$, it becomes zero. Up to this point the reaction has been exothermic—that is to say, giving out heat—but from this point on it absorbs heat, the sign of H becoming negative, and the reaction is said to be endothermic.

If we take the reaction as running from B into A the same sequence of events in the reverse order occurs. Here C is negative, and RT log $\frac{P_B}{P_A}$ becomes RT log $\frac{P_A}{P_B}$, so that the equation runs

$$H = -C - RT \log \frac{P_A}{P_B}.$$

Starting with nearly all the substance in the Form B, P_A is very small; RT log $\frac{P_A}{P_B}$ has hence a large negative value. Accordingly $-C - RT$ log $\frac{P_A}{P_B}$ has a positive value, and the reaction runs exothermically until RT log $\frac{P_A}{P_B} = -C$, or RT log $\frac{P_B}{P_A} = C$, when the heat of reaction is zero, and from this on the reaction is endothermic. It is hence evident that the reaction runs exothermically from either end down to the same point, where $C = RT$ log $\frac{P_B}{P_A}$, and at this point where H $= 0$, energy is neither given up to nor taken up from the surround-

---

[1] That is, the energy set free in the reaction, which need not necessarily all be set free as heat energy; it is merely for simplicity that energy set free in the reaction is spoken of in the text as heat of reaction.

ings. This point is accordingly the equilibrium point of the reaction.

The equation for equilibrium is accordingly $RT \log \frac{P_B}{P_A} = C = \text{const.}$[1]

If the chemical energy involved in the passage from the form A to the form B, or *vice versa*, is so small as to be negligible, as is usually the case in the passage of a substance from one isomeric form to another, we can write $RT \log \frac{P_B}{P_A} = C = 0$, and hence $\log \frac{P_B}{P_A} = 0$, $\frac{P_B}{P_A} = 1$, or $P_B = P_A$ —that is, under such conditions equilibrium is attained when the osmotic pressures, and hence the molecular concentrations in solution, are equal.

If we write p_A and p_B for the osmotic pressures of the two substances at the equilibrium point, and P_A and P_B as before for the corresponding pressures at any given point in the reaction, another form can be given to the fundamental equation for the heat of reaction at any given point in the reaction.

For now $C = RT \log \frac{p_B}{p_A}$, and hence on substituting this value we obtain

$$H = RT \left(\log \frac{p_B}{p_A} - \log \frac{P_B}{P_A} \right), \text{ or } H = RT \log \frac{p_B}{p_A} \cdot \frac{P_A}{P_B}.$$

2. Let us take next the cases where two substances A and B interact to form reversibly two other substances C and D, and let P, with the appropriate suffix of the letter denoting the substance, represent the osmotic pressure of each substance.

Then since A and B disappear from solution and diminish the volume energy or osmotic pressure energy, and C and D appear and increase the osmotic pressure energy, the equation becomes

$$H = C - RT \left(\log \frac{P_C}{P_0} + \log \frac{P_D}{P_0} - \log \frac{P_A}{P_0} - \log \frac{P_B}{P_0} \right),$$

or

$$H = C - RT \log \frac{P_C \cdot P_D}{P_A \cdot P_B}.$$

The reaction, as before, can be shown to run exothermally from either end until $C = RT \log \frac{P_C \cdot P_D}{P_A \cdot P_B}$, at which point energy is neither given to nor taken up from the surroundings; hence at this point there

---

[1] This equation may also be written $\log \frac{P_B}{P_A} = \frac{C}{RT}$, or $\frac{P_B}{P_A} = e^{\frac{C}{RT}}$.

is equilibrium, and the equation of equilibrium is

$$RT \log \frac{P_c \cdot P_D}{P_A \cdot P_B} = C = const.[1]$$

At any other point in the reaction the heat of reaction for a grm. molecule changing form at the given pressures is given by the equation

$$H = C - RT \log \frac{P_c \cdot P_D}{P_A \cdot P_B},$$

or

$$H = RT \left(\log \frac{p_c \cdot p_D}{p_A \cdot p_B} - \log \frac{P_c \cdot P_D}{P_A \cdot P_B} \right),$$

or

$$H = RT \log \frac{p_c \cdot p_D \cdot P_A \cdot P_B}{p_A \cdot p_B \cdot P_c \cdot P_D}.$$

If at the beginning of the reaction A and B are present in equal molecular concentrations, then since an equal number of molecules of each always disappear in the reaction, and an equal number of C and D appear as the result, at every stage $P_A' = P_B$ and $P_c = P_D$. Hence the equation of equilibrium simplifies to $C = RT \log \frac{P_A^2}{P_c^2} = 2RT \log \frac{P_A}{P_c}$, and that for the heat of reaction to $H = C - 2RT \log \frac{P_A}{P_c}$, or $H = 2RT \left(\log \frac{p_A}{p_c} \cdot \frac{P_c}{P_A} \right)$.

3. Take next a type of reaction which is one of the commonest, and which is almost universally met in the problems of biological chemistry—namely, the type in which a single compound on one side of the equation breaks up into two or more on the other side, or a reaction in which, although two substances react on each side of the equation, one of them is identical with the solvent, so that it causes no change in volume energy when it appears or disappears in the reaction, such a reaction occurring in aqueous solution, for example, as

$$C_{12}H_{22}O_{11} + H_2O \rightleftharpoons C_6H_{12}O_6 + C_6H_{12}O_6$$
$$\text{(Maltose)} \qquad \text{(Dextrose)} \quad \text{(Dextrose)}$$

Using the same notation as before, let P_A be the osmotic pressure at any stage in the reaction of the single substance which undergoes change in osmotic pressure on the left-hand side of the equation, and

[1] As before, this quotation may be put in the form $\frac{P_c \cdot P_D}{P_A \cdot P_B} = e^{\frac{C}{RT}}$, which if $P_A = P_B$, and $P_c = P_D$, may be further simplified to $\frac{P_c}{P_A} = e^{\frac{C}{2RT}}$.

P_B the osmotic pressure of either of the two substances produced on the right-hand side, for these being produced in equimolecular proportion, their osmotic pressures at any given stage in the reaction will be equal in value.[1]

Here, as a result of the reaction, a grm. molecule of A disappears, lowering the volume energy by $RT \log \dfrac{P_A}{P_0}$, and a grm. molecule of each of the two substances formed appears at a pressure P_B, raising the volume energy in each case by $RT \log \dfrac{P_B}{P_0}$, or in all by $2RT \log \dfrac{P_B}{P_0}$. Accordingly our equation becomes

$$H = C - RT \left(2 \log \frac{P_B}{P_0} - \log \frac{P_A}{P_0} \right),$$

or

$$H = C - RT \log \frac{P_B^2}{P_A \cdot P_0}.$$

As before, the reaction runs exothermically from either end until $RT \log \dfrac{P_B^2}{P_A \cdot P_0} = C$, at which point there is equilibrium.[2]

For the heat of reaction at any other point we have

$$H = C - RT \log \frac{P_B^2}{P_A \cdot P_0},$$

or, using the same notation as in the other cases,

$$H = RT \left(\log \frac{p_B^2}{p_A \cdot p_0} - \log \frac{P_B^2}{P_A \cdot P_0} \right),$$

or

$$H = RT \log \frac{p_B^2}{p_A \cdot p_0} \cdot \frac{P_A \cdot P_0}{P_B^2}.$$

But the zero pressure P_0 and p_0 is always the same, hence

$$H = RT \log \frac{p_B^2}{p_A} \cdot \frac{P_A}{P_B^2}.$$

---

[1] If unequal quantities of the two substances formed on the right-hand side are present at the beginning along with the single substance, or a certain amount of one of them, then the osmotic pressures of these two (B and C) will not be equal; but if they are represented by the pressures P_B and P_C the only difference is that we will have $P_B \cdot P_C$ in the final equation instead of P_B^2, so that the equation becomes: $H = C - RT \log \dfrac{P_B \cdot P_C}{P_A \cdot P_0}$, which for equilibrium leads to $\log \dfrac{P_B \cdot P_C}{P_A \cdot P_0} = \dfrac{C}{RT}$, or $\dfrac{P_B \cdot P_C}{P_A \cdot P_0} = e^{\frac{C}{RT}}$.

[2] As before, the equilibrium equation can accordingly be written

$$\frac{P_B^2}{P_A \cdot P_0} = e^{\frac{C}{RT}}, \text{ or } \frac{P_B^2}{P} = P_0 \cdot e^{\frac{C}{RT}}.$$

4. The most general form of the equation is where a number of substances, A, B, C, etc., react with one another to form a number of other substances, A′, B′, C′, etc., and where the number of molecules of each substance entering into reaction varies

Let the chemical equation be represented by

$$aA + bB + cC + \text{etc.} \rightleftharpoons a'A' + b'B' + c'C' + \text{etc },$$

in which the small letters represent the numbers of molecules of each substance respectively entering into reaction. Then the expression for the change in volume energy becomes

$$RT\left[a'\ \log\ \frac{P_{A'}}{P_0} + b'\ \log\ \frac{P_{B'}}{P_0} + c'\ \log\ \frac{P_{C'}}{P_0} + \text{etc.} - (a\ \log\ \frac{P_A}{P_0} + b\ \log\ \frac{P_B}{P_0} + c\ \log\ \frac{P_C}{P_0} + \text{etc.)} \right].$$

This expression can be written

$$RT\ \log\ \frac{P_{A'}^{a'}.P_{B'}^{b'}.P_{C'}^{c'}.\text{etc.}}{P_A^a.P_B^b.P_C^c}.P_0^{[a+b+c+\text{etc} -(a'+b'+c'+\text{etc })]}$$

For equilibrium, as before, this expression is equal to C, the energy evolved when a grm. molecule of each substance changes from the left-hand side of the equation to the right, and hence

$$RT\ \log\ \frac{P_{A'}^{a'}.P_{B'}^{b'}.P_{C'}^{c'}.\text{etc.}}{P_A^a.P_B^b.P_C^c\ \text{etc.}}\ .\ P_0^{[a+b+c+\text{etc} -(a'+b'+c'+\text{etc })]} = 0,$$

or

$$\frac{P_{A'}^{a'}.P_{B'}^{b'}.P_{C'}^{c'}.\text{etc.}}{P_A^a.P_B^b.P_C^c.\text{etc.}} = P_0^{[a'+b'+c'+\text{etc.} -(a+b+c+\text{etc })]}\ .\ e^{\frac{C}{RT}}.$$

Now the right-hand side is a constant, so the general equation of equilibrium becomes

$$\frac{P_{A'}^{a'}.P_{B'}^{b'}.P_{C'}^{c'}.\text{etc.}}{P_A^a.P_B^b.P_C^c\ \text{etc.}} = \text{constant}$$

The results which can be derived from the types of reaction that we have considered may now be discussed. Writing K for the constant, we have the following results

I. Where a single substance A undergoes molecular rearrangement to form a single substance B

$$\frac{P_B}{P_A} = e^{\frac{C}{RT}} = K, \text{ or } P_B = KP_A.$$

If the chemical energy of transference from substance A to substance B is zero, the constant becomes unity and the equation is $P_B = P_A$. This condition is probably attained with stereo-isomers, and hence when the two isomers are formed in any reaction they are turned out in the condition of equilibrium—that is, in equal quantities—and we get, as in the case of the synthetically prepared sugars, the indifferent compound consisting of an equimolecular mixture of the two isomeric bodies.

II. Where two substances, A and B, interact to form two others, C and D:

$$\frac{P_C \cdot P_D}{P_A \cdot P_B} = e^{\frac{C}{ET}} = K, \text{ or } P_C \cdot P_D = K P_A \cdot P_B$$

—that is, the product of the osmotic pressures of the one pair of substances is proportional to the product of the osmotic pressures of the other pair of substances.

If the substances A and B at the commencement are in equimolecular concentration, then $P_A = B_B$, and since the substances C and D are then also formed in equimolecular concentration also $P_C = P_D$, and hence the equation for equilibrium can obviously be simplified to $P_{(C \text{ or } D)} = K \cdot P_{(A \text{ or } B)}$. That is, the osmotic pressure of the substances formed always bears the same ratio to the osmotic pressure of the substances from which they are formed when the equilibrium point is reached.

It follows that for reactions of the type I., and for those of II. when the substances are present in the proper equimolecular proportions for combining, the equilibrium point is not affected by the concentration of the solution. That is, whether the reaction occurs in very dilute or in concentrated solution (within the limits at which the gas laws hold for osmotic pressures), the same proportion of A is turned into B in type I., and of A and B into C and D in type II. This is obvious, for if $P_A = K P_C$, then if P_A is doubled, so must P_C be in order that the equation may still hold, or, in other words, no matter what is the original concentration of the reacting substances, the same percentage is always turned into the substances formed before equilibrium is reached.

The law that the equilibrium point is fixed where the reaction is of the types I. or II., and is independent of the concentration, has been proved experimentally for the reaction between gaseous hydrogen and bromine vapour. Here a molecule of hydrogen and a molecule of bromine unite to form two molecules of hydrogen bromide, and there is no change in number of reacting molecules; thus $H_2 + Br_2 = HBr + HBr$; accordingly we have $P_{(H, or Br)} = K P_H$,, and no matter how the pressure of hydrogen, bromine, and gaseous hydrobromic acid are altered, the percentage of the three reacting constituents ought to have the same ratio—that is, there ought always to be the same percentage of bromine vapour converted into hydrobromic acid   This is found to hold experimentally, within fairly wide limits, no matter how the pressure is varied, the percentage of conversion remains the same

III. Where a single compound splits up into two compounds, or *vice versa* when the reaction is proceeding in the opposite direction. Under this class are also included those reactions in which, although there are two substances on each side of the reaction, one by passing out of solution or by blending with the solvent with which it happens to be identical, develops no change in osmotic pressure, and hence there is no work done on or by it, and it does not come into the reaction   Such a reaction would be included, for example, as a disaccharide splitting into its constituent hexoses, or in the reverse direction, although the molecule of water added to or taken away from the disaccharides in the reaction makes the number of molecules *apparently* equal on the two sides of the equation. The molecule of water in the reaction, however, comes from or is returned to the great mass of water forming the solvent for the disaccharide molecule, and hence has no osmotic pressure before, during, or after the reaction. Accordingly, it does not come into the equilibrium equation, for no change of osmotic energy takes place in connection with it, and hence such reaction is practically one in which one molecule forms two or *vice versa.*

Nearly all the reactions of digestion and metabolism also belong to this type of reaction, with the slight modification that the number of simpler molecules formed is often three or more instead of two, and all the conclusions deduced for the simpler splitting into two molecules, or the reverse, can be applied to such reactions with but slight modification. For example, the hydrolyses of neutral fats or triglycerides into fatty acids and of starches into sugars belong to this category.

When a disaccharide is hydrolysed (for example, maltose into two molecules of dextrose), as in the equation

$$C_{12}H_{22}O_{11} + H_2O \rightleftharpoons C_6H_{12}O_6 + C_6H_{12}O_6,$$

the equation of equilibrium is, as deduced above, $\dfrac{P_B^2}{P_A} = P_0 \cdot e^{\frac{C}{RT}},$

where P_B is the osmotic pressure of the hexose at equilibrium, and P_A that of the disaccharide; this may be written $\dfrac{P_B^2}{P_A} = K,$

or $P_B^2 = K P_A.$ Expressed in words, there is a constant ratio between the osmotic pressure of the disaccharide and the *square* of the osmotic pressure of the hexose. As a result, the point of equilibrium is not fixed and independent of the concentration of the reacting substances as in the types of reaction previously discussed, but varies with the initial concentration of the solution, in such a way that in dilute solutions the equilibrium lies where the whole of the disaccharide is dissociated into its constituent hexoses, while as the solution becomes more concentrated the equilibrium point lies more and more towards complete conversion into disaccharide. This is obvious, for if the concentration of disaccharide in the solution be doubled so that P_A becomes $2P_A$, then P_B only becomes $\sqrt{2} \cdot P_B$—that is, with increasing concentration P_B increases in a less ratio than does P_A; conversely on dilution, P_B decreases in a less ratio than P_A, and hence in dilute solutions P_B increases relatively to P_A.[1]

In the case of a neutral fat or triglyceride hydrolysing in solution,[2] three molecules of fatty acid and one of glycerine are formed from each molecule of the fat, and the equation of equilibrium becomes $P_B^4 = K \cdot P_A.$ Accordingly, the effect of concentration

---

[1] It may be pointed out that an electrolyte, such as sodium chloride in aqueous solution, behaves similarly and for the same reason. In dilute solution, the electrolyte is practically dissociated into its ions, while in concentrated solution an amount proportional to the osmotic pressures of the different reacting substances is undissociated. The type of reaction is the same as that discussed above. If at equilibrium, the osmotic pressure of the undissociated molecules is represented by P_S and that of each ion by P_I, then as above for equilibrium we have $P_S = K \cdot P_I^2$, and the same reasoning as given above shows that P_I increases relatively to P_S with increasing dilution.

[2] The neutral fats are practically insoluble in water, but the reasoning holds for fats in solution in the cell protoplasm.

becomes still more accentuated, and the tendency is still greater to form the fat in concentrated solution, and the fatty acid and glycerine in dilute solution. Similar results follow in the formation, or *vice versa*, of the starches and proteins from their component simpler molecules.

It follows from the above considerations that, in order that hydrolysis may proceed under the most favourable conditions, as in digestion, then the reaction should proceed in dilute solution; while in order that recombination may occur, as in storage in the cell, the process should take place in concentrated solution. Further, that any drop in concentration of a substance in solution in the cell will tend to produce again hydrolysis and re-solution of the stored-up substance. In fact, on the supposition that the enzymes are not capable of utilising any other forms of energy in the transformations which they induce, and merely act in hastening passage to the equilibrium point, hydrolysis during digestion, and building up again in the cell during metabolism can only proceed if the concentrations are low in digestion, and high in the cell during metabolism and accompanying storage

The truth of the law deduced theoretically above with regard to the effect of concentration upon the point of equilibrium of reactions can also be shown by experiments. Thus Croft Hill found that *in very concentrated solutions*, the ferment of malt, maltase, caused the formation of a disaccharide from glucose. In his earlier work Croft Hill thought the disaccharide formed was maltose—viz., the disaccharide on which the ferment naturally works in the grain—and that the process was hence a direct reversal of the action of the same ferment upon maltose in dilute solution. Emmerling, who repeated the experiments, thought the disaccharide formed in the concentrated solution of glucose was isomaltose. Then Croft Hill himself in later work found that the substance formed was a new disaccharide which he termed *revertose*. The important fact, however, remains that a ferment which in dilute solutions of a disaccharide causes a hydrolysis into hexoses or monosaccharides, in concentrated solution acts upon the hexose and causes a condensation to disaccharide. It was further shown by Croft Hill that in dilute solutions, containing less than 4 per cent. of glucose, the formation of the disaccharide does not occur.

It has since been shown by E. Fischer and E. F. Armstrong that lactase, a ferment obtained from kefir, causes under like conditions a formation of isolactose from a solution containing a mixture in equal concentration of its constituent hexoses, glucose, and galactose; and even from glucose alone a disaccharide was obtained.

Similar evidence has been obtained of reversibility in the case of certain esters of *somewhat* analogous constitution to the fats, by the action of lipase, the fat-splitting enzyme of the pancreas; from which by analogy the inference has been drawn that similar syntheses of neutral fats by reversed enzymic action may occur in the body.

Thus, Kastle and Loevenhart digested a mixture of butyric acid and ethyl alcohol with a fresh aqueous extract of pancreas, and were able to detect ethyl butyrate by its odour, and, operating on a large scale, were able to obtain a few drops of a light oil with the odour and general properties of the ester. The changes did not occur when boiled pancreatic extract was used, and since in dilute solutions the same lipase can be used to convert ethyl butyrate into butyric acid and ethyl alcohol, it becomes evident that the action is a reversible one. In a later paper, Loevenhart showed that a similar reaction was obtainable with a large number of different tissue extracts.

In a similar fashion, Hanriot showed that lipase is capable of forming monobutyrin from butyric acid and glycerine.

In so far, however, as the syntheses of simple esters by lipase are considered to have a bearing upon the synthesis of neutral fats by the same enzyme in the body, it must be pointed out that the reactions are of somewhat different type, and that the equations of equilibrium, taken in conjunction with the solubilities of the neutral fats, show that the synthesis of neutral fats is a much more difficult process, and one which, granted that it may occur by reversed action of the enzyme under the conditions existing in the cell, is exceedingly unlikely to occur in aqueous solution in the test-tube.

The difference arises from the fact that the two syntheses achieved by the authors mentioned above of ethyl butyrate and monobutyrin are produced in reactions in which single molecules of each of the constituents unite to form a molecule of the ester; while in the case of the neutral fats three molecules of the fatty acid concerned unite with one molecule of the glycerine. If we represent the osmotic pressures (which are proportional to the molecular concentrations) by P_E, P_A, and P_B, for ester, acid, and base respectively, then the equation of equilibrium for the ethyl butyrate and monobutyrin becomes $P_E = K . P_A . P_B$ or $P_E = K . P^2_A$, and that for the neutral fat is $P_E = K . P^3_A . P_B$, or, assuming that the constituents are present in the proper concentrations for combination, $P_E = K . P^4_B$.

Contrasting the two formulæ $P_E = K . P_A^2$ and $P_E = K . P_A^4$, we see that in the case of such a reaction as that in which a neutral fat is formed, the tendency to remain dissociated in dilute solution and to remain combined in concentrated solution is more exaggerated than in the simpler reaction. Accordingly, as we pass from a concentrated solution to a dilute solution the value of P_E falls very rapidly compared to the fall in P_A, or the relative amount of neutral fat becomes very small. In excessively concentrated solution practically all would be neutral fat, but very rapidly on reducing the concentration nearly all would be hydrolysed to free fatty acid and glycerine.

Hence a synthesis of neutral fat from fatty acid and glycerine is only possible in a highly concentrated solution. But the physical property of the fatty acids and neutral fats of being insoluble in water renders the attainment of such concentrated solutions an impossibility in all attempts at synthesis hitherto made, and for this reason no satisfactory proof of syntheses of neutral fats by lipase have hitherto been furnished.

The theory of equilibrium in solution proves, however, that given the possibility of obtaining more concentrated solutions of the fatty acids, the synthesis of neutral fats by enzymes is quite possible; and in the conditions obtaining in the cell, where the solvent is not water but the cell protoplasm, and where also other solvents, such as the bile salts, may be present in concentrated solution, the synthesis of fats may well occur by such means.

The synthesis of neutral fat from soap and glycerine solutions has been claimed by C. A. Ewald, and by Hamburger, by the action of the isolated cells of the intestinal mucous membranes; but similar experiments by the writer, in which both the cells and cell-free extracts of the cells were used from the intestinal mucosa, lymphatic glands, and the pancreas, demonstrated that no trace of neutral fat was ever formed, the only action observable being a setting free of fatty acids from the soaps used. The observations of the authors quoted above, being obtained by difference between total ethereal extract and free fatty acid, were shown to be due to unaltered soaps dissolved out by the ether.

IV. The most general case of equilibrium in solution is that where an indefinite number of substances react together, and the equation, as demonstrated on p. 150, becomes

$$\frac{P_{A'}^a . P_{B'}^{b'} . P_{C'}^{c'} . \text{etc.}}{P_A^a . P_B^b . P_C^c . \text{etc.}} = K,$$

which may be written

$$P_{A'}^a . P_{B'}^{b'} . P_{C'}^{c'} . \text{etc.} = K . P_A^a . P_B^b . P_C^c . \text{etc.};$$

that is, at the equilibrium point the products of the osmotic pressures of the substances reacting upon the one side of the equation, raised in each case to a power corresponding to the number of molecules entering into the reaction, bear a constant ratio to the similar products of the substances on the other side of the equation of reaction.

All the other special cases previously considered can obviously be deduced from this general equation of equilibrium. Otherwise it is of little practical interest, for reactions more complicated than those given under the special types are too difficult to deal with experimentally.

It may be pointed out that since the osmotic pressures are proportional to the molecular concentrations of the reacting substances, in all the above equations the P representing osmotic pressure may be replaced by a C representing the molecular concentration. This is the form in which such equations are usually given, but since the energy changes which are responsible for bringing about a reaction and establishing an equilibrium are dependent upon the osmotic energies of the dissolved substances it has been thought advisable to give the equations in the form shown above.

Before passing from the subject of equilibrium in solution to that of velocity of reaction, and the effect of enzymes and other energy transformers upon reaction and velocity of reaction, it may be profitable to consider briefly the conditions which determine whether a reaction is *practically* reversible or not—that is to say, which determine whether the equilibrium point shall lie at an appreciable and practically measurable distance from either extreme end of the reaction.

In the first place, it is clear from the form of the general equation of equilibrium that the osmotic pressure, and therefore the molecular concentration, of none of the reacting substances on one side can be zero,[1] unless the osmotic pressure of one or more of the reacting substances on the other side also became zero. But a zero value on both sides could only mean that substances taking part in the reaction are absent, and this condition is therefore impossible. Hence there is theoretically an equilibrium point in all reactions, and every reaction is reversible. But the value of the constant may be, and in many reactions is, such that the point of equilibrium lies so near one of the end points that the position is indistinguishable experimentally from that of complete passage into the substances found on one side of the equation of reaction. Hence *practically* reactions may be divided into reversible or incomplete and irreversible or complete reactions, and we now proceed to consider the conditions which tend to cause a reaction to become practically reversible or incomplete.

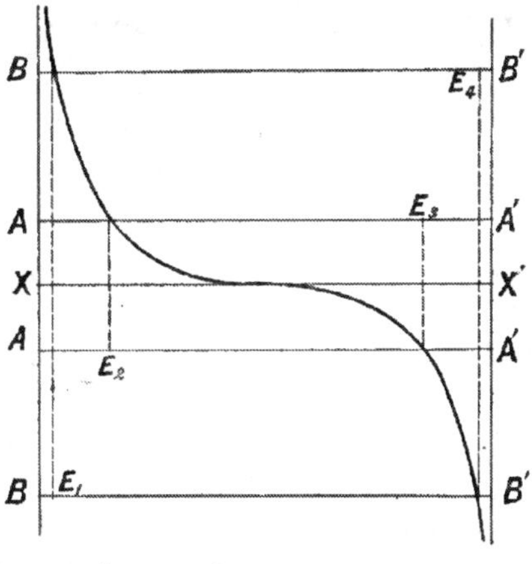

Fig. 2.—Graphic Representation of the Energy Changes in the Course of a Reaction.

We have already seen that in those reactions in which, as a result of the reaction, the number of molecules in solution changes, the concentration of solution changes the equilibrium point, and that such reactions tend to become reversible or incomplete in concentrated solutions and in dilute solution to become irreversible in that phase in which the number of molecules in the solution is largest, and the osmotic energy accordingly at a maximum. It follows for all reactions of this type, which involves by far the greatest number of reactions, that reversibility or the presence of the two phases is impossible in sufficiently dilute solution. This

---

[1] For if any one factor in the product $P_A . P_B . P_C$, etc., becomes zero, the value of the whole product is zero, and this cannot be equated to any finite value on the other side.

follows because in the equation $P_A = K . P_B^n$, where n is greater than unity, that as P_A and P_B diminish together P_A must get relatively smaller compared to P_B, and with sufficient dilution tends to become infinitely small relatively to P_B.

The other factors which affect the position of the point of equilibrium and determine whether a reaction shall be practically reversible or not are the value of C, the chemical energy involved in the change from the one phase to the other, and the absolute temperature of the reaction; for changes in either of these affect the value of the constant K.

The effects of changes in C and T upon the point of equilibrium can best be understood by following out the energy changes as the substances pass in the reaction from the one condition to the other. The matter can best be understood by graphic illustration as in the diagram on p. 158, in which are represented the energy changes at each instant as the substance passes from the one form to the other according to the simplest type of equation, that in which $H = C - RT \log \frac{P_B}{P_A}$.

The base-line XX' represents the zero line of energy exchange, ordinates above the base-line representing quantities of energy set free by the reaction at any stage, and ordinates below, energy required in order that the reaction may proceed. At X the substance is all in the form A and at X' in the form B; at intermediate points fractions are in the two forms proportionate to the distances from X and X'. The horizontal line above or below XX' represents by its height above or below XX' the amount of chemical energy set free (positive when above XX' and negative when below) when a grm. molecule passes from the form A to the form B. The curved line represents the osmotic energy set free at each point in the reaction when a grm. molecule changes form at the particular osmotic pressures present at that point. The height of this line above or below XX' is given numerically by the expression $RT \log \frac{P_B}{P_A}$, and the sign is reversed in plotting it so that at each stage the difference in the heights above XX' of the straight line and the curved line give the value of H, the energy set free at that stage in the reaction, for a grm. molecule changed, according to the equation $H = C - RT \log \frac{P_B}{P_A}$. Tracing now the value of the amount of energy set free in the reaction at each stage, we have at X $P_B = 0$, and therefore $\log \frac{P_B}{P_A} = \log 0 = -\infty$. Therefore at

X, and points close to it, $-$ RT log $\frac{P_B}{P_A}$ has a large positive value, which is to be added to the constant C in order to give the energy set free. Hence no value of C positive or negative can cause the equilibrium point to lie quite at X   As the reaction proceeds, however, and more and more of B is present, P_B rises in value, and the positive value of $-$ RT log $\frac{P_B}{P_A}$ rapidly drops. If now the value of C is negative—that is, if chemical energy is absorbed on change of substance A into substance B—then an equilibrium will be reached as soon as the value of $-$ RT log $\frac{P_B}{P_A}$ equals C. This will occur nearer X, as at E_1, if C has a large negative value than if C has a small negative value, as at E_2 Beyond the point of equilibrium so defined the positive value of $-$ RT log $\frac{P_B}{P_A}$ becomes still smaller, and hence·II, which is C $-$ RT log $\frac{P_B}{P_A}$, becomes negative—that is, energy is absorbed, the reaction is endothermic, and cannot proceed without external energy being added, which is excluded under the conditions we are considering. But if C has a positive value the reaction will run farther towards X′ before the equilibrium point is reached.   As it so runs P_B continually increases and P_A decreases So long as P_A is greater than P_B, the fraction $\frac{P_B}{P_A}$ is less than unity, its logarithm is negative, and hence $-$ RT log $\frac{P_B}{P_A}$ has a positive value; but at the position where $P_B = P_A$, log $\frac{P_B}{P_A} =$ log $1 = 0$, and the curved line representing the change in the osmotic energy crosses the base-line, for the osmotic energy set free at this point in the reaction is zero

From this point onward osmotic energy is absorbed instead of being given out in the reaction, for log $\frac{P_B}{P_A}$ now becomes positive and goes on increasing in value, at first slowly, and later very rapidly as P_A becomes very small in the neighbourhood of X′ and the curved line becomes asymptotic to the ordinate   Hence at a certain point the distance of the curved line below the base-line becomes equal to the distance above the base-line of the horizontal line representing the positive value of C. Also the smaller the positive value of C the farther from the end point will be the point of equilibrium

The same reasoning applies if we start at X′ with the substance all in the form B, and proceed towards X   The diagram to suit progress in this direction is the mirror reflex in the base-line of the one given for the opposite direction (X to X'). For if the value of C was positive in passing from A to B, it will be negative in passing from B to A, and value of $-\mathrm{RT} \log \frac{P_A'}{P_B}$ will be positive at the X' end and negative at the X end, precisely as $-\mathrm{RT} \log \frac{P_B}{P_A}$ was positive at the X end and negative at the X' end. Hence the same equilibrium point is reached from whichever condition, A or B, we choose to travel. The positions of the lines AA' and $-$ AA' and of BB' and $-$ BB' illustrate the effects of a small and a large value of C either positive or negative, and it is evident that a small value increases the distance of the equilibrium point from the end point, and hence increases the reversibility or incompleteness of the reaction.[1]

We learn accordingly that for a reaction of type $P_B = K \cdot P_A$ the smaller the chemical energy involved in the change from A to B, the more does the reaction become practically reversible. The same statement is also true, within certain limits, for other types of reaction.

Now the value of the chemical energy is not measurable experimentally, for heats of reaction as usually measured do not give either C or H of our equations, but instead the heat of reaction for a grm. molecule changed at varying values of P_A and P_B. This figure, which is the only experimental datum we possess, gives us an integration of a small fraction of H at each stage throughout the process.

However, the heat of reaction must vary somewhat in the same manner as C, and a small value of heat of reaction indicates a small value of chemical energy, and a large heat of reaction a high value of chemical energy

Using this criterion as the best available, we find that experiment bears out the above conclusion   In all the typically reversible actions, such as the formation of esters, the polymerisation and hydrolysis of carbohydrates, and such reactions as we have seen above are reversible by enzymes, the heat of reaction is excessively low, so low indeed that it cannot be measured experi-

---

[1] The shape of the curved line varies with the expression for the value of the osmotic energy, so that the effect of changes in low values of C is complicated to follow   But high values of C will always land the equilibrium point upon the asymptotic portion of the curve close to one or other of the two end points

The effect of change in temperature is *on the whole* opposed to that of change of chemical energy; a rise in temperature having the same effect as a drop in chemical energy and tending to increase the reversibility of the reaction.

This is seen from the fact that the part of the constant K, which changes with alterations in chemical energy C and temperature T, is the expression $e^{\frac{c}{RT}}$, in which it is clear that similar changes in C and T balance each other. In the simple form of reaction $P_B = K.P_A$, illustrated in the diagram (p. 158), this is quite clear, for increase in T will cause similar increase in the expression $RT \log \frac{P_B}{P_A}$, and hence will place each point on the curved line farther from the base-line, and so bring the equilibrium point—that is, the point where the curved and horizontal lines lie at an equal distance from the base-line XX'—nearer to the mid point. Accordingly increase of temperature acts like low value of chemical energy and increases reversibility.

In the more complex forms of reaction, such as $P_B = K.P^2_A$, etc.. the form of the curved line representing change in osmotic energy varies; it is still asymptotic at both ends, but no longer crosses the zero line at the mid point between X and X'. Hence increases from zero in the value of C in one definite direction only will up to a certain limit bring the point of crossing nearer the mid point, and so increase reversibility. Similarly, if the value of C is taken as fixed, increases in T up to a fixed limit will decrease the reversibility, but later for higher values will increase it. Hence in those cases where the number of molecules is altered in the reaction there is at a certain given point in each case of change in C or change in T, a reversal in the effect. For higher values of C or T, however, effects of increase of C to high positive or negative values is to throw the crossing farther along towards the asymptotic portion of the line at either end, and so diminish the reversibility; while effects of increase of T at higher values, C being fixed and moderately low, is to throw the crossings farther from either end point and so to increase reversibility.

CHAPTER XI

VELOCITY OF REACTION, AND THE COMPARATIVE ACTION OF ENZYMES AND CELLS

EXPERIMENTAL OBSERVATIONS ON VELOCITY OF REACTION, AND THEIR DISCUSSION — ALTERATION OF CONCENTRATION OF ENZYME.

THE investigations of the conditions of equilibrium have shown that at a certain point in the reaction, at which the molecular concentrations or osmotic pressures of the different substances in solution and taking a part in the reaction bear a definite proportion to one another, there is no energy set free as a result of the reaction, and hence that the system is in equilibrium at this point At all other points or stages in the reaction energy is set free as the result of the reaction, and hence the question arises, Why is a stationary position possible in the system at any other point in the reaction than the equilibrium point ? If a system contains substances capable of reacting with one another and present at other concentrations than those of the equilibrium point, energy will be set free by any movement towards the equilibrium point; why then is the equilibrium point not instantly reached and the energy set free ? Why, in some instances, is there a slow and measurable velocity of reaction towards equilibrium which may not be reached for days or weeks ? Why, in other cases, is there no measurable movement at all towards the position of equilibrium, although the substances are left in solution for an indefinite time, until certain substances not permanently altered themselves in the slightest degree are added to the solution, and after the addition of such substances why does the reaction at once commence and continue until equilibrium is attained ? That is, why do catalysts in general (and enzymes, which form a particular class of catalysts formed by the agency of living cells) induce reactions which cannot be shown to proceed in their absence, or cause reactions which proceed with infinite slowness to be hastened into a measurable velocity? Finally, in many reactions in living

164

cells, and notably in the anabolic processes of chlorophyll-containing cells of living plants, why does the reaction proceed *away* from the equilibrium point with storage of chemical energy, instead of energy being set free ?

There is no shadow of doubt as to the experimental facts which suggest these queries, all of which form a connected whole, and must receive their explanation on a common basis.

Sterilised solutions of cane-sugar, maltose, lactose, and starch can be preserved indefinitely without any measurable change into their simpler components. On the other hand, solutions in molecular proportions of the constituent hexoses which build up these more complex carbohydrates can similarly be kept in solution with no observable change for indefinite periods. There is hence no movement towards the equilibrium point from either side of that point. But let the appropriate catalyst be added under the proper conditions and at once the reaction towards equilibrium occurs.

Still more striking are the examples derived from the metabolism of living cells.

Carbon dioxide and water or water vapour may be left together indefinitely at such temperatures and physical conditions as obtain in the chlorophyll-containing cells, and no formation of organic compounds occurs. Similarly, the organic compounds produced can be left under like conditions, and no chemical changes are observed. But in the green plant cell, under the influence of the solar energy, movement *directly away from the equilibrium poin!* of undirected chemical and osmotic energy takes place, and gives the origin to the whole system of vital processes on the planet.

The fundamental groundwork for an answer to the problems stated in the paragraphs above may thus be outlined. *For energy exchanges to occur it is necessary that there should be present the properly adapted machines or energy transformers.* It is not sufficient that there should be differences in energy potentials in the system in order that a reaction may occur; these give but the *possibility* for the reaction, which can never take place unless in addition conditions are present which allow the transference between the forms of energy possessing differences in potential.

The equations with which we have been dealing under the heading of chemical equilibrium teach us that, at other positions than equilibrium, as a result of reaction, energy will be set free, and the energy so set free is the driving-force towards equilibrium, or a tendency towards chemical equilibrium. But whether there will be any movement towards equilibrium or the reverse, and the velocity of that movement, depend entirely upon how far there is opposition to such movement, by the resistance of other forms of energy present in or brought to bear upon the system by any agency such as a catalyst, or upon how far such resisting forms of energy are diminished by the action of any such agent which may be present in the system.[1]

Chemical energy is not peculiar in this respect, and does not stand isolated from other forms of energy. Water standing in two reservoirs, unconnected by a channel through which the water can flow, will remain at a constant difference in hydrostatic pressure for ever, and if there be a channel of communication between them, the rate of flow—that is, the velocity with which the potential difference is equated out—will vary not only with the difference in potential but with the resistance to the flow of water in the connecting channel. Further, if there is a turbine, or properly constructed reversible pump, on the channel of communication between the two reservoirs, then the water as it flows from the higher to the lower level can be made to give out energy which by suitable transforming machines can be changed into any form of energy; or conversely, if external energy is supplied to the pump, at a sufficiently high potential, it can be made to work the pump in the opposite direction, and the absorbed energy can so be utilised to force the water in the opposite direction from the lower reservoir to the higher reservoir, so that the difference in hydrostatic potential increases instead of diminishing, as it would do if the system were not operated upon by other forms of energy from without.

Similarly in the case of electrical energy, if there is no path of conduction between two charged conductors at different potentials, there can be no equalisation of potential between the two conductors; if a path is provided the velocity of the energy reaction

---

[1] Lest the reader should think that, because these equations do not lead directly to expressions for the velocity of reaction, they are therefore useless, it may be pointed out that they do give the conditions for equilibrium quite truly when no energy is imparted to the system from without   For although variations in resistance will alter the velocity with which equilibrium is reached, at the equilibrium point itself the velocity becomes zero, and the resistance has accordingly no effect upon the equilibrium point.

varies with the resistance of the path; also by giving various forms to the conducting path, the electrical energy may be transformed into various forms; and lastly, if a sufficiently powerful dynamo be placed upon the conducting path and worked in the right direction, instead of the path being a means for equating potential it is converted into a means for heaping up difference in potential.

So also for any type of mechanical engine or motor, however driven: if the load is taken off, the engine races; as the load is increased the velocity lessens, and with a sufficiently heavy load the movement stops entirely. Always when the potential differences of the opposing forms of energy become greater than those of the form of energy driving the motor, the latter becomes ineffective and the engine must stop, or, if built so as to be capable of reversal, must run in the opposite direction.

Exactly similar reasoning applies to every known type of energy, and since the law of conservation of energy holds and a definite amount of chemical energy is equivalent to a definite amount of any other form, it is clear that the reasoning must hold for chemical energy also.

Hence we see that while the difference in chemical energy gives the driving force tending to cause chemical reaction, and a passage towards a definite point of equilibrium, there is present something in the nature of a resistance or load upon the engine, which determines by its amount whether a reaction shall occur at all, if it occurs the speed at which it shall occur, and according as the resistance is modified by other factors, the path of the reaction is determined and the very qualitative nature of the compounds formed by the reaction.

It is hence necessary for our purpose to inquire what is the nature of the resistance to chemical reaction, what are the forms of energy opposed to the reaction, and how is the action of these opposing forms of energy altered under different circumstances, so that the velocity of reaction becomes changed, the reaction stopped or its actual direction reversed, or finally the path of the reaction altered so that, under different conditions, different products may be formed.

The obvious forms of energy opposed to chemical reaction are: (1) molecular cohesion or chemical affinity, which must be overcome before the molecule breaks up or is rendered capable of react-

ing with another molecule, which also may require similar changes
in its molecular constitution before it is fitted to react, and (2) the
physical forms of energy which act between the dissolved molecule
and its solvent, such as the velocity of movement of the molecule
through the solvent, and, at any rate in the case of the colloidal
molecule, probably surface tension at the surface between the
dissolved molecule and its solvent

Action between the dissolved molecule and its solvent, which
must also come in as a factor in preparing for chemical reaction, or
altering the resistance to chemical reaction, is seen in the different
ionising powers of different solvents for salts, and in the different
degrees of association of different dissolved substances in different
solvents. For example, the ionisation of inorganic salts in water
as compared to organic solvents, and the duplicate and higher
molecular weights of organic substances in an associating solvent,
such as benzol, compared with another solvent, such as alcohol.
As proof of this connection, it may be pointed out that the more
ionised a dissolved substance is the more quickly it reacts, showing
that the molecular resistance to reaction has been broken down,
and the very different velocities of reaction of the same substances
in different organic solvents must be due to corresponding
differences in molecular resistance to reaction in these different
media

The first of these factors is that which will probably be most
effective in entirely stopping a reaction, and the latter that which
is effective in rendering reactions in solution as a general rule much
slower than those which occur in gaseous mixtures

It is by modifying the action of these opposing forms of energy,
in some way,[1] that the catalyst or enzyme or living cell produces

----

[1] The mode of action is at present unknown to us the hypotheses thereon
will be given later, the important fact to realise here, apart from any hypothesis, is that the catalyst acts as an energy conductor or transformer for
chemical energy, and varies the amount of energy necessary to be transformed into other channels before the reaction can ensue. It only makes
the path easy between forms of energy Further, it may be pointed out
that the *modus operandi* of energy transformers lies always without the pale
of our knowledge in the case of other forms of energy, just as much as in the
case of chemical energy, where the matter has given rise to so much thought
and discussion. We do not really know, for example, the mode in which an
electric current heats a wire, or how an electric current magnetises iron, and
no other substances; all we have is hypothesis, just as we have for how a
catalyst produces its transformations of chemical energy.

its remarkable effect upon the duration and course of the reaction.

If the catalyst is not capable of acting upon external forms of energy, such as light energy in the case of the green plant cell, but can only utilise chemical energy and convert this into heat energy and osmotic energy, then the catalyst can only work towards the equilibrium point and not away from it. It can start a reaction held stationary by molecular attractions, or can modify a reaction already running by hastening or slowing it, but it must act in all cases towards the equilibrium point from either end. Also dependent upon the power of the enzyme, the reaction may be slowed and stopped at other points, usually corresponding to some definite stage in the reaction, which are called false equilibrium points (see p. 186). This follows, because as the reaction comes nearer the equilibrium point, the chemical potential aiding the catalyst in its work becomes less, and hence always the velocity becomes less, but also the resistance may become so great as to be insuperable for a particular enzyme, and the reaction may come to a dead stop. Take, for example, the relative action as catalysts upon starch solutions of dilute acid and of diastase of malt. The diastase is powerless as a catalyst when all the starch has disappeared and been replaced by a mixture of dextrin and maltose, the resistances, for this catalyst, have been increased beyond the power it possesses and the reaction ceases. But the acid proceeds farther, and converts the dextrin and also the maltose into dextrose; it possesses the power of breaking down the resistance which was insuperable for the diastase.

In both these cases, however, the movement is towards the point of chemical equilibrium, and it is by acting as a transformer of chemical energy into other forms that the catalyst does its work. The only difference is that at a certain stage the potential factor of the molecular energy of the substance being broken up becomes too powerful for the diastase, and the reaction is stopped so far as that catalyst is concerned; but the more powerful hydrogen ion of the acid is still able to overcome the molecular cohesion, and to continue the reaction a stage farther.

But there are catalysts or transformers which can convert other forms of energy into chemical energy, and these form a distinct class from the others; for although they are similar to the former in not being themselves altered by the reaction they induce, they differ in that they require external energy in order to do their work; instead of causing energy to be given out from the chemical system, they cause the system to take up energy, and instead of assisting the system towards the equilibrium point towards which it tends in their absence, they cause a movement away from the equilibrium point.

To this class of catalysts the living cells of plants and animals belong, and although the process is most clearly seen where chlorophyll is present, and is masked in other cells by preponderating action in the opposite direction, there is probably no cell in which anabolic processes do not occur, as shown by the building up, accompanied by storage of chemical energy, of complex organic substances, such as the organised proteid or protoplasm of the cell, and the granular deposits in the cell of amyloses, fats, and other reserve foodstuffs, from the soluble constituents of the plasma or of the circulating fluids by which the cell is nourished. In most types of cell the energy required for the anabolic processes is derived from chemical energy obtained by an oxidation process affecting a portion of the nutrient matter, the energy obtained from this reaction being used to run the anabolic reaction.

The linkage together in this way of a variety of complex chemical reactions is what distinguishes the cell as an energy transformer from the simpler soluble enzyme, which is so often a product of its activity. Such linkage of reaction is never seen in the case of enzymes, which are exceedingly fixed and selective in their action. The enzyme acts usually upon one type of molecular arrangement only, often failing in attacking even the stereo-isomer, but the cell carries on a wide commerce of reaction with many types of matter, and modifies the reactions in varied ways; and also differently at different periods according to its condition, and the manner in which it is affected by concurrent reactions taking place in other cells in the body, or by the influence of the nervous system upon it.

Actions similar to those of the cell in storing up chemical energy are also seen in physical transformers; an example of such is the synthesis of compounds by the electric current and the electrolysis of conducting solutions. Here the electrodes, two conductors at different potentials, act as energy transformers for converting electrical into chemical energy.

The analogy between chemical energy transformations and those of other forms of energy is so clear and the action is so obviously of the same nature, that we may summarise the action of a catalyst or energy transformer as follows:

1. *The action of the soluble or unorganised catalyst or enzyme may consist (a) in commencing a reaction which does not proceed at all in its absence; (b) in altering the velocity of a reaction which does proceed in its absence, and such action may be positive, increasing the speed of the reaction, or negative, diminishing the speed of the reaction; but (c) the direction of reaction must always be towards the point of equilibrium, as defined in the previous section, because the enzyme does not yield energy itself, and is unable to act as a transformer to external energy, or to link two chemical reactions so as to obtain energy from one for the performance of the other.*

2. *The living cell as an energy transformer, in addition to the actions (a) and (b) of the enzyme, can store up chemical energy, either by using energy in other forms and converting it into chemical energy, or by linking several reactions together and transforming the chemical energy obtained from some back to chemical energy which is stored up in others. Finally, the cell can modify its activities, and alter in its action as a transformer, changing entirely the course of the reactions it induces and the products obtained, while the type of action of the enzyme is simple, selective, and entirely fixed.*

There is no doubt whatever that the cell makes use of the action of many intracellular enzymes for the chemical transformations it induces, but in all cases the action of such enzymes is adapted, controlled, and co-ordinated by the cell.

It is necessary to point out that the above view as to the action of enzymes is different in many essential points from the one which is usually accepted at the present time.

The currently accepted view is that any reaction which is influenced by catalysts is already proceeding in the absence of the catalyst, and that all the catalyst can do is to alter the speed of reaction, and bring the reaction more quickly or slowly to that equilibrium point which it would inevitably have attained in its own time in the absence of the catalyst.

The statement is based on the fact that the catalyst is not itself altered in the reaction, and hence neither takes up nor gives out energy to the system; accordingly it cannot alter the amount of energy in the system, and must lead to the same equilibrium point. For if the equilibrium point differed in the presence and absence of the enzyme, then by working a cycle with the catalyst in the solution, then removing the catalyst and excess products of activity, and replacing the catalyst again, energy could be continually manufactured from nothing, or working in the opposite direction energy could be destroyed; both which results are obviously contrary to the law of conservation of energy.

To this reasoning the following objections may be taken:

1. The assumption is wrong that because the catalyst is not permanently altered in the process it cannot therefore take up or give out energy to the system, because it excludes (a) the possibility of the catalyst operating upon external energy, which is done, for example, by the chlorophyll-bearing cell; (b) the possibility of the catalyst using part of the chemical energy of the system, to run another reaction in which energy is absorbed, as is done by all living cells.

2. Even for catalysts in the restricted sense, there is nothing in the reasoning to show that the catalyst cannot take up and give out energy in a vibratile fashion, so that as a net result its own condition and amount of energy is unaltered, and its condition at the end is the same as at the beginning, and yet by this means it can induce a reaction which would not occur at all in its absence. For example, an electro-motor is not altered at the end of a period of running from what it was at the beginning, but by intermediately taking up an amount of energy it is capable of converting a large amount of electrical energy into mechanical energy which would never have occurred if it had not been in the electric circuit. So when a chemical reaction is *absolutely* stationary on account of opposed molecular attractions present in the molecule having a tendency to react, the enzyme, by imparting momentarily a small amount of energy to the molecule, may overcome the molecular attractions, and in the break-up of the molecule may receive back all the energy previously given out, so as to remain unchanged in the process.

Finally, as has been pointed out above, the presence of the catalyst may not cause the reaction to proceed completely to the equilibrium point, because as the reaction proceeds, and the concentration of the substance reacting changes, the potential tendency backing the action of the catalyst may fall to such a level that the energy in the first stage which the catalyst is capable of yielding is insufficient to cause the cleavage to occur. Hence the reaction may cease at a different point with different catalysts.

The only point essential with the simple type of catalyst is that it shall work towards the equilibrium point; but it can cause movement towards that point not occurring before, alter velocity of reaction, and may fall short of reaching the equilibrium point.

The experimental evidence with regard to the action of enzymes is entirely in accord with the view here expressed.

If, as has already been pointed out, the appropriate solutions on which the digestive enzymes act be kept in sterilised condition, not the slightest change is observable in any one case, no matter how long the solution is preserved, but if the enzyme is added its effect is apparent in a few minutes.

Further, the nature of the reaction and of the products formed, as well as the relative amounts of the latter, are often determined by the nature of the catalyst added to the same medium. As, for example, in the catalysis of protein by pepsin, trypsin, acid, and alkali respectively. Here, in all cases, the products and their amounts are different. Are we, then, to suppose that all these different reactions to as many different equilibrium points are running concurrently in any given protein solution, but at so slow a rate as not to be observable ? It is an interesting theoretical speculation; but it would appear more probable that these different catalysts possess a specific affinity for attacking some definite molecular groupings in the complex protein molecule, and in each case *started* a reaction which was not possible until that particular catalyst was present in the solution.

Equations for Velocity of Reaction.

The various expressions deduced for the value of the energy set free in the reaction give us the driving agent in the reaction, but the unknown values of the resistances opposed to this, and the effect of the amount of catalysts upon them, render the velocity theoretically indeterminate from a knowledge of the energy set free in the reaction only. We have hence, in order to obtain formulæ for the expression of the velocity of reaction under different conditions, to introduce empirical constants to denote the resistance to reaction of the substances concerned, or rather the reciprocals of these resistances—that is, the chemical conductivities. The velocity of change of each substance is then proportional to the product of the osmotic pressure or molecular concentration of that substance and the constant[1] which represents the reciprocal of the resistance to change. For (as is shown in deducing the conditions of equilibrium) the energy set free by the reaction will vary with the osmotic pressure, and the resistance is inversely proportional to the constant, and accordingly the product of these two is proportional to the velocity of reaction.

In all cases the tendency to react is proportional to the osmotic pressure or molecular concentration of each substance in solution, and this, the fundamental law of chemical kinetics, is called *the law of mass action*. When two or more substances tend to unite to form a single substance, the tendency on the part of each substance is by the law of mass action proportional to its pressure or concentration in the solution, and hence the velocity of formation of the combined substance will be proportioned to the *product* of the concentrations of the uniting constituents. Accordingly, in any equation of velocity, the velocity of formation of a substance may be set down as equal to the product of the concentrations of its constituents in the solution, multiplied by a constant (k) which represents, and is the reciprocal of, the resistance to the reaction. The value of k will vary with the amount of catalyst present, with the temperature and other factors which alter the resistance ; but these factors being supposed kept constant, the value of k will remain constant throughout the reaction.

We are now in a position to state equations for the velocity of reactions.

Let two substances, A and B, in solution react to form two others, C and D, according to the equation

$$A + B \rightleftharpoons C + D.$$

Further, let the molecular concentrations of the four substances (or their osmotic pressures, which are proportional to these concentrations) be represented by c_A, c_B, c_C, c_D, and the constant of reaction for conversion of A and B into C and D (as explained above) be k_1, and the constant for reaction in the opposite direction of C and D into A and B be k_2. Then the rate of formation of C and D is given by $k_1 . c_A . c_B$, and the rate of formation of A and B—that is, of disappearance of C and D—is given by $k_2 . c_C . c_D$. Hence the net velocity

---

[1] It will be shown later that the assumption that the resistance is constant throughout the reaction is only an approximation, and that the resistance really varies somewhat with the ratio between enzyme and substratum.

of formation of C and D is the difference of these two expressions, or $k_1 c_A . c_B - k_2 c_C . c_D$. But the velocity of reaction is the limit of the change in concentration divided by the change in time when both change in concentration and in time are infinitely small—that is,

velocity $= -\dfrac{dc_A}{dt}$, the negative sign being used because c_A is decreasing.

Accordingly, the equation for the velocity of reaction is

$$-\frac{dc_A}{dt} = k_1 \, c_A . c_B - k_2 \, c_C . c_D. \tag{1}$$

This equation holds, under the conditions as to constancy of resistance laid down above, throughout the course of the reaction, and hence if a, b, c, and d be the initial molecular concentrations of the four substances, and at the end of a time t the molecular concentrations of A and B have changed by an amount $-x$, and become $a-x$ and $b-x$ respectively, while C and D have changed also by an equal amount $+x$, and become $c+x$ and $d+x$ respectively, then the equation becomes

$$\frac{dx}{dt} = k_1 (a-x)(b-x) - k_2 (c+x)(d+x). \tag{2}$$

If the initial concentrations and the values of k_1 and k_2 are known, the course of the reaction can accordingly be determined, and the amount of x after any given time be determined by integration of the above equation, remembering that when $t=0$, $x=0$. The values of k_1 and k_2 can be determined by making measurements at sufficiently close intervals of the value of x at different times during the reaction, the initial concentrations being known and substituting in the equation.

The ratio of the two constants k_1 and k_2 in the equation for velocity of reaction is equal to the value of the constant K of the equation of equilibrium, for at equilibrium $-\dfrac{dc_A}{dt}$ is zero, because no change is occurring in the substance, therefore from the equation $-\dfrac{dc_A}{dt} = k_1 c_A . c_B - k_2 c_C . c_D$, we have at equilibrium $k_1 \, c_A . c_B - k_2 \, c_C . c_D = 0$,

or
$$\frac{c_C . c_D}{c_A . c_B} = \frac{k_1}{k_2},$$

but in the equation of equilibrium

$$\frac{c_C . c_D}{c_A . c_B} = K,$$

therefore
$$K = \frac{k_1}{k_2}.$$

It follows from this that the resistances k_1 and k_2 bear the same values in whichever way the reaction is going, and that anything which slows or hastens the reaction in the direction $A + B \longrightarrow C + D$ must also equally hasten or slow it in the direction $A + B \longleftarrow C + D$.

Hence a catalyst or enzyme which at one set of concentrations increases the velocity of a reaction in one direction must equally hasten it at another set of concentrations in the opposite direction. In other words, all catalytic action must be reversible, although in most instances the equilibrium point lies so near one end that the action of the enzyme on the velocity of reaction in one of the directions cannot be demonstrated experimentally.

The equation for the velocity of reaction between two pairs of substances A, B and C, D, given above, can be much simplified, if A and B be present in the proper molecular concentration for reacting upon each other at the commencement and C and D be initially absent. For then the initial molecular concentration of A and B will be the same; let it be represented by a and let x be the change in molecular concentration at time t after the commencement of the reaction. Then the equation for the velocity of change in x at time t, by using equation (2) and remembering that $a = b$, and $c = d = 0$ becomes

$$\frac{dx}{dt} = k_1 (a - x)^2 - k_2 . x^2 \qquad (3)$$

Similar equations for the velocity of reaction can be deduced, by using the same processes of reasoning, for the other types of reaction which have been discussed under the heading of equilibrium.

For example—

1. For a single substance undergoing conversion by molecular rearrangement into another single substance—such, for example, as an isomeric change:

$$\frac{dx}{dt} = k_1 (a - x) - k_2 (b + x),$$

where a and b are the original molecular concentrations of the substances A and B, and x the change in molecular concentration at time t. This equation obviously takes the form

$$\frac{dx}{dt} = K' - K''x.$$

2. For a single substance A undergoing conversion into two substances B and C, the common type of action of enzymes and many other catalysts:

$$\frac{dx}{dt} = k_1 (a - x) - k_2 (b + x) (c + x),$$

where a is molecular concentration of single substance, b and c those of substances into which it is converted, and x the change in concentration in time t. If, as is usually the case, B and C are absent in the beginning, and a still stands for the initial concentration of substance A, then the equation obviously simplifies to

$$\frac{dx}{dt} = k_1 (a - x) - k_2 x^2 \tag{4}$$

3. For completeness we may add the formula deduced at length above, for when two substances A and B react to form two others C and D—

$$\frac{dx}{dt} = k_1 (a - x) (b - x) - k_2 (c + x) (d + x).$$

When initially $a = b$ for A and B, and $c = d = 0$ for C and D, then the equation becomes

$$\frac{dx}{dt} = k_1 (a - x)^2 - k_2 x^2 \tag{5}$$

The integration of the above equations of velocity is necessary in order to obtain x, the quantity of the substance (or substratum) changed in a given time t by the action of any catalyst, which is the quantity usually observed in experiments on reaction velocity, and is used to determine the constant or constants of reaction. Such integration is, however, difficult, and leads to complicated expressions for the value of x, on account of the presence of the second member on the right-hand side prefixed by the negative sign. Now this expression, which introduces the difficulty, arises from the supposition that the reaction is reversible; it is the expression in the equation which represents the tendency of the substances to react in the reverse direction from right to left instead of from left to right.

Accordingly, if the degree of reversibility is small—that is, if the equilibrium point lies close up to the end point corresponding to the substances being practically all converted into the forms represented on the right-hand side of the equation of reaction—the value of the second expression on the right-hand side of the equation of velocity becomes very small compared to the value of the first expression, and may be neglected. That is, the reaction may be taken as running irreversibly, and this is what is usually done in obtaining the equations for the velocity of most reactions which concern us.

This means that in those equations which run almost to completion, the value of the constant k_2 is small compared to k_1. Now

12

the constants are the reciprocals of the resistances to the reaction running in the two opposed directions, and hence this means that the resistance to such a reaction running from left to right is small compared to the resistance for it running from right to left.

It must be pointed out, however, that in the later stages of the reaction running from left to right, when $a - x$ has become very small compared to x, although k_1 is large compared to k_2, the second expression may cease to be negligible, and hence, although the equation obtained by neglect of the second expression may truly represent the course of the reaction throughout the greater part of its length, there may be a difference between observed and calculated results at the later stages of the experiment.

The discrepancy will be less the lower is the initial concentration of the substratum, and, as we have seen in speaking of equilibrium in dilute solutions of type 2, where one substance is resolved into two others, the equilibrium point lies close up to complete resolution into the two substances. Accordingly for this type of reaction in dilute solution, which includes all the digestive processes, the second expression can be allowed to drop without sensible error.

In concentrated solutions, for this type of reaction, as the reaction approaches completion, and the *tendency* to reversion begins to become potent, the velocity of reaction must, however, fall off, and the velocity constant calculated by neglecting the reversibility expression (k_2x^2) must fall off in value, as it is actually found to do by experiment.

This important fact has been neglected by most experimenters, and the drop in velocity has been attributed to combination between the catalyst and the products of reaction. This explanation of the effect of products of reaction in slowing the reaction is no doubt experimentally correct, for the enzyme does combine with the products or one of them. But such combination is also the preliminary stage in the process of reversal, and the ferment must equally combine with the substratum when the reaction is running from left to right. The subject will be returned to when the results of experiment upon strong solutions of carbohydrates are considered; for the present, with this word of warning as to the danger of neglecting the reversal factor in such experiments, we may proceed to the derivation of the equations, connecting x the quantity converted in time t, and the velocity constant, when the second expression is neglected as small in value. Since the second constant falls away in this process, we can replace k_1 by k, when the typical equations become:

Nos. 1 and 2. Where a single substance undergoes change into either one or two others:[1]

$$\frac{dx}{dt} = k\,(a - x).$$

In words, this means that the velocity of reaction is proportional to the molecular concentration, at the moment, of the substance undergoing change.

The above equation can be written

$$\frac{dx}{a - x} = k\,dt;$$

this when integrated gives $-\log$ nat. $(a - x) = kt + \text{const.}$, and since when x is 0, t is 0, the constant is $-\log$ nat. $a = \text{const.}$ Subtracting, we get $\log$ nat. $a - \log$ nat. $(a - x) = kt,$

or

$$\log \frac{a}{a - x} = kt,$$

and, for the value of the constant of reaction,

$$k = \frac{1}{t} \log \frac{a}{a - x}.$$

The curve showing the quantity of substance changed in different times, for such reactions in which only one substance undergoes change, is accordingly a logarithmic curve.

Such reactions are termed *mono-molecular*, and include all those reactions induced by enzymes, in which a single substance breaks up into two or more, and the quantity of ferment active throughout the reaction remains constant.

No. 3. Where two substances on the left-hand side of the equation of reaction react to form two (or more)[2] substances on the right-hand side.

Here the velocity equation becomes

$$\frac{dx}{dt} = k\,(a - x)\,(b - x) \tag{1}$$

---

[1] Or indeed any number of others; the same equation would hold, for example, for a triglyceride, breaking up into three molecules of fatty acid and one of glycerine. This arises because there is only one substance changing on the left-hand side, and the back action of those on the right side is negligible.

[2] As before, the number of substances on the right-hand side has no effect if these do not react back on the progress of the reaction from left to right.

or if the substances concerned (A and B) are in equi-molecular concentration a at the outset—

$$\frac{dx}{dt} = k\,(a-x)^2 \tag{2}$$

The first equation (1) may be written

$$\frac{dx}{(a-x)\,(b-x)} = k\,dt;$$

and this

$$\frac{1}{a-b}\left(\frac{dx}{b-x} - \frac{dx}{a-x}\right) = k\,dt,$$

on integrating this equation yields

$$-\frac{1}{a-b}\left[\log\,(b-x) - \log\,(a-x)\right] = kt + \text{const}$$

To obtain the value of the integration constant, we have when $t=0$—that is, at the start of the experiment—$x=0$, for x is the amount changed at time $=t$, and hence when $t=0$, $x=0$. Therefore, substituting these values in above equation, we get

$$-\frac{1}{a-b}\left[\log\,b - \log\,a\right] = \text{const.,}$$

and subtracting the two equations we obtain

$$\frac{1}{a-b}\left[\log\,(a-x) - \log\,(b-x) + \log\,b - \log\,a\right] = kt,$$

which is

$$\frac{1}{a-b}\,\log\frac{b\,(a-x)}{a\,(b-x)} = kt,$$

giving for the velocity constant k

$$k = \frac{1}{(a-b)\,t}\cdot\log\frac{b\,(a-x)}{a\,(b-x)}.$$

The second equation (2) (above) may be written

$$\frac{dx}{(a-x)^2} = k\,dt,$$

or since $dx = -\,d\,(a-x)$

$$-\frac{d\,(a-x)}{(a-x)^2} = k\,dt,$$

which on integrating yields

$$\frac{1}{a-x} = kt + \text{const.},$$

as before when $t = 0$, $x = 0$, hence $\frac{1}{a} = \text{const.}$, and on subtracting the two equations

$$\frac{1}{a-x} - \frac{1}{a} = kt,$$

or

$$\frac{x}{a\,(a-x)} = kt,$$

and for the reaction constant k

$$k = \frac{x}{t \cdot a \cdot (a-x)}$$

These reactions, where two substances undergo change in concentration on the left-hand side of the equation of reaction when the reaction is proceeding from left to right, are spoken of as *bimolecular reactions*. The best known examples are where an ester, containing two monad radicles, such as ethyl acetate, is saponified by an alkali. The reaction is different from that with an acid, for the alkali as well as the ester is changing its concentration during the reaction, while in the hydrolysis by the acid, the hydrogen ion concentration which affects the change in the ester remains constant, and the water produced being merely added to the water of the solvent has no effect on the progress of the reaction.

Tri-molecular reactions and higher are rare, from the tendency of the reaction to break down into stages. For a tri-molecular reaction, in which three molecules react together on the left-hand side of the equation, the equation of velocity, supposing the three substances present in equi-molecular proportions at the outset, would be

$$\frac{dx}{dt} = k\,(a-x)^3,$$

The pursuit of these higher reactions would, however, only be an exercise in mathematics, and so may be left on one side to pass on to experimental work.

Experimental Observations on Velocity of Reaction induced by Enzymes.

We may now proceed to the examination of the experimental results on chemical kinetics, and to the investigation of the extent to which such observations are in accord with the equations theoretically deduced above.

At the outset we are met by great apparent divergence of experimental results, and different statements by different observers. More recent work has, however, tended to show that the apparent discrepancies are due to different observers having worked at different portions of the reaction, that there are several different factors involved which disturb the velocity of the reaction when there is not due attention given to the relative amounts of catalyst and the substratum on which it acts, or to the conditions obtaining at the extreme ends of the reaction.

In the case of the enzymes it has recently been shown, particularly by the researches of Horace Brown and Glendinning and of E. F. Armstrong, that the simple logarithmic law deduced above holds only at some distance from the beginning or end of the reaction, and when there is a due proportionality between ferment and substratum.

The experiments on velocity of reaction may be divided into— (1) those in which, with a constant amount of catalyst throughout the experiment, the course of the reaction is followed from the initial point at which only the substratum or substance upon which the catalyst acts is present, to the end-point at which the substratum has been as completely converted into the products of reaction as is possible under the conditions of experiment; (2) those in which the effects upon the velocity of varying the concentration (a) of ferment and (b) of substratum are observed in the earlier stages of the experiment; and (3) those in which the effects of addition of one or other of the products of reaction at the initial stage are studied, or the effect of addition or removal of such products upon the end-point or apparent equilibrium point of the reaction. The experimental measurement in all cases is that of the quantity or percentage of the substratum converted in a given time, and this has been measured in many different ways. The enzymes which have been most employed have been those which act upon starches or sugars.

The results of experiment may be stated either in the form of a curve in which the co-ordinates represent time from the commencement of the experiment and percentage of substance converted, or by calculating the values of the constant of reaction k at each period at which a determination is made.

In the case of dilute acids, acting upon esters or upon disaccharides, the reaction is mono-molecular, and the curve showing the ratio of percentage conversion to time of reaction is, as the formula indicates, a logarithmic curve.

The velocity is proportional in each case to the dissociation of the acid—that is to say, to the concentration of the hydrogen ions; but the proportionality is by no means exact. Thus a 0·5 normal hydrochloric acid inverts cane sugar at 6·07 times the rate of a 0·1 normal solution, although its concentration in hydrogen ions is only 4·64 times as great. Hence the negative ions of the acid must also possess a certain secondary action in increasing the power of the hydrogen ions as catalysts, as suggested by Arrhenius. That this is the cause of the discrepancy is further shown by the action of the ions of the neutral salt when present along with the acid, for, although the neutral salt alone does not catalyse, the presence of an equivalent amount of the neutral potassium salt of the acid used increases the rate of catalysis by the acid alone by about 10 per cent.

An application of this inverting power of the acid or hydrogen ion, as a test for free hydrogen ions or acidity, is of great importance to the biological chemist. The method is of highest value when dealing with a secretion of acid reaction,[1] where it is important to determine whether and in how far the reaction may be due to the presence of a feebly dissociated acid, such as carbonic, acetic, lactic, etc., or to a strongly dissociated acid, such as hydrochloric.

Here the usual methods of titration of the acid entirely fail; for example, a decinormal solution of acetic acid will give on titration in presence of an indicator the same acidity as a decinormal solution of hydrochloric acid. But the real effective acidity of the two solutions is entirely different, the acetic acid only possessing about 3 per cent. of the hydrogen ion concentration of the hydrochloric acid, and being in consequence for most physiological purposes correspondingly weak in its action.

---

[1] A similar application can be made in the case of alkaline solutions, in determining by inversion the concentration of the alkali, or hydroxyl ion.

Could the two acids be obtained in pure solution the determination of their relative effective acidities could easily be made by measuring their relative conductivities; but as the physiological chemist has to deal with them, as, for example, in the gastric juice, they are present in solution with inorganic salts of high conductivity, such as sodium chloride, and hence the electrical conductivity method fails.

It is just here that the method of determining concentration of hydrogen ions and corresponding effective acidity, first suggested by Ostwald and carried out experimentally by F. A Hoftmann, becomes of such immense value in enabling a determination of this important point to be made in gastric juice.

The best substratum to employ is methyl acetate, and in using the method recently in a large number of pathological cases for the determination of the amount, and, by means of control with ordinary titration methods, the nature of the acid in the gastric contents, the writer has found it a most reliable method.

The recognition of the fact that it is not the total amount of acid or alkali in a secretion or body fluid, as shown by titration with an indicator, which confers upon the fluid its activity or modifies its activity as a catalyst, or as an active agent upon living cells, but rather its effective concentration in hydrogen or hydroxyl ions, is of the highest importance, and the supplying of methods for determining such factors, of which an example has been shown above, is one of the most important services that physical chemistry has rendered to biology.

On passing from the action of the simpler catalysts, such as acids, alkalies, and inorganic salts, to the enzymes, we find that the disturbing elements, of which we have had some evidences above in the action of the negative ion, and of neutral salts, in effecting the catalytic power of the hydrogen ion, become more predominating, and often, especially at certain stages in the reaction, the velocity does not experimentally obey the logarithmic law at all, although the reaction is quite clearly a mono-molecular one

As a result of measurements with different strengths of solutions and of enzyme, and of the experiment only being carried through the earlier stages by some observers, while others carried on observations until the reaction came to a standstill, very different expressions were obtained for the law of velocity of reaction of the same enzyme upon the same substratum, and it was only later by the observations of Henri, Horace Brown and Glendinning, E. F. Armstrong, and Bayliss that we began to understand the results, and so bring the different observations into accord with one another.

O'Sullivan and Tompson were the first observers who studied the velocity of action of an enzyme quantitatively throughout the course of the reaction.[1] They employed the action of invertase on cane sugar, and found that the reaction was mono-molecular, obeying the mass action law, and giving a logarithmic curve. Henri, however, who later worked at the same subject, found that the value of the constant K, derived from their figures, by using the formula deduced above, $K = \frac{1}{t} \log \frac{a}{a-x}$, did not remain quite constant throughout the reaction, but slowly increased in value in the ratio, for example, of 298 near the beginning to 332 near the close of the reaction, thus showing that the velocity of reaction only approximated to the logarithmic law.

Tammann, in a series of researches, investigated not only the action of invertase on cane sugar, but of emulsin on different glucosides (salicin, amygdalin, arbutin, æsculin), and found that the reaction never proceeded to completion. He observed that the velocity of reaction was retarded in increasing amount by the presence of the products of reaction as these accumulated in solution. The percentage which remained unconverted varied with the temperature, the concentration of ferment, and the concentration of substratum. Increasing the temperature caused the reaction after it had come to rest at the lower temperature to recommence and proceed farther towards completion. With a constant quantity of enzyme (emulsin) increased concentration of substratum (amygdalin) increased the total quantity converted, although not proportionately, the percentage conversion being diminished; also, addition of substratum after the reaction had ceased caused a fresh quantity to be converted.

Removal of the products of conversion also had the effect of causing conversion of further quantities. This last result is confirmed by other observers.

---

[1] That is to say, the progress of the reaction when a definite amount of enzyme had been added initially; the effects of variation in amount of enzyme acting for equal times had previously been studied by Brücke, Schütz, and others.

These results of Tammann with regard to the alteration of the position of the incomplete end-point by precisely such factors as influence a true equilibrium point, are interesting in view of the usual statement that the points of rest in such incomplete reactions are so-called *false* equilibrium points. That the equilibrium point is false in the sense that it cannot be reached by the same catalyst working in the reversed direction must be admitted, but it is a false equilibrium point in this sense only; and as far as the entire system, *including the catalyst*, is concerned, for the given concentrations and temperature it is in true equilibrium at this point, else why should the system come permanently into rest and the reaction cease ? As has been pointed out above, the action of the catalyst is to diminish the resistance opposed to the driving force due to energy set free in the reaction. Now, as the system approaches the true or absolute equilibrium point which it would reach in the absence of resistance, the driving force diminishes, and the movement against resistance will cease at a point,

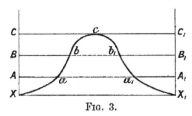

FIG. 3.

dependent upon the power of the catalyst in diminishing the resistance short of the equilibrium point for no resistance, in whichever direction the reaction is proceeding.

The matter may be illustrated graphically, as in the annexed diagram. Let the horizontal line XX_1 represent the path of the reaction, the substance being supposed to be all in one form at X and all in the other form at X_1; at intermediate points varying percentages are in the two forms. Let the curved line, by its height above XX_1, represent the opposition to reaction[1] at each stage. Then the opposition where it is low will be overcome up to a certain distance from either side, dependent upon the power of the catalyst. A catalyst of sufficient power will carry the reaction up to the same point (c), in no matter which direction the change is going: *this* point is what is ordinarily called the equilibrium point or true equilibrium point. But for a less powerful catalyst the diagram shows that there will be two points of equilibrium, one on each side, according to the direction in

[1] That is, $\frac{R}{P}$, where R is resistance and P the potential tending to reaction, of which R remains approximately constant while P continually diminishes as the equilibrium point is approached; hence, as shown in the diagram, the opposition to reaction $\frac{R}{P}$ increases as the equilibrium point is approached.

which the reaction is proceeding, each falling short of the true or absolute equilibrium point. For example, a catalyst which by reason of its properties and concentration has a power represented as at AA_1, will when the reaction is proceeding in the direction from left to right (X to X_1) carry the reaction up to the point a, and the system will be in equilibrium there, and when the reaction is proceeding in the opposite direction (X_1 to X) will carry the reaction up to a_1, and leave the system in equilibrium there. Hence it is quite erroneous to speak of these equilibrium points in incomplete reactions as *false* equilibrium points, for under the given conditions the system is as truly in equilibrium as it would be if all resistance to reaction were removed and it had reached the absolute equilibrium point in the absence of a catalyst.

Barth, and later Duclaux, found that in the earlier part of the reaction induced by invertase upon cane sugar, when moderately concentrated solutions were used, the amount of the sugar hydrolysed was not proportional to its concentration. Thus Barth observed that, using the same amount of invertase, and varying the concentration of sugar, between 5 per cent. of sugar and 15 per cent. practically the same amount was hydrolysed in equal time. Below 5 per cent. the amount hydrolysed increased with the concentration, but not proportionately, so that the percentage hydrolysed was less, and with percentages higher than 15 the absolute amount hydrolysed actually fell off. Duclaux further showed that with the same concentration of enzyme and sugar, the amount hydrolysed up to the point at which 20 per cent. had been inverted was simply proportional to the time, so that the curve representing the progress of the reaction up to this point was a straight line and not a logarithmic curve. At a later stage, as a result according to Duclaux of the retarding action of the products of reaction, the curve began to obey the logarithmic law. Henri later showed, however, that even in this portion Duclaux's results do not give the logarithmic law, the constant K all the time increasing with the progress of the reaction.

In an extensive series of experiments on the inversion of cane sugar by invertase, Henri showed that the value of K calculated on the basis $K = \dfrac{1}{t} \log \dfrac{a}{a-x}$ continually increased throughout the reaction.

He based on the fact that the value of the constant increased with the percentage of invert sugar an empirical formula in which the constant K was replaced by $K_1\left(1+\epsilon\dfrac{x}{a}\right)$, so that the equation for velocity of reaction became $\dfrac{dx}{dt}=\epsilon\left(1+\epsilon\dfrac{x}{a}\right)(a-x)$, leading on integration to $K_1(1+\epsilon)=\dfrac{1}{t}\left[\log\dfrac{a}{a-x}+\log\left(1+\epsilon\dfrac{x}{a}\right)\right]$. Calculating the value of the empirical constant ϵ from his experimental results, Henri found that it varied within narrow limits around the value unity, and hence the above formula simplifies to $K_1=\dfrac{1}{2t}\log\dfrac{a+x}{a-x}$.

In accord with O'Sullivan and Tompson, Henri found that within limits in which the enzyme was not too concentrated the amount of hydrolysis in the case of invertase and cane sugar was directly proportional to the concentration of the enzyme. The laws governing the velocity of reaction have also been studied by Adrian Brown in the case of zymase for conversion of glucose into alcohol, and for the action of invertase upon cane sugar. In the case of the alcoholic fermentation it was found by this author that the velocity of reaction was not represented by a logarithmic curve, but by a straight line—that is to say, the velocity of reaction was constant. On the other hand, it was found, as in Henri's experiments, that the velocity of reaction in the case of invertase and cane sugar increased more rapidly than it ought on the basis of the logarithmic law, the value of $K=\dfrac{1}{t}\log\dfrac{a}{a-x}$ increasing steadily throughout the series. Adrian Brown also obtained similar results to those of Barth, Duclaux, and Henri for variations in concentration of the cane sugar in not too dilute solutions, the amount converted showing a constant weight and not a constant proportion for equal times. To explain this result, he supposed that a compound is formed between enzyme and sugar which persists for a time, and that as a result a molecule of enzyme can effect only a limited number of complete molecular changes in unit time. Accordingly, whatever the available concentration of sugar may be at any given instant, no increase of conversion above a fixed maximum can occur. It is hence only when the concentration of the sugar falls below a certain definite level relatively to the amount of enzyme present that the amount of conversion can fall below this maximum, and the velocity of reaction can begin to obey the logarithmic law. It is hence only in dilute solutions (compared to the amount of enzyme) that the amount of sugar converted per unit time can be proportional to the amount present, and this condition Adrian Brown found to be experimentally realised.

It is clear that this conception of A. Brown's is really coincident with that of Arrhenius of the " active mass."

The catalysis of starch by the action of diastase was next studied by Horace Brown and Glendinning, who showed that the velocity curve in this case also is at first represented closely by a straight line, but later approximates to the logarithmic curve. These authors also assume a combination between the enzyme and its substratum, and that at first the concentration of enzyme is small compared to that of the substratum. As before, as long as the amount of substratum is large, the amount of combined substratum and enzyme will remain constant, the amount therefore converted in unit time will remain constant, and the velocity curve will be a straight line. Later, when the concentration of substratum falls off, the amount in combination will begin to vary directly as the concentration at any moment of the substratum and the logarithmic law will begin to hold.

An extensive series of observations on the hydrolysis of various proteids, chiefly caseinogen and gelatin, by the action of trypsin has been published by Bayliss. The method used was that of measuring the increase in electrical conductivity, and it appears from his statements to be both convenient to carry out experimentally and to give reliable results.

With regard to the course of the reaction, Bayliss found that the curve representing quantity converted and time fell off continuously and rapidly throughout the experiment from the logarithmic curve, the velocity constant decreasing in value to the end. The form of the curve (which tends to become asymptotic to the base-line) shows that the velocity of reaction tends to become zero—that is to say, that there is an equilibrium point with the reaction incomplete. It was found that the position of this point of rest altered with the same factors as have already been described as causing an alteration in Tammann's experiments— viz., alteration of concentration of substratum; alteration of concentration of enzyme; alteration of concentration of the system as a whole; removal of products of reaction; and alteration of temperature.

A certain amount of evidence in favour of the reversibility of the reaction was obtained by subjecting a 40 per cent. solution of the products of reaction of caseinogen and trypsin to the action of fresh trypsin, when in a period of four days a considerable diminution of conductivity was observed, which is the reverse of the increase in conductivity observed when the caseinogen is acted upon, and is presumptive evidence that the reaction was proceeding in the reverse or synthetic direction.

Discussion of Experimental Results on Velocity of Reactions induced by Enzymes.

It is clear from the foregoing account of the experimental results obtained by different authors, that in the case of the enzymes the simple logarithmic law fails to suit the general course of the reaction from beginning to end.

It may be inquired, therefore, whether any assumption has been made in the deduction of the velocity equation for such reactions as we have been considering which has been the means of introducing the differences between theory and experiment.

The equation from which the simple logarithmic expression, $k = \frac{1}{t} \log \frac{a}{a-x}$, is derived is $\frac{dx}{dt} = k (a-x)$, which simply expresses that the rate of change at any moment is proportional to the concentration of the unchanged substratum at that moment. The entire action of the enzyme, as far as the formula is concerned, is contained in the constant k; the more powerful the enzyme the greater is the value of k, and the less powerful the less is the value of k. Regarding the ferment as acting by reducing the resistance to reaction in the system, as described above, we may regard k as the conductivity factor in the reaction. Hence by writing $\frac{dx}{dt} = k (a-x)$, we have assumed that the effect of the enzyme upon the conductivity is constant throughout the reaction. Expressed in another way, the assumption has been made that throughout the whole of the reaction, no matter what the concentration of the substratum, the effect of the enzyme is the same *upon each molecule of the substratum.* Now this need not necessarily be the case experimentally, and probably is not so; for as the number of molecules of substratum decreases, there will be continually a larger number of enzyme molecules relatively, and there may be in consequence a greater amount of action upon each substratum molecule —that is, the value of k on this account will increase throughout the reaction. Thus indirectly k becomes a function of x, the quantity inverted. There is no experimental basis for the assumption that the effect of the enzyme upon each molecule of substratum is the same, no matter what the concentration in substratum; and when the concentration of the substratum falls in the course of the reaction, then the available material upon which the enzyme acts being lessened, the effect upon each molecule must be increased. Therefore although the velocity of change diminishes as the mass action law indicates, on account of the diminution in unchanged material, there is a factor of increase on account of greater activity being exercised by the constant number of enzyme molecules upon each of the now smaller number of substratum molecules.[1] A second assumption which is made in applying the law $\frac{dx}{dt} = k\,(a-x)$ to enzymic action has already been alluded to in the derivation of the equation (see p. 52),—viz., that the action is taken to be irreversible, or that the tendency to reversion may be neglected.

This assumption is in all probability not experimentally justifiable, especially at the later stages of the reaction. For it does not follow that, because a reaction runs practically to completion —as, for example, that induced by invertase upon cane-sugar— therefore the effect of the *tendency* to reversion in decreasing the velocity of reaction in the late stages can be neglected.

The same causes which produce the actual reversibility seen in the case of strong solutions must be present in dilute solutions, and emphasis must be laid upon the fact that, on either side of the equilibrium point for some distance, the tendency for the reac-

---

[1] A kinetic analogy may make the contention clearer. Suppose the enzyme molecules are a fleet of battleships, firing at a number of targets which are gradually sunk as a result. Then, as the targets sink, the rate of disappearance will decrease, and provided the number of targets is large enough the rate will be proportional to the number at any instant—that is, the law $\frac{dx}{dt} = k\,(a-x)$ will hold. As the firing goes on, however, there will come in a factor of increase in the rate of sinking, because each target will be attacked by an increased number of ships.

tion to run in the opposed direction must be present and ever-increasing in amount as the equilibrium point is neared, so as to stop the reaction at the equilibrium point. Hence before the equilibrium point is reached there must be a decrease in velocity due to the tendency to reversion.

Accordingly it is not safe to assume that, because a reaction runs to 99 per cent. and over before equilibrium is reached, and is therefore regarded as a complete reaction, it will run up to 99 per cent. with the same velocity as if there were no equilibrium point and no tendency to reverse near that point.[1]

As pointed out above, Bayliss has shown that there is a tendency, at least, to reversion in the case of caseinogen and trypsin, and actual reversion has been shown with other enzymes, and even in the case of the action of acids upon disaccharides E. F. Armstrong and R. J. Caldwell have demonstrated that there is a tendency to reversal indicated by the rotation of the plane of polarised light beyond the maximum value corresponding to complete hydrolysis.

In fact, the retardation due to products of reaction which causes the velocity in the later stages to fall off from the logarithmic expression may in all cases probably be ascribed to the tendency to reversion. The usual view that the drop is due to removal of enzyme from the sphere of action by its combination with one or more of the products of reaction is not incompatible with this supposition. For just as it is supposed that, in order that the action may proceed from left to right, it is necessary for the enzyme to enter into some relationship or combination with the substratum, so it must be supposed that some such relationship is necessary with the reaction products, or one of them, in order that the reaction may proceed in the opposite direction from right to left. Nor is it any objection to the view that slowing by the products of reaction is due to the tendency to the establishment

[1] Visser (quoted by Hamburger, *Osm. Druck und Ionenlehre*, vol. iii., p. 97, 1904) found that the action of invertase upon cane-sugar was not quite complete, as always 1 per cent. of the cane sugar was left. Visser deduced a formula which gave a constant with his own results and those of Henri. In this he first, as recommended above in the text, retained the reversibility expression; and secondly, introduced a variable for the alteration in intensity of action of the enzyme throughout the reaction. The method suggested in the text for making the second of these two corrections is different from that of Visser.

of the reverse reaction, that such slowing is caused by one only of these products in each case; but rather the contrary, for the enzyme in whichever direction the reaction is going will probably act upon one of the cleavage products only, and dependently upon the relative concentrations, either attach it to the other cleavage product or detach it from it. But while there is nothing in the formation of chemical compounds between the ferment and either the substratum or one of its cleavage products to negative the view that the retardation caused by the products is anything else than the expression of a tendency to reversion, it must be pointed out that the formation of such chemical compounds is an hypothesis invented *ad hoc* to explain the retardation, and that there is no experiment as proof of the existence of such compounds.

That the enzyme enters into some relationship with the substratum, as a result of which the velocity of reaction is established or increased, is certain; and it is equally certain that the enzyme also enters into some relationship at a later stage in the reaction with one of the products of the reaction, as a result of which the reaction is slowed, or when a position is considered beyond the equilibrium point, as a result of which the action is made to proceed in the opposite direction. But it is by no means certain that this relationship is that of a chemical compound in the ordinary sense of the word; no such compounds have been isolated, there is no exact relationship pointing to any chemical combination between enzyme and substratum, and the amount of enzyme compared to that of the substratum which it can act upon at the same instant or in an exceedingly short time interval is such as to preclude in all probability the existence of a chemical compound in the ordinary sense of the term.

It is hence most probable that the influence of the enzyme as an energy transformer is one of a physical character, and at any rate the formation of chemical compounds must at present be taken as unproven. Accordingly it is much safer to make use of a point of view which leaves the question open, and to regard the retardation due to products of reaction as the sign of the tendency to reversal or influence of the products tending to react in the opposite direction, rather than being due to removal of enzyme by combination with such products in a reaction which is regarded as irreversible.

The matter becomes clearer when we consider the reaction as

proceeding in the opposite direction, as, for example, in any of the syntheses by enzymes mentioned on previous pages. Here the reaction slows down also as it nears the equilibrium point, and we might consider the slowing as due to the product of reaction, and state that this combined with the enzyme and removed it from the sphere of action. But for the reaction proceeding from left to right, it is just this combination of enzyme and product of reaction (now substratum) which is regarded as giving rise to the action of the enzyme. It is evident, then, that our explanation must be symmetrical on both sides of the equilibrium point, and that it is better to regard the relationship between enzyme and substratum on the one hand, or cleavage product on the other, as favouring the reaction in a determinate direction in each case, rather than as doing this in one case, and simply inertly removing enzyme in the other.

Returning to the mathematical consideration of a formula to suit the entire course of the reaction, it becomes clear after the above discussion that in the first place we must not remove the expression $k_2 x^2$ representing reversibility in those formulæ deduced earlier in the work, or there will be experimental obscuration in the later stages increasing as the equilibrium point is neared; and, secondly, that into the portion of each expression which represents the action of the enzyme we must introduce a factor expressing that this action is not constant throughout, but intensifies as the concentration of the substratum diminishes; and here it must be remembered that for the expression $k_1(a - x)$ the concentration of the substratum is $a - x$, and for the second expression in the equation of velocity of reaction $k_2 x^2$, the concentration of the substratum is x. In other words, the influence of the enzyme in either direction is not a constant, but is some function of the concentration of the substratum. As a simple approximation the factor introduced by Henri $\left(1 + \epsilon \dfrac{x}{a}\right)$ may be used, so that k_1 becomes $k_1\left(1 + \epsilon \dfrac{x}{a}\right)$; only it must be remembered that such a correction equally applies to the reversed reaction, and hence instead of k_2 we must put $k_2\left(1 - \epsilon_1 \dfrac{a - x}{a}\right)$, when the equation for velocity of reaction becomes

$$\frac{dx}{dt} = k_1\left(1 + \epsilon \frac{x}{a}\right)(a - x) - k_2\left(1 - \epsilon_1 \frac{a - x}{a}\right)x^2.$$

This formula is too complicated for application to experimental results on integration, but it includes all the observed experimental cases—

that is, it shows a stage when x is small where the reaction is linear, a stage where the reaction is more rapid than the simple logarithmic law demands, as in Henri's own experiments, a stage showing a falling off from the logarithmic values, as in the later stages of the experiments of Armstrong and of Bayliss, a zero stage at the equilibrium point, a reversed velocity, which also at the very end tends to become linear.

To make the investigation of the equation easier,[1] we may suppose, since Henri found experimentally that the value of e was approximately unity, that $e = e_1 = 1$, when the equation becomes

$$\frac{dx}{dt} = k_1 \left(1 + \frac{x}{a} \right) (a - x) - k_2 \left(1 - \frac{a - x}{a} \right) x^2.$$

This may be written

$$\frac{dx}{dt} = k_1(a - x) + \frac{x}{a}[k_1(a - x) - k_2 x^2],$$

and in this form we may now investigate how the velocity—that is, the value of $\frac{dx}{dt}$—will vary at different stages of the reaction.

First, let the value of x be small compared with a as in the earlier stages of the reaction, then x^2 and higher powers of x may be neglected as small magnitudes of the second or higher orders and the equation reduces to

$$\frac{dx}{dt} = k_1(a - x) + x . k_1 = a k_1.$$

That is, the velocity of reaction is constant, and the curve expressing it is linear.

Secondly, for higher values of x (that is, later in the reaction), but where x is not yet large compared to $(a - x)$, since k_2 is small compared to k_1, $k_2 x^2$ is small compared to $k_1(a - x)$ and may be neglected when the formula becomes

$$\frac{dx}{dt} = k_1(a - x) + \frac{x}{a} . k_1(a - x).$$

This may be written

$$\frac{dx}{dt} = k_1 \left(1 + \frac{x}{a} \right) (a - x),$$

which is Henri's formula—that is to say, during this period when $k_2 x^2$ is small compared to $k_1(a - x)$, or, in other words, when reversion may still be neglected, Henri's formula holds. The curve of velocity shows a greater value than is given by the simple logarithmic law, and the

[1] The same results follow with the formula as it stands, only the expressions are more complicated.

" *constant* " calculated on the simple logarithmic basis will increase in this stage of the reaction, while a " *constant* " calculated on the above formula will remain approximately constant.

As x goes on increasing, however, the value of k_2x^2 will cease to be negligible as compared with $k_1(a - x)$, and in the end $k_1(a - x)$ will become less than k_2x^2, when the expression within the square brackets will become negative in value. Just around the point where $k_2x^2 = k_1(a - x)$, the simple logarithmic law will approximately hold, for then the expression in square brackets will be almost zero and negligible in comparison to $k_1(a - x)$, so that the equation becomes $\frac{dx}{dt} = k_1(a - x)$, which yields the simple logarithmic formula. But as x goes on increasing, and $a - x$ diminishing, it is obvious that the negative value of the expression in square brackets will rapidly increase, and that the reaction will proceed much more slowly with ever-increasing deviation from the logarithmic law.

Finally, the reaction will come into equilibrium, and beyond this point will be reversed

For the reversed reaction *near the end-point*, since $a - x$ is small compared to x and hence $\frac{a}{x} = 1$, the equation becomes $\frac{dx}{dt} = k_2a^2$, or the velocity of reaction is constant and the curve expressing it a straight line as at the beginning of the reaction Since, however, the whole of the reversed stage is short, and an appreciable amount of $a - x$ relatively to x is soon formed since the reaction runs $\frac{dx}{dt} = k_2x^2$, and x is here large, the straight line portion on this side is infinitely short and cannot be demonstrated experimentally

The equation given above hence serves to demonstrate that the law governing the reaction is the same throughout, and that the deviations from the logarithmic law arise from the assumptions having been made in the derivation of that law—(1) that reversibility can be neglected, and (2) that the intensity of action of the enzyme, per molecule of substratum, can be taken as constant throughout the reaction.

EFFECTS ON VELOCITY OF REACTION OF ALTERATIONS IN THE CONCENTRATION OF ENZYME.

The effects of variation in the amount of enzyme initially added upon the velocity of reaction, in the case of the sucroclastic enzymes and of trypsin, have been already mentioned in describing the experiments upon the course of the reaction. Experiments upon this question, to be comparable with one another, should be made under such conditions that the concentration of the sub-stratum remains constant throughout the experiment. Otherwise the ratio of enzyme and substratum is continually varying during the experiment, and the effect of variation in concentration of enzyme is not obtained pure, but a combination of this with variation in concentration of substratum. Also the effects of accumulation of products of reaction must be avoided. Hence the ideal condition is that in which there is excess of solid substratum, the products of action are continuously removed by dialysis, and the enzyme is present in constant strength throughout each experiment. Such an arrangement as is suggested, for example, by Bayliss, of a bell-jar filled with solid gelatine containing the enzyme and dialysing into a larger vessel (the bell-jar being attached to one end of a lever which records the rapidity of action by the loss in weight, and writes a record on a smoked paper surface) would be an ideal arrangement for such a purpose, on the supposition that the enzyme did not dialyse out, as would probably be found to be realised within the experimental limits, as the rate of dialysis of enzymes is so slow.

Such experiments have, however, not been yet carried out, and the next best are those in which the observations have been recorded at the initial stages of the reaction where the amount of substratum has been large and not very widely varied before the measurement has been taken, and especially those in which, where possible, a solid substratum has been employed.

As Bredig has pointed out, the result would be more certain, and more definite conclusions could be drawn if, in such experiments, instead of measuring the different amounts of substratum converted in *equal* times by varying amounts of enzyme, determinations were made of the varying intervals of time necessary to convert the same percentage of substratum as the concentration of enzyme is changed. For in the latter case whatever the law may be governing the course of the reaction, and as we have seen above this may be somewhat complicated, since the reaction in such case runs to the same stage, in deducing the ratio of the increases in velocity, due to the two different concentrations of enzyme, this complicated factor eliminates out, being the same in each case, and the ratio in the activation by the two quantities of enzyme is simply inversely proportional to the two time-intervals for production of the same percentage change.

While it must be admitted that this method of varying time-interval and constant percentage of conversion is the more scientific, it must, however, be stated that it is in most cases of zymolytic action most difficult or impossible to carry out experimentally. For in most such cases we have no indicator to show when a certain definite percentage of the total change has occurred, and a somewhat elaborate method of determination must be introduced[1] in order to discover the state of affairs in the solution, so that the experimenter is reduced to making measurements at definite time-intervals instead of at definite amounts of conversion Nor will it do to take the end-point of the reaction in most cases on account of the slowness with which that point is reached, although in certain cases where the end-point has special physical or chemical characteristics this has been used—as, for example, the coagulation point for an enzyme such as rennin, or the disappearance of the colour test with iodine in the case of starch and diastase

It may be further added that in many cases the objections of Bredig have little practical weight—as, for example, where solid substratum is used in determining activity in varying concentration of proteoclastic enzymes, or where the amount of substratum is initially large compared to the amount of enzyme, and the measurements are taken early in the course of the reaction before there is any large alteration in percentage of the substratum. In such cases none of the variations in the reaction detailed above occur in the short stage of reaction utilised for the determinations, and the degree of activation by the enzyme may be safely taken as directly proportional to the amounts converted in equal times

The law connecting velocity of action and concentration of the enzyme varies with the nature of the enzyme. In many cases where the question has been accurately examined in recent times, the ordinary law which applies to inorganic catalysts applies also to enzymes—viz., that the effect is in simple direct proportion to the concentration in enzyme. There is this difference, however, in the

---

[1] This does not apply to the electrical conductivity method of Bayliss, who has utilised the method suggested by Bredig, and determined the times at which equal changes in conductivity occur

case of enzymes, that a maximum is soon reached beyond which further addition of enzyme produces no noticeable effect whatever, and it is hardly necessary to add that for concentrations somewhat short of the maximum, the linear law does not hold, as the linear portion of the curve gradually rounds off to the asymptotic line which marks the maximum velocity with increasing concentration. Having regard to the high molecular weight which enzymes possess and correspondingly low molecular concentration, and also the low percentage amount present when the maximum amount of increased effect with concentration is obtained, we have here incontrovertible evidence of a difference in mode of action of enzymes and inorganic catalysts—such, for example, as sucroclastic enzymes and the hydrogen ion of acids. Here the sucroclastic enzyme is already in possession of its maximum effect at a molecular concentration, at which the action of the hydrogen ion is practically imperceptible, and the hydrogen ion goes on increasing in effect, as the concentration is increased, at a rate considerably greater than corresponds to the increased ionic concentration, while the action of the enzyme remains at a constant level.

The enzymes which within the limits indicated above obey the law of direct proportionality between concentration and activity are: Invertase (O'Sullivan and Tompson, Henri, E. R. Armstrong), Rennin (Segelcke u. Storch, Soxhlet, Lörcher, Duclaux, Fuld), Lipase (Kastle u. Loewenhart), Trypsin (Bayliss).

In the case of other ferments, however, although the same falling off to a maximum value at an upper limit, at which the percentage of ferment is still very low, is observed in all cases, it is found that even well below this limit of maximum effect the linear law is not obeyed of direct proportionality between concentration of enzyme and intensity of action.

In most such cases, the majority of experimenters have arrived at the conclusion that the law first empirically deduced from experiments upon pepsin by E. Schütz, and known as " Schütz's law," is that which best expresses the effects of concentration upon intensity of action within a certain range. The law is that the intensity is directly proportional to the square root of the concentration, or put conversely, that the relative concentrations of enzyme are directly proportional to the squares of the intensities (that is, the amounts changed in equal times). Expressed in an equation, if k_1 and k_2 are the velocity constants (or quantities converted in equal times) at two different concentrations of enzyme c_1 and c_2, then " Schütz's law " is that

$$\frac{k_1}{k_2} = \left(\frac{c_1}{c_2}\right)^{\frac{1}{2}}, \text{ or } \frac{c_1}{c_2} = \left(\frac{k_1}{k_2}\right)^2.$$

The law has been most worked out in the case of pepsin by E. Schütz, J Schütz, Huppert and J. Schütz, and Borissow; but according to Pawlow and his co-workers, using Mett's method, it also holds for the tryptic and diastatic enzymes of the pancreas, in addition to pepsin.

The whole subject, however, deserves to be thoroughly worked out anew, for there is a want of concordance in methods and results amongst the different workers, who have not only employed different methods and different stages in the reaction for different enzymes, but also for the same enzyme. Thus in the case of trypsin Bayliss finds, as stated above, that the law at any rate for dilute solutions is approximately a linear one, while Pawlow, using a different method (Mett's), finds the " Schütz law " followed. Again, while Huppert and J. Schütz found the Schütz law followed for not too concentrated solutions on using dissolved proteid (egg albumin), they found with the Mett's tube method on coagulated egg albumin, that this law was not obeyed, but rather that the length of albumin dissolved was nearly directly proportional to the concentration in enzyme On the other hand, Borissow, using the Mett's method, found that pepsin in its action in dissolving coagulated egg-white obeyed Schutz's law

In the writer's own experience with the Mett's method, and active preparations of commercial pepsin of various origin, the Schutz's law is by no means followed. With stronger solutions, the length of egg-white dissolved off is approximately equal, as the concentration in enzyme is diminished, the intensity of action falls off very slowly, much less than in direct linear proportion, but there is no period at which the Schütz law is closely obeyed, and with very dilute solutions the length of egg-white is so little as not to be accurately measurable, so that the method is useless for testing very dilute solutions. Even in stronger solutions the slowness of fluid diffusion in the narrow tubes tending to accumulation of products of digestion at the active interface, and the irregularity with which the column of egg-white is eaten away, form grave objections to the employment of this oft-described method.

The explanation of the " Schütz law " is that it holds for a certain range only, and in this range is an empirical law which gives an approximation to the truth.

The conclusion may therefore be drawn that in the case of each enzyme, there is in dilute solutions a range of concentration throughout which the activity increases approximately directly as the concentration, and as the concentration increases a further period in which there is also an increase but at a less rapid rate than the concentration, and that finally a maximum effect is obtained beyond which increasing the concentration has no action in increasing the activity.

CHAPTER XII

INFLUENCE OF OTHER FACTORS UPON ENZYMES AND CELLS

TEMPERATURE—PHYSICAL AND CHEMICAL AGENTS—NEGATIVE
CATALYSTS, ANTI-CATALYSTS, ANTI-FERMENTS, AND ANTI-
ENZYMES—ZYMO-EXCITATORS OR KINASES—AUTO-CATALYSIS
AND INFECTION—SPECIFIC NATURE OF CATALYTIC ACTION—
THE CHEMICAL AND PHYSICAL NATURE OF ENZYMES—THE SO-
CALLED INORGANIC ENZYMES OR METAL-SOLS.

It is characteristic of all enzymes that they are very sensitive to
changes of temperature both as regards their stability and as
regards their rapidity of action.

The stability of the different enzymes varies very widely, but
as a general rule it may be stated that the rate of destruction
rapidly increases with the temperature, although this may lie much
below that at which they are most rapidly destroyed. The amount
of enzyme destroyed also varies with the substances present in
solution; thus the products of reaction in all cases exercise a protective action against rise in temperature which has been ascribed
to the formation of a compound between the enzyme and the
products of its activity.

All enzymes in aqueous solution are rapidly destroyed at about
the coagulation temperature of proteids (65° to 75° C.) and a
coagulum usually appears in the solution.

Even at body temperature and below it many are, however,
rapidly destroyed, especially in the absence of a protective substratum. Thus Vernon has shown that trypsin in nearly pure
solution is rapidly destroyed at 38° C., but is protected from such
rapid destruction by the presence of protein. The subject has
been further investigated by Bayliss, who finds that trypsin in
solution slowly loses activity even at 0° C.

The action of heat upon enzymes in organic solvents is much
less marked than in aqueous solutions; thus Pavy found that
the diastatic ferments of the liver and pancreas are not destroyed

by boiling in alcoholic solution, and Fermi and Pernossi that enzymes are only slowly acted upon in amyl alcohol solutions.

In the dried condition it has been shown that some enzymes can be heated to as high as 160° C. without losing their activity.

Exposure to low temperatures does not appear to have any marked effect upon enzymes.

With regard to the effect of alterations of temperature upon the rapidity of action of ferments, it is found that each ferment is most active at a temperature called the *optimum* temperature, which varies in the case of each ferment, and also in the same ferment with the conditions of solution, presence of neutral salts, reaction, and temperature to which the solution has previously been exposed. As a general rule the optimum temperature lies between 35° and 45° C., but according to Roberts the action of trypsin increases even up to 60° C., at which temperature it is, however, rapidly destroyed.

It is stated by Bredig that the existence of the optimum temperature and the decrease in rapidity of reaction at higher temperatures than the optimum is due to two opposing factors. The first factor is the increase in reaction velocity which rise in temperature always occasions, and the second is the destruction of a portion of the enzyme which gradually occurs, more rapidly as the temperature is increased, and finally outbalances the positive effect due to increased temperature *per se*. Ernst working in Bredig's laboratory tested the rate of action of Bredig's platinsol upon water-gas, and found conformably to this view that it also possessed an optimum temperature of action, the exact position of which varied with the previous history of the platinsol, the period during which it had been kept at the higher temperature previously to starting the reaction, etc.

Accordingly it would appear that the optimum temperature is not a peculiar characteristic of enzymes, but depends upon their instability at the optimum temperature and above it. It must be added, however, that in presence of their appropriate substrata, some ferments are very stable at their temperature of optimum activity—*e.g.*, pepsin—the rate of destruction being practically inappreciable, and hence it appears to the writer that although Bredig's view may hold in some cases it is not a universal explanation of the existence of an optimum temperature of action for all ferments.

The temperature coefficient—that is, the variation in the velocity constant with the temperature—which is usually expressed for each 10° C., has been measured by Bayliss in the case of trypsin. It was found that it required 5·3 times as long to effect an equal change at 20·7° C. as at 30·7° C.; between 30·7° C. and 38·7° C. the ratio of velocities was 2·6 : 1, giving 3·3 as the coefficient for an interval of 10° C.; also a determination of the velocity of 0° C. gave a coefficient for each 10° interval between 0° C. and 30° C. of 12. In the case of emulsin, between 60° and 70°, Tammann found for the temperature coefficient the value of 7·14, and Senter for the peroxidase of blood the value of 1·5, between 0° C. and 10° C.

The living cell in its reaction to temperature changes, in so far as it is not controlled in the higher animals by the temperature regulating mechanism, obeys exactly the same laws as the enzyme. Its activity is only possible, as in the case of the enzyme, between certain well-defined limits, which vary from cell to cell, as from enzyme to enzyme, and somewhere in the range there is an optimum point of maximum activity which is variable under like conditions as in the case of the enzyme. Also at the point of maximum activity, the living cell is working above its safety point, and prolonged action at this level leads to a breakdown in the cell's activity and to death.

There is an apparent exception in the case of warm-blooded animals in the fact that a slight fall in temperature leads to increased activity, but this is merely due to the action of one cell upon another, to stimulation by the nervous system; and when on account of continued fall in temperature the regulatory mechanism is overcome, the cells of the warm-blooded animal obey the general law just as do those of cold-blooded animals.

On account of the regulatory mechanism, as a result of the action of which the cells of the warm-blooded animals are rarely exposed to any appreciable variations in temperature, the cells have lost their power to respond to temperature variations throughout so wide a range, the minimum and maximum points are close together, and so arises the great danger of temperature variations after the regulating mechanism has been overpowered by greater than normal variations in temperature of external surroundings.

It is, therefore, in unicellular organisms, and in the earlier stages of development of multicellular organisms, that the variation in activity with alteration in temperature is most clearly seen. Here it is found that at a certain minimal temperature the activity just begins to be perceptible, as the temperature rises the activity increases with it until an optimum point is reached, lying usually, as in the case of the enzyme, a few degrees above the usual temperature of the action of the organism, and beyond the optimum temperature the life of the organism becomes again more sluggish, its activities lessened, and if the high temperature is maintained it dies. The optimum point of activity for the living cell probably arises in the same manner as in the case of some enzymes, by the simultaneous action of two opposing causes—viz., (1) the hastening of all chemical reactions by rise in the temperature, (2) a similar hastening from the same cause of the by-reactions which lead to a using up and diminishing of the cell substances which act as catalysts to these reactions. As a result of this it follows that in the earlier stages of the range of temperature, as the temperature rises, the chemical reactions in the cell will increase in velocity, while as yet there will be no appreciable destruction of the more stable cell substance, or of the catalysts. But in the later stages, at the optimum point and beyond it, destruction of catalysts, cellular enzymes, and cell substance will also proceed at an ever-increasing rate, and although the velocity of reaction of the catalysed reactions is still increasing, the diminution in concentration of catalyst more than outbalances this, and the cell activities are lessened.

The same differences are to be noted at the two extreme ends of the range in the case of enzymes and living cells; as the temperature falls, the enzyme and living cell merely become dormant and temporarily pass out of activity, but neither is killed unless the fall in temperature is enormous compared to the rise in temperature which would cause total permanent loss of activity or death upon the other side of the active range. Nor is the reason far to seek; the lower limit is reached by gradual fall in activity until the zero point is reached, while the upper limit is reached by gradual increase in activity, accompanied by gradual destruction finally surpassing increase in activity, until the cell stops from destruction in hyper-activity.

The level at which living cells are *rapidly* destroyed by increased temperature closely resembles that at which enzymes are similarly destroyed, and lies around the coagulation temperature of proteins. As in the case of enzymes, the point varies with the nature of the cell, some cells being more resistant than others. The resistance appears to vary inversely as the state of activity of the cell, inactive spores being more resistant than the active cells.[1] As in the case of enzymes, the amount of water present has a powerful effect upon the rate of destruction. Dried bacteria, and their spores in the dried condition, can be raised to temperatures above the boiling-point for an appreciable time without destruction, although in suspension in aqueous fluids they are readily destroyed by such a temperature; and dried seeds can be exposed to low temperatures without injury, while in the moist condition they lose their vitality. The latter effect is probably a physical one due to disruption of the cell by the expansion of the water in freezing.

Influence of various Physical and Chemical Agencies on Enzymes and Living Cells.

Many enzymes are rapidly destroyed in aqueous solution by sunlight. The subject has been investigated in the case of the diastases by Green, who found that all parts of the spectrum are not equally active in this respect; the most active part is the ultra-violet, but the green rays are also destructive. Certain portions of the red, orange, and blue appear at first to increase the amount of diastase, but this positive effect soon disappears and is followed by a destructive action. Green ascribes the first stage to a conversion of zymogen into active enzyme. The different diastases are not equally affected: thus the destruction in the case of malt diastase amounted to 68 per cent., in salivary diastase to 45 per cent., while diastase from green leaves was only affected to the extent of 8 per cent., but in this latter case it is probable that the chlorophyll acted as a protective.

A similar action is seen in the case of the living cell in the marked germicidal action of sunlight upon bacteria of many kinds, and in the higher animals in the subtle influence of sunlight in the preservation of a normal physiological condition of the body; in the formation and action of pigment cells; in the powerful effect upon epidermal cells of sunlight apart from the heating effect; in the probable effects of insufficient sunlight, in producing the cretinism found in the inhabitants of certain valleys; in the effects

---

[1] The more active an enzyme preparation is the more rapidly it is destroyed by variations in external conditions.

of light under certain conditions in producing ophthalmia. Here may be mentioned also the action of various other forms of radiant energy upon living cells, such as the X rays and Finsen rays, and the radiations of radium, which act as such powerful stimulants upon living cells.

Action of Acids and Alkalies and of Neutral Salts upon Enzymes and Living Cells.—In considering the value of foodstuffs such as protein, carbohydrates, and fats as sources of energy to the body, we are too apt to forget that energy is not the only thing required, and that in order to use this energy, the integrity of the mechanism for its conversion or transformation—viz., the living cell—is no less important. For the preservation of this integrity, the simple inorganic salts, and a due proportionality between acid and alkali, are no less important, and such simple substances are no less indispensable than the organic foodstuffs. It has been shown by Ringer and others that normal physiological activity is not possible in the presence of the organic or energy-yielding constituents alone, that these may be present in abundance, and yet the tissue be entirely incapable of functionating unless it is also fed with certain inorganic constituents. Ringer further showed in the case of the frog's heart that there must be a certain balance maintained between the various inorganic constituents, that sodium chloride alone could not maintain the activity, but that it was necessary to have present both potassium and calcium in certain balanced proportions. Working on the basis of his experiments, he devised " Ringer's solution," containing these substances in the proper concentrations for the preservation of physiological activity, which has since, in various modifications, been employed by most subsequent workers on the subject.

The work begun by Ringer has been continued by many workers, and extended into observation of the effects of variation of the inorganic salts, and of acids and alkalies, not only upon a maintenance of physiological activity, which was the problem chiefly studied by Ringer, but also of the effects upon rapidity of cell growth and division and of reproduction.

The physiological balance of salt solutions first discovered and investigated by Ringer, in the case of the frog's heart, was later extended by him to skeletal muscle and to marine organisms, and shown by the same observer to be a general law.

The valuable results obtained by many independent later

observers show the immense importance to the growth and activity of living cells of their inorganic constituents, and this division of biochemistry is rapidly acquiring an immense literature of its own.[1]

In such an action due to variation in inorganic salts, the writer believes that the key will ultimately be found to the secret of the cause of irregular cell division in the body, giving rise to malignant growths. For the production of what must be described as a pathological division in unfertilised eggs, and the production of pathological cell divisions such as have been noted by Galleoti by the action of inorganic salts such as the iodides, must be problems of the same order as the causation of the ungoverned and pathological divisions, often of very similar type, found in malignant growths.

As a general rule it may be stated that for the same enzyme the intensity of action of a given concentration of an alkali or acid varies approximately directly as the concentration in $\overset{-}{HO}$ or $\overset{+}{H}$ ions, the effect of the other ion being only of secondary importance. Thus in all cases free alkalies such as sodium or potassium hydrate are many times more powerful than the corresponding carbonates in consequence of their almost complete ionisation as contrasted with the low ionisation of the carbonates.[2] Again, ammonia, which is but feebly ionised (about $\frac{1}{88}$ of that of sodium hydrate) has a correspondingly feeble destructive action. The same holds in the case of acids, the effect here being mainly due to the hydrogen ion; thus organic acids solutions, such as acetic, which are only ionised to the extent of 2 or 3 per cent., have a correspondingly weak destructive effect, while inorganic acids, such as hydrochloric, which in dilute solution are almost completely ionised, break up the enzymes with great rapidity.

The degree of resistance as compared in different ferments is subject to wide variation, dependent doubtless upon the chemical constitution of the different enzymes, and arising usually from the environment in which the enzyme has been developed. The

---

[1] Another class of substances, organic in nature but not acting through transformations of organic energy, are the " accessory food factors." For a most excellent account of these the reader is referred to the Special Report Series of Medical Research Council, No. 38, H.M. Stationery Office, 1919.

[2] In decinormal solutions sodium carbonate has only about 3 per cent. of the concentration in hydroxyl ions found in sodium hydrate (Shields, *Zeitsch. f. physik. Chem.*, vol. xii., p. 167).

most exceptional enzyme in this respect is pepsin, which is most active in a concentration of acid (*i.e.*, of hydrogen ion) which would be almost instantly destructive to nearly all other enzymes.

The great majority of enzymes are produced and act in media of alkaline reaction, and although in certain instances it has been shown that even in the case of these ferments the degree of activity is increased by a slight decrease in hydroxyl ion and increase in hydrogen ion beyond their usual normal reaction, there is no doubt that they act well in fluids of alkaline reaction, and according to some observers are at their maximum activity in such media.

While there is no doubt that all the enzymes occurring in alkaline media in the body are quickly paralysed in their action and rapidly destroyed by more than the merest trace of free acid, and also, that a slight trace of *free* alkali above the amount necessary to form bicarbonate with the carbonic acid present has a similar effect; there is much difference of opinion in the literature of the subject as regards the point of optimum action of each ferment. The subject is made very hazy by the fact that earlier workers, not realising that the all-important point was the concentration in the solutions tested of the hydroxyl and hydrogen ion, have worked indiscriminately with free alkalies in some cases and carbonates in others.

It is interesting to observe that the same effect of acids and alkalies, and the same dependence upon hydroxyl and hydrogen ions, is observable in the case of living cells as has been described above in the case of the enzymes.

The rate of growth and cell division, and the regularity of the latter process, are dependent in large measure upon the reaction of the medium which bathes and permeates the cell. Solutions of various neutral salts in addition have a marked influence upon cell growth and upon the maintenance of a physiological condition of normal metabolism in the cell, but it is the alkalies and acids, and these proportionately to their concentration in hydroxyl and hydrogen ions, which exercise the profoundest influence.

A normal balance in the ratio of hydroxyl and hydrogen ions must be maintained, or the whole of the metabolism and life of the cell becomes abnormal and morbid.

The position of pioneer in this subject must be ascribed, as mentioned above, to Sidney Ringer, who first showed the enormous importance of even minute doses of certain inorganic salts in

14

maintaining a normal condition and proper performance of physiological functions in living cells.

Ringer, working before the advent and about the time of the introduction of the modern ionic theory of solutions, did not express his results in the language of that theory, and spoke of " the action of calcium or of lime of potassium or of potash salts," instead of, as in modern terminology, " the effects of molecular concentration of the calcium or potassium ion," and of the effects of acids and alkalies instead of those of hydrogen and hydroxyl ions   But there is no doubt that Ringer thoroughly appreciated that the effects he obtained were due to the one ion of the combination he used although he did not speak of it by that name, and that he recognised without naming them as such the antagonistic action of different ions

It is necessary to point out the importance of this early and classical work of Ringer's, because it appears to be in danger of becoming forgotten by modern workers, who often do not refer to him in their account of previous work, and appear to use " Ringer's solution," or modifications of it, with little knowledge of its history, or of the fact that Ringer by its use had shown the all-importance of ions for the maintenance of physiological activity, and had demonstrated the action of sodium, potassium, and calcium ions, and recognised it though not by name as ionic activity, when yet the ionisation theory had obtained but little credence

Ringer's experiments upon the effects of acids and alkalies were, however, confined to the action of these in maintaining physiological activity, and it remained for Loeb to demonstrate upon the fertilised eggs of the sea-urchin that the rate of growth is appreciably increased by very minute amounts of alkali added to the sea water, larger amounts stopping the growth entirely.

The writer, led to the subject from its relationship to malignant growth, by the fact that the secretion of the acid in gastric juice was suppressed or diminished, and the alkalinity of the blood increased in cancer, has carried out, in conjunction with H E Roaf and E Whitley, a series of observations on the effects of acids and alkalies, and of acid and alkaline salts upon the rate of growth and character of the cell division in the fertilised eggs of *Echinus esculentus*.

It was found that a mere trace of added sodium hydrate—viz.,

$\frac{1}{1000}$ normal[1]—increased markedly the growth even in the earlier stages, and not merely after one or two days, as Loeb had previously found, while the addition of half as much more sodium hydrate practically stopped the growth altogether, the cells not proceeding beyond the four-cell stage. Addition of double the quantity, $\frac{1}{500}$ normal, stopped the growth entirely. Addition of hydrochloric acid slowed the growth from the beginning, and at $\frac{1}{800}$ normal the growth was stopped entirely, all the cells remaining in the single-cell stage.

The action of alkaline and acid salts, such as the phosphates and carbonates, corresponding to their lessened concentration in hydroxyl or hydrogen ions, was less effective, and these salts had to be added in greater concentration.

In addition to the alteration in rate of growth, it was found that the addition of alkali, in more than the minimal concentration of $\frac{1}{1000}$ normal, led to marked irregularity in the size and shape of the cell, and to irregular nuclear division. In the large undivided cells, multiple nuclei were found, and many division figures were seen with the chromatin reduced in quantity, and in number of chromosomes. In many cases division with three and four centrosomes was observed.

In the cells to which acid has been added, no such increase in nuclei was observed, nor nuclear division figures, and in many cases the chromatin appeared to have been acted upon chemically and to have disappeared.

The experiments illustrate the extreme sensitiveness of the living cell to variations in concentration of the hydroxyl and hydrogen ion, and the importance of a normal reaction of the medium for cell growth and division

Action of Antiseptics and Protoplasmic Poisons.

There is here a great *quantitative* difference in action upon enzyme and living cell respectively, which probably has for its cause the more complex and highly organised chemical structure of the cell, causing it to enter more readily into combination with the antiseptic. That the difference is a quantitative and not a qualitative one, however, is shown clearly by many experiments which go to prove

[1] That is, 1 c.c. of $\frac{N}{10}$ alkali per 100 c c. of sea water: this amounts to only 1 part by weight of sodium hydrate in 25,000 parts by volume of sea water.

that many of those substances which affect cells, and either render them inert or permanently destroy them, have in greater concentration a similar action upon enzymes. Thus alcohol, chloroform, salicylic acid, carbolic acid, thymol, and sodium fluoride, which were at one time regarded as affecting living cells only and without action upon enzymes, have now been shown by various observers to more or less retard the action of enzymes also, and to destroy them in greater concentration, although the action varies in degree in different instances and is always less than that upon the cell The greater degree of action of such substances upon cells has been often taken advantage of as an experimental aid in observing the nature and products of reactions of enzymes, especially of those proteoclastic enzymes which act in an alkaline medium. For such substances stop the growth of the putrefactive bacteria at a concentration in which they have little action upon enzymes. This experimental use of antiseptic agents was first made by Kuhne in studying the products of action of trypsin. In choosing such an antiseptic, one ought to be selected which possesses a strong action upon cells, but as little as possible upon enzymes, and one which is now often used for the purpose on this account is toluol Another substance said to be almost without action on enzymes, but most toxic for cells, is hydrocyanic acid; it stops, however, the property of acting upon hydrogen peroxide which is common to nearly all enzymes Such substances as antiseptics and anæsthetics produce their effects by combination with protein or protoplasm, and since all enzymes and cells must be allied in consisting of colloids related in character to protein, it is evident that an ideal substance which will affect the cell and not the enzyme is an impossibility. As a result, we have no hard-and-fast criterion as to whether a given effect is produced by an enzyme or a living cell, except where living cells can be ruled out by microscopic examination. For, while active cells are thrown out of activity by protoplasmic poisons much more readily than enzymes, there exists, bridging over the interval, the sporing form of the cell, which shows the same resistance to the chemical reagents that we have already seen in the case of changes in temperature.

The only true test is that of being able to grow and produce the cell in pure culture, and then obtain with it the previously observed chemical or biological effect. Unfortunately, this in many instances fails, notably in the case of many of the commonest infectious diseases, and we are left unable to trace with certainty the causation of the disease to any particular micro-organism

A good example of this is to be met with in the case of ordinary vaccine. As is now well known, thanks to the labours of Copeman and of Green, this can be kept in contact with glycerine, or, better, with chloroform water, until all extraneous organisms have perished, and nothing can be grown from the preparation in culture media; yet the virus is still present in almost unabated power, as is shown by obtaining the typical effect on vaccination.

The virus may here either be a very resistant spore, which remains alive after all the other organisms have been destroyed by the chloroform, which cannot be cultivated upon ordinary nutrient media, and only commences to develop in the serum of the living body after vaccination, or it may be that the virus of vaccine, as suggested by the writer,[1] is an enzyme with the property of reproducing itself in the manner indicated under the heading of autocatalysis.

The theory of infection held at the present day includes as an axiom that all infection must be carried by micro-organisms or parasites. Now, although this has been incontrovertibly demonstrated in many cases, in just as many others, and these including the most common infectious diseases, in spite of innumerable attempts no causal connection with any definite parasite or micro-organism has been shown to exist.

If the above-mentioned axiom is granted, then it follows that vaccine prepared with chloroform must contain an undemonstrable living germ, but otherwise the experimental evidence is far more strongly in favour of the virus being an enzyme, reproducing itself in the manner described under Autocatalysis.

At any rate for the present, the case may serve as an example of how difficult it often is to decide whether a given action is the result of an enzyme or a living cell, because the same agencies which affect one similarly affect the other.

NEGATIVE CATALYSTS.

The catalysts which we have hitherto been considering are those which, by their action in diminishing resistance, increase the velocity of a reaction, but a number of substances are known

[1] " A Chemical Theory as to the Propagation and Development of certain Infectious Diseases," *The Journal of State Medicine*, April, 1904.

which increase the resistance and so diminish the velocity of the reaction without being changed themselves in the process. Such bodies have been termed by Ostwald negative catalysts. In the language of our formulæ these bodies diminish the value of k, the constant of reaction velocity. That these substances are truly catalytic in their action is demonstrated by the extremely minute quantities necessary to slow the reaction in comparison with the quantities of substratum acted upon. Thus Bigelow has shown that the presence of such a minimal trace of mannite as 0 000,001,4 grm. per cubic centimetre reduces the velocity of oxidation of 800 times as great an amount of sodium sulphite in solution by one-half, and S W. Young has shown that the oxidation of stannous chloride or sodium sulphite is similarly reduced by mere traces of many organic substances, such as nicotine, brucine, morphine, quinine, aniline, mannite, and potassium cyanide. As first shown by Graham, the oxidation or ignition of phosphorus is also prevented by traces of organic substances, such as turpentine, alcohol, ether, and ethyl iodide.

The number of such negative catalysts known to us is not so large as that of those which increase the velocity, but this is perhaps due to the fact that the interest and attention of the chemist have been chiefly directed towards those substances which cause or hasten reaction rather than to such as stop or retard it.

We have already seen that the reactions caused by enzymes do not proceed with a measurable velocity in the absence of the enzymes, in fact, do not appear to occur at all, and hence there is no necessity for the existence of negative enzymes in the body, and none such have hitherto been described.

It will be pointed out later that the existence of negative catalysts, as has been urged by Ostwald, is a point of evidence against the view that the mode of action of catalysts is *in all cases* by the formation of intermediate compounds.

Anticatalysts, Antiferments, and Anti-enzymes.

Under the name of " Anti-catalysers," or " Paralysers," Bredig has designated those substances which by their presence in small quantity retard or stop the action of a catalyst Such bodies differ from the " negative catalysts " mentioned above in that they do not retard the reaction by directly acting upon the substratum, but by acting upon a positive catalyst which is present and preventing or retarding its action. Bredig places these substances in analogy with the antitoxins. Strictly speaking, all those substances ought to be placed in this group, which have already been described above as affecting enzyme action, such as acids and alkalies, neutral salts, anæsthetics and antiseptics; but it is better to reserve the term, if it is to be used at all, for substances which act after the fashion of catalysts of a second order, so to speak, in quantities small compared to the amount of the primary catalyst.

An example of such an action is the " paralysis " of the action of solutions of colloidal platinum upon hydrogen peroxide, by the addition of traces of hydrocyanic acid. Thus, Bredig, Müller von Berneck, and Ikeda found that the addition of 0·000,000,001 grm. hydrocyanic acid per cubic centimetre to a colloidal platinum solution containing 0·000,006 grm. platinum per cubic centimetre reduced the intense action of the platinsol upon hydrogen peroxide to half its original value. Here it is to be noted that although the quantities of both platinum and hydrocyanic acid are small, that of the platinum is 6000 times as large as the hydrocyanic acid; hence there is no stoichiometric relationship, and the action cannot be ascribed to any chemical combination in definite molecular relationship between the colloidal platinum and the hydrocyanic acid. The paralysing effect of the hydrocyanic acid can be removed by passing a stream of air through the solution and so removing the hydrocyanic acid. The " recovery " shows that the catalyst is not destroyed by the " poison " of the anticatalyst but only inhibited during its presence.

The catalytic action of platinum upon hydrogen peroxide or water gas is also anticatalysed by traces of many substances, of which the following list is given by Bredig: Iodine, mercuric chloride, hydrogen sulphide, sodium thiosulphate, carbon monoxide, phosphorus, hydrogen phosphide, hydrogen arsenide, mercuric cyanide, carbon bisulphide.

In this group must also be placed the antiferments or antienzymes which have been shown to exist in the case of the majority of the enzymes. These have usually been obtained by the process of injection into an animal of solutions containing the enzyme in question for a period, and then separating the animal's serum and demonstrating that it contains a substance capable of stopping the action of the enzyme.

The first anti-enzyme was shown to exist by Morgenroth in

the case of antirennin (" Antilab "); he obtained it in a similar
fashion to an antitoxin by injection of increasing doses of rennet
solution, and found that both the serum and the milk of the injected animal possessed in a high degree the power of preventing
the coagulation of caseinogen by the action of rennin. Antibodies have since been obtained to pepsin, trypsin, fibrin ferment,
laccase, urease, and tyrosinase

It has been urged that this reaction of the tissue cells to ferments shows that the toxins of disease and various poisons of
animal and vegetable source act similarly to enzymes, and produce
their effect in a similar catalytic fashion, until their action is paralysed by the production by the tissue cells of the appropriate
antitoxin   Although there is no doubt whatever as to the production of the antitoxins and of the anti-enzymes, we do not yet
know enough regarding the processes to generalise as to the action
of toxins and enzymes being the same, and the wide generality
in the reaction of the cells in producing an antibody to almost
anything which is presented to them, as has now been demonstrated
for hundreds of bodies, indicates that the formation of the antibody is a general act of protection of the tissue cells and not one
specially directed against catalysts or enzymes only.

Weiland states that antitrypsin exists ready formed under
normal conditions in the cells of intestinal worms, and in the cells
of the intestinal mucosa, as shown by the fact that cell-free extracts
of these protect fibrin against tryptic digestion. The proteins
of the serum in unaltered form show a great resistance against
trypsin, which is lost when they have been chemically altered
by coagulation, or the action of chemical reagents, and this resistance has been ascribed to the presence of an antitrypsin.

Since the discovery of enterokinase the view has been advanced
by Dastre and by Delezenne that the effect of preventing the
action of the trypsin is not due to an antitrypsin but to an
antikinase, which prevents or opposes the activation of the
trypsin by the enterokinase.

ZYMO-EXCITATORS OR KINASES.

The various enzymes are not at first produced in an active
form in the cells of the glands which secrete them, but as inactive
substances called zymogens or proferments   This was first shown

by Langley in the case of pepsin, and the precursor of the enzyme was termed pepsinogen. The method of separating pepsinogen and pepsin, by their varying resistance to alkali, which attacks pepsin with much greater rapidity than it does pepsinogen, was later given by Langley and Edkins. Trypsinogen, the zymogen of trypsin, was later shown to exist by Heidenhain, and since then the existence of a proferment has been shown for most of the enzymes. These zymogens, as has been stated, are inactive while in the cell and exist in granular form visible under the microscope; they are converted into the active form, either at the time of secretion or later, on coming in contact with certain substances which have been termed zymo-excitators, or, in certain cases, kinases.

This action is possessed by all dilute acids, and it is probably in this way that pepsinogen and prochymosin, the zymogens respectively of pepsin and of rennin or chymosin, are activated in the stomach.

In the case of the trypsinogen of the pancreatic juice it has been shown by Pawlow and Chepowalnikoff that the activation takes place by means of a substance secreted by the intestinal mucosa It was found that while the secretion from a pancreatic fistula had scarcely any action upon protein, the addition of a small quantity of succus entericus caused it rapidly to become very active. Such action took place only upon the trypsin and not upon the other proferments of the pancreatic juice, but an increase in the activity of the lipoclastic enzyme occurred on the addition of bile.

The substance which so behaved as a zymo-excitator or kinase to trypsinogen was called *enterokinase* by Pawlow, and has since been the subject of much investigation and discussion as to whether it is itself a true ferment, a " ferment of ferment," as it was styled by its discoverer, who regards it as a ferment on account of the small quantity necessary to activate a much larger amount of trypsinogen, and the fact that it is destroyed, although slowly, at the usual temperature of destruction of enzymes (65° C.).

Delezenne and Dastre and other French observers deny that enterokinase is an enzyme, but consider that it forms a compound with trypsinogen, which is the active proteoclastic ferment trypsin This view is based upon the observations that a definite amount of enterokinase is required to develop the maximum amount of activity in a given amount of trypsinogen. They hence regard the enterokinase as a co-ferment, which serves to link together the attacked protein and the trypsinogen, and so invokes the protein cleavage. A further support for this view was the supposed observation that enterokinase combines with fibrin and can be so removed from solution.

Other French observers have pointed out as evidence against enterokinase being an enzyme, that it is much more slowly destroyed by heat than are most other enzymes. Thus Largnier des Barcels claims to have obtained activation although in lessened degree on extraction of the mucous membrane with boiling saline, and Biery and Henri state that they have heated enterokinase for twenty minutes to 120° C. without entirely destroying its action

Bayliss and Starling, however, have brought forward strong evidence in favour of enterokinase being a ferment Thus, they have shown that there is no stoichiometric relationship between the amount of trypsinogen and the amount of enterokinase necessary to activate it, as little as 0·0001 c.c. of an active enterokinase being capable of activating 5 c.c of pancreatic juice provided it was allowed two or three days to act. The rate of activation was also found to be proportioned to the amount of enterokinase added. Bayliss and Starling accordingly consider that the observation of Delezenne, that a definite amount of enterokinase is required to produce full activation, was due to a sufficient attention not having been given to the time relationships of the reaction, so that the full effects of the smaller quantities of added enterokinase were not allowed to develop, and secondly to slow auto-destruction of the trypsin first formed in the longer period necessary to effect the conversion with the smaller quantities of enterokinase

It is an observation dating back to Kuhne's earlier experiments that in preparing active extracts of pancreas, the trypsinogen of the fresh gland cells can be activated by extraction with very dilute acids, such as acetic acid, and that such treatment always yields more powerful extracts.

Since the discovery of enterokinase, Vernon has also shown that an inactive pancreatic extract can be rendered active by addition of an active preparation, or of an active commercial trypsin preparation. This was attributed by Vernon to the presence of an enterokinase different in some of its reactions, such as greater sensitiveness to alkalies, from intestinal entero-kinase.

Bayliss and Starling found, however, that this did not apply to pancreatic juice, which they found remained inactive not only when treated with active glycerine pancreatic extract supplied by Vernon, but also when acidified with weak or strong acid and then neutralised or made alkaline after varying periods, or when left in contact with fibrin, yeast, takadiastase, platinum black, gastric juice in acid or alkaline media, saliva, hydrogen peroxide, and sodium amalgam. The juice stood most of these treatments extremely well—that is, it could be activated afterwards by entero-kinase. The authors accordingly regard the action of enterokinase as absolutely specific.

They were unable to confirm the statement of Delezenne mentioned above, that fibrin took up enterokinase from solution, as also that enterokinase could be obtained from lymphatic glands or Payer's patches as stated by Delezenne, but found it specific-ally confined to the mucous membrane of the small intestine in its upper portion, extracts of the mucous membrane of the ileum being inactive.

Further evidence brought forward later by Bayliss and Starling against trypsin being considered as any compound of trypsinogen and enterokinase was derived from the formation of the antibody (antikinase) in the animal's serum, as a result of subcutaneous injection of enterokinase. On the view of Delezenne, the anti-tryptic action of normal serum must be due to antikinase, trypsin consisting of kinase (enterokinase) and trypsinogen, and hence subcutaneous injection of kinase (enterokinase) should increase the antitryptic action of serum. This, however, it was not found to do, but to produce a directly antikinasic body instead, neutralis-ing enterokinase if it were allowed to act upon this before the mixture was added to a trypsinogen solution.

The authors, therefore, conclude that the antitrypsin of normal serum is really antitrypsin or the antibody of a specific sub-stance trypsin, and not antikinase.

Activation in the case of the superoxydases is produced by minute traces of alkalies, which cause a marked increase in the action upon peroxide of hydrogen possessed by the solutions of most enzymes and tissue extracts.

The action of the manganese salts in increasing the power of laccase, and of calcium salts in increasing the rapidity of action of the coagulating enzymes, may also be mentioned in this connection

In inorganic reactions examples of similar effects are seen in the action of minute traces of copper salts in aiding the catalysis of hydrogen iodide and hydrogen peroxide by iron salts, and in the action of traces of alkali in increasing the power of colloidal platinum solutions upon hydrogen peroxide

AUTOCATALYSIS AND INFECTION

In the course of any reaction the products formed may themselves in certain cases act as catalysts and alter the velocity of the reaction. For example, in the hydrolysis of esters by water, the process is at first so slow as to be inappreciable, but as the process goes on, the hydrogen ions of the acid set free in the reaction itself act as a catalytic agent upon the portion of ester still undecomposed and hasten the reaction. To such a process Ostwald has assigned the term of " autocatalysis," and has pointed out that such a process may play an important rôle in biological processes, and that the course of such autocatalytic reactions bears a close analogy to the phenomena of fever

If the substance produced acts as a negative catalyst it will have only the effect of making the reaction run more slowly, and as its effect will increase with rising concentration, the result will be that the course of the reaction will resemble that of an ordinary reaction, save that the tendency to run more slowly as the equilibrium point is approached will be increased.

When, however, the substance formed in the reaction acts as a positive catalyst, the course of the reaction becomes markedly changed in a most interesting fashion.

For while in the ordinary non-catalysed reaction, or a reaction in which the concentration of catalyst remains constant, as in all those which we have previously considered, the velocity of reaction diminishes steadily onward from the beginning, in an autocatalytic reaction, as the quantity of autocatalyst increases as the reaction proceeds, the reaction is correspondingly hastened. Hence a reaction of this type may begin by being barely perceptible, but gathering way as it proceeds like a descending avalanche, may in the end become stormy or explosive

Examples of such autocatalytic reactions are seen in the tendency of many explosive substances to spontaneous explosion. Thus if gun-cotton be not most carefully washed from oxides of nitrogen, these products, present in too minute quantity at first to cause any change, may set up a slow and at first inappreciable reaction, which, slumbering at first, gradually increases in velocity and finally fires off the gun-cotton.

A good example of autocatalysis is quoted by Ostwald in the case of the action of nitric acid in dissolving metals. As has been noticed by several observers, pure nitric acid free from nitrous acid at first scarcely attacks many metals, such as copper, mercury, and zinc, although the impure acid readily oxidises them with production of nitrous acid. If a trace of a nitrite be added, however, the reaction at once commences and momentarily becomes more energetic, as it is continually autocatalysed with increasing energy by the nitrous acid formed in the reaction.

The writer has pointed out that such a process of autocatalysis, induced by a trace of enzyme, may be the means of infection, and of the reproduction of the virus in many of those infectious diseases, such as the acute exanthemata, in which notwithstanding much bacteriological research no causal connection of any living organism has yet been demonstrated.

The incubation period would be that required for the production of the autocatalyst in sufficient quantity to cause a general reaction with the tissue cells. The autocatalyst, which would act as the toxin of the disease, would still go on increasing in quantity until it had attained the concentration for maximum effect; but at the same time the tissue cells would react to it as to an ordinary toxin and produce the antitoxin, by which the toxin would be neutralised and rendered inert, and so the course of the disease would be limited.

The length of time and the exactness of duration of the incubation period form no objection to such a view, for the time of the initial period of autocatalytic reactions is often prolonged, and the duration of the incubation period would be determined by the reaction of the tissue cells affected, and would but little depend upon the amount of the trace of autocatalyst which originally carried the infection, unless this were very large.

Further, it may be pointed out that in many cases in which the toxin arises from the products of bacterial growth, the length of the incubation period depends upon the period of reaction of the tissue cells, and not upon any cycle of development of the parasite—as, for example, in enteric fever, where the *Bacillus typhosus* possesses no period of growth corresponding to the period of incubation.

Finally, variations in immunity in different individuals here, equally as in parasitic infection, will depend upon the individual variations in the blood as a suitable medium for such a reaction, upon the presence or absence of an antibody at the outset capable of neutralising the trace of autocatalyst bearing the infection, and upon the reactive power of the tissue cells to the autocatalyst or toxin.

THE SPECIFIC NATURE OF CATALYTIC ACTION

It has already been mentioned that enzymes are very specific in their action, and in the character of the products which they produce from the substratum.

It has been well pointed out by Bredig that this cannot be converted into a criterion for distinguishing the action of an enzyme from that of an inorganic catalyst. For although such specific action is seen at its maximum in the enzymes, it is also observable in the action of many inorganic catalysts. Thus while certain catalysts, such as the hydrogen ion, are very general in their action, catalysing most hydrolytic reactions, such as cleavage of all disaccharides, amyloses, and esters, other catalysts are quite selective in action. Examples quoted by Bredig are potassium bichromate, which energetically catalyses the oxidation of hydriodic acid by bromic acid, but does not act upon that of the same acid by iodic acid or potassium persulphate; iron and copper salts, which intensely catalyse the oxidation of potassium iodide by potassium persulphate, but not the oxidation of sulphurous acid by the same oxidising agent.

On the other hand, as also pointed out by Bredig, emulsin in addition to hydrolysing the glucoside amygdalin with which it is naturally associated, similarly acts upon many other substances, such as arbutin, helicin, salicin, phloridzin, daphnin, coniferin, æsculin, and lactose.

There is no doubt, however, although no fundamental difference can be deduced therefrom, that the vast majority of the enzymes are more highly selective in their action than the inorganic enzymes.

Thus, as has been beautifully shown by the researches of E. Fischer, an enzyme may act upon one stereo-isomer and not upon the other, the action being thrown out by the changes in position of a single group.

To use Fischer's striking analogy, the ferment and its substratum must fit like key and lock, or the reaction does not occur.

A similar selective action is seen in the case of the organisms which induce fermentation, as was known before the date of Fischer's researches upon the enzymes, as a result of the investigations of Pasteur, who showed that only dextrorotatory racemic acid was attacked, and was able to separate the lævorotatory stereo-isomer by such means. It is only those sugars with six or nine carbon atoms that are fermentable, and of these only certain of the stereo-isomers belonging to the " d " series. This fact has been used by Fischer for the purpose of separating the " l " stereo-isomers from the inactive mixture of " d " and " l " sugars obtained by synthetic procedures.

It can accordingly be predicted, when the constitution and stereo-chemical relations of a body are known from its derivation, whether it will be attacked by a given enzyme or not.

It is worthy of note that it is not whether a sugar is artificial or natural which determines the attack, but whether it possesses a certain molecular configuration the identity of which must extend even into stereochemical exactness. Hence it follows that the specific action does not mean that an enzyme can attack one substance only; it may attack many hundreds if only they all possess a given molecular and stereo-identical grouping, and it is this relationship upon which the specific action is based. Also the extent of action depends on the group attacked. Thus both invertase from yeast, and emulsin from bitter almonds, attack the glucoside, amygdalin; but invertase only detaches a molecule of glucose, leaving the remainder untouched, while emulsin, attacking a different grouping, breaks the amygdalin up into benzaldehyde, hydrocyanic acid, and glucose. Other natural glucosides, not possessing the particular grouping attackable by invertase, are resistant to that enzyme, and are attacked only by emulsin.

An interesting fact in the case of the cell, showing physiological adaptation to environment and nutrition, is that the action depends upon the food-supply; the cells forming in all probability enzymes to suit the configuration of the molecules at their disposal. Thus, *aspergillus* cultivated on a nutrient medium containing lactose or β-methyl galactosid acquires the property of hydrolysing these, while if grown upon a-methyl galactosid the property is acquired of attacking this substance.

The outcome of these investigations appears, then, to be that by specific action must be understood *entire* conformity between the particular enzyme and a corresponding molecular grouping or structural arrangement in the molecule attacked, and not that a single substance only is attacked by the same enzyme.

It may perhaps, in conclusion, be pointed out that this serves to explain what sometimes seems a most fantastic distribution of certain enzymes in nature. Thus the stomach of the fish contains a milk-curdling enzyme, similar to that of the mammalia, although such an enzyme never comes in contact with milk, and never has in the development of the fishes. The presence of such an enzyme can scarcely be regarded as a provision of Nature for the coming mammalia, and points to the fact that the milk-curdling enzyme must have other functions than the coagulation of milk. Since such ferments are also found in plants, it follows that they must, like the sucroclastic enzymes, be adapted to some definite molecular grouping upon which they act, and that milk coagulation can be but one example of their activity.

There is room for research in this region of biochemistry.

The Chemical and Physical Nature of Enzymes.

Little is known regarding the chemical nature of enzymes, because all attempts to isolate them in a state of purity have hitherto failed. In fact, there is nothing to give certainty that at the end of any process the product in the case of such complicated substances is pure, a remark which applies equally to ordinary proteins. None of the criteria of purity in the case of an ordinary crystalloid apply in the case of a colloid of complex constitution, except constancy of percentage composition. It does not crystallise out,[1] it has no definite melting-point, it does not affect the freezing-point or boiling-point,[2] it cannot be synthesised by reactions which can be followed in their course, and it is probably

---

[1] Unless when in combination with other bodies which confer crystalloid properties.

[2] At least to such an extent that measurements can be made.

polymerised to a high degree. Hence it would be more correct to say that we do not know whether protein and enzymes have ever been prepared in a state of purity, rather than, as is usually done, that they never have been so prepared.

One of the great difficulties in freeing enzymes from other substances, such as proteins, is that they share the common property of colloids, of being easily thrown mechanically out of solution, by electrolytes or organic precipitants of proteins.

The methods of attempted separation have differed in the case of different enzymes, and cannot all be gone into in detail here.

One general method is that of allowing the ferment to digest out any substratum present naturally with it as much as possible where it can be made to do this, as in the case of the proteoclastic enzymes, and then to precipitate it by means of some indifferent precipitate such as calcium phosphate in the case of pepsin, or by the addition of collodium or cholesterin dissolved in a mixture of alcohol and ether. Another method when the ferment does not rapidly undergo alcohol coagulation is to remove the accompanying protein by allowing the mixture to stand for some weeks under alcohol, and then dissolve the ferment by means of water, as in the case of fibrin ferment (thrombase). Another method is to allow the strong solution to remain standing at the freezing-point for some days, when the enzyme falls out in granular form, as in the case of fibrin ferment precursor (prothrombase) in oxalated plasma, or of pepsin from pure gastric juice.

The investigations have shown that enzymes are not in all cases proteins. Thus the purer preparations of pepsin and invertase do not give the protein colour tests. In elementary composition the enzymes do, however, resemble the proteins more than any other class of bodies. In addition to being salted out, or precipitated out like colloids, the enzymes are further shown to be colloids by the fact that they do not diffuse through parchment paper, or diffuse with great slowness.

THE SO-CALLED INORGANIC ENZYMES OR METAL SOLS.

It has already been repeatedly stated that the enzymes are a particular class of the bodies known as catalysts, which modify the conditions of a reaction. The enzymes differ from most of the inorganic catalysts, however, in that they are colloids, and to this certain of the differences in action between inorganic catalysts and enzymes are due.

The method of Bredig for obtaining, in the case of certain metals, catalysts of inorganic nature in colloidal solution as metal sols is hence of high interest. These metal sols have been termed inorganic enzymes by Bredig from their close resemblance in many respects to the enzymes produced by living cells; but it is questionable whether the use of such a term is justifiable, since the properties of such colloidal solutions are only exaggerations, probably on account of increased surface, of the action of the finely divided metals when not in solution, and most of the reactions destroying or removing the properties of such solutions may be ascribed to the throwing of the metal out of solution or to alteration of the active surface.

We have no proof that the similar actions in the case of the enzymes are due to similar causes. Also, we have no case where these colloids act upon another colloid as in the case of enzymes, nor of any hydrolytic action upon organic bodies caused by their agency as in the case of enzymes. In fact, their action is confined to simple reactions upon inorganic bodies, such as the catalysis of hydrogen peroxide into water and oxygen, or of hydrogen and oxygen to form water. Such reactions are shown by the metals concerned in finely divided form apart from solution, and the increased activity is merely due to finer division, and is removed by anything which interferes with the action of the large surface. Accordingly, it appears to the writer that the term " inorganic enzyme " is not a very appropriate name for a colloidal solution of platinum, since it indicates that we possess more knowledge of the mode of action of enzymes than we really do.[1] The same applies to the term " poisoning " as supplied to the action of hydrocyanic acid and sulphuretted hydrogen in stopping the action of such metal sols when added in minute traces, for this term is one which has hitherto been applied to the destruction of life by reagents, and until we know that the stopping of the action of

---

[1] The suggestion of Oppenheimer (*Die Fermente*, p. 46), that it would be better to call the enzymes " organic catalysts," is much better if any change must be made. For it is much better to retain the name catalyst as a general class name, including both inorganic and organic, and the enzymes now form a well-defined group of organic catalysts for which the name ought to be retained.

colloidal platinum by hydrocyanic acid arises from the same causes as the poisoning of a living cell by that reagent, it is dangerous to apply the same term to both processes. By a strange process of reasoning this same " poisoning " of the colloidal platinum by hydrocyanic acid has been put forward as supporting the view that the platin sol is an " inorganic enzyme " Now, if the process of " poisoning " proves anything at all, it proves that the colloidal platinum is a living cell, for it is living cells and not enzymes that are destroyed by the action of hydrocyanic acid, by which in such minute concentrations most enzymes are entirely unaffected. The only action related to enzymes which is stopped in the same degree by hydrocyanic acid is the identical one to that stopped in the case of colloidal platinum—namely, the action upon hydrogen peroxide —which is found not only in practically every enzyme but in nearly all tissue extracts. This action is ascribed usually to enzymes called " oxydases " or " peroxydases," occurring generally in all tissues where oxidative processes occur; but our knowledge of the subject is scarcely sufficient to state whether it is to be ascribed to any particular enzyme or group of enzymes, or is a general property attaching to all enzymes. The action, as has been stated, is stopped by a trace of hydrocyanic acid without interfering with the specific action of the enzyme accompanying the " peroxydase "; it is also stopped by the action of heat similarly to that of an enzyme, but it has not clearly been shown that the substance causing the oxidation is not altered in the process, nor that there is no stoichiometric relationship between the quantity of " peroxydase " and the amount of hydrogen peroxide changed. In fact, it appears that the " peroxydases " are very sensitive, and that after conversion of a certain amount of peroxide the action ceases

Whether the " peroxydases " be specific enzymes or not, the action of hydrocyanic acid in stopping or " poisoning," both in their case and that of colloidal platinum, is confined to one reaction, that of the conversion of hydrogen peroxide into water and oxygen, and it appears to the writer that this is a narrow basis on which to lay any weight as a proof of identity in mode of action between enzymes and colloidal platinum. It has not even been proved, for example, that hydrocyanic acid does not act directly as a negative catalyst to the reaction concerned.

While it cannot be admitted, therefore, that the terms " inorganic enzyme " and " poisoning " can be legitimately employed in connection with these metallic catalysts, the effects obtained with them are of high interest in regard to the manner in which a colloid in solution can act as a catalyst.

It was already known to Faraday that all porous bodies, and especially certain metals, such as platinum, possessed the property of absorbing large amounts of gases. The velocity with which the gases are absorbed increases with the state of subdivision of the metal, and is best seen in the case of platinum when this is used in the finely divided form of platinum black. Faraday pointed out also that this subdivision favoured the action of the platinum black as a catalyst by increasing the local concentration of the substances to be catalysed, and even showed that the action of catalysis by platinum black of an explosive mixture of hydrogen and oxygen was stopped by the presence of traces of carbon bisulphide or sulphuretted hydrogen. It is wonderful how closely this view of Faraday comes to the modern view with regard to the mode of action of a colloidal catalyst or enzyme.

The catalytic action of finely divided metals was taken up by Bredig and Müller von Berneck, and tested in the case of platinum and hydrogen peroxide. For this purpose, finding platinum black difficult to subdivide and suspend in solution, they evolved the ingenious method of obtaining the platinum in colloidal solution. Colloidal solutions of metals had already been prepared by Carey Lea by chemical means, such as colloidal silver by reduction of silver nitrate by ferrous sulphate; but Bredig discovered the much simpler method of detaching the metal from the negative electrode by means of a high potential in distilled water.

The process consists in establishing an electric arc between stout metallic electrodes of the metal of which it is desired to make a colloidal solution, in as pure as possible distilled water, which must be maintained at a low temperature. The conductivity of the water must be low, or otherwise electrolytic conductivity comes in and destroys the process, and, further, the presence of electrolytes tends to precipitate the colloidal metal.

The process can be best carried out by utilising the electric lighting mains (the usual 110 volt, constant current, circuit), and placing in the circuit an ammeter, a flat crystallising dish containing about 100 c.c. of pure distilled water which has previously been boiled to expel dissolved carbon dioxide, and a variable fluid resistance which is regulated to give a current of 4 or 5 ampères after the electric arc has been established under the distilled water. The electrodes consist of stout platinum, gold, or silver wire from 1 to 2 mm. in diameter, and can either be passed through two glass tubes so as to be easily handled, or sealed into two glass tubes which are filled with mercury by means of which electric contact is made with the platinum.

In using the apparatus a short circuit is made between the two electrodes under the distilled water, and then separated, when an electric arc is established, and glows beneath the water; minute particles of metal are now detached from the negative pole, some of which pass to the positive pole, but others remain in the distilled water and form an exceedingly fine suspension or colloidal solution of the metal.

The colloidal suspension begins at once, and in a few minutes a fluid of a deep dark colour is obtained, which in the case of platinum resembles the colour of reduced osmic acid solutions. Accompanying the colloidal particles there is always a certain amount of metal in coarser suspension, which may be removed by allowing to stand, filtering, or centrifugalising. The dark-coloured solution remaining is perfectly clear; it may deposit a little more platinum in the first day or two, but the rest remains in solution for months, and apparently indefinitely.

In the case of gold the colloidal solution has a deep dark-red colour, while the silver sol varies in colour from dark reddish-brown to olive-green, according to the dilution and fineness of the subdivision.

All the metal sols are extremely sensitive to the presence of electrolytes; they cannot be prepared in normal saline, and even addition of normal saline to them when prepared precipitates them entirely from solution.

The catalytic reactions of metal sols which have been studied are the conversion of hydrogen peroxide into water and oxygen, and of hydrogen and oxygen to water. These have been most studied in the case of the platin-sol by Bredig and his pupils.

The action of platin-sol upon peroxide was found to follow approximately the logarithmic law for a monomolecular reaction, but in the case of hydrogen and oxygen Ernst found that the velocity was proportional to the absolute amount of platinum present, and in the peroxide experiments it was found that the activity did not vary in simple direct proportionality to the concentration in platinum, but was expressed by the empirical law, $\frac{k_1}{k_2} = \left(\frac{C_1}{C_2}\right)^b$, in which k_1 and k_2 are the velocity constants corresponding to concentrations in platinum of C_1 and C_2, and b, instead of being unity, is a constant, the value of which lies between 1·6 and 1·3. Hence we see that there are abnormalities in the action of these inorganic catalysts, similar to those already described in the case of the enzymes. The abnormalities are explained upon the basis of intermediate compounds between catalyst and substratum, or products of reaction.

Even equal platinum concentrations do not always lead to the same velocity of reaction, this depending upon variations in fineness of subdivision of the platinum, and upon the previous history of the solution, such as its age, the temperature at which it has been preserved, etc.; to this variation van Bemmellen has in analogy with similar phenomena in magnetisation applied the term " hysteresis."

The dilutions in which these colloidal platinum solutions exert their catalytic effects are enormous. Thus a solution containing only 0·000,01 grm.—that is, $\frac{1}{100}$ mgrm. per c.c.—acting upon a solution of hydrogen peroxide containing 0·06 grm. per c.c., converted more than the half in forty minutes. The action of $\frac{1}{10000}$ to $\frac{1}{100000}$ mgrm. of colloidal platinum upon more than 1,000,000 times its weight of hydrogen peroxide could still be detected.

Ernst also found that $\frac{1}{10}$ mgrm. of colloidal platinum catalysed 50,000 times its own weight of hydrogen and oxygen to water at ordinary temperature without losing its activity in the least.

The retarding action (or so-called " poisoning " action) of certain substances upon the catalytic action of these inorganic colloidal catalysts is also remarkable on account of the minute quantities required to stop the reaction.

For example, the addition of 0·000,000,014 grm. per c.c. of hydrocyanic acid, to the above-mentioned experiment, in which 0·000,01 grm. per c.c. of platinum was acting upon 0·06 grm. per c.c. of peroxide, served to decrease the rate of change by one half, and the addition of 0·000,000,001 grm. per c.c. of hydrocyanic acid in another experiment had an equal effect upon the velocity of conversion by a colloidal platinum solution in concentration of 0·000,006 grm. per litre. It is to be noted that the hydrocyanic acid produces its marked effect in amounts of $\frac{1}{200}$ to $\frac{1}{100}$ of that of the platinum in these experiments, so that there cannot be an ordinary chemical compound between the catalyst and the " paralysator." It must be remembered, however, that even at these dilutions the platinum is present not in molecular form but in suspended particles, and that to stop the reaction it is only necessary for the hydrocyanic acid to combine with the surface layer of each platinum particle, which may explain the small amount necessary. Such combination might be either of a chemical or physical nature, but the latter is the more probable.

Before leaving the subject of the action of hydrocyanic acid it may be recalled that it possesses a similar action in minute traces, as shown by Schönbein in the case of the peroxydases accompanying ferments. Now if these peroxydases are responsible in the tissue cells for the uptake of oxygen by the protoplasm, it may well be that the poisonous action of hydrocyanic acid in such minute doses is due to interference with the action of the peroxydases.

A large number of other substances were also quantitatively tested by Bredig and his co-workers as to their action upon the catalytic power of colloidal platinum. Thus so little as one part of sulphuretted hydrogen in 300,000,000 parts showed clearly a retarding effect upon the catalysis. The colloidal platinum is capable of recovery from the action of some of the reagents employed and not from others. Thus if a stream of air be passed for some time through a solution of colloidal platinum which has been rendered inert by addition of a trace of hydrocyanic acid, so as to remove the latter, the activity is again restored.

A similar effect is probably found in what has been termed the " oligodynamic " property of heavy metals, as a result of which a trace of certain metals in distilled water, too minute for all chemical analysis, leads to the death of living organisms. Thus mere immersion of a strip of clean copper in a vessel of distilled water containing a number of tadpoles, which would otherwise live therein for weeks, is sufficient to kill the animals in a few hours.

CHAPTER XIII

THEORIES AS TO MODE OF ACTION OF CATALYSTS AND ENZYMES

CORRELATION OF THEORIES—MEANS OTHER THAN CATALYSIS BY WHICH CHEMICAL REACTIONS CAN BE INDUCED, OR REACTION VELOCITY VARIED.

I. *The Theory of Molecular Vibrations.*—Theories having a bearing upon catalytic action first began to be formulated for the purpose of giving some explanation of the processes of fermentation which at the time occupied the attention of the chemist more than of the biologist. The brilliant work of Pasteur had not as yet illuminated the action of micro-organisms in these processes, when Liebig, searching for some explanation of the action of yeast upon glucose, evolved the theory that such action arose because the yeast was itself involved in a process of chemical activity or decay and provoked as a result chemical activity in the sugar. In support of his theory Liebig adduced many examples from inorganic chemistry of where the chemical activity of one body influences that of another, and of cases where even mechanical vibration causes changes, as in explosive bodies, such as the iodide or chloride of nitrogen.

It is not to be wondered at that Liebig in those early days looked upon those activities, which are now known to be due to micro-organisms, as due to chemical action entirely.

Many of the experiments carried out by Liebig and others of his school of thought, to attempt to exclude the possibility of micro-organisms being present, were well and scientifically thought out, and if they led the distinguished chemist into error, it was only because of failure to realise, at that early date, the difficulty not only of maintaining but of preserving complete sterility. When one reads the experiments by which it was sought to prove that it was the access of air and not the presence of micro-organisms which conditioned fermentation, one is forced to admit that they

232

were made with great ingenuity, and to acknowledge that the errors to which they led were due to the stage of advancement of scientific knowledge at the time, and not to want of care on the part of the experimenter

The indisputable proof by Pasteur that fermentation is due to the life processes of micro-organisms and the strong position which Liebig took in combating this led to the theory that catalytic activity was due to the activity of one body being transferred to another, and so to the catalysis of the latter, falling into disrepute, until this view was revived in the form of the theory that the decomposition by a ferment is due to a transference of " molecular vibration " from the ferment to the substratum. The molecules of the substance undergoing the fermentation were supposed to be already in a condition of vibration which became increased by the sympathetic swingings or vibrations in the ferment to such an extent that the vibrations passed the point of equilibrium, and the substance accordingly underwent decomposition This revival of a part of Liebig's view by Nägeli was only applied by him to the organised ferments, and he stated that it was the living protoplasm which acted directly in increasing the molecular vibrations He maintained the view that the living cell and the enzyme were different both in mode of action and in their physiological rôle, the enzymes preparing the foodstuffs for use in physiological activity, and the organised ferment or living cell making use of the material so prepared.

It is now clear that Liebig was wrong in regarding the yeast as being in a process of decay and giving rise to accompanying chemical changes in the substratum which lay apart entirely from any life processes.

But if we strip Liebig's statements free from this error there is much in them which even to-day demands attention.

We shall see later that no single theory which has ever been put forward is capable of accounting for all cases or classes of catalytic action, and it is quite probable that catalysis is due in one case to one cause or factor, and in another case to quite a different one, so that different theories may by no means be incompatible

It seems to the writer that for those cases of almost instantaneous reaction due to mechanical vibration or friction, or to contact with another chemical substance, Liebig's view of the *vis inertiæ* to reaction—or, as we would term it, of the resistance being overcome by an enhancing of molecular vibration—fits the facts better than any other theory.

A concise account of the view can perhaps best be put in Liebig's own words:

" It is well known that there are chemical compounds of so unstable a nature that changes in temperature and electrical condition, or even simple mechanical friction or contact with bodies apparently totally indifferent, cause such a disturbance in the attraction of their constituents, that the latter enter into new forms, without any of them combining with the acting body. These compounds appear to stand but just within the limits of chemical combination, and agents exercise a powerful influence on them which are completely devoid of action on compounds of a stronger affinity. Thus, by a slight increase of temperature the elements of hypochlorous acid separate from one another with evolution of heat and light; chloride of nitrogen explodes by contact with many bodies which combine neither with chlorine nor nitrogen at common temperatures; and the contact of any solid substance is sufficient to cause the explosion of iodide of nitrogen, or of fulminating silver.

" It is evident that the active state of the atoms of one body has an influence upon the atoms of a body in contact with it; and if these atoms are capable of the same change as the former, they likewise undergo that change; and combinations and decomposition are the consequences. But when the atoms of the second body are not of themselves capable of such an action, any further disposition to change ceases from the moment at which the atoms of the first body assume the state of rest—that is, when the changes or transformations of this body are quite completed."

It is worthy of note, in view of modern opinion upon the subject, that Liebig was well aware of the fact (and actually deprecates the use of the term *catalytic force* for this very reason) that a catalytic agent need not necessarily start a reaction, but only increase the rapidity of one already in progress; instancing as an example the catalysis of hydrogen peroxide by platinum or silver.

There is no other theory which appears to the writer to cover the case of detonating substances in which the mechanical percussion acts as a catalyst in inducing chemical reaction; similar action can in many instances be induced by contact with a chemical substance, and by analogy it is probable that in a certain number of cases the explanation of catalysis may lie in molecular kinetics.

In any case the theory does not deserve dismissal in the cavalier fashion in which it is often treated by modern physical chemists.

Other instances of mechanical movements effecting chemical or physical change are the effects of motion in causing crystallisation from supersaturated solutions. While this action is not marked in some cases, it is conspicuous in others, as in the two cases quoted by Liebig, of acid potassium tartrate on shaking mixed solutions of a potassium salt and tartaric acid, or on stirring with a glass rod the sides of a beaker containing ammonio-magnesium phosphate, when the crystals separate out on the parts rubbed by the rod. Similar effects are seen in the crystallisation out from amorphous solids (or solid solutions) of sugar, glass, or sulphur on mechanical stimulation.

II. *The Theory of Intermediate Reactions.*—This theory of catalytic action, in its application at least to one classical reaction— viz., that of production of sulphur trioxide from sulphur dioxide and oxygen by the catalytic action of nitric oxide—was introduced even before the previous one, although it does not appear to have occurred to anyone to invoke it as a general theory of catalysis until long after Liebig's theory had been propagated. As early as 1806 Clement and Désormes described this process in the leaden chamber sulphuric acid process as arising from an alternating -reduction and oxidation of the nitrogen oxides. Another classical example is the formation of the intermediate ethyl-hydrogen sulphate shown by Williamson to occur in the etherification process for the production of ethylic ether from ethyl alcohol.

Although bodies corresponding to such intermediate reactions have been isolated in some cases by slightly varying the conditions of reaction, it has frequently been disputed whether or not they actually occur in the reaction as it takes place under usual conditions. Further, Ostwald has rightly pointed out that the mere fact of the occurrence of such a body is by no means a proof that it is the cause, or a step in the process, of the quicker catalytic reaction. It may not be an intermediate product: it may merely be a by-product. In order that such a body can be shown to be a part of the catalytic reaction, it must be shown not only that it occurs, but that the *sum* of the times, for its formation and its breaking up again to form the final products of the reaction, is less than the time of the direct non-catalysed reaction. Otherwise it is clear that the reaction will run more quickly without the intermediate body being formed.

It is clear that this condition is satisfied in those cases in which the reaction does not go at all in the absence of the catalyst, or does not go within appreciable experimental limits, as in the case of sulphur dioxide and atmospheric oxygen mentioned above. Here it is obvious that the reaction without the catalyst runs more slowly than the sum of the formation of nitrosyl-sulphuric acid, and the decomposition of this to form sulphuric acid and nitric oxide, without any quantitative work on the substrate. Also in one case of a reaction which does run at a measurable rate by itself —viz , that between hydriodic acid and hydrogen peroxide in which water and iodine are formed, but which is catalysed into much greater velocity by molybdic acid—it has been shown by Brode that an intermediate compound permolybdic acid can be isolated, and also that the *sum* of the times of formation of (1) permolybdic acid from molybdic acid and peroxide, and (2) the oxidation of hydriodic acid by permolybdic acid to iodine with regeneration of molybdic acid, is less than the time of direct oxidation of hydriodic acid by peroxide in the absence of molybdic acid

Although a proof that the sum of the times was *greater* than the direct time would rule out the intermediate compound, it must be clearly pointed out, however, that the times being *less* does not necessarily prove that the intermediate compound formation actually occurs and is the cause of the catalysis What it does prove is that the formation of the intermediate compound would increase the velocity of the reaction by a definite amount; but such increase might be due to other causes, and the increase by such other means might be greater than that by the path of the intermediate reaction.

Still, an experimental proof that the path by intermediate reaction is quicker is presumptive evidence that the reaction probably occurs by such intermediate reaction.

It is only in a comparatively few of the known catalytic reactions, however, that such intermediate compounds have been shown to exist, and in a few others they have been introduced as an hypothesis to explain irregularities of reaction In the majority of cases there is no experimental proof for the existence of such compounds. Further, as Ostwald has pointed out, the theory

of intermediate reaction fails entirely to account for the action
of negative catalysts, for here the indirect action *must* go more
slowly than the direct one. Accordingly the direct reaction would
run at its own undiminished rate by itself, for the quantity of
catalyst is too small to take all the substratum at the beginning
and compel its conversion by the slower rate.

The conclusion may accordingly be drawn that although intermediate reaction may and probaby does occur, and increase reaction
velocity in a considerable number of catalytic reactions, it is evident
that this does not furnish a universal explanation of catalysis
applicable to all cases.

III. *Theory of Altered Solubility and Different Reaction Velocity
of the Substratum in the Catalyst.*—The outline of this theory was first
given by Faraday, who showed that all porous and finely divided
bodies, such as porcelain clay, wood charcoal, animal charcoal,
and some metals, notably platinum, possessed the property of
taking up different gases and condensing them, and ascribed to
this property the power such bodies were known to possess of
inducing or favouring chemical reaction—as, for example, in causing
the union of a mixture of hydrogen and oxygen at ordinary temperatures in the case of spongy platinum. Such an effect can obviously
only obtain in a heterogeneous system—that is, a system in which
there is discontinuity of structure and chemical composition—for
in a homogeneous system there is no opportunity for variation
in concentration of the components of the system. For example,
in the above case of spongy platinum, there are portions of the
system where on account of the presence of the platinum within
molecular distance of action, the hydrogen and oxygen can become
condensed in the metal or on its surface, and the action can therefore proceed more rapidly than in those parts of the system outside
the range of action of the platinum where the reaction, if it proceeds
at all, can only proceed at the rate at which it takes place in the
absence of platinum.

Similarly, in the case of a colloidal catalyst, such as most
enzymes are supposed to be, it may be supposed that the catalyst is
present in the form of ultra-microscopic particles suspended in the
solution, and that the substratum possesses a higher solubility in
the particles of the ultra-microscopic emulsion, or by surface tension
is attracted in increased concentration to the surface of the particles.
In either case a portion of the system is obtained in a state of

higher local concentration than in the absence of the catalyst, and accordingly the reaction will proceed more rapidly in this portion of the system. If now the relative solubilities of the substratum and products of reaction in the colloidal catalyst portion and the remainder of the solution are such as to give sufficient rapidity of diffusion, of the substratum into, and of the products of reaction out of, the colloidal particles, then the reaction as a whole will be hastened by the condensation within or upon the colloidal particles.

This view as to the mode of action of colloidal catalysts has in recent times been prominently put forward, and the chemical kinetics of reactions in such heterogeneous systems studied by Bodenstein, Bredig, Goldschmidt, Findlay, von Ernst, and others.

It has been shown by Menschutkin that the nature of the solvent exercises an enormous influence upon the velocity of the reaction, so that the same reaction running at the same temperature but in different media may occur at excessively different rates. Thus the velocity of reaction between tri-ethylamine and ethyl iodide was tested in eight different organic solvents and found to be different in all of them, the extreme variation between acetophenone in which it was greatest, and hexane in which it was least, being no less than 720 times.

Accordingly, if we may regard the colloidal enzyme and the solution in which it is present as a heterogeneous system with two distinct phases in which the substratum to be acted upon possesses different reaction velocities, and also different solubilities, a scheme is at hand by which the catalytic reaction can receive an explanation *in such cases.*

It may here be pointed out, as an extension of such a theory, that it is not necessary that the catalyst should be colloidal *provided that the substratum is in such a case a colloid* All that is necessary is that there shall be a heterogeneous system with two phases present, in one of which the velocity can be increased by the presence of the catalyst. Thus in the case of a colloidal solution, such as starch, undergoing catalysis by a non-colloidal catalyst, such as dilute acid, the starch particles may be regarded as a phase to which the hydrogen ions are attracted and become concentrated, and in which they increase the velocity of reaction, the products of reaction then rapidly diffusing out, through the large surface of starch particle compared to its mass, and so fresh starch molecules undergoing attack [1] ;

It must be admitted, however, that such differences in velocity of reaction in colloidal catalyst or colloidal substratum as compared with the other phase of the solution have never been experimentally demonstrated. Also all attempts to demonstrate, as a model, an artificial emulsion consisting of two phases by the operation of which a reaction took place more rapidly than in a homogeneous solution of one of the phases only, have hitherto failed.

Bredig has postulated such an emulsion somewhat as follows: It should consist of two media, A and B, of which B should form a suspension menstruum for A, the reaction to be tested should run more quickly in A than in B, and the reacting substance should be more soluble in A than in B, and if possible the products of reaction should be more soluble in B than in A. Could such an emulsion be constructed, there is no doubt that the reaction would run more quickly in it than in a homogeneous solution in B alone, and it would illustrate the foregoing theory as to the mode of action of colloidal enzymes.

In conclusion, regarding this most ingenious theory, which in all probability does hold in certain cases of colloidal catalysts, particularly those in which a concentration or condensation of the reacting substance occurs in or upon the catalyst, it must be emphasised, however, that it cannot form an explanation of all catalytic action, because it is a necessary premise of the theory that either the catalyst or substratum must be colloidal.

SUMMARY REGARDING THEORIES OF CATALYTIC ACTION AND CORRELATION OF THESE THEORIES.

A review of the theories of catalysis such as is given above appears to indicate that the explanation lies not in any one of them but in a correlation of all. Each of them supplies a different path

---

[1] Attention may be drawn to the fact that in cases where the substratum is colloidal, we have experimental evidence of an attraction between this phase of the system and the catalyst, similar to that seen between the colloidal catalyst and reacting substance in the case of platinum and gases. Thus, the strong attraction of fibrin for pepsin is analogous to the attraction of the reacting gases by the platinum. In one case the catalyst is attracted and concentrated in the substratum; in the other the substratum is attracted and concentrated in the catalyst.

which may be used in different special cases to reach the same end. The end to be reached, in order that the reaction velocity may be increased, is to diminish the resistance to reaction.   The potential factor, or *vis a tergo*, is dependent upon the energy freed in the reaction, and this in turn upon the initial and final chemical energies of the reacting substances; hence this factor may be regarded as constant.   But the velocity with which equilibrium will be reached, and in fact whether it will be reached at all, depends, as pointed out previously, upon what the value of the resistance is to the reaction. Now all the above theories are explanations of various means by which the resistance may be altered, and so the reaction velocity varied, and which of these means is taken must vary with the circumstances of each case.[1]

Thus, increase of molecular vibration, as in chemical reactions induced by detonation, or by mere contact with a chemical catalyst, may decrease the molecular stability, and so increase the velocity, and by analogy this may also occur in less easily provoked reactions; again, the formation of intermediate products may break up the molecular stability, producing compounds in which the resistance to reaction is lessened; change in the properties of the solvent may induce or hasten reaction by bringing new attractions to bear upon the constituent groups of the molecule, so that the resistance to these parting company may be increased or diminished, and the reaction velocity correspondingly varied; this change may be occasioned by the presence of a heterogeneous system with different reaction velocities due to different solvents in its two phases; varying concentration may alter the relationships and attractions between solvent and substratum and so alter resistance and reaction velocity.

There is hence nothing incompatible between the different theories of catalytic action, and these must be regarded as theories of the means by which the one common factor of chemical resistance to reaction can be changed.

[1] It is not meant here that the means by which chemical resistance may be studied are not of the highest value, and call for most careful study, but only to point out that all these lead to the same end.

Catalysis is not the only means by which a reaction may be induced, or the resistance to a reaction be reduced. We have seen that provided any energy transformer is included in the resisting system whereby energy can be added to the reaction, the reaction need not run towards the equilibrium point, but instead the chemical energy may be increased, and complex chemical substances possessing more chemical energy may be built up from simple and completely oxidised inorganic substances, and we have instanced the chlorophyll-containing cell of the plant as an example of such an energy transformer which is capable of converting radiant solar energy into chemical energy. In all living cells we have, however, examples of such reaction in which energy set free from one reaction is utilised to run another.

To consider, accordingly, that all the reactions of cell life are catalytic is to take a narrow and incomplete view of the problem of the chemical life of the cell. Important to the cell economy as are those reactions induced by enzymes, they form but one portion of the whole, and if the chemistry of the cell included only such reactions as could be induced by enzymes, there would be no building up of compounds with greater chemical potential such as actually occurs: the whole process would become katabolic.

It is the linkage of one reaction with another, and the using of the free energy of one to run another, which specially characterises the cell and differentiates the cell from the enzyme.

In such a connection of two reactions there is something therefore superadded to the action of a catalyst. The catalyst can only alter the resistance to the induced reaction. An inducing reaction can in addition add energy to the reaction induced because it itself gives out free energy.

Hence the old idea of Liebig, that a body which is itself in a state of reaction may induce reaction in another body, although not a necessary part of a theory of catalysis, because both bodies are altered, must not be lost sight of, since it is of high importance to chemical kinetics, and more especially for the chemistry of the cell.

It may be noted that an induced reaction by such a body may

16

either be similar to that produced by a catalyst, in that it also runs downhill like the reaction inducing it with energy being set free, or may run in the opposite direction away from its equilibrium point, taking up the energy set free in the inducing reaction.

Even in the first case, where both inducing and induced reaction run towards their respective equilibrium points, and energy is set free in both, it is evident that the inducing reaction, other things being equal, will be a more powerful agent in increasing velocity of reaction than a catalyst. For if the catalyst, which can add no energy to the reaction because it remains unchanged itself, can diminish the resistance so as to start or increase the velocity of a reaction, still more can a substance undergoing change and giving out free energy start or hasten a reaction.

This is not mere theory or hypothesis, but experimental fact, verified by many chemical experiments in everyday laboratory use; the subject seems, however, to be often forgotten or lost sight of from the preponderating attention given to catalytic action.

No better example can be given than that quoted by Liebig in 1840, of the action of nitric acid upon silver in inducing a similar action upon platinum.

"Platinum, for example, does not decompose nitric acid; it may be boiled with this acid without being oxidised by it, even when in a state of such fine division that it no longer reflects light (black spongy platinum). But an alloy of silver and platinum dissolves with great ease in nitric acid; the oxidation which the silver suffers causes the platinum to undergo the same change; or, in other words, the latter body, from its contact with the oxidising silver, acquires the property of decomposing nitric acid."

"Electrical action ought to have retarded or prevented the oxidation of the platinum in contact with silver, but, as experience shows, this action is more than counterbalanced by chemical action."

Examples are also not wanting in inorganic chemistry of where the energy set free in one reaction is used to cause another reaction to proceed away from the direction of its equilibrium point, as in the reduction actions often induced by oxidising agents. For example, in the action of hydrogen peroxide upon certain metallic oxides, such as silver, gold, and peroxide of lead. Here the reaction of formation of water and oxygen from hydrogen peroxide which goes on slowly by itself, and gives out free energy, is actually enormously increased in velocity[1] by another 'reaction which absorbs energy in the process. The induced reaction runs the inducing reaction backwards away from its equilibrium point by means of the energy which would be otherwise set free. The reason for the increased velocity is the same as in the case of catalytic action; although free energy from the induced reaction is taken up by the inducing reaction, the resistance in the process of the intermediate stage due to setting free of nascent oxygen is removed, and in this respect, although undergoing alteration itself with absorption of energy, the metallic oxide acts as does a catalyst in catalysed reactions.

But it is in the metabolism of the living cell that we meet with examples of such linked and induced reactions in greatest numbers. Even in the animal cell, although the balance-sheet of metabolism is in favour of oxidation with liberation of free energy, it is a mistake to suppose that there are no reactions running in the reversed direction. We have seen earlier, that with the varying conditions of concentration in the cell the equilibrium point may alter so that syntheses forming the reversals of simple hydrolytic cleavages may readily occur in the cell, simply by the action of enzymes. Such, for example, as maltose formation from glucose, of glycogen formation from glucose, of protein from albumose, or even of neutral fat from fatty acids and glycerine. Such syntheses demand little or no energy, because the chemical energy of the substances upon one side of the equation is practically identical with that of the substances upon the other, and hence variations in osmotic energy with changes in concentration may easily make the balance, so that an enzyme which adds no energy may affect the conversion. But in such cases of metabolic change—as, for example, the conversion of carbohydrates to fats, where, weight for weight, the energy is almost double, or in the conversion of carbon dioxide and water into organic compounds, as in the green leaf, where energy is also taken up—such energy must be provided from other sources and a more complex mechanism than that of the enzyme, capable of linking together different chemical reactions, or of acting as a transformer of other energy forms into chemical energy, must be present.

[1] We cannot say catalysed, because the inducing substance does not remain unaltered but takes up energy, but the difference is only in definition, for, as far as chemical kinetics go, the action is virtually catalysed.

This is the part taken by the living cell, which in one oxidising action obtains free energy, and in an accompanying reducing action stores this energy up, at least in part, in a new synthesised body at a higher potential of chemical energy than that from which it came. In this process enzymes may freely be used by the cell, but they are co-ordinated and regulated in the process.

Further, in the process, a set of energy manifestations peculiar to life appear, which cannot be reproduced elsewhere than in living cells, and as this is the sole criterion which differentiates one form of energy from another in the inorganic world, it may justly be maintained that we are here dealing with a peculiar type of energy, although this arises from, and ultimately passes back again into inorganic forms.

CHAPTER XIV

SECRETION AND GLANDULAR MECHANISMS

Correlation of Secretion, Absorption, and Excretion, and their Relationship to Osmotic Energy.—The processes of secretion, absorption, and excretion are distinguished from one another only by their object or physiological function, and not by anything intrinsically different in their nature or in the mechanism by which these processes are carried out in the body   The purpose of secretion is to prepare an active substance in solution for use in assisting a process which is of service to the organism in some other part, such as a digestive secretion; a secretion of a substance which has a guiding influence upon chemical change in other tissues, and hence affects the state of activity of those tissues—as, for example, the internal secretions, adrenalin, secretin, etc.; or a secretion which acts by mechanical means, such as the secretion of the tears in the lachrymal gland, the mucous secretions on the mucous surfaces, and the serous and synovial secretions of the serous and synovial cavities.   The purpose of absorption is to take up for the service of the body generally and of the absorbing cells the materials in solution which have been prepared and modified by the secretions.   Lastly, the purpose of excretion is to remove from the body materials which have passed through, or been formed in, the cycle of metabolism in the body, and have become waste products for which the body has no further use.   In addition, the purpose of excretion is to maintain in normal amount and concentration in the circulating fluid of the body, the blood, those products which *are* of service, for in abnormal concentrations these useful bodies become as injurious to the living cells as effete products of metabolism, or foreign substances of actively poisonous nature.

Respiration also is essentially identical in its nature with these three processes, being a combination of absorption, secretion, and excretion, the only difference being that the products concerned in respiration exist in the form of gases before being taken into the body and after being removed from it, but in the process of respiration itself the substances concerned—oxygen and carbon dioxide—

are as truly in aqueous solution as are the substances involved in secretion, absorption, and excretion. It is clear, then, that the purposes served in the processes of secretion, absorption, excretion, and respiration differ, but we shall see that in so far as the intrinsic nature of these processes and the mechanisms by which they are carried out are concerned, they are closely similar or identical, and · are governed by the same laws

At the outset it may be pointed out that not only in respiration, where the differentiation of the process into two parts—an external respiration and an internal or tissue respiration—has been clearly recognised, but also in the other processes of secretion, absorption, and excretion, there are two parts to the process—viz, (1) an internal or cellular part, in which chemical changes, and processes involving energy changes within the cells active in the process, occur, and (2) an external or mechanical part in which the products acted upon are brought to or carried away from the cell and transferred to other parts of the organism, and by means of which, through the activity of mechanisms external to the cells concerned in the active process, the internal or cellular part is modified and regulated.

Thus, in the case of secretion, we may point out as the internal or cellular part of the process. (1) the formation and storage in the cell of the intrinsic organic constituents of the secretion, as zymogens, etc., in which process the cell acts as an energy transformer upon the chemical energy supplied by the organic constituents of the plasma, and builds up its own special products from these constituents, (2) the formation from the inorganic constituents of the plasma of the inorganic constituents of the secretion against the laws of diffusion and osmosis, so that the osmotic energy is increased by the separation of a secretion containing substances in greater concentration than they possess in the plasma, the cell here again acting as a transformer, and converting chemical energy derived from its absorbed and oxidised food into osmotic energy.

But we have also in secretion the external part of the process in which agencies outside the secreting cell come into operation, and either modify the action of the cell, or produce an effect apart from the cell entirely.

The agents which come into operation in the external part of secretion may be classified as follows:

(1) The alteration in the supply of fluid or solvent and of dissolved and nutrient matter to the cell, such as variations of the

blood-supply to the secreting cells; or alterations in the concentration of the dissolved substances in the blood-supply—for example, alteration of percentage of glucose in the blood which influences the glycogen-secreting power of the liver cells

(2) Alterations in the secretory activity of the cells due to external causes, when the supplies of solvent and nutrient remain constant or do not change proportionately to the change in secretory activity, such as the stimulation of the special secretory nervous mechanism of the secretory cells, or the effects upon secretion of chemical substances—for example, *secretin* upon the pancreatic cells, or *gastrin* upon the gastric cells—or drugs such as pilocarpin or atropin upon secretory cells in general.

(3) Most external in character of all are the mechanisms by which the secretions in certain cases are carried away from the secreting cells, diverted into different channels so as to be carried away to different parts of the body, or by certain muscular arrangements in the different ducts, are retained ready and already secreted for use at intermittent periods. Examples of such external mechanisms of secretion are found in the ducts of secreting glands, often, when of an appreciable length, supplied with muscular walls which by means of peristaltic contractions pass on the secretion, or by sphincters at definite parts along their course, provide for its retention until a reflex stimulus causes it to be discharged when there is physiological occasion for its use Storage sacs for the secretion are found in the gall-bladder, in the organs of generation, in the dilated ducts of the mammary gland, and in the poison glands, etc., of many animals.

Exactly the same division into an intrinsic indispensable cellular or internal part is seen in the processes of excretion and absorption, together with a more or less expanded and varying accessory or external part.

Thus, in absorption, we have in the intestinal columnar cells an active cellular absorption, with accompanying chemical change, and work done against osmotic pressure, and the external part of carriage of the products to the tissues, where again cellular processes of absorption occur modified by the operation of the nervous system, and new products are given out which are carried by an extra-cellular process to other cells. Similarly in excretion, we have cellular activity in which the excretory products are formed in the various cells; external processes by which these are carried to the liver; cellular processes, again, in which the excretory products are chemically modified; external processes by which the products are carried to the excretory organ, such as the kidney; and, lastly, in the special excretory organ itself, we have cellular processes again in which the excreting cell provides energy for work to be done against osmotic pressure with corresponding increase in osmotic energy, at the expense of chemical energy obtained from oxidation of nutrient matter. Throughout the processes, in addition to external carriage in the blood-stream, there is also the play from without upon the active cells of the external agencies (a) of the nervous system directly, or indirectly through the vasomotors, and (b) the stimulus of chemical substances in the circulation, which may also act upon the cells, or intermediately through varying the blood-supply.

It is in the external parts of the processes that the chief differences in their mechanisms are to be found, and this statement holds not only in contrasting the processes of respiration, secretion, absorption, and excretion with one another, but in regard to the variations between one type or case of secretion, etc., and another. The variations in the external mechanisms are manifold between one process and another, and from one animal species to another, with regard to how the same fundamental process is carried out; but in all cases the essential cellular processes are very much alike, and the same types of phenomena are to be found. There is in every case a living cell involved in the process, and by this living cell the processes of diffusion and osmosis are profoundly modified. Substances are separated often at higher concentrations than in the bathing fluid, which can only take place on the condition that energy is transformed by the cell and converted into osmotic energy. New substances are produced in many cases which are typical of the action of the cell involved, and can only be produced as a result of energy transformations induced by the cell. Even where the concentrations of every single instance in the secretion may be less than in the bathing fluid, and no new substance is produced in the passage through the cell,[1] the rate of secretion or transmission is so much subject to variation apart from purely physical factors, that the cell must be regarded as something more than simply an inert membrane, because its permeability for different dissolved substances, and for the solvent, varies from time

---

[1] It is improbable that this condition ever is completely realised in the action of living cells.

to time as the cell is acted upon either by the nervous system or by substances in solution in the plasma. Such specific substances dissolved in the plasma possess the power of affecting permeability for other and quite different substances in a manner never seen in the case of non-living membranes or apart from living cells.

The consideration of the mechanism of secretion may accordingly be divided into two parts—viz , (1) the intrinsic activity of the cells concerned in secretion, and (2) the accessory mechanisms by which the rate of secretion is varied and controlled.

INTRINSIC ACTIVITY OF SECRETING CELLS.

That secreting cells do not act in a passive, inert manner as filtering mechanisms, or as membranes possessing different and constant permeabilities for different dissolved substances in the plasma, or as media in which different substances possess different solubilities, is proven by many experimental observations. Thus that the rate of secretion is not merely passively dependent upon blood-pressure and blood-supply (although under normal conditions it is subject to variations corresponding to changes in these physical factors) is shown by the observation of Ludwig that the secretion pressure in the submaxillary salivary gland, when the outflow is resisted by fluid in a manometer, may rise much above the arterial pressure. Also by the observation that after administration of a drug, such as atropin, the blood-supply may be increased as much as before administration of the drug on stimulation of the secretory nerve, without, however, calling forth any flow of secretion. In other cases, such as the kidney, where the secretion pressure cannot be raised above arterial pressure, this is due to the nature of the minute anatomical structure, as a result of which all supply of fluid is cut off from the secreting cells before the pressure in the ductules can exceed that in the bloodvessels, and so the stoppage of secretion is a purely mechanical effect.

These experiments prove that, although secretion under normal conditions may be aided by filtration, yet the process in its nature is not one of passive filtration.

That it is not passively dependent upon osmotic pressure is shown (1) by the fact that the total osmotic pressure of the secretion, as shown by depression of freezing-point, is in many cases greater than that of the plasma; (2) that even in cases—such, for example, as the saliva—where the total osmotic pressure is less than that of the plasma, the osmotic pressure of certain constituents is higher than their pressure in the plasma—for example, in the saliva, the pressure of dissolved carbon dioxide, of calcium salts, and of the sulphocyanide; (3) that new constituents appear in the secretion as a result of chemical activity in the cell which are entirely absent in the plasma, and are not sent into the plasma, but into the gland duct, by means of cellular activity and in opposition to the operation of osmotic energy; (4) the alteration in many cases of chemical reaction by concentration of hydrogen or of hydroxyl ions in the secretion high above the concentration which they possess in the plasma, may be quoted as an example of cellular activity producing an effect in opposition to osmotic pressure.

Now it is clear that while the source of energy residing in the blood-pressure might separate a secretion, with concentration possessing any value up to that of the same dissolved constituent in the plasma, it cannot produce a concentration in even a single constituent exceeding the value of the concentration of that same constituent in the plasma, and certainly cannot produce a new constituent not present in the plasma. When the results of experiment are taken in conjunction with this statement, it is found that in every secretion in the body cellular activity must be brought into action—in other words, the secreting cell must furnish energy in the process of secretion—and this not only holds obviously for the new constituents, but also for all those crystallised and inorganic constituents which are found in the secretion at a higher concentration than in the plasma, and hence possess more osmotic energy.

Not only does the increase in concentration of certain constituents in the secretion above their concentration in the plasma rule out, as far as these constituents are concerned, the operation of filtration and osmosis, but it also rules out any passive view of the secretion whatever which does not involve work done by the cell as an active energy transformer.

If any single substance is increased in concentration in a secretion above the concentration which it possesses in the plasma, then such increase in concentration involves the performance of work against osmotic pressure,[1] *and in consequence the expenditure of energy by*

---

[1] This does not mean that the osmotic pressure is balanced or overcome by hydrostatic pressure in the cell, but that osmotic or volume energy must be replaced by energy in another form by the agency of the cell.

the secreting cell and the secretion of such substance cannot be explained by any theory which does not take into account the work of the cell as an energy transformer

A recognition of this principle would save much error in not recognising the limitations of certain theories which have been put forward in explanation of absorption and secretion by the cell.

In the first place may be mentioned the selective absorption theory of Overton, for the explanation of the selective uptake by the cell of different ions, salts, crystalloids, and nutrient matter, and the retention of certain salts or ions in the cell—such, for example, as potassium salts—in greater concentration than in the plasma.

Overton supposes that there exists, enclosing the cell or separating off in some manner its protoplasmic constituents from the plasma, a thin envelope or layer of lipoid substances, chiefly lecithin, which possesses selective permeabilities for different substances and ions in solution, being impermeable entirely for some, easily permeable for others, and in other cases permeable with difficulty. This theoretical lipoid membrane or " Plasmahaut " is supposed in this way to determine the uptake and output of the cell and its osmotic behaviour with regard to different substances, and has also been invoked in explanation of the toxicity or otherwise of different substances for the cell, and of the effects of anæsthetics.

Taking the theory first from the experimental point of view, although it must be admitted that " lipoids " (if by this term is meant merely substances soluble in ether) are present in all cells, and lecithin in all of those in which it has been experimentally sought, although often only in small traces; yet it has never been shown experimentally that this forms a separating membrane between plasma and cell protoplasm, as has been assumed by Overton. Further, it has never been shown that this hypothetical membrane possesses for different ions and crystalloids the permeabilities and impermeabilities ascribed to it.

In order to attempt to test the Overton theory with regard to salt solutions, the writer has prepared a lecithin membrane by thoroughly impregnating a membrane of parchment paper with lecithin, so that the pores of the paper were thoroughly soaked with the lecithin, and there was a continuous layer of lecithin on both sides of the paper, and using this as a membrane between sodium chloride solution and water, or between two sodium chloride solutions of different strengths, so as to avoid action of the water upon the lecithin.

According to Overton's view, the lecithin membrane, like the cell, ought to be impermeable to the sodium chloride, and in solutions of different strengths an osmotic pressure effect ought to have been obtainable with such a membrane.

It was found, however, when the membrane was used in an osmometer (1) that no osmotic pressure whatever developed on the sodium chloride solution side, or on the side of the stronger solution, and (2) that sodium chloride did pass through the membrane.

Accordingly, the presence of a lecithin membrane, even were such shown experimentally to exist, would not explain the osmotic phenomena of the cell or the impermeability of the cell for the sodium ion.

Taking next the membrane hypothesis from the theoretical point of view, the following arguments may be urged, which apply not only to the lipoid membrane but to any other conceivable membrane by which an attempt may be made to explain upon such a passive basis the active work of the cell in maintaining a different composition and concentration of the crystalloids and ions within it to that which obtains in the medium in which the cell lives. It is on account of this general applicability against an explanation by any passive membrane theory and not merely against the lipoidal membrane theory that the arguments are here given at length.

Take, first of all, the position that the cells are *entirely* impermeable to certain ions (and to other non-dissociated organic crystalloids), and that it is on account of such perfect impermeability that these are found only within or only without the cell, or in such very different and fixed concentrations within and without the cell. For example, that potassium salts are found in the cell in excess, and sodium salts in the plasma in excess, and that this is due to a membrane refusing passage entirely to sodium and potassium ions. This then excludes all exchange of such ions between cells and plasma, and there is neither any explanation on such a basis of how the present state of affairs with such an unequal distribution of potassium and sodium ions occurred in the first instance when the cells were formed and growing; nor any explanation of how more potassium ion is taken in and sodium ion excluded when cell division takes place and new cells are growing and causing increased volume of cellular tissue without any drop in potassium ion concentration. The explanation on the ground of complete impermeability can obviously only hold so long as the cell is in complete equilibrium with the plasma as regards the inner and outer levels in potassium and sodium salts But there is no explanation whatever of how that equilibrium was attained initially, nor how it is maintained when the cell volume increases as cell multiplication occurs. Are we to suppose that the original fertilised ovum contained all the potassium salts of the adult organism ? Obviously such a conclusion is absurd, and it must be admitted that the cells must have at some time taken up potassium and continued to reject sodium ions.

In fact, it is quite clear that so far from being impermeable to potassium ions, up to the period at which the cell attained its maximum saturation, it must have greedily taken up potassium ions, from an exceedingly low concentration in the plasma, by an *active* process of selective absorption against osmotic pressure and with corresponding expenditure of energy by the cell, in the same fashion as a diatom concentrates the silica for its skeleton from the trace present in sea water, or as the bone-forming cells take up the calcium salts from the circulating plasma. Once the cell has attained its normal level of potassium ion concentration this action ceases and equilibrium is attained; but this condition is preserved only so long as the cell is resting in size There is no evidence that there is an impermeable membrane formed, or that the cell is really impermeable to potassium salts, because it does not give them out or take them up any more in appreciable quantity; all this means is that there is a balance being maintained dependent upon the nature and active properties of the particular cell protoplasm involved. When such a cell is immersed in a solution of a potassium salt it takes practically none up, because it has already attained its balance in potassium ions, and *actively* preserves this Did it behave as an inert membrane, as when it is killed, it would take up more potassium ions in a strong solution; but the living cell does not do so to any appreciable extent; it actively preserves itself against osmotic invasion. On the other hand, when such a cell is placed in a solution not containing potassium salts, such as a solution of sodium chloride, it does not part with its potassium salts in appreciable amount; but this need not be because it is surrounded by a membrane impermeable to potassium ions but because it actively retains its potassium ions on account of that affinity or activity by which it originally took them up when they were present in traces only in the plasma.

Thus the balance of concentration for each individual ion and salt and dissolved substance within and without the cell is maintained, and readjusted when it changes, not by means of any hypothetical inert impassable membrane stopping any reaction between the cell contents and the constituents in solution within and without, but by the play of the cell's activities upon the medium in which it lives.

This, it may be remarked, is not theory but experimental fact; we *see* that the growing cell takes up certain definite constituents from the medium and rejects others, that the constituents taken up are often taken up in opposition to osmotic pressure, and hence only possible by the expenditure of energy by the cell.

Why, then, should the basis of explanation be changed, and when the cell comes into a position of *labile* equilibrium with its media should it be supposed that, instead of those forms of energy which brought it to that state being still active, the mechanism of a hypothetical membrane or permeability be invoked ?

The condition is analogous to that of a chemical reaction which has come into equilibrium; here we do not suppose that the reaction is frozen rigid, so to speak, at the equilibrium point, or that membranes of an impermeable type are formed around the molecules which keep them from reacting. No, the reaction is preserved by the balance of opposing factors, reactions still occur between the molecules, but these are equal and opposite.

So also in the case of the living cell in equilibrium: the case is not that of an impenetrable membrane through which an ion of potassium or sodium never passes, but a labile equilibrium with both potassium and sodium ions passing in and out all the time, but the numbers passing in and out are equal, so that the concentrations are preserved unaltered.

That this is the true state of affairs there is abundant experimental proof. For let the resting cell divide, and the two daughter cells commence to grow, then the supposed impermeable membrane for potassium ions quits the scene of action, and the growing cell readily takes up potassium ions.

Further proof of the existence of a labile balance of equilibrium is seen in the physiological behaviour of the cell when the appropriate ions are absent from its circulating fluids.

As we have seen in the preceding chapter in describing the effects of inorganic salts upon living cells, in order that the physiological properties of tissues may be maintained in a normal condition, it is necessary that normal amounts of different ions shall be present in the circulating medium. Thus the normal heart-beat cannot be retained unless a certain definite low concentration of potassium ion is maintained in the perfusing fluid. What explanation of this can be given on the basis that the active cells are impermeable to potassium ions ? If the cells of the heart muscle are impermeable to potassium ions, how can the presence, or absence, or variation in concentration, of such ions in the circulating fluid affect the physiological activity of the cells ? Obviously the cells *are* permeable to the potassium ions and in both directions; for when there is no potassium ion in the circulating fluid, the balance, for potassium ion between circulating fluid and cell contents, becomes upset, and corresponding to the low pressure in potassium ion in the circulating fluid potassium ion must be given out by the cell until a new equilibrium is reached. On the other hand, if potassium ion is present in the circulating fluid at the proper concentration to correspond to and balance the concentration in the cell, then exchange will be equal, the concentration of potassium ion in the cell will not change, and the cell will preserve its normal activities. Finally, if the concentration of the potassium ion in the circulating fluid be greater than that required to balance the concentration within the cell, then more potassium ion must enter the cell than leaves it, and the effect becomes evident in a change in the action of the cell.

But how, it may be asked, is such a statement to be correlated with that upon which the supposed impermeability of the cell for potassium ions is based, with the fact, namely, that the cell does not appear, as far as chemical investigations go, to take up, for example, potassium ion from a solution of a potassium salt in which it is immersed ? The correlation of the two sets of experimental facts is not, however, a difficult task. The explanation lies in the fact that the cell possesses different affinities for the different ions and other dissolved constituents of its circulating fluids, so that at the equilibrium point for normal conditions the concentrations for each constituent within and without the cell are never equal but bear a definite ratio to each other, and further that these constituents enter into unstable physical or chemical relations with the protoplasm, so that there is a more or less definite minimal concentration for each constituent ion or dissolved substance in the plasma, at which the protoplasm becomes combined with it.   There is an unstable chemical or physical combination formed between the protoplasm and each of the active constituents of the plasma, the existence of which depends upon the osmotic pressure or concentration of the particular constituent in the plasma; just as the existence of the compound oxyhæmoglobin in the red blood-corpuscles depends upon the partial osmotic pressure of oxygen in the plasma.

In the case of oxyhæmoglobin but little oxygen is given off until the pressure of oxygen in the plasma has fallen to the level of commencing dissociation of oxyhæmoglobin similarly; in the case of the tissue cells in general but little potassium ion, for example, is given off until the osmotic pressure of that ion has fallen in the plasma below a certain limit, when the range of dissociation of potassium ion commences [1]   Accordingly it is only at this limit that the change in physiological action of the cell due to diminution of potassium ionic pressure in the plasma begins to become evident.

On the other hand, with increasing osmotic pressure of oxygen in the plasma above the point at which oxyhæmoglobin has been completely formed, there is but little further uptake of oxygen by the red blood-corpuscle; and similarly in the case of the potassium ion, or any other active ion, in the plasma above the concentration at which the protoplasm of the tissue cell has been saturated, the uptake of potassium ion by the cell will be small and inappreciable to chemical investigation, so that even in an isotonic or somewhat hypertonic solution *of potassium salt alone* the amount of potassium ion taken up by the cell will not be appreciably greater to ordinary chemical analysis than that taken up from normal plasma where the osmotic pressure of potassium ion is many times lower, but still sufficiently high to cause almost complete association between the protoplasm and the potassium ion   Although the difference in uptake of either oxygen or potassium ion is so small as to escape chemical determination, it may, however, produce in both cases profound physiological effects, probably from the rapid increase in osmotic pressure of the constituent concerned in the cell after the

----

[1] The concentration of potassium ion in Ringer's solution lies above this limit.

saturation point has been passed. Thus, although at two atmospheres of oxygen pressure the amount of oxygen dissolved in corpuscles, plasma, and tissue cells is not very appreciably higher than when the oxygen pressure is about 100 mms , yet the activities of the cells become affected and the animal dies in convulsions. So although the uptake of potassium ion by the cell may not be appreciably affected quantitatively when the concentration in the plasma is increased compared to the uptake at a lower concentration, yet the physiological action of the small additional amount upon the cell may be enormous

It must be remembered that just as in the case of oxyhæmoglobin there is no absolutely definite pressure which can be spoken of as the dissociation *point*, but rather a definite range of pressure, throughout which association of the oxygen and hæmoglobin occurs, so in the case of other dissolved constituents (ions, organic crystalloids, and anæsthetics) and the tissue cells, there is not a sharp point, but a range of association with increasing pressure, and the curve of osmotic pressure and association varies with each dissolved constituent and each type of tissue cell.

In the case of every active drug, and every active constituent of the plasma, some such association must occur as the pressure of such constituent in the plasma rises, and dissociation (with recovery in the case of a drug) take place as the pressure falls. No drug or other substance can be active unless it either enters the cell, and forms some combination with the protoplasm, or else prevents in some manner association and dissociation of a like type in the case of some other important constituent necessary to normal protoplasmic activity.

The action of different drugs, their rapidity of action, and their dosage, will depend on the nature and extent of the association between them and the cell protoplasm. If the saturation point of the drug and protoplasm is attained at a low pressure and with a low amount of drug, then the amount of the drug necessary to produce the full effect will be small, and in all probability the cell will take up but little of the drug, so that to chemical analysis the uptake may appear to be zero, and yet physiological methods of examination may show that the effect is very profound.

For example, in the case of salts of iron, the saturation pressure must be excessively low, and a protein substance fully combined with iron contains but a very low percentage of iron, hence the

17

physiological effect of iron may be very large, although the uptake is infinitesimal, and the time required for uptake is large. Thus, in an individual weighing, say, 60 kilograms, the weight of blood would be approximately 4 kilograms, that of hæmoglobin about 500 grms., and in this the iron would be about 0·4 per cent., or 2 grms. Therefore in a course of iron treatment lasting over some weeks the amount of iron necessary to be taken up in order to produce a marked effect would obviously be so small as to be entirely beyond the bounds of determination under the conditions of experiment

Nor does the view of varying permeability of the cell to different dissolved substances, of high permeability for some and low permeability for others, give any better solution to the real problems of secretion and absorption than that of complete impermeability, for the simple reason that variations in permeability form a passive factor like the variation of a resistance, and hence can at most alter the time relations of the process, and not the end results, and so there can on such a basis be no explanation of the fact that work is done by the secreting cell in the process, as when a constituent dissolved substance is secreted at higher concentration and pressure than in the plasma   Thus if a cell is immersed in a fluid containing any given constituent in solution, it will, if it possesses any degree of permeability whatever for that constituent, become ultimately saturated to the equilibrium point with the constituent, and the point of equilibrium will not vary with the permeability; the only thing which will vary with the permeability will be the time in which equilibrium is attained. In considering the effects of change in permeability upon the time relationships of absorption and secretion, the factors to be borne in mind are the thickness of the layer through which diffusion has to occur, the difference in concentration of the diffusing dissolved substance or ion at the two surfaces bounding the layer through which diffusion is taking place, and the coefficient of diffusion for the particular substance through the layer. The rate of diffusion, regarded as a purely physical process unaided by the cellular activity (and dependent only upon the difference in osmotic pressure at the two sides of the layer or membrane, the thickness, and the coefficient of permeability or diffusion), may be said to be directly proportional to the difference in osmotic pressure and to the coefficient of permeability, and inversely proportional to the thickness of the layer or membrane—that is, the length of the absorbing or secreting cell.

Hence diffusion can only occur so long as there is a fall in osmotic pressure in the direction in which diffusion is taking place; when the two pressures become equal diffusion must stop, and if by any chance the pressure became greater in the direction in which diffusion had been taking place, then the purely physical process of diffusion would carry out or tend to carry out the process in the opposite direction. Accordingly any separation of a constituent at a higher osmotic pressure must be carried out against diffusion, with increase in osmotic energy, and heaping up of difference in osmotic pressure or increase in the potential factor of osmotic energy.

It is, then, only when the concentration of a substance, either secreted or passing through as an absorption product to the other side of the active cell, is diminished that diffusion due to osmotic pressure can be regarded as a factor in the process, and it is here only that we have to consider the possible effects of changes in the permeability of the cell   If the secreted or absorbed product is carried rapidly away from the other side of the cell after having passed through, so that it does not tend to approach in concentration, as a result of stagnation, that concentration it possesses in the fluid from which secretion or absorption is occurring, then the rapidity of secretion or absorption of the substance will be greater the thinner the secreting or absorbing cell and the higher its coefficient of permeability. In other words, accordingly as the cell grows thinner and more permeable, the more nearly will the secretion approach in concentration of its constituents to the fluid from which the secretion has been formed.

In so far as the cell has a lower permeability than the plasma or lymph, it will form a resistance of varying amount upon the rate of secretion, and in so far as the cell has a greater permeability than these fluids it will form a less resistance than a layer of equal thickness of these fluids, and to this extent the increased permeability will aid the rate of secretion. But it must clearly be pointed out that change in permeability can only act as a variation in resistance, and hence the concentration can never be increased, nor the dissolved substance be expedited through het cell at a greater rate than if the cell did not exist on the path—that is, than if the resistance for the length of the cell were zero—in other words, as far as diffusion is concerned the cell can have no positive effect, such as is actually seen for some constituent or other in every secretion.

Further, it may be pointed out that the extent of the secreting or absorbing surface is in all cases so large, and the thickness of the layer so small, amounting to the length of a single cell, that increase in permeability *above* the value for a layer of lymph or plasma of equal thickness can possess but a very secondary value in determining rate of secretion or absorption. Let us imagine the layer of secreting or absorbing cells spread out so as to form a huge plane lamina, the thickness of which is that of a single secreting cell, and the area of the side that of the total secreting area of cells, and that this lamina forms a membrane between lymph upon the one side and secretion upon the other; then, if this lamina were supposed to have the same resistance to diffusion through it as a lamina of lymph of equal thickness, such resistance would be excessively low, and with a rapid removal of fluid from the secretion side the concentration of each constituent upon the secretion side would be practically the same as upon the lymph side of the lamina. Hence the supposition of a higher permeability or selective permeability of the secreting cell above that of the lymph (or water) can have but an infinitesimal effect, since it cannot increase, as we have seen, the concentration above the value in the lymph, and if it had the value of the lymph (or water) in permeability, the concentrations would be practically the same. It is when the permeability changes in the opposite direction, and the degree of permeability of the secreting or absorbing cell becomes progressively less and less than that of a layer of lymph or water of equal thickness, that the only and indeed an important effect of cell permeability becomes obvious, in slowing, never in hastening, the rate of secretion of constituents. For as the permeability of our imaginary secreting or absorbing lamina to any constituent becomes less and less, its resistance to the passage of that constituent becomes greater and greater, and the concentration of the constituent in the secretion or absorbed fluid less and less, until in the limit none may pass through at all.

It is in such a resisting action that the value of differences in permeability comes in, by causing the retention of substances in the lymph, and not in a high degree of permeability causing increased rate of passage, and increased concentration of substances in secretion. Examples are the retention of the plasma proteins in the glomerular secretion or filtration, and the prevention of ingress of poisonous substances in many cases to the tissue cells.   But the greater concentration of substances and ions in the secretions cannot be explained by the application of the principle of altered permeability.   Diffusion and permeability can accordingly explain the passage of such substances as are already contained in the plasma up to the concentrations at which they are contained in the plasma, but furnish no means for obtaining substances not present in the plasma, or for concentrating crystalloids or ions in solution to osmotic pressure higher than in the plasma   The latter effects, which are universal in processes of secretion and absorption, can only be obtained from expenditure of energy by the cell

An attempt has been undertaken by Overton and Meyer and by Friedenthal to explain the secretion and absorption of substances by the cell on the basis of varying solvent powers of the cell or certain of its constituents for such substances.

Thus Overton would explain the effects of anæsthetics as arising from the high solubility of the anæsthetic in the *lipoids* or lecithin of the cell, and also the absorption or non-absorption of other substances by the cell as dependent upon whether they dissolve or not in the lipoid membrane, and hence can obtain ingress to the cell   The author does not state in the case of the anæsthetics whether the action is to be ascribed to the physical action upon the lipoids themselves, or whether it is due to a passage through the lipoids to the cell protoplasm

Friedenthal has evolved a similar theory for the absorption of fats in the intestine, which he ascribes to the high solubility · of the fats in the protoplasm of the absorbing cells.   The theory is also extended to other substances taken up in solution for absorption or secretion, so that these processes are placed in dependence upon the peculiar and selective properties of the cell as a solvent

The two theories of the lipoid membrane acting as a selective solvent and of the cell protoplasm playing a similar rôle may be taken together, as the same arguments apply to both views.

Neither of these theories furnishes any basis of explanation of how energy is expended in concentrating any secreted or absorbed substance.   For the fact that a substance, such as the lipoids or cell protoplasm, is a good solvent for a given constituent does not give any power to the solvent to pass that substance through the cell in more concentrated solution, or indeed to alter the concentration of the dissolved substance anywhere *save in the solvent itself*.   Further, increased concentration in the solvent has no effect whatever upon rate of passage of the substance through the solvent or through the cell, and will indeed delay passage through the cell until the lipoid or cell protoplasm has become saturated with the dissolved substance, and after that will behave in an inert manner, without any effect either upon uptake of dissolved substance, rate of passage of dissolved substance through the cell, or output of dissolved substance at the other side.

In the statement of the two theories there is a complete confusion of solubility and permeability, which are quite distinct processes. ,

The matter may perhaps be most easily made clear by means of a diagram.

Suppose we have a sphere of fluid C, surrounded by a continuous layer of a different fluid B, and immersed in a vessel containing a

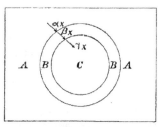

FIG. 4.

quantity of fluid A, and that A contains a substance x in solution. Further, that the substance is also soluble in the fluids B and C, and that the coefficient of distribution of the substance x is such between the three fluids, that the concentrations of βx in B and of γx in C correspond to the concentration αx in A, so that there is equilibrium when the ratio of concentrations is $\alpha x : \beta x : \gamma x$ in the three fluids A, B, and C.   Now if at the commencement there is none of x in B or C but x is present in A, diffusion into B will take place, and as soon as the concentration of x in B commences to rise there will be diffusion from B into C.   Also, the higher the value of the ratio $\beta : \alpha$, the more rapid, other things being equal, will be the rate of entry of x into B; *but* if β be increased so as to increase the ratio $\beta : \alpha$, the ratio $\gamma : \beta$ which determines the rate of output into C will be correspondingly *diminished,* and hence the rate of passage from A to C is entirely independent of the solubility in B, and depends only upon the rate of *transmission* or diffusion through B.[1]   Also the final condition of equilibrium is independent of the solubility in B, for A and C are

[1] The matter may also be put thus—the rate of solution from A into B is given by $k_1 \dfrac{\beta}{\alpha}$, that of solution from B into C by $k_2 \dfrac{\gamma}{\beta}$, therefore that from A into C is given by $k_1 \dfrac{\beta}{\alpha} \cdot k_2 \dfrac{\gamma}{\beta}$, or $K \dfrac{\gamma}{\alpha}$.

cach in equilibrium with B, and hence are in equilibrium with one another, so that when the final concentrations are attained the ratio of concentrations in A and C must be the same as if B were left out and A and C had been placed in contact and allowed to come into equilibrium   The only factor which affects the result apart from equilibrium is the rate of diffusion of the substance x through the layer B, and this may not bear any constant relationship to the solubility of x in B.

We see, therefore, that a high solubility of any dissolved substance in a supposed lipoid membrane or in the cell protoplasm, will cause a corresponding accumulation of that substance in the lipoid membrane or in the cell protoplasm, but cannot act as an engine or energy producer for sending the substance through the cell as a secretion or an absorbed product.

The substance taken up as a result of higher solubility, such as an anæsthetic absorbed in lipoids, or by fat in ordinary adipose tissue, is hence imprisoned to that same extent in the fat or lipoid, and kept from attacking or combining with the protoplasm; and accordingly the presence of such bodies, instead of aiding or causing anæsthesia, acts in the opposite sense by forming a reservoir for the anæsthetic where it is inert so far as the cell protoplasm is concerned, which is its real objective so far as production of anæsthesia is concerned.

The view expressed above, that those substances which are actively absorbed and retained by the tissue cells form unstable physical or chemical compounds with the cell protoplasm dependent upon the osmotic pressure of such substances, cannot any more than the others which have just been criticised be put forward as an explanation of the active work of the cell in secretion and absorption, when the product is not to be retained in the cell, but is to be turned out in greater concentration than that at which it entered. For substances in such unstable combination, although subject to different laws of relationship between concentration and osmotic pressure, obviously come into equilibrium also at a given point of concentration and osmotic pressure, and hence their formation cannot be turned into a continuous source of energy for the performance of work by the cell, such as is required to fit the case of secretion

The formation of such unstable compounds is capable of explaining the selective uptake and retention of constituents by the cell, just as the different solubilities of different constituents by the cell protoplasm or lipoids may explain such uptake or retention, but neither view can explain more than this. Before passing on to a consideration of the energy changes involved in secretion, and the possible explanation of such changes, it may be well to point out that the view of the formation of unstable chemical combinations between cell protoplasm and selectively absorbed and retained constituents, fits the observed facts much better than the alternative view of solution in cell protoplasm or in cell lipoids. For if the explanation were solution, then the osmotic pressure and amount of substance taken up must be in simple ratio to each other. On doubling the osmotic pressure of any constituent in the lymph, the amount taken up or secreted by the cell ought to be doubled, since for simple solution the coefficient of distribution between cell and lymph must be constant, or, in other words, the relationship between osmotic pressure and amount absorbed by the cell should be a linear one.

This is not found, however, experimentally to be the case; the absorption at first rises very rapidly with increasing osmotic pressure, then later the rise in amount absorbed for equal increments of osmotic pressure is much decreased, an almost maximum value is later reached, after which there is hardly any appreciable increase in absorption. This sequence of events is precisely what would occur if formation of an unstable or reversible chemical combination took place at a certain range of pressure, and is seen, for example, typically in the combination between hæmoglobin and oxygen. Hence it is most probable that such a type of combination exists in the case of those ions and other cell constituents which are selectively absorbed and retained.

THE ENERGY CHANGES INVOLVED IN SECRETION.

The work done by the secreting cell in the process of secretion may be considered as divided into two fractions—viz., (1) the work done in increasing the volume energy, or work done against osmotic pressure in increasing the concentration of dissolved substances already present in the lymph, and (2) the work done in increasing chemical energy by the formation in the cell of *new* substances not present in the lymph from other substances and by means of the chemical energy supplied by other substances present in the lymph.

It is only for the first of these types of energy production by the cell that accurate quantitative estimations can be made ; because for the second type the chemical energy and amounts of the organic substances formed in the cell, and the chemical energy and amounts of substances used by the cell in their formation, are at present unknown to us.

Method of Estimating the Work done against Osmotic Pressure in separating each Constituent of a Secretion —The amount of work done in separating each constituent of a secretion can easily be deduced when the pressure of the substance in the lymph and in the secretion are known, and the total volume of the secretion. But such estimation must be made for each constituent of the secretion separately, and the total work done is the sum of the work done in the separation of each constituent. It leads to quite a fallacious result to take the two depressions of freezing-point of the lymph and secretion respectively, calculate the total osmotic pressure of lymph and secretion from these two values, and then assume that the work done is the product of the volume of the solution and the difference in pressure. For the amount of volume-energy change, as has been pointed out in a previous chapter, depends upon the two pressures for each constituent between which pressure has varied for that particular constituent, and since in the formation of a secretion the same ratio is not preserved between the pressures of the various constituents as exists in the lymph, but one constituent is far more compressed or concentrated than another, it cannot be taken that the lymph is compressed or concentrated as a whole as it were by a piston impermeable to all the dissolved constituents, and the work done obtained from the total initial and final osmotic pressures and the change in volume, but instead the work done upon each pressure-giving constituent must be taken separately, and the total work calculated as the sum of all these fractions.

As demonstrated in a previous chapter, the work done when a grm. molecule of substance is compressed from pressure p_1 to pressure p_2 is given by the expression $RT \log \dfrac{p_2}{p_1}$, and if Q be any other weight in grms. of the substance and M the molecular weight, then the number of grm. molecules will be $\dfrac{Q}{M}$, and the expression for the amount of work done in changing the pressure of the quantity Q grms. in solution at pressure p_1 to pressure p_2 will be $RT \dfrac{Q}{M} \log \dfrac{p_2}{p_1}$.

If now there are any number of substances A, B, C . . . N in solution in the secretion in quantities Q_a, Q_b, Q_c . . . Q_n, and the molecular weights of the substances be M_a, M_b, M_c . . . M_n, and the pressures of the substances in the lymph be represented by p_a, p_b, p_c . . . p_n, and the corresponding pressures in the secretion by p'_a, p'_b, p'_c . . . p'_n; then the expression for the work done upon each substance in its production from the pressure in the lymph to the pressure in the plasma will be the same as that given above for a single substance; for example, for substance A the expression will be $\dfrac{Q_a}{M_a} RT \log \dfrac{p'_a}{p_n}$. Accordingly the value of the total amount of work done against osmotic pressure (W) will be given by:

$$W = RT \left(\frac{Q_a}{M_a} \log \frac{p'_b}{p_a} + \frac{Q_b}{M_b} . \log \frac{p'_b}{p_b} + \frac{Q_c}{M_c} \log \frac{p'_c}{p_c} \cdots \frac{Q_n}{M_n} \log \frac{p'_n}{p_n} \right)$$

or

$$W = RT\Sigma \frac{Q_a}{M_a} \log \frac{p'_a}{p_a}.$$

If any of the constituents is electrolytically dissociated, then Q in the expression for the work done in separating it must be multiplied by the dissociation factor, because the osmotic pressure will be higher on account of the dissociation, and correspondingly more work will be done in the separation; thus in the case of the sodium chloride of the urine, for example, at the concentration at which that salt is there separated it is almost completely dissociated, and Q must be multiplied by the factor 1·9 approximately in order to obtain the amount of work done.

The above investigation of an expression for the amount of work done against osmotic energy in separating a secretion is entirely different from that usually given, which is quite erroneous in that it supposes all the constituents of the secretion to be equally concentrated in the process of separation from the plasma. Such a supposition is wrong in fact, and leads to quite a wrong expression for the total amount of work done, as well as for the work done upon each constituent. For example, while the concentrations of urea in plasma and urine are respectively 0·04 and 2·0 per cent. in the human organism, the similar concentrations of sodium chloride are 0 55 and 1·10 per cent.; and hence in the expressions for the work done in secreting urea and sodium chloride respectively the factor $\log_e \dfrac{p_2}{p_1}$ has quite a different value in the two cases, being $\log_e 50$ in the case of the urea and $\log_e 2$ in the case of the sodium chloride. As a result, taking the average daily quantities to be 30 grms in the case of urea, and 16 grms. in the case of sodium chloride, and correcting for the almost complete dissociation of the sodium chloride, a calculation of the work done in the separation in the two cases shows that the amount of work done in separating the urea is nearly six times as great as that done in separating the sodium chloride

This is quite different from the usual type of treatment, in which it is taken in calculating the work done merely from the lowerings of freezing-point of serum and of urine respectively, that the calculation may be based on the supposition that the secretion may roughly be regarded as a concentration of sodium chloride.

The reason of the fallacy is not far to seek: the urea solution is, roughly speaking, concentrated fifty times in the process of secretion, while the concentration of the sodium chloride is barely doubled. If then we imagine the urea and sodium chloride as being separately removed from the plasma by the action of a semipermeable piston, in the first case impermeable to urea and in the second case impermeable to sodium and chlorine ions and to sodium chloride; then, to separate in each case 1500 c c. of secretion containing in one case 2 per cent of urea, and in the other case 1 1 per cent of sodium chloride, from a plasma containing 0·04 per cent of urea and 0·55 per cent. of sodium chloride, we should require to take in the case of the urea $1500 \times \dfrac{2}{0 04} = 75{,}000$ c.c. of plasma and compress down to 1500 c c., while in the case of the sodium chloride we should only have to take $1500 \times \dfrac{1 \cdot 1}{0 \cdot 55} = 3000$ c c of plasma and compress down to 1500 c.c.

Hence to get the true expression for the work done against osmotic pressure in secretion, each constituent must be treated separately, and the work done depends in large degree upon the pressures of the separated constituent in plasma and secretion respectively, and the total molecular amount separated. So that as a result, for example, in the case of the urine, the separation of the urea involves more work than the separation of all the other constituents combined.

As an example of the method of calculating the work done in secretion against osmotic pressure, we may give the calculation of the amount done in secreting the normal daily amount of urea— viz., 30 grms. in a 2 per cent. solution, measuring accordingly 1500 c.c. The molecular weight of urea is 60, and it is not dissociated, so that there is no correction for dissociation, also the usual figure of 0·04 per cent. may be taken for the concentration in the plasma.

The expression for the work done is

$$W = RT \frac{Q}{M} \log_e \frac{p'}{p}.$$

If we express this amount of work as heat energy in small calories the value of the constant R becomes 1·98, if T be taken at 40° C., the value of T in absolute scale becomes 273+40=313, and hence the value of RT is 620 at this temperature;[1] Q is 30 grms., and the value of M, the molecular weight in grms., is 60, so that $\frac{Q}{M}$ becomes 0·5; the value of the ratio of $\frac{p'}{p}$ is the same as that of the two concentrations of the urea in secretion and plasma respectively $= \frac{2}{0·04} = 50$, and for $\log_e 50$, we can substitute $\log_{10} 50$; on dividing by the Briggs modulus for transference from Napierian to common logarithms, the value of $\log_{10} 50$ is very closely 1·7, and the value of the modulus is 0·434; so that we

---

[1] The value of 5·8 rational calories or 580 small calories, given in a previous chapter, was the usual value based on a temperature of 15° C.; the value 620 small calories used above is that which the expression RT has at a temperature of 40° C., the approximate temperature of secretion of the urine. The value of 1·98 for R is obtained by using the formula PV=RT, or $R = \frac{PV}{T}$, and then substituting the values for P, V, and T for a grm. molecule at any given values of pressure, volume, and temperature corresponding to one another. Thus a grm. molecule at 0° C. has a volume of 22,330 c.c., a pressure of 76 cms. of mercury $= 76 \times 13·4 \times 981$ dynes, and T is 273 on absolute scale. Also 1 small calory $= 42 \times 10^6$ dynes, and on substituting these values in the above equation we obtain for the value of R in small calories:

$$R = \frac{22330 \times 76 \times 13·4 \times 981}{273 \times 42 \times 10^6} = 1·98.$$

finally get on making all these substitutions in the above equation, for the value of the work done expressed in small calories:

$$W = 620 \times 0\ 5 \times 1\cdot 7 \div 0\ 434 = 1214 \text{ calories.}$$

This amount of energy may be expressed as mechanical work by remembering that the small calory is approximately equivalent to 0 042 kilogram-metres, and multiplying by this factor, we obtain $1214 \times 0\ 042 = 50\ 9$ kilogram-metres as the work done by the kidneys in secreting the urea against osmotic pressure. The work done in similarly secreting the sodium chloride is less than 10 kilogram-metres, as can be shown by a similar calculation, and these two form the chief amount of the work done against osmotic pressure, because the amount of the other constituents is comparatively low.

The estimate of 100 kilogram-metres would therefore be certainly above the amount of total work done by the kidneys against osmotic pressure in the twenty-four hours, and it must be pointed out that this amount is by no means large. Expressed as heat it would only, if it were all taken as heat from the urine secreted, lower the temperature of that excretion between $1°$ and $2°$ C.

The osmotic pressure of a secretion expressed as a hydrostatic pressure may give a very high value; thus Dreser found in the morning urine of man a lowering of the freezing-point amounting to $2\ 3°$ C., which corresponds to an osmotic pressure of 282 metres of water, or over 30 atmospheres of pressure.

In the urine of other animals still higher osmotic pressures are obtained; thus in the cat an osmotic pressure of 49,800 grms. per square centimetre was calculated by Dreser, and the statement is made that if the work of concentration were carried out by the cells of the kidney tubules, these results would imply that these cells can exert a force six times greater than the absolute force of human muscle (8000 grms. per square centimetre).

Such a statement and such a view as to the action of the cells of the tubules, is, however, a highly absurd one. The kidney cells do carry out the work of concentration, but we have no evidence that they exert or resist the least possible pressure in the process. Although the osmotic pressure is so high, the amount of energy change, as is shown by the calculation given above, is comparatively very small, and the work of the kidney cell consists in supplying this small amount of energy, from energy in another form, by transformation of a corresponding small amount of the energy which it takes up as nutrient matter from the plasma. That anything approximating to the osmotic pressure of the separated urine develops in this process of energy transformation, or indeed that there is any pressure developed whatever, we possess not the smallest fraction of experimental evidence. All that is known is that there is a small increase in osmotic energy, provided by the expenditure of energy by the secreting kidney cell. The view that the kidney cell is something in the nature of a semipermeable membrane with a difference in pressure upon its two ends of many atmospheres of pressure is an entirely erroneous one; no cell in the body could withstand such a difference in pressure for a moment; there is no evidence that such a pressure exists in the kidney tubules —in fact, it most certainly does not exist. Finally, no arrangement in the nature of a semipermeable membrane could form the secretion with accompanying concentration of dissolved substances. In the first instance, because for such an operation, as has already been pointed out, energy is required which a semipermeable membrane cannot yield. Since an energy machine such as the cell must be utilised for producing the secretion, we at once lose on the introduction of such a machine all necessity for the maintenance of hydrostatic pressure in opposition to osmotic pressure, and there is no more reason why the kidney cells should be supposed to be exposed to the osmotic pressure than there is to suppose that the walls of the bladder should have to withstand the osmotic pressure of the urine after it has been secreted and passed into the bladder.

In an exactly similar manner, the work done in the secretion of any constituent of any secretion can be calculated if the pressures or concentrations in plasma and secretion and the amount of secreted substance and volume of secretion are known.

As to the mechanism or type of energy transformation by which the cell does its work nothing is known ; similar phenomena of concentration of ions and of dissolved colloids by means of movement in the electric field have long been known, and it is probable that it may be the case that the living secreting cell, by developing differences in electrical potential at its two ends, or by developing differences in energy potential of some other form of energy such as that which intrinsically belongs to the living cell, may establish a directive influence upon substances in solution, as a result of which, and of energy potentials upon the dissolved molecules themselves, they may be caused to move in a definite direction and at a definite speed through the cell, different from that of the water in which they are dissolved. A similar directive movement, in fact, to that seen in the case of dissolved ions and colloidal molecules in the electric field may occur

Or the energy changes may be brought about by chemical combinations and dissociations in the cell.

But whatever view be taken as to the mode of operation, it is clear from the experimental study of the selective rates of passage of dissolved substances through the cell that what might be termed " polar " properties must be ascribed to the cell in its phenomena of secretion and absorption. This is not theory but experimental fact. It is seen that many substances pass through the cell several times more rapidly than the solvent, while others pass through more slowly. In the case of those which pass through more rapidly, work in giving velocity to these molecules or ions and in increasing osmotic energy must be done by the cell. It is clear from this that the amount of solvent in which any given quantity of a constituent is dissolved need never enter the cell, but instead the dissolved substance may be attracted and moved through the solvent towards and into the cell by the energy of the cell, just as independent velocities are given to the ions towards the electrodes by the electric potentials on the electrodes without the solvent between the electrodes moving at the same rate towards either electrode. Thus there may only be a slow current of water through the cell, with a slow uptake of water from the lymph, and a much more rapid current of dissolved substances and corresponding increase in concentration of these in the secretion or absorbed fluid

If the water containing the dissolved substances were taken up at the same rate by the secreting cell, then in order that the secretion could become more concentrated in any constituent it would be necessary that at intervals water should be returned or pressed out again at the side of the cell at which it entered, containing the constituent which was to be concentrated in more dilute solution. It hence appears more probable that instead of such a to-and-fro movement of water, the dissolved substances are taken up upon the entrance side of the cell more rapidly than if they passively moved in with a corresponding amount of water.

That this view is probable is seen from the enormous amount of water which would have to pass into and out of the cell alternately if only passive absorption of water and its dissolved substances formed the first stage in the process of secretion Thus in the secretion of hydrochloric acid in the gastric juice, the concentration of the hydrogen ion has to be increased from an almost immeasurably low concentration in the plasma up to almost the strength of a deci-normal solution, and to do this by passive absorption an enormous amount of water must enter the secreting cell and be again rejected at the same side at which it entered. Again, in the secretion of urea in the urine 75 kilograms would have to enter and pass through the kidney cells and be reabsorbed in order to concentrate and separate the daily output of urea. Also, in absorption from the intestine, to take up a meal of 150 grms. of carbohydrate or fat in 1 per cent. solution, which is probably in excess of the concentration at which these foodstuffs are normally absorbed, it would be necessary for 15 kgrms. of water to be taken up by the absorbing cells, and either returned by alternating back streams into the intestine free from carbohydrate or fat, or else poured into the blood-stream Such an amount is much in excess of the total of the water swallowed with the food and the combined digestive secretions

Hence we must suppose that the cell, whether absorbing or secreting, does not undergo passive infiltration by the fluids in contact with it, and allow these, or even the water, to stream through passively, but is an active energy machine, and takes up the various constituents and their solvents in definite and well-regulated proportions.

For the reason stated at the outset, the amounts of energy involved in the formation by the cell of the new organic constituents of the secretion not present in the plasma cannot at present be estimated, and so we pass to a consideration of the extrinsic mechanisms of secretion.

The Extrinsic Mechanisms of Secretion.

Alterations in the Blood-Supply to the Secreting Gland —Accompanying the increased amount of physiological work which the secreting cells have to perform, there is always during secretion an increase in the amount of blood supplied. This increase was estimated by Chauveau and Kaufmann in the case of the submaxillary salivary gland as amounting to three times the blood-supply in the resting condition of that gland, but according to more recent experiments by Barcroft, it may in the dog be set down as amounting to more nearly six times the blood-supply in the resting condition.

Comparative analyses of the blood-gases in the arterial blood and the venous blood passing from the gland show also, according to Barcroft's experiments, that the amount of oxygen used by the gland, and also the amount of carbon dioxide formed, as shown by the sum of the increase in the venous blood and the amount in the saliva, both increase during activity much above the amounts similarly determined in the case of the resting gland, pointing to increased chemical activity during secretion.

Thus, Barcroft found that during secretion of saliva by the submaxillary gland, induced by stimulation of the chorda tympani, the oxygen taken from the blood was increased to an amount which was three to four times that taken up by the resting gland. The carbon dioxide given out by the gland was also increased under the same circumstances to an equal or even greater amount. While after an injection of atropin sufficient to cause paralysis of the secretion the intake of oxygen was not increased by stimulation of the chorda tympani, on the other hand the output of carbon dioxide was increased, at least for a time.

In the case of the pancreas Barcroft and Starling found that the secretion was also accompanied by an increased oxygen absorption from the blood, and that this increased oxidation took place irrespective of increased blood-flow through the organ. These observers also found that the normal oxidation in the pancreas was much greater than in the body generally, and about the same as that of the submaxillary gland.

In experiments upon the metabolism in the kidney, Barcroft and Brodie found that the production of diuresis was accompanied by a marked increase in the absorption of oxygen, although there was no direct proportionality in oxygen absorption and degree of diuresis. The authors found no definite relation between the oxygen taken in and the carbon dioxide given out, and also that the onset of diuresis was not necessarily accompanied by an increase in the rate of blood-flow through the kidney, and even where an increased flow was found it was never proportional to the acceleration of the urinary flow

18

The profound influence of the nervous system upon secretion is in the case of certain glandular structures a matter of common experience. Thus it is well known to us that the sight or smell of food often provokes salivary secretion, or causes the mouth to water, in everyday parlance; but the effect of the nervous system is in the case of other glands most difficult to prove, and may be said in certain cases not even yet to have been unequivocally demonstrated. Certain it is in some cases from the recent experiments of Bayliss and Starling that this nervous stimulation cannot be regarded as the sole, if indeed the most fundamental and important, factor; and we shall see in the next section that it must be regarded as supplemented or replaced by the important action of chemical stimulation and the production of specific secretory substances which act upon the secreting cells after having been absorbed by the circulating blood.

As has been well pointed out by Pawlow, it is dangerous, in the case of the nervous mechanisms of secretion, to generalise from the somewhat simple mechanism of salivary secretion for the secretory innervation of the whole secreting system of glands, for in the case of other glands, such as the gastric glands and probably the pancreas, the influence of inhibitory nervous mechanisms comes into play and complicates the problem. Hence we are forced to consider separately the nervous mechanisms in the case of each important secreting gland.

Before proceeding to the separate accounts, however, it may be well to point out the general resemblances.

In each case where an influence of the nervous system upon secretion has been clearly demonstrated, it has been shown that a complete reflex arc exists. The nervous stimulation is excited at the peripheral endings of afferent fibres, which excite nerve cells in the central nervous system and cause stimuli to be discharged along efferent paths to the secreting cells. In the case of the salivary glands the afferent channels are nerves of special sense, either the optic or ophthalmic nerves, or the endings of the gustatory nerves in the mucous membrane of the mouth. In the case of the gastric secretion the afferent impulses arise at the mucous membrane of the stomach by the stimulation of peripheral nerve endings through the medium of digestible substances present in the stomach, or through nerves of special sense by the sight of appetising food, as has been shown by the experiments of Pawlow.

In all cases, the efferent nervous impulses by which secretion is excited pass along one of two paths, one coming directly from the central nervous system and the other indirectly through the sympathetic nervous system

In the case of the salivary glands, our knowledge of the efferent paths belongs to classical and well-established physiological history, while in the case of the gastric and pancreatic secretions the efferent channels may be said still to be in dispute.

The Innervation of the Salivary Glands.—Each of the important paired salivary glands receives efferent fibres from two sources—viz , directly from a cephalic nerve, and indirectly from the sympathetic system. About eighty years ago Carl Ludwig showed in the case of the submaxillary gland that the gland possessed a special secretory nerve, the chorda tympani, which on stimulation called into activity a copious secretion of saliva. The flow of saliva was large in quantity but poor in organic constituents and in the specific ferment. Some twenty-five years later Heidenhain demonstrated that the gland also received secretory fibres from the cervical sympathetic, which evoked a flow of saliva small in total quantity but rich in organic constituents and in the specific ferment produced by the gland

As a result of his experiments, Heidenhain evolved the theory that the salivary glands possessed two sets of secretory fibres, one obtained from the cephalic nerve and possessing the property of evoking a flow of water and saline, and the other, which he termed the " trophic " or " anabolic " nerve, obtained from the sympathetic system and responsible for stimulating the secretion of organic substances and the specific ferment

This view of Heidenhain's was subsequently generalised for secretion in general without adequate experimental proof. In the case of the submaxillary gland, however, it must be admitted from the clear experimental evidence, that of the two efferent sets of fibres which govern the secretion of the gland, one induces a free flow of dilute saliva poor in organic constituents, while the other causes a scanty flow of a richer saliva. Also, as shown by Langley, alternate stimulation of the two nerves causes an increase in the amount of saliva which would arise from stimulation of the sympathetic only, and indicates that in normal secretion there is a conjoint action of the two efferent nerves, giving rise to the usual secretion. Hence we must regard the chorda tympani as largely responsible for the flow of water and saline constituents, and the sympathetic as responsible for the stimulation of the gland cells to the production of the organic constituents and ferment.

The Innervation of the Gastric Glands.—The gastric glands, like all the other digestive glands, are supplied by two sets of nerve fibres, one cerebrospinal and the other sympathetic. In the case of the stomach the cerebrospinal fibres are supplied by the vagus and the sympathetic fibres are derived from the solar plexus.

The proof that these fibres possess an effect upon the process of secretion by the gastric glands has, however, been exceedingly difficult to obtain unequivocally by experiment, mainly on account of the important nerve supplies to other organs and regions which accompany the gastric nerve fibres in the vagus. As a result of this, section or stimulation of the vagus gives rise to profound effects other than those upon the secreting cells of the gastric mucous membrane, which obscure and mask, or interfere with, the effects upon secretion, and hence it was only by ingenious methods of avoiding such results that Pawlow and his co-workers were able to demonstrate that the vagus contained excitatory fibres for the secreting cells. Several of the earlier workers upon the subject found that section of both vagi in the neck led to suppression of the gastric secretion; but this double operation performed at one time leads to such profound disturbances that, as Pawlow points out, it had little effect in encouraging a belief in a causal connection between the vagus fibres and gastric secretion, since it is not to be wondered at that an operation which in a short time brings the whole functions of the organism to a standstill should amongst other things disturb the action of the gastric glands. An attitude of caution towards the results of an experiment with such drastic consequence was suggested by the further experiment of Schiff, of dividing the vagi beneath the diaphragm in dogs, when, especially in young animals, there was good recovery and the animals lived in excellent health after the operation. Also Rutherford found that gastric secretion could be formed after section of both vagi or of both splanchnics. Similarly Pawlow found much more recently that even after double vagotomy the stomach is capable of preparing its specific secretion in the absence of vagal influence.

But, as Pawlow points out, this does not settle the problem as to whether the vagus contains fibres which influence the secretion, and he adduces evidence going to show that the vagus probably contains both excitatory and inhibitory fibres for the secreting cells of the stomach.

It is only by careful comparison of the secretory activity of the stomach before and after vagotomy, and by stimulation of the peripheral end of the nerve in such a manner, or after such procedures, that other effects upon the heart, etc., are not excited, that we can judge as to any possible effect upon secretion.

Previous to Pawlow's more detailed experiments as to the paths along which efferent stimuli pass to the secreting cells, it had been shown fairly clearly that the gastric secretion could be called forth by reflex nervous mechanism. Thus Richet showed in the case of a boy with an inoperable and complete stricture of the œsophagus occasioned by swallowing caustic alkali, upon whom a gastrotomy had been performed, that soon after taking anything sweet or acid into the mouth a secretion of pure gastric juice occurred, which could accordingly only be excited by a reflex nervous stimulus. Bidder and Schmidt also showed that the sight of food to a dog with a gastric fistula led to a flow of gastric juice. The experiment of Richet was, however, an isolated one, and in those of Bidder and Schmidt the stimulus might have been a direct one due to swallowed saliva.

To Pawlow belongs the credit of having devised most ingenious methods for studying the secretion of the gastric juice, the reflex influence of the nervous system upon the secretion, and the efferent path by which the reflex travelled ; as also the effects of different forms of food upon the amount and properties of the secretion.

A method for studying the secretion apart from any influence of the contact of saliva or swallowed food was obtained by making a fistula of the œsophagus in the neck in addition to the usual gastric fistula. After the double operation the effect of " *physical* " stimulation could be studied by *showing* appetising food to the animal but not allowing it to chew or swallow it, when a copious flow of gastric juice resulted after a latent period of about five minutes. Also the effect of *sham* feeding was investigated, in which the animal, in addition to being shown the food, was allowed to chew and swallow it ; but the food dropped out at the œsophageal fistula and did not enter the stomach and so excite it by direct contact. In this method of sham feeding the flow of gastric juice was somewhat greater in most cases than where the afferent stimulus occurred from the sight of food only ; but the increase was never very marked, and in the case of some foods which greatly excited the appetite the psychical juice or " appetite juice " was as great as or even exceeded slightly that from sham feeding.

Again, Pawlow was able to study by this method the effect of stimulation of the gastric mucous membrane by means of direct contact of the food, which was introduced into the stomach through the gastric fistula without the knowledge of the animal, when it was asleep, or when its attention was strongly excited in some other direction. In this case there is an absence of the ordinary excitants of appetite in the sight and smell of food and in the operations of chewing and tasting it. Here it was found that the effect upon secretion varied with the character of the food, and that, contrary to what might perhaps have been expected, digestible protein food did not always prove to be a strong excitant to a flow of gastric juice. Thus milk or a solution of white of egg introduced into the stomach gave rise to scarcely any secretion, not more than would a quantity of water or dilute saline solution. But meat-broth, meat-juice, or solutions of meat extracts gave rise in all cases after a latent period of a few minutes to a considerable flow of gastric juice. The number of such direct excitants of a flow of juice was, however, found by Pawlow to be small, being almost confined to certain constituents of flesh food, which are also found in meat extracts. Thus, fats, carbohydrates, and ordinary proteins were without any effect.

In the case of flesh food, Pawlow showed that the amounts of secretion obtained by sham feeding and by direct introduction of the flesh into the stomach, when added together approximately equalled the amount of secretion when the animal ate the food, and the food which dropped out at the œsophageal fistula was placed in the stomach.

Accordingly the excitation to secretion through the nervous system may be divided into three fractions—viz., (1) that due to the sight and smell of the food ; (2) that due to the taste, mastication, and swallowing of the food ; and (3) that due to the contact of the food with the stomach. And of these three the first, according to Pawlow's experiment, is responsible for the greater portion of the flow of secretion.

The statement that mere mechanical irritation of the gastric mucous membrane by contact with foreign bodies is an efficient stimulus to provoke a flow of gastric juice is so often made in physiological textbooks that it may be well to state that Pawlow entirely denies such an influence, and states that the most thorough and prolonged irritation of the mucous surface, with a glass rod or feather, or by the blowing of sand into the stomach, is incapable of causing a single drop of secretion.

Another experimental method of great importance devised by Pawlow, both for investigating the effect upon secretion of various forms of foods and for studying the innervation of the glands, was that of forming a miniature stomach completely lined by mucous membrane, and possessing its nerve-supply intact, yet completely shut off from the main stomach [1] Different foods could be introduced into the main stomach by the usual process of feeding, or, in certain other animals in which the method of operation above described of œsophagotomy and ordinary gastrotomy had been performed in addition to the formation of the miniature stomach, the food could be introduced directly into the stomach, or psychical or sham feeding could be carried on.

Since the mucous membrane is not injured in the operation, and the nerve-supply is left intact, the small pouch of mucous membrane isolated becomes a faithful mirror or index of what is occurring in the main stomach Accordingly the rate of secretion and the quality of the secretion can be studied throughout the whole process of digestion of a meal of any type, and also the innervation of the glands can be tested by observing the effects of section and stimulation of the nerves supplying the stomach.

We may now return, after the above short sketch of the methods by which Pawlow prepared the stomach for experimentation, and observed the reflex effects of the nervous system upon gastric secretion, to the experiments by which the same observer studied the efferent path in the vagus of the reflex excitation of the secretion.

As has already been stated, the other functions of the vagus nerve

[1] For the details of this ingenious operation the reader is referred to that most interesting book, " The Work of the Digestive Glands," by J F Pawlow, English translation by W H Thompson; Griffin, London, 1902.

are so important that the effects upon gastric secretion cannot be observed by the usual simple methods of section and of stimulation of the nerve, without certain preliminary operations which allow of section and stimulation without calling forth an interference at the same time with other important functions. The procedures differ somewhat according to whether the effects of section or of stimulation of the vagus are to be tested, and hence it is better to describe each experiment separately.

Effects upon Gastric Secretion of Section of the Vagal Fibres.— The operation is carried out upon a dog in two stages. In the first stage an ordinary permanent gastric fistula fitted with a metallic cannula is made, and in addition an œsophageal fistula, so that the mouth is cut off from all communication with the cavity of the stomach. At the same operation the *right* vagus nerve is divided below the point of exit of the recurrent laryngeal and cardiac branches, so that on any subsequent section at a later stage of the *left* vagus the control of the larynx and heart will still be left in action. If at some time after recovery from the operation food is offered to the animal and is eaten, it of course drops out by the œsophageal fistula and nothing reaches the stomach. Under such circumstances, however, and although the gastric fibres of the vagus on the right side have been completely severed, a copious flow of gastric juice is obtained which starts about five minutes after the commencement of the sham feeding. If now the left vagus be dissected out and severed there is no profound general disturbance of functions, because, although the pulmonary and abdominal vagal fibres on both sides are paralysed, the laryngeal and cardiac fibres on the right side are still intact. If now a process of sham feeding be commenced, although the dog takes and swallows the food greedily, no secretion of gastric juice is evoked by the process: not a single drop flows from the gastric fistula.

In the same animal in which the above procedures had been carried out the right vagus was at a later period divided *in the neck*, yet the animal continued in perfect health and enjoyed its life to the full, although both cervical vagi were now severed. Double cervical vagotomy was also carried out in similar fashion upon a second dog, which survived the double operation for months. In both these animals, after the severance of the second vagus, sham feeding was found never to give rise to a secretion, although often tested.

In addition to demonstrating that the vagus is at any rate the most important efferent channel for reflex stimulation of the gastric secretion, these experiments demonstrate the most important fact that the profound and fatal effects of double cervical vagotomy carried out at one operation are due to the sudden shock of complete removal of vagal control upon the heart, respiratory, and alimentary systems, and that compensation can and does occur and prevent the fatal result, if the operation be carried out piecemeal.

Although sham feeding calls forth reflexly no flow of secretion after the vagal fibres have been completely severed, it must not, however, be hastily assumed that no secretion can occur under any circumstances after the vagal fibres have been so thrown out of action, for both Pawlow and other observers have observed secretion under such conditions. Whether such secretion is due both to stimulation through other nervous channels, such as the sympathetic fibres, or to absorption of chemical substances which cause direct chemical stimulation of the gland cells, may still be disputed. Recent work shows that such direct chemical action upon the cells is a cause of secretion.

Effects on Gastric Secretion of Stimulation of the Peripheral End of the Severed Cervical Vagus.—The experiment of vagus stimulation yields results entirely confirmatory of those obtained by section of the nerve, but similar preliminary precautions are necessary.

After gastrotomy and œsophagotomy have been previously carried out as before described, one vagus (the right) is cut through as before below the cardiac and laryngeal branches, then the other vagus is cut through in the neck, and after a length has been dissected out and attached to a ligature it is left *in situ*, and the wound closed up for a period of three to four days   The stitches are then carefully removed, exposing the nerve for stimulation, and this is stimulated with slow rhythmic induction shocks at intervals of one to two seconds. A secretion of juice is invariably obtained from the empty stomach as a result of such stimulation. The object of waiting for three or four days after section of the vagus is to allow time for the cardiac fibres to degenerate, which process appears to occur earlier than the degeneration of the secretory fibres of the stomach.

After obtaining positive results regarding the efferent function of the vagus in gastric secretion by this so-called "chronic" method, Pawlow and his co-workers returned to the attempt to obtain evidence by the so-called " acute " method of stimulation of the

peripheral vagus immediately after section. The experimental procedure was to perform tracheotomy, so that artificial respiration
could be carried on, to cut the spinal cord beneath the medulla so
as to throw out reflex action upon the gastric glands, to sever the
vagi, keeping the peripheral ends attached to ligatures for stimulation, to establish an ordinary gastric fistula, and to ligature off
the stomach from the œsophagus and pylorus. The results of
stimulation of the vagus in these acute experiments were not,
however, invariably the same; in more than half of the experiments
a flow of secretion was obtained, but the latent period was prolonged
from the usual five minutes to from fifteen minutes to an hour or
more, and the causal connection of a secretion occurring an hour
after stimulation has commenced is, to say the least of it, very
doubtful. After the nerve had once commenced to work, however,
the dependence of the secretion upon the stimulus became more
apparent, for on removal of the stimulus the process of secretion
gradually stopped, and on renewal of the stimulus, secretion now
appeared with greater rapidity. Administration of atropin stopped
the secretion. Pawlow explains the long latent period on the
assumption that the vagus contains inhibitory fibres as well as
excitatory fibres for the gastric glands.

Nothing is known worth recording regarding the action upon
the secretion of the sympathetic fibres which run to the stomach.
It is almost impossible to find and stimulate these after they leave
the solar plexus. It has been stated that gastric secretion still
persists after section of the splanchnics ; but this fact alone proves
nothing as to the possible effect of these nerves in initiating,
inhibiting, or controlling gastric secretion.

Innervation of the Pancreas.—The study of the influence of its
nerve-supply upon the secretory activity of the pancreas has proved
one of the most difficult and perplexing of the problems of gland
innervation, and we cannot yet be said to be in possession of clear
and complete information as to the influence of its nerves upon
the physiological activity of this most important gland. But
the study of the subject has indirectly led to most important results
in the discovery of the fact that gland activity may be called out,
apart from nervous activity, by the chemical action directly upon
the gland cells of substances which are formed in cells in other
regions away from the gland, and are carried by the blood-stream
directly to the gland cells.

The subject of chemical stimulation will be treated in a subsequent section, and we shall here deal with the subject of pancreatic innervation which properly leads up to it.

The nerve-supply of the pancreas is similar in plan to that of the stomach, being provided by cerebrospinal fibres coming from the vagi, and sympathetic fibres derived from the solar plexus.

The methods for studying the effect of these nerves upon the secretion of pancreatic juice devised by Pawlow and his co-workers closely resemble those employed in the case of the gastric secretion, with one important exception—namely, that no means was devised similar to the œsophageal fistula for preventing escape of material from the stomach into the duodenum, as a result of, or accompanying, the stimulation of the nerves. This difference is of importance, because it was shown by the workers of the St Petersburg school themselves that the application of dilute acid solutions or of acid chyme to the duodenal wall gives rise to a copious and long-continued flow of pancreatic juice This flow was ascribed by these experimenters to a stimulation by the acid of afferent nerve endings of a local reflex nervous mechanism in the duodenal wall; but it was later shown by Bayliss and Starling, as we shall see in detail in the next section, that the flow of pancreatic juice so obtained was not due to a direct action of the acid upon afferent nerve endings in the duodenum, nor indeed to nervous mechanism at all, but to a chemical action of the acid upon a substance formed in the duodenal mucous membrane cells which they named *prosecretin* This prosecretin is formed during rest in the duodenal cells, and when acid arrives from the stomach is converted into an active substance called *secretin*, which enters the blood-stream, is carried to the pancreatic cells, and excites these cells to secretion by acting as a direct chemical stimulus

For the present, what concerns us here as a preliminary to the description of the experiments of the Pawlow school upon the effect of stimulation of the vagus and sympathetic nerves on the process of pancreatic secretion, is the experimental fact that passage of acid chyme from the stomach to the duodenum is capable of calling forth a secretion of pancreatic juice It is accordingly just as important, in experimenting upon the effects of nerve stimulation upon secretion by the pancreas, to make certain that no chyme passes from the stomach to the duodenum, as it is in similar experiments upon gastric secretion to make certain that no food or saliva passes from the mouth to the stomach, upon the importance of which Pawlow himself lays great stress and against which the œsophageal fistula was intended to guard.

The absence of such a precautionary measure seriously invalidates the result of many of the earlier experiments of Pawlow and his collaborators on the effects of vagal stimulation upon pancreatic secretion. Thus, while Pawlow invariably obtained a positive effect upon pancreatic secretion as a result of vagus stimulation after certain preliminary procedures, which will presently be described, had been carried out, Bayliss and Starling were quite unable to find any result upon pancreatic secretion from stimulation of the peripheral end of the vagus. It must hence be regarded as a possibility that in Pawlow's experiments, as a result perhaps of stimulation of movement of the stomach by the vagal excitation, that acid which had escaped from the stomach set free secretin from the duodenal mucous membrane, and this in turn directly stimulated the pancreatic cells. Bayliss and Starling, while not explicitly denying a control of secretion by the vagus, state that they have not in several experiments been able experimentally to demonstrate the fact, and certainly regard the chemical stimulus as the adequate and efficient one.

Hence judgment must be reserved regarding the control of the pancreatic secretion upon the nervous side. Still the methods used may here be described from their interest as leading up to the discovery of the chemical control, and as the experimental basis of any future attempts at a study of the influence of the gland nerves, when the additional safeguard has been provided of a fistula between pylorus and duodenum, or the separation of these by ligation.

In preparing the permanent pancreatic fistula in the dogs used for the experiments, Pawlow employed a modification of the method used by Heidenhain. Heidenhain, in preparing his fistulæ, had completely resected the intestine in order to obtain a short piece of the intestine into which the pancreatic duct opened, and which was then, after splitting open, attached to the abdominal wall, the continuity of the intestine having of course been restored by suturing together the two ends of the intestine after the removal of the short piece containing the opening of the pancreatic duct. Pawlow improved upon this by merely cutting out a small oval patch of the intestinal wall around the entrance of the pancreatic duct, and then reclosing the intestine, which was only slightly narrowed by this procedure. ⟩The small oval patch so removed was then implanted on the outside of the muscular abdominal wall, so that the pancreatic secretion was now poured out to the exterior.

By careful nursing, adaptation of the food, and administration of sodium bicarbonate so as to make good the loss of alkali due to the flowing away of the secretion to the exterior, dogs with such fistulæ could be preserved alive and in good health for a long time, and after recovery could be used for the study of the effect of alterations in the nature of the food upon the amount and quality of the pancreatic secretion, and for the investigation of the effects of the gland nerves upon the process of secretion.

In such an animal, the preliminary procedure to studying the effect of stimulation of the vagus upon the secretory process is to dissect out a portion of the nerve in the neck and cut it, attaching a ligature to the peripheral end. The nerve is then preserved under the skin for a period of four days, in order to allow time for the cardiac fibres to degenerate After the lapse of this time, the stitches are removed and the nerve stimulated with slow induction shocks. As a result of stimulating, it is found that after a latent period of about three minutes a flow of pancreatic juice commences and gradually increases in quantity. On stopping the stimulus the flow does not instantly stop, but continues in decreasing quantity for a period of four or five minutes from the cessation of the stimulus. Positive results were also obtained by Pawlow by the use of the so-called " acute " method, provided the spinal cord was cut to avoid reflex inhibition from the operative procedures, and the vagus was stimulated below the cardiac nerves so as not to produce disturbance of the heart and circulation, the order of procedure being tracheotomy, severance of cervical spinal cord below medulla, artificial respiration, opening of thorax and preparation of vagus below the heart, insertion of pancreatic cannula, and slow rhythmic excitation of the nerve.

In using the acute method, evidence of the presence of inhibitory fibres was obtained similar to that mentioned above in the case of the gastric secretion. Thus it was found that after a steady flow of secretion had been set up by stimulation of one vagus, similar and simultaneous excitation of the other vagus often led after a latent period to a suppression of the flow.

An inhibitory influence of the sympathetic fibres was also demonstrated in the case of the acute experiment. The first effect of stimulation of the sympathetic by an induced current was a slight increase in flow ; this, however, lasted only for a few seconds, and was followed later, and especially after stopping the stimulus, by a suppression of the secretion. Similar inhibitory results were obtained as a result of mechanical stimulation with the tetanometer, and in a nerve in which degeneration had been allowed to proceed for three or four days a purely inhibitory effect was obtained as a result of electrical stimulation.

The presence of inhibitory fibres in the vagus was also shown by Popielski, by the employment of another method. This observer caused a continuous flow of pancreatic secretion by injection of dilute hydrochloric acid into the duodenum, and then strongly stimulated the vagus, when a slowing of the secretion was always obtained, often to a complete standstill. Excitation of the sympathetic under like circumstances did not produce such a marked effect, but usually gave rise to decrease in rate of secretion after a long latent period.

The important fact that the presence of acids in the duodenum gives rise to a copious and long-continued flow of pancreatic juice was established by Dolinski in Pawlow's laboratory in 1894. The whole mental aspect of the workers in Pawlow's laboratory at that period was directed towards the discovery of the innervation of the pancreas, and hence naturally the flow of pancreatic secretion caused by the presence of the acid in the duodenum was looked upon as a reflex act in which the stimulation of the acid upon peripheral nerve endings in the duodenal mucous membrane give rise to the afferent impulses.

The secretion set up by the presence of acid in the duodenum was further studied by Popielski and by Wertheimer and Lepage, who showed that secretion was still evoked by the introduction of acid into the duodenum even after section of both vagi and splanchnics, or destruction of the spinal cord, or after complete extirpation of the solar plexus.

These experiments clearly shut out the central nervous system from participation in the supposed reflex, but the observers, still clinging to the belief that the phenomena before them arose from nervous activity, accommodated their views to the additional experimental facts, by receding to the conclusion that the secretion arose from a *peripheral* reflex act. Popielski concluded, from finding that the secretion occurred after removal of the solar plexus, and also after separating the duodenum with the pylorus from the stomach, but not if the duodenum were cut across a short distance below the pylorus, that the centres for the supposed peripheral reflex were in the scattered ganglia of the pancreas of which the most important were to be found near the pylorus, and were cut off when the duodenum was cut across near to the pylorus. Wertheimer and Lepage accepted the peripheral reflex explanation, but as they found that injection of acid into the jejunum also called out a secretion diminishing in intensity as the distance from the duodenum increased, they came to the conclusion that the centre for the supposed reflex varied according to the region of intestine stimulated by the acid, and that while the secretion in the case of the duodenum might result from stimulation of pancreatic ganglia, that from the jejunum probably was set up by stimulation of the solar plexus. The experiment of injection of acid into a loop of jejunum, after extirpation of the solar plexus, or after severance of the mesenteric nerves of the loop, was not performed by these observers. They found that the secretory effect was not abolished by administration of atropin, but instead of arousing any suspicion that the secretion might not after all be of nervous origin, this fact was only correlated to the absence of effect of this drug upon the sympathetic salivary secretion.

The possibility of the secretion induced by acid in the duodenum being due to chemical action was not unthought of entirely, however, by the St. Petersburg school, and is discussed by Pawlow in his book, in which he states that the acid works either locally by exciting the peripheral end-apparatus of the centripetal nerves in the mucous membrane, or else it is absorbed into the blood and stimulates either the secretory centre or the gland cells directly. The view that the acid produces its effect by absorption into the blood is then negatived by Pawlow, from theoretical considerations, as well as from the fact that injection of acid into the rectum was without effect upon pancreatic secretion.

It did not occur, however, to the discoverers of the secretion of the pancreas as a specific result of the presence of acids in the duodenum, that there was a third hypothesis—namely, that the acid might awaken an internal secretion in the duodenal cells, and that the substance so secreted might travel in the blood-stream to the pancreatic cells and set them in activity.

This view did occur to Bayliss and Starling, who, on testing it experimentally, found it to be the correct one, and so not only brilliantly supplemented the work of the St. Petersburg school on pancreatic secretion, but made a new departure in our knowledge regarding secretory processes, and opened up a new field to research.

The Chemical Mechanisms of Secretion—Chemical Excitants of Secretion or Hormones.

Pancreatic Secretion and Secretin.—The apparently local character of the reaction when acid was placed in the intestine, described in the preceding section, led Bayliss and Starling to experimentation upon the subject, from the view that there might here be an extension of the local reflexes, the action of which in movements of the intestinal wall these observers had already investigated. It was soon found, however, that the phenomenon was one of an entirely different order, and that the secretion of the pancreas is normally called into action not by nervous agency at all, but by a chemical substance formed in the mucous membrane of the upper parts of the small intestine under the influence of acid, and carried thence by the blood-stream to the gland cells of the pancreas. To the active substance the name *secretin* has been given by the authors.

In the earlier experiments of Bayliss and Starling, dogs were used, but in a later research other animals were employed (rabbit, cat, and monkey), and it was demonstrated that the reaction is a general one for all vertebrates.

The animals received an injection of morphia previous to the experiment, and during its course were anæsthetised with A.C.E. mixture. In order to keep the condition of the animals constant during the experiment, artificial respiration was resorted to, and a constant depth of anæsthesia was attained by placing the anæsthetising bottle in the air circuit ; this procedure is especially necessary when the vagi have been cut. The animals in the earlier experiments had not been fed for a period of eighteen to twenty-four hours, but in later experiments it was shown that secretin is active no matter what may be the state of digestion. In order

˙to avoid shock and to keep up the temperature, the animal was immersed in a bath of warm physiological saline throughout the experiment; the level of the fluid was above that of the abdominal wound, so that the intestine was bathed with the warm fluid. The arterial pressure was always recorded by means of a mercurial manometer connected with the carotid artery in the usual way. The pancreatic juice was obtained by placing a cannula in the larger duct which enters the duodenum on a level with the lower border of the pancreas.   To the cannula was connected a long glass tube filled at first with physiological saline ; the end of this tube projected over the edge of the bath so that the drops of the secretion fell upon a mica disc cemented to the lever of a Marey's tambour; this was in connection by means of rubber tubing with another tambour which marked each drop upon the smoked paper of the kymograph   A time tracing was taken showing intervals of ten seconds, and an injection signal was arranged to indicate the point at which acid was injected into the intestine, or a preparation of secretin into a vein, in which a venous cannula had been placed in the usual way.

The authors first confirmed the results of previous experimenters as to the effects of injection of acid into the duodenum or jejunum, and found that the result of injecting from 30 to 50 c.c. of 0 4 per cent. hydrochloric acid into the lumen of the duodenum or jejunum is to produce, after a latent period of about two minutes, a marked flow of pancreatic juice.   This effect is still produced after section of both vagi, section of the spinal cord at the level of the foramen magnum, destruction of the spinal cord, section of the splanchnic nerves, extirpation of the solar plexus, or any combination of these operations.

The next step in the chain of evidence was to test the effect of injection of acid into a loop of the upper part of the intestine after severing the mesenteric nerves.   Such a procedure was impossible for anatomical reasons in the duodenum, but was successfully carried out with a positive result on a loop of jejunum.

In this crucial experiment the loop of intestine was completely cut off from all nervous connection with the pancreas, and hence the conclusion is an inevitable one that the effect must be produced by some chemical substance finding its way into the circulation, and then either directly or indirectly stimulating the pancreatic cells.

19

It must be admitted here that the process of severing all the network of sympathetic nerve fibres surrounding the blood-vessels passing to the intestinal loop is a difficult one, and it is hard to make certain that it has been effectually carried out, so that it would have been well to insert in this experiment small cannulæ into the completely severed artery and vein of the loop. But, as Bayliss and Starling point out, the experiment was that which led to the discovery of *secretin*, the specific chemical excitant, or *hormone*, of the pancreatic secretion. Also the effects about to be described of injection of extracts of the duodenal or jejunal mucous membrane prepared by the action of dilute acid clearly demonstrate a local action of the secretin upon the pancreas.

The positive result obtained in the experiment with the nerve-less loop of intestine, taken in conjunction with the result obtained by Wertheimer and Lepage, that acid itself introduced into the circulation has no effect upon the pancreatic secretion, led Bayliss and Starling to the view that the acid must give rise to some active substance in the cells of the mucosa which is taken into the circulation and produces the specific effect. This view was then abundantly confirmed by the results of experiment. The loop of jejunum from which the positive result was obtained was cut out, the mucous membrane scraped off, rubbed up with sand and 0·4 per cent. hydrochloric acid in a mortar, filtered through cotton-wool, and the extract injected into a vein. The result was a flow of pancreatic juice at more than twice the rate produced at the beginning of the experiment by introduction of acid into the duodenum. Two further results were obtained in the same experiment: first, it was shown that the acid extract could be boiled without losing its activity, so that the active substance (secretin) was shown not to be a ferment ; and secondly, it was shown that the activity of extracts of portions of the small intestine taken at different levels showed a decreasing amount of activity as the intestine was descended, corresponding to the known effects upon the pancreatic secretion of injection of acid into these various portions. Thus injection of acid into a loop from the lower end of the ileum gives rise to no pancreatic secretion, and, corresponding to this, an acid extract from the mucous membrane of the lower end of the ileum possesses when intravenously injected no exciting effect upon the pancreatic secretion.

With regard to the seat of action of secretin, Bayliss and Starling have traced it as far as possible towards the periphery, and conclude that it acts in all probability directly as a chemical excitant

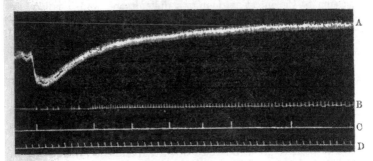

FIG. 5.—ACTION OF ACID EXTRACT OF BOILED AND WASHED MUCOUS MEMBRANE OF DUODENUM.

A, Blood-pressure; B, drops of pancreatic juice; C, drops of bile; D, time tracing.   (Bayliss and Starling.)

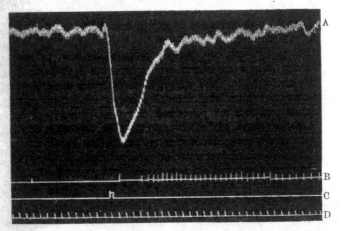

FIG. 6.—ACTION OF ACID EXTRACT OF MUCOUS MEMBRANE OF DUODENUM WHICH HAS BEEN DRIED AFTER DEHYDRATION BY ALCOHOL.

A, Blood-pressure; B, drops of pancreatic juice; C, injection signal; D, time tracing.   (Bayliss and Starling.)

upon the secreting cells of the pancreas. It is impossible with our present experimental methods to exclude a possible action upon the nerve cells and fibres in the pancreas itself ; just as it is impossible to do so in the case of tracing towards the periphery the seat of action of any drug or other active substance—for example, to exclude an action of adrenalin upon nerve cells or endings upon the muscular walls of small arteries rather than upon the muscle cells directly. But it has been shown that the excitatory effect upon the pancreatic secretion is still obtained after the gland has been cut off, as far as is experimentally possible from its anatomical relationships, from connection with nervous mechanisms, both central and peripheral. The sensitiveness of the pancreas renders practically impossible the experiment of perfusion of whipped blood containing secretin through the excised gland.

Certain physical and chemical properties of secretin solution have also been investigated by Bayliss and Starling and W. A. Osborne, as well as the properties of the pancreatic juice secreted as a result of the action of secretin ; the results are summarised in the following conclusions :

1. The secretion of the pancreatic juice is normally evoked by the entrance of acid chyme into the duodenum, and is proportional to the amount of acid entering (Pawlow). This secretion does not depend on a nervous reflex, and occurs when all the nervous connections of the intestine are destroyed.

2. The contact of the acid with the epithelial cells of the duodenum causes in them the production of a body (secretin), which is absorbed from the cells by the blood-current, and is carried to the pancreas, where it acts as a specific stimulus to the pancreatic cells, exciting a secretion of pancreatic juice proportional to the amount of secretin present.

3. This substance, secretin, is produced probably by a process of hydrolysis from a precursor (prosecretin) present in the cells, which is insoluble in water and alkalies and is not destroyed by boiling alcohol.

4. Secretin is not a ferment. It withstands boiling in acid, neutral, or alkaline solutions, but is easily destroyed by active pancreatic juice or by oxidising agents. It is not precipitated from its watery solutions by tannic acid, or alcohol and ether. It is destroyed by most metallic salts. It is slightly diffusible through parchment paper.

5. The pancreatic juice obtained by secretin injection has no action on proteins until " enterokinase " is added. It acts on

starch and to some extent on fats, the action on fats being increased by the addition of succus entericus. It is, in fact, normal pancreatic juice.

6. Secretin rapidly disappears from the tissues, but cannot be detected in any of the secretions. It is apparently not absorbed from the lumen of the intestine.

7 It is not possible to obtain a body resembling secretin from any tissues of the body other than the mucous membrane of the duodenum and jejunum.

8. Secretin solutions, free from bile salts, cause some increase in the secretion of bile. They have no action on any other glands.

9. Acid extracts of the mucous membrane normally contain a body which causes a fall of blood-pressure. This body is not secretin, and the latter may be prepared free from the depressor substance by acting on desquamated epithelial cells with acid.

The Chemical Mechanism of Gastric Secretion—Gastrin.—It has long been known that the introduction of certain substances into the stomach provokes a secretion of gastric juice, and the effect has been ascribed to a nervous mechanism stimulated by the effect of absorbed substances upon peripheral nerve endings in the gastric mucosa. Soon after the discovery of secretin it was shown by Edkins that intravenous injection of extracts prepared in special manner from certain parts of the gastric mucous membrane leads to a flow of gastric juice Edkins considers this action to be due to a substance which he has named *gastrin,* and which acts as a chemical excitant or " hormone " for the gastric secretion, in a similar fashion to secretin in the case of the pancreatic juice. It is hence possible that those substances shown by Pawlow to excite the gastric secretion when introduced into the stomach so as not to call forth a psychical flow, as by the use of a sound or, better, through a gastric fistula without attracting the animal's attention, produce their effect not by exciting peripheral nerve-endings in the gastric mucosa, but by means of a chemical action upon the secreting cells This action may either be a direct one of the substances themselves or, more probably, according to Edkins's observations, an indirect action in which these substances, similarly to hydrochloric acid in the case of the duodenal mucosa, set free an active substance chiefly from the pyloric portion of the gastric mucosa. This substance, after being absorbed by the blood-stream, is carried to the secreting cells lying deeper in the mucosa, and also to the secreting cells of the fundus, where it acts as a chemical stimulant, and calls forth secretion.

Edkins has studied the effects of intravenous injection of extracts made from different parts of the gastric mucosa. He placed a certain amount of saline in the stomach, and then determined the amount of acid formed in the stomach, after the injection of each extract to be tested into a vein, by titrating this saline for total acidity.

The results obtained were as follows:

"If an extract in 5 per cent. dextrin of the fundus mucous membrane be injected into the jugular vein, there is no evidence of secretion of gastric juice. If the extract be made with the pyloric mucous membrane there is evidence of a small quantity of secretion. With dextrin by itself there is no secretion.

"Extracts of fundus mucous membrane in dextrose or maltose give no secretion; extracts of pyloric mucous membrane give marked secretion; dextrose or maltose alone brings about no secretion.

"If extracts be made with commercial peptone, it is found that no secretion occurs with the fundus mucous membrane, a marked secretion with the pyloric mucous membrane; the peptone alone gives a slight secretion.

"If the extracts be made by boiling the mucous membrane in the different media, the effect is just the same—that is to say, the active principle, which may be called ' gastrin,' is not destroyed by boiling.

"Finally, it may be pointed out that such absorption as occurs in the stomach apparently takes place at the pyloric end. In the pig's stomach, in which the cardiac region differs from the ordinary type in only having simple glands as in the pyloric, extracts of the cardiac region in general have the same efficiency in promoting secretion as do pyloric."

The media most powerful in calling forth secretion in these experiments are hence those containing the products of advanced salivary digestion, or of peptic digestion—viz., glucose, maltose, and commercial peptone—and the region from which active preparations can be prepared being the pyloric mucous membrane, which also is the region in which any slight absorption in the stomach occurs, the indication of the experiments is that the precursor of the active gastrin is formed in the pyloric mucosa, and is activated by the absorption of these digestive products, and discharged into the blood-stream, whence it reaches the gastric secreting cells.

The earlier experiments of Pawlow upon those substances which excite gastric secretion on introduction into the stomach are of interest in the light of these later experiments on intravenous injection. Thus introduction of water into the stomach, *even after section of both vagi*, always gave rise to a secretion, although not a very copious one; here there is a good deal cut off from central control, as the vagi are clearly, from Pawlow's other experiments, the most important efferent nerves for gastric secretion, and it would be most interesting to know if this secretion on the introduction of water also occurred after more profound interference with the central nervous system connections—*e.g.*, if it still took place after destruction of the spinal cord and extirpation of the solar plexus.

Alkaline solutions, such as sodium bicarbonate, were found by Pawlow to exercise an inhibitory effect upon gastric secretion. Fresh meat and meat extracts were the most powerful excitants, and research is still required to test whether this action is nervous or chemical in origin. Starch and fat were found by Pawlow not to excite secretion on direct introduction without psychical stimulation Bread and solution of egg-albumin also appeared to be nonexcitants, but the fluid digestive products from the stomach of another dog which had eaten egg-albumin, when introduced without psychical effect directly into the main stomach, gave a stronger and more constant effect than a like quantity of water.

The above experiments upon the effects of chemical stimulants formed in the cells of the body itself upon the activity of the secreting cells of pancreas and stomach open up to physiological research a field of great importance, and one with practical bearing for medicine and organotherapy Doubtless similar actions occur elsewhere in the body which will in the future be brought to light. Bayliss and Starling in their paper briefly draw attention to what they term the *chemical sympathies* between uterus and mammary gland, and to the modifications in the composition of the pancreatic juice accompanying long-continued change in the diet—such, for example, as the production of a lactase as the result of milk feeding—and call attention to the advisability of a renewed investigation of these facts from the point of view of the production in such cases of bodies allied to secretin. There is no doubt that in many cases the stimulus to seasonal functional activity of organs may be a chemical one. In this connection also might be mentioned the occurrence of menstruation, and the seasonal recurrence of rut in cattle, also the absence of these during pregnancy accompanying the changed chemical metabolism at such a period, and the chemical changes going on in the corpus luteum of the ovary.

Thus the field of " internal secretion," which first began to be explored in the case of the ductless glands, the thyroid and suprarenal, goes on widening in scope, and we learn afresh that an organ or cell, in addition to its most conspicuous function, may possess other and no less important chemical activities.

Effects of Food upon the Production of the Digestive Secretions.—A number of most interesting and valuable observations have been published from the Pawlow school, upon the effects of different foods on the rate of secretion, and variations in this during the period of digestion, and on the alterations in the quality of the secretion resulting from the intake of different foods, and continuance upon different diets for more prolonged periods. The series of experiments upon these points are very extensive, and only a summary of results can be included in this article; a good account of the matter is contained in Pawlow's book on " The Work of the Digestive Glands " above referred to.[1]

1. Secretion under normal conditions only commences as a result of food being taken into the alimentary canal. The miniature stomach does not secrete during inanition, but commences a few minutes after a meal. The quantity of juice from a pancreatic fistula during hunger amounts to only 2 or 3 c.c. per hour, but some time after a meal increases to many times that amount.

2. The quantity of juice secreted in the case of the same food is directly proportional to the quantity of food taken. Thus for raw meat, for 100 grms., 26 c.c. of gastric juice were secreted; for 200 grms., 50 c.c. of juice; and for 400 grms., 106 c.c. On a mixed diet of meat (50 grms.), bread (50 grms.), and milk (300 c.c.), 42 c.c. of gastric juice were secreted; for double these quantities 83·2 c.c. were secreted.

3. The secretion is not all poured out rapidly at the beginning, but is distributed throughout the period of digestion, and the curve of quantity secreted and time varies for the different types

[1] See p. 279.

of food Each food possesses a modifying effect both upon the quantity and quality of the secretion. Also the presence of one food has a modifying power upon the secretion called forth by another, and on the whole course of digestion.

Thus in the case of gastric secretion on a meal of flesh, bread, or milk respectively, each separate food corresponds to a definite hourly rate of secretion, and calls forth a characteristic alteration of the properties of the juice Flesh and bread diet produces a maximum rate during the first hour of digestion, while milk gives the maximum rate during the second or third hour. Tested as to maximum content in ferment during the period of digestion, the greatest activity is found with flesh diet in the beginning ; with bread in the second and third hours ; and with milk in the last (or sixth) hour. Contrasting the digestive power of the juices for protein at corresponding periods of digestion in the case of the three foods, the greatest power is found in the case of the flesh diet, the bread comes second, and, in the earlier stages at least, close to the meat, while that on the milk diet is much feebler in proteolytic power.

In the case of the pancreatic secretion, a similar adaptation of the secretion to the nature of the food is seen, and here the changes become more striking, because there is a ferment for each class of food-stuff, and relative variations can be contrasted.

The following table of results by Walther, quoted by Pawlow, gives the variation in secretion (quantity and ferments) of pancreatic juice on milk, bread, and flesh respectively. The quantities of each food given are based on the percentages of nitrogen contained in each variety :

Diet.	Quantity of Pancreatic Juice	Proteoclastic Strength.	Amyloclastic Strength	Steatoclastic Strength
Milk, 600 c c	48	22·6	9 0	90·3
Bread, 250 grms	151	13·1	10·6	5 3
Flesh, 100 grms.	144	10·6	4·5	25·0

The adaptation of the secretion to the nature of the food requires no comment Attention may be drawn to the high proteoclastic power of the secretion called forth by the milk, and to a contrast of this with the low proteoclastic power produced by milk in the case of the gastric secretion. In the case of flesh there is the reverse effect. It looks from the figures as if the protein of the flesh were digested chiefly in the stomach and that of the milk in the intestine.

Similar variations in the curve of rate of secretion and time are found in the case of the pancreas as in the stomach, the curve being characteristic for each food. The form of this curve is altered by the simultaneous presence of different food-stuffs; thus the curve of gastric secretion for lean meat, consisting chiefly of protein, becomes profoundly modified if a small amount of fat or oil be also given: the rate of secretion and amount of pepsin being reduced, and the maximum point of secretion being pushed back to a later point in the period of digestion. Similarly the curve of secretion for flesh is modified by the addition of starch to the flesh meal, so as to come to resemble fairly closely that of a bread meal.

4. When an animal is kept for a long period (some weeks) upon a definite and constant diet, the ferment content of the pancreatic juice becomes adapted to the character of the food. If, for example, an animal which has been fed for some weeks entirely upon bread and milk is brought on to an exclusively meat diet, which in contrast with the other diet contains more protein but scarcely any carbohydrate, it is found that the power of the pancreatic juice for digesting protein increases from day to day, while the digestive power for starch progressively diminishes. On reversing the diet again to bread and milk, similar but inverse changes are observed. The moral from this for practical medicine, which experience had already indicated, is that a sudden change from one régime to another may have a disastrous effect upon the digestive process, by subjecting the glands to a strain to which they have not been adapted. Hence changes in dietary should be brought about slowly and progressively wherever possible, and not by a sudden and sweeping change.

The physiological causes and mechanisms of this interesting adaptation in quantity and quality of the digestive fluids to the nature of the food are as yet obscure to us.

Pawlow, their chief discoverer, ascribed them to a differentiated peripheral nerve-supply in the mucous membrane of the alimentary canal, whereby the absorption of different digested food-stuffs stimulated different nerve endings, fibres, and cells, and caused a discharge of correspondingly different efferent stimuli to the gland cells, as also to the variation in amount and kind of psychical stimulation by the variation to sight and smell of different sorts of food.

This explanation was given, however, before the days of Bayliss and Starling's discovery of the chemical excitants to secretion, and the question now remains an open one whether the nervous system has anything, and if so how much, to do with the adaptation of secretion to food, and with the characteristic variations above described of rate and progress of secretion with the nature of the food.

In the light of our new knowledge the whole subject of secretion stands ripe for investigation, and is rich in promise of new additions to our knowledge of the highest value to physiology and to medicine.

CHAPTER XV

THE EQUILIBRIUM OF COLLOID AND CRYSTALLOID IN LIVING CELLS

THE living cell may be regarded from the physicochemical point of view as a machine or mechanism through which there constantly is taking place a flux of energy. The cell is continually taking energy up from its surroundings in certain forms, and redistributing this energy in other forms, but in the process it itself undergoes little or no permanent change. Certain changes, it is true, do occur slowly in the cell in the course of its life-history which have the effect of permanently altering the character of the energy discharged through it ; but these structural changes are so slow that they can be put aside in the study of the cell as an energy machine acting upon the energy at any given moment.

If the case of the green plant cell acting as an energy transformer for light energy be placed on one side, it may be stated that the energy supplies of the cell always come to it in the form of organic compounds capable of yielding energy in the process of oxidation in the cell.

In order that the cell may be capable of oxidising these chemical compounds of organic character coming in from its environment, it is, however, absolutely essential that its own integrity be preserved; and this integrity is just as completely dependent upon the presence of the ions of certain simple inorganic salts in the cell and its surrounding fluid media, as the exhibition of the typical phenomena of cell activity is upon the supply of energy in the form of the organic compounds to the living cell. In fact, in point of time, the physiological activity of the cell is more rapidly destroyed by removing or altering the supply of inorganc ions than it is by interfering with the supply of organic food-stuffs. For, in the latter case, the cell can oxidise the combustible materials present in storage within it, and even use up a portion of its own intrinsic substance before its activities come to a standstill; but when the inorganic ions, forming a constitutional part of the living cell, are altered,

300

and the equilibrium between protoplasm and ion thus destroyed, the cell activities are immediately affected, and after a short period of pathological activity everything comes to rest.

An analogy with another form of energy transformer may make this clearer. If the fires are banked under the boiler of a steam-engine the head of steam in the boiler will for a longer or shorter period keep the steam-engine going. this is comparable to stopping the organic food-supply of the cell; but if there is a sudden burst in the boiler, if the cylinder blows off, or if there is a break in any essential part of the machinery, then there is a sudden stoppage of the engine, often preceded by a very brief period of excessive activity : this is comparable to interference with the inorganic ions of the cell. The inorganic ions form in fact an intrinsic and indispensable part of the cell's structure, in the absence of which it can no longer utilise its food-supply, however abundant that supply may be or suitably adapted for the nutrition of the normal cell.

These effects, although they may be demonstrated in any living tissue, are seen perhaps most typically in the case of the isolated and perfused heart muscle. If the fluid caused to flow through the heart consists of distilled water, to which organic foodstuff, in the form, say, of dextrose, has been added, the heart-beat ceases almost instantaneously. If next the experiment be repeated upon a fresh heart, using instead a solution of pure sodium chloride in distilled water, of such concentration that it is isosmotic with the natural serum of the animal, there ensues a considerably longer period of perhaps some minutes' duration before the heart-beat disappears. The sodium chloride solution, however, although possessing the proper osmotic pressure, is unable for any considerable time to preserve the heart-muscle cells in normal condition. By supplying the proper osmotic concentration it has prevented the cells being suddenly broken up, but it has a zero pressure for certain ions indispensable to the heart's activity; these have slowly diffused out, and the period of the heart's action has been determined by that moment at which the concentration in the protoplasm has reached a certain minimal value.

The most important of the ions which have been washed out of the cardiac muscle cells by the current of pure sodium chloride solution are the potassium and calcium ions. It still possesses abundance of combustible organic material to furnish the energy for its contractions, but the structural mechanism or machine for oxidation has been interfered with and the cells can no longer draw on their supply of stored energy.

That this is the true state of the case is shown by the effects of adding quite minimal traces of soluble salts of calcium and potassium to the pure sodium chloride solution, when the spontaneous beating of the heart commences and goes on for hours, and even days, in a regular and automatic manner.

The amounts of potassium and calcium salts necessary to bring out this profound difference in behaviour of the heart muscle are strikingly small, the optimum amount of potassium chloride required being only about 1 part in 10,000. More than an exceedingly minute trace must not be added or the heart will be stopped by the excess. There is only a certain range of concentration which must not be passed in either direction or the heart will not beat normally. The meaning of this range will be pointed out later.

These important experimental results were first demonstrated by Sidney Ringer in the case of cardiac muscle of the frog heart; the complete generality of their application in all cells and tissues, and the causes underlying them, are only in recent times becoming generally appreciated, but the delicate and lightly balanced labile equilibrium between the colloids of the cell protoplasm and the osmotic pressures or concentrations of the inorganic ions and other crystalloid constituents is perhaps the most important and fundamental fact in the whole of biology.

The inorganic ions are sufficient in the case of the more slowly oxidising cardiac muscle of the heart of the cold-blooded animal to maintain for lengthened periods an automatic rhythmic beat; the sufficient amount of oxygen for the oxidation being capable of being carried at the partial pressure of one-fifth of an atmosphere that the atmospheric oxygen possesses, and the combustible organic material coming from the store in the cardiac muscle cells. But in the case of the mammalian heart, the oxygen pressure must be increased to nearly a whole atmosphere of pure oxygen by bubbling oxygen gas through the Ringer's saline heated to mammalian body temperature in a flask attached to the perfusion cannula, before a normal heart-beat can be obtained. This increased oxygen pressure supplies the place of the red blood-corpuscles which in the body are able to carry a sufficiency of oxygen at the lower pressure of oxygen present in the lungs. Also, in the case of the mammalian heart for a prolonged experiment, it is well, as recommended by Locke, to add dextrose to the Ringer's solution to prevent exhaustion of organic combustible material which occurs earlier in the case of mammalian muscle on account of the greater expenditure of energy which here occurs at each heart-beat.

Before leaving the classical example of cardiac muscle for more general considerations, the similar action of anæsthetics may be mentioned as an example of the relationship of drugs to the cell protoplasm.

The conditions which govern the action of chloroform upon the isolated mammalian heart have been beautifully demonstrated by Sherrington and Sowton. These observers have shown that at a fairly definite concentration of chloroform in the circulating saline the heart-beat becomes affected, and if this concentration be passed the beat is stopped. If now the chloroform be cut off and pure Ringer's solution be perfused instead of it, after a short time, sufficient to reduce the osmotic pressure of the chloroform in the cardiac cells below a definite limit, the heart recommences its beating and soon becomes normal once more. The conditions of action here are obviously the same as in the case of the inorganic ions above mentioned, except that the result is reversed, and that whereas in the case of the inorganic ions a certain pressure or concentration of ions was essential in order to keep the heart functioning normally, here a certain pressure of anæsthetic is required to still its activities. As soon as the osmotic pressure of the anæsthetic passes below a certain limit, the cells cease to be anæsthetised. In other words, some grouping in the protoplasm is free from the anæsthetising influence and open to continue other chemical interchanges which give rise to its activity. Within certain well-marked limits there is a certain reduced activity or anæsthesia. On one side of this is free activity or absence of anæsthesia; on the other side there is complete anchoring of protoplasm by anæsthetic or complete bondage from oxidising activity, resulting finally in death of the cell.

The action of chloroform upon nerve cells in the production of surgical anæsthesia is shown, by the known physiological effects connected with induction of and recovery from anæsthesia, to be similar in nature, and hence in producing safe anæsthesia we stand

upon that bridge or interval of partial combination between protoplasm and anæsthetic, where there is just sufficient combination
between the two to produce the stilling of activity which gives
the absence of pain, but not sufficient to cause complete stilling
of activity nor that degree of combination which cannot become
reversible and dissociate off when the pressure of anæsthetic is
lowered by discontinuing the administration and allowing the
process of respiration to lower the pressure of anæsthetic in the
nerve cells.

There is fortunately here, as in the case of all drugs, a degree
of selective absorption by different types of cells, and the cells of
the higher nerve centres are affected before other lower centres,
and these again before cardiac and other forms of muscle cells.
It is on this selective effect that all the benefits of anæsthesia as
an accessory of surgery depend, for if the heart, for example, were
affected at the same level of concentration of the anæsthetic as the
higher nerve cells, anæsthesia would become impossible. Precisely
at the same moment as anæsthesia set in the heart would stop
beating.

In general terms it may be stated that the actions of all specific
drugs depend upon this delicate selective action between the cells
of different tissues, or parasitic cells, and the drugs. The problem
of practical therapeutics is to find a drug or chemical combination
which by its peculiar chemical conformation is capable of undergoing adsorption at a lower pressure by a specific type of cell
protoplasm. This subject will be treated more in detail later on
when we have considered the general conditions governing the
relationships of the protoplasm to crystalloids, and to the other
substances with which it is brought in contact in the cell either
naturally, or as a result of disease, or in the treatment of disease.

We may now turn to a consideration of the general chemical
nature of protoplasm in so far as this bears upon its power of
adsorbing or combining with inorganic ions or other substances
which may be present in common with it in the living cell.

The most essential and as it were the central constituents in
building up the excessively complex physicochemical aggregation
which we term protoplasm or bioplasm are the protein bodies.
By means of the proteins, the fats and carbohydrates are knitted
together with the variously constituted proteins themselves and
with the ions of the inorganic salts to form a united system. The

component parts of this system are only lightly held together ; each is held in by the pressure of a free portion of it in the cell fluid, and for the life and activity of the cell it is essential that the osmotic pressure of each constituent should be within a certain range, so that it neither becomes fixed quite permanently nor so completely liberated as to be absent from the cell when it is required for the chemical transformations which yield the supply of energy to the cell. During the molecular vibrations which accompany this labile equilibrium in which the intensities of attachment of the various constituents to the bioplasm are all the time varying, the organic oxidisable substances—viz , the proteins themselves, the fats and carbohydrates—suffer temporary molecular disruptions during which the oxygen also held in the bioplasm comes into union with them, and the oxidised products as they increase in pressure are shed off from the cell.

As has been stated above, the inorganic ions exercise the function in the cell of favouring these chemical disruptions, for when by lowering their osmotic pressure in the cell fluid they are dissociated off from the bioplasm, the oxidation processes which form the chemical basis for the cell's activities also come to an end.

Although it is impossible at the present time artificially to synthesise any of the proteins of the cells or body fluids, and still less to build these up synthetically with the other constituents mentioned above into bioplasm, or living matter, yet we have even now obtained much insight as to the general character of the constitution of proteins, and the main plan upon which details are still to be worked out lies before us.

This knowledge has been arrived at by two different channels of approach—viz , that of studying the cleavage products of proteins in which Schutzenberger was the great pioneer, followed by a host of others ; and that of building together such cleavage products into bodies closely resembling in many respects the naturally occurring proteins, in which Emil Fischer led the way, and, by the synthesis of the polypeptides, there has already been demonstrated the lines on which proteins must be built together.

Under the influence of hydrolytic agents, such as heating with either alkalies or acids under pressure, the proteins take up the elements of water and yield a large number of simple organic substances; and conversely by the action of dehydrating or condensing agencies these simpler organic substances or organic

20

radicles of the proteins can again be made to unite. In the latter direction the process cannot be carried back quite to that degree of complexity which yields the naturally occurring protein, mainly because at that level the degree of chemical association of the constituents is so delicately balanced that the chemical manipulations cause splitting off and decomposition.

The synthesised products are in fact beginning to possess that delicately balanced power of associating and dissociating which is characteristic in still higher degree of living matter, and it is for this reason that only the living cell has hitherto been able to put the finishing touches upon the delicate unions which finally yield proteins, and beyond these up to living protoplasm, where the complexity and corresponding instability reach their acme.

The organic radicles, which form the building stones, so to speak, for the structure of the protein molecules, may be divided into three classes—viz., those which are purely organic bases, those which are entirely organic acids, and a third and most characteristic class which possess both the properties of organic acids and organic bases in modified degree. The compounds of this third class are known as the amino- or amido-acids, and it is to them that the proteins owe their peculiar property of building up into such complex bodies of higher molecular weights.[1] The simplest type of amino-acid contains one organic acid radicle and one basic radicle, the acid character being given by the carboxyl group (COOH) and the basic character by the amidogen group (NH_2). As the simplest example, glycocoll, or glycine, which is the amino-acid of acetic acid, may be quoted. Acetic acid is $CH_3.COOH$, and is purely acid in its properties, combining with bases—such, for example, as ammonium—to form the acetate ($CH_3.COO.NH_4$). If the ammonia, instead of neutralising the carboxyl group, becomes attached, with the loss of one atom of hydrogen, as the group amidogen (NH_2) in the methyl group (CH_3), there is formed instead the body $CH_2(NH_2).COOH$, which is the amino-acid. The carboxyl group (COOH) being still free, the amino-acid retains acid properties, but in lessened degree, on account of the presence in the molecule of the basic group (NH_2). The presence of the basic group also at the same time confers the properties of a base, so that the amino-acid now has the peculiar property of being able to function

---

[1] The terms amido-acid and amino-acid have the same meaning, and are used indiscriminately in describing members of this class of compounds.

either as acid or base Thus with copper it forms a deep blue soluble compound called copper glycocoll, and when in union with other organic acids it forms well-known and important substances found in the body—for example, the compound with benzoic acid known as hippuric acid, and the compound with cholalic acid occurring in the bile as glycocholic acid.

Amino-acids possessing only one amidogen group are termed mono-amino-acids; others exist possessing two such basic groups in their molecule, and these are called di-amino-acids. A number of both classes occur amongst the products of hydrolytic cleavage of the proteins. Again, there is in the majority of cases only one acidic or carboxyl group, but there are sometimes two or more such acid groups, and then the amido-acids are referred to as mono- and di-basic, etc., as in the case of ordinary organic acids.

The most striking chemical characteristic of all these amino-acids, and that which from the point of view of proteid formation interests us most at present, is that of undergoing conjugation or condensation with one another or with other organic bodies to form long chains in single series, or it may be main chains with side or branch chains arising from them

In each union of this kind the elements of a molecule of water are eliminated, a hydrogen atom being yielded by one of the two combining molecules and a hydroxyl radicle by the other, and in the great majority of instances the union occurs between the amidogen group of one and the carboxyl group of the other.

For the reader who is not acquainted with the technical terms of organic chemistry, the nature of the process of combination to form protein, and further of proteins to form bioplasm, may be illustrated by the use of electrical terms The amino-acid, on account of its possessing both an acidic and a basic group, may be considered as possessing a sort of polarity (indeed it does possess a kind of chemical polarity); as a result of this polarity a chemical attraction exists between acidic pole and basic pole of different molecules, so that these tend to unite with the elimination of the elements of water above mentioned Now it is clear, since each combining amino-acid had two free poles, that after this union has occurred there will still be left, in the new combine of double the molecular size, two opposite poles free, and if this larger new molecule is brought, under suitable conditions, in chemical contact with more molecules, that further additions of like nature can occur.

If it be remembered that a certain number of the amino-acids possess more than one basic group, or more than one acidic group, it is further obvious that it is not necessary for this process of growing to extend out in a single chain; but that branching may occur, and union of branches, so that a ramification or network can be formed in all three dimensions of space.

There is no limit but the stability of the whole chemical system to this growth proceeding until a point is reached at which, with the particular chemical agencies for union and condensation at hand, there is an equilibrium between the forces building up or synthesising and the forces tending to disrupt.

In the same way by protein unions the substances of the protoplasm or bioplasm can be formed, until new limiting conditions again fix a maximum, and, it may be added, though the agencies at work may differ in type, similarly the bioplasm can increase in aggregation until a maximum cell volume has been reached for a particular cell, and cell division becomes essential for further multiplication.

In this process of growth it will be observed that there must be left at the end of the process a number of poles of opposite type. These poles, although they are chemically saturated (for as pointed out above the elimination of the elements of water is required at each union), must still possess what has been termed residual affinity,[1] and have sufficient power to attract a group of opposite polarity and hold it very loosely attached.

[1] This residual chemical affinity is seen when compounds, saturated as regards ordinary chemical values, combine with one another, such as neutral salts with their molecules of water of crystallisation. The energy of such residual combinations is seen when dehydrated salts are dissolved in water, for this process always causes heat development although the crystallised salts after the residual combination is once completed always cause cooling when dissolved on account of energy going latent as osmotic energy from development of pressure* in the given volume of water. Similar heat effects are seen in dissolving alcohol in water, and in the solution of free acids and caustic alkalies in water. Other examples are the union of anæsthetics such as chloroform with proteins, where the chloroform or other anæsthetic is in all cases a chemically saturated body, yet the proofs of union with protein are indisputable, there being finally obtained with sufficient pressure of chloroform actual precipitation, the precipitate containing chloroform in high percentage.

* Pressure signifies in this chapter osmotic pressure.

When this feeble attachment has once occurred it may become altered in different ways. First, if the growing protein aggregation has not yet reached its full size, there may be a swing into tru chemical union with the elimination of a water molecule.

If chemical union does not take place, a diminution of pressure of one of the constituents may occur, causing dissociation or disruption, or conversely an increased pressure may lead to firmer attachment, increasing association at the expense of dissociation, and favouring chemical combination.

The form of union described above as " feeble union " or union by " residual affinities " is usually spoken of as *adsorption*, although often a number of processes which may be dissimilar in nature are placed together under this term

Thus, the invisible layer of moisture that collects on the surface of glass, the adhesion of gases on the inner surface of glass vessels which are in process of exhaustion; the moisture taken up by textile fabrics; the gases occluded by certain metals such as platinum, palladium, and iron; the concentration of dyes upon the surfaces of fibres and tissues being dyed; the union or adhesion between inorganic salts or other crystalloids and colloids of various kinds—these and a great many other phenomena are variously given as examples of adsorption, and it is maintained that this process is physical in character and essentially different from chemical combination

If extreme cases of adsorption on the one hand and of chemical combination on the other be taken for comparison, it becomes obvious at once that there exist great differences between them —such, for example, as the hygroscopic absorption of water by a glass surface compared with the combination of hydrogen and oxygen to form water. In the former case the glass remains unaltered, and by heating the water molecules can be removed unaltered from the surface; while in the latter case the water is quite different in all its physical and chemical properties from either of the two gases which have united with great evolution of energy to form it

But if the comparison be made between chemical reactions

Other examples are the dyeing of tissues and fabrics by dyes, where a saturated dye combines with a saturated colloid substratum In all such cases the best effects are obtained where the chemical sign of dye and substratum are opposite.

and adsorptions which lie close together, it is found that the characteristic differences become diminished in degree, there are all possible gradations, and many instances in which it is impossible definitely to say whether the union which takes place ought to be described as an adsorption or a chemical combination.

If the various criteria of a physical or chemical nature which are usually taken as decisive of whether any union is a chemical combination or an adsorption be examined, it is found that they one after another break down.

To take an example of interest to the biologist, it was taught for many years in all the physiological textbooks that hæmoglobin formed with oxygen an easily dissociable compound. The chemical combination was said to be complete at a certain pressure of oxygen, and as the oxygen pressure fell this compound, called oxyhæmoglobin, dissociated off into oxygen and hæmoglobin, or " reduced hæmoglobin," the dissociation occurring over a definite range of pressures. So certainly established were the facts regarding this that the proofs of the formation of the compound formed a stock question of the examination room. One of the strongest proofs of this formation of the compound oxyhæmoglobin was supposed to be that the amount of oxygen absorbed by hæmoglobin was not directly proportional to the partial pressure of the oxygen, absorption occurring in relatively greater amount at the lower pressures and falling off rapidly to nearly a zero increment as the dissociation range was passed. So that when oxygen pressures were graphically plotted as abscissæ and amounts absorbed as ordinates, instead of a straight line, as, say, in the case of absorption of oxygen (or other inert gas) by water, a curve was obtained.

But recent research has shown that in many cases where the phenomena ought to be classed under the head of adsorption, the plotted curve of pressure (or concentration) and of amount absorbed is not a straight line but a curve, and hence the new criterion is not a simple linear relationship between concentration and amount absorbed, but that the plotted curve shall show kinks or breaks upon it—that is to say, regions at which there is a sudden change in the equation of the curve. Now the oxygen-hæmoglobin curve is a smooth curve, and for this reason it has recently been maintained by Wolfgang Ostwald that in the case of oxygen and hæmoglobin the phenomenon is one of adsorption. Yet in the case of oxygen and hæmoglobin there exists at the point where absorption is complete an exact stoichiometric relationship of one molecule of oxygen to one molecule of hæmoglobin, the molecular weight of hæmoglobin being fixed by the iron determinations, which can be carried out with great exactitude   Now the existence of exact stoichiometric relationships is usually supposed to be one of the strongest criteria for chemical combination   Further, there is the very definite and distinctive oxyhæmoglobin spectrum, quite definitely different from that of " reduced hæmoglobin," and the fact that other gases, such as carbon monoxide, replace oxygen at saturation point in exactly equal volume to the oxygen required to saturate

It would appear from this conflicting evidence that the form of the pressure absorption curve as a criterion between adsorption and chemical combination breaks down, rather than to be proved that the uptake of oxygen by hæmoglobin is adsorption and not chemical combination

The other supposed criterion that there shall exist simple stoichiometric relationships at the saturation point between the two substances uniting also breaks down in the case of unions between colloids and crystalloids for several reasons.

For the apparent absence of stoichiometric relationship may be fallacious, and there may exist such relationships quite definitely, and true chemical union where there is apparently absorption, because the *total* mass of the colloid may not be identical or proportional to its *active* mass.   For example, the crystalloid, such as a dye, may not penetrate the aggregate of the colloid, and the chemical reaction may occur on the surface of the colloid only; and since it is impossible to estimate the active mass lying on the surface and participating in the reaction, exact relative molecular masses may be involved and yet there be apparently no such relationships.   Conversely, there may be no true chemical union and yet the masses of the two substances bear quite definite molecular relationships   For if we consider, for example, the protein molecule, with a given number of amidogen groups each chemically saturated as to valency, and yet each possessing a certain residual amount of basic affinity, and if now to this protein we add in increasing quantity a substance with weak and chemically saturated acidic groups, then we have a definite number of anchorages, and when the saturation point of absorption is reached there must appear stoichiometric relationships although there has occurred no condensation, and breaking apart would readily take place if the osmotic pressure or concentration of either constituent were reduced.

In this way a salt which crystallises with water of crystallisation has exact stoichiometric relationships with the water, and yet the water and salt, which are both saturated compounds, can only be held together here by residual affinities.

To carry this short sketch of the controversy as to adsorption *versus* chemical combination into detail would lead us far beyond the limits of this chapter, so we may sum up with the statement that between bodies of different chemical constitution there are varying grades of affinity for union. At the one end of the scale there are the typical chemical compounds, and at the other the more physical unions[1] of a weaker type, and dependent upon the maintenance of certain appreciable pressures or concentrations of the substances uniting, which have been called *adsorptions ;* but between these two there are all possible gradations, just as there are all possible stages between crystalloids and colloids.

Whether the theories and terminology of adsorption be accepted or those of the formation of easily dissociable chemical combination, or the middle view be taken that in some cases one occurs and in other cases the other, the important experimental fact which remains indisputable is that a type of union occurs which is only stable so long as a certain pressure (concentration) is maintained, and breaks up as the pressure diminishes, showing a range therefore at which association and dissociation of the union occur in a fluctuating way accompanying variations in pressures within the range.

---

[1] A great deal has been written as to the mode of physical union and how it is brought about. It has been shown that any substance which lowers the surface tension at a bounding surface or interface will tend to increase in concentration at that surface.   In this way the formation of surface films of protein and other colloidal solutions can be explained, similarly the formation of a layer of dye on a fabric may meet with explanation, and a great many if not all other cases of adsorption.   But the question remains, Why does the substance lower the surface tension ? and the view is still tenable that the surface tension is lowered because of chemical affinity for the substance forming the surface, or because the conditions on the surface favour chemical condensation of the substance to form larger molecules or aggregates than in the body of the solution.   Also, an attraction of residual affinities may attach the substance by adsorption, and after this anchorage true chemical union may follow,

This type of union occurs *par excellence*, and in endless variety both as to number of substances so uniting and ranges of pressure for union and disunion in the case of colloid with crystalloid, and in particular in living cells. Also in the building up of protein and bioplasm there occur endless varieties in the modes of grouping of the constituent radicles, which give rise to the selective affinities of the cells, and cause one cell to enter into selective union with one constituent of the plasma at a different level of pressure (concentration) from another, or to possess affinities of such a difference in order, that a substance is taken up with avidity by one cell and apparently refused altogether by another. The groups in cell and in substance entering into union with it are often so delicately arranged that the change of a single radicle alters the result entirely—as, for example, in the action of strychnine at very low pressure upon the nerve cells of the central nervous system changing at once and practically disappearing when a methyl group is added to the strychnine molecule, or the more slightly poisonous action of piperidine passing into the most virulent action of coniïne, when a propyl group (C_3H_7), in itself a harmless enough constituent, replaces one of the hydrogen atoms as a side chain

We may now pass to the consideration of the evidence that the various organic and inorganic constituents in tissue cells and plasma are held in loose union by the bioplasm or proteins.

First, in regard to the carbohydrate material present in the blood, it has been shown that if a stream of carbon dioxide be passed through a sample of blood, or if an anæsthetic such as chloroform or ether be added to it, and then it be subjected to dialysis, the amount of sugar passing into the dialysate is considerably increased above the amount in the case of untreated blood. It was at first supposed that this increased amount of sugar came from the blood-corpuscles, but more recent work has demonstrated that there is practically no sugar present in the corpuscles, and, further, a similar and equal increment in amount of sugar dialysing out can be obtained when clear serum is used for the experiment instead of whipped blood. If now a stream of air be passed through the serum in order to remove the carbon dioxide or anæsthetic before the serum is subjected to dialysis, it is found that the yield of sugar in the dialysate has passed back again to the normal amount.

This experiment would appear to demonstrate that the sugar in the serum exists in some form of feeble union with the protein which the action of the mild acidity of the carbon dioxide or the residual affinity of the anæsthetic is sufficient to break up, so leaving the sugar free to dialyse out.

This union of carbohydrate and protein throws a light on the glycosuria which follows hyperglycæmia. For in hyperglycæmia there is an excess of sugar above that which can enter into union with the protein, and it is this excess which is seized upon and thrown out into the urine by the kidney cells. From this point of view it is interesting to note that in the living animal, when there is more than a certain percentage of carbon dioxide in the respired air for a given period, even though there be in the air breathed more than the atmospheric proportion of oxygen, then there invariably appears sugar in the urine in very considerable amount. Also in the case of prolonged anæsthesia, especially if the concentration of the anæsthetic administered be increased to the maximum limit, there always appears sugar in the urine, often in high percentages. The author has found as much as 11 per cent. of sugar in the urine of dogs after ether anæsthesia, and has shown that the reducing material present is undoubtedly glucose by obtaining and separating typical glucosazone crystals in abundance.

In the liver cells there is undoubtedly union between the bioplasm and the sugar before glycogen is formed. The glycogen up to a certain maximum limit at which it separates as granules can also exist in union in the cell, for considerable amounts of glycogen can be separated from the tissues long before separated glycogen can be shown by histochemical methods.

Similar evidence has been obtained by different authors as to the formation of unions between cell proteins and fats. By certain procedures, such as partial interference with blood-supply (Bainbridge and Leathes), it has been possible to make the cells of certain organs, notably those of the liver, take on the appearances of fatty degeneration. The cells become loaded with obvious fat globules, which stain with all the usual histochemical staining reagents for fatty substances. It looks at first sight as if the amount of fat in the organ had been enormously increased, but the interesting point is that comparative analyses of normal liver with no appearance of fat in the cells, and of such liver cells apparently loaded up with.

fat, demonstrate that the amounts of fat in the two cases are about equal.

The normal liver tissue is capable of holding 5 to 10 per cent of fat in such form that it is quite transparent and invisible in discrete form, being in fact an integral part of the bioplasm. This can be done in no other way than by some type of union, for a fraction only of this fat in free condition would give a thick emulsion, showing obvious globules under the microscope, as it does when conditions are interfered with as above described, and the feeble union of the fat with the tissue broken up.

Similar results are seen in the chemical phenomena accompanying nerve degeneration Again in the plasma or serum itself a certain amount of union must take place, for, from a perfectly clear serum, showing no oil globules whatever under the microscope, as much as 0 5 to 1 per cent of fat may be taken out by organic extractives, such as alcohol and ether. Now this amount of fat, were there no agency to hold it in clear solution, would be sufficient to give a white milky emulsion. It is only when the capacity of the serum for holding fat in solution by feeble union with proteins is surpassed that the milky serum often found after a heavy fatty meal is obtainable, and this excess of fat is so soon taken into union by the bioplasm of the liver and other tissue cells, that in an hour or two no trace of any microscopically visible fat is seen in the serum or elsewhere.

In this capacity of the serum for holding in union in invisible form a certain amount of fat is found the solution of the problem of fat transference in the body from one tissue to another without any obvious carriage as an emulsion. By this power of solution of fat in bioplasm is also provided the mechanism for the oxidation of fats, for it is obvious that previously to oxidation the fat must pass into simple molecular form, and that it cannot be oxidised as globules of liquid fat

Apart from direct oxidation to furnish energy for the cell's work, it is obvious that these lightly held unions of the organic food-stuffs furnish the means for the chemical changes in the cell which give rise to those syntheses of one organic body from another which occur in animals as well as in plants; for the synthesis of new proteins by the union of protein radicles rich in amido-acids with carbohydrate radicles; for the synthesis of fats from carbohydrates; and for the elaboration of those products of cell activity which we know as internal secretions, lysins, antibodies, toxins, hormones, etc.

Turning now from the organic food-stuffs and the synthesised products of metabolism to the inorganic crystalloids of the cells and body fluids, we find abundant evidence of union in labile equilibrium between these and the organic constituents of the body—unions which are absolutely essential to the life and work of the cell, specific in character from one type of cell to another, and which owe their peculiar and effective functional power in the life of the cell to the very feebleness of the union which allows of interchange and reaction. So that we have stability of the whole system in the midst of and indeed as a consequence of the instability of the constituent parts.

The first evidence which may be quoted in favour of this form of union is the peculiar distribution of the inorganic salts and ions as between tissue cells and their environing fluids, the plasma and lymph.

Although the same inorganic salts are present in the cells of the tissue and in the blood-corpuscles as are found in the lymph and plasma, the quantitative distribution is very different in the two cases. The cells are rich in potassium and phosphatic ions, and relatively poor in sodium and chlorides, while the converse holds in the case of the bathing fluids of the cells.

This peculiar distribution finds an easy explanation on the basis that the proteins of the cells are so constituted chemically that they possess affinities for absorbing or uniting with potassium and phosphatic ions, and have no such power for holding sodium and chlorine, while the converse holds for the proteins of the plasma. For under these conditions, with the same osmotic pressure of dissolved constituents within and without the cell, any particular ion will increase in amount in the absorbed or united form in that particular region where protein is found possessing an affinity for it.

No other view which has been put forward furnishes an adequate explanation of this peculiar distribution of the salts. The other view which has obtained most adherence is that there exist membranes with peculiar and specific properties surrounding the cells which present a varying resistance to the passage of different ions. These membranes, which recently have been regarded as consisting of bodies called lipoids,[1] related to the fats and lecithins, are supposed to be easily permeable for some substances such as urea, ammonia, carbonic ions, and the anæsthetics; but difficultly or almost impermeable for other substances such as the usual inorganic ions of the plasma—viz., potassium, sodium, phosphates, and chlorides. As a result of this difficult permeability it is supposed that the potassium is retained in the cell and the sodium in the plasma, while anæsthetic, ammonia, and urea, for example, rapidly pass through.[2]

There are, however, fatal objections to this membrane view—viz., first, that while it makes some attempt at an explanation of the maintenance of the *status quo*, it fails entirely to explain how that condition was originally arrived at; secondly, it inextricably confuses factors which are of value in the velocity with which equilibrium is arrived at with the final conditions of equilibrium; and thirdly, it fails to explain the phenomena of cell interchange and the rapid physiological effects upon the cells of variations in the concentration of the ions in the external medium.

If the cell is almost impermeable to potassium ions, for example, it is difficult to see how it has become fully charged with them, and to many times the amount that these are present in the nutrient fluid outside.

Again, however poor the permeability, if there is no union between constituents within or without and the ion in question, it is obvious that when equilibrium has finally been attained, the concentrations at the two sides must be equal. Variations in permeability can only alter the time required to reach equilibrium, and not the final conditions of accumulation on the two sides corresponding to the equilibrium.

Further, anæsthesia cannot, as has been suggested by the up-

---

[1] The text merely refers to lipoids regarded as semipermeable membranes Using lipoid as a generic term to include the class of the lecithides and other forms of compound fats, there is no doubt that these play an important rôle in the life of the cells by means of their power of entering into combination or absorption with organic poisons and toxins But this is entirely different from a membrane action, being a formation rather of easily dissociable unions of the kind shown in the text to exist between bioplasm and organic bodies.

[2] The questions of cell permeability, and the arguments for the membrane view, may be found in detail in Hamburger's "Osmotischer Druck und Ionenlehre" For the reasons given in the text they have not been stated at length.

holders of the membrane theory, arise from greater solubility of the anæsthetic in the membrane, because that would only delay the arrival of the anæsthetic at the active part of the cell until the lipoid membrane had first been saturated with anæsthetic.

For this reason also greater solubility of any constituent in the cell substance itself will not explain the greater amount of concentration of any particular substance or ion in the process of secretion or excretion. Such greater solubility would serve to fill the cell up with it *and keep it there*, but would not hasten passage through the cell, and after the solubility in the cell substance had been satisfied, diffusion would then go on until the free concentration on the secretion side equalled the concentration on the lymph side, but not a fraction beyond this point.

With regard to increased or specific solubility in the cell substance as an agency in statically loading the cell up with a given constituent or ion, as distinct from passing it out again in heightened concentration in a secretion, it may be admitted that this would explain the accumulation; but this on closer examination is essentially the same view as that of union or adsorption with the protein, except that the adsorption or combination view goes a step farther and attempts to give a basis for the increased or specific solubility.

Even in the simpler case where a substance in solution divides itself in different concentrations between two solvents which do not mix with each other,[1] giving rise to the quotient of distribution, it is obvious that there is an equilibrium between the concentrations in the two media depending upon the relative affinities (or residual affinities) of the molecules of two solvents respectively for the molecules of the solute or dissolved substance.

One may therefore quite justly assign the unequal distribution of the various ions in cell and environing fluid respectively to different solubilities in the two media; apart from membrane action which is out of the question unless the somewhat absurd hypothesis be made that the accumulation remains and resides in the membrane. But knowing the nature of the constitution of the protein constituents, and that these must possess residual affinities or absorptive powers, it appears feasible to go a step farther and assign the distribution and different solubility to the formation of unions between protein or bioplasm and the ions.

[1] As, for example, an organic acid dividing itself between water and ethylic ether.

On this view the cell of any tissue or the blood-corpuscle is a system in equilibrium regarding ions with its surrounding medium, and the equilibrium is maintained by the pressure of each particular ion, acting independently, in the surrounding medium. Also variations in concentration of any of the ions will cause reaction and variation in the equilibrium of the whole, and may cause such disturbances as will alter the distribution of other ions and soluble substances, and so cause variations in the character and types of reaction of the protein or bioplasm.

Two chief factors determine the equilibrium between each ion and the cell, one of these is the concentration of the ion, the other the constant of association or adsorption between the cell substance and the ion   This constant changes its value specifically from one ion to another with a constant type of cell or bioplasm; and with the same ion kept constant varies from type of cell to type of cell, so giving rise to the specific picking out of particular cell types by particular ions or other bodies [1]

In addition to these chief factors, there is some evidence that certain ions can replace each other, or in other words compete for the same vacant places in the protein or bioplasm. This is known as the antagonistic action of drugs. Usually the ions so replacing must be of the same order of valency, a monad being unable to take the place of a dyad, but one dyad can replace another, and

---

[1] This might be put in simple mathematical form thus: If C_1 be the concentration of the protein or other substratum in a given cell, C_2 the concentration of the ion to be absorbed in the medium outside (lymph), and C_3 the concentration of the substance adsorbed, then $C_3 = KC_1C_2$, where K is a constant dependent on the chemical and physical affinities of the ion and other substance for each other, and hence having a different value when either ion or type of protein is changed   If now we keep the same ion, as in the distribution of any naturally occurring ion in the body, or in the action of any given drug which can only be given so that it is free to act on all cells in the body, then for a different cell, using small letters, we can write as before $c_3 = kc_1c_2$ where the suffixes show the same meaning as before. But now C_2 and c_2 the concentration of the ion or drug in the circulating medium is the same in both cells, and hence if we want to get the relative concentration in the two types of the cell we have $\dfrac{c_3}{C_3} = \dfrac{k}{K}\dfrac{c_1}{C_1}$, and further if we take it that the protein concentration is the same in the two cells, we finally have $\dfrac{c_3}{C_3} = \dfrac{k}{K}$, or the relative distribution is in proportion to the affinities between ion or drug and particular type of protein

especially two dyads in the same periodic group of elements are interchangeable. For example, one heavy metal can take the place of another, and even the paradox is arrived at that the poisonous action of one of these heavy metals is decreased by the simultaneous presence of another, so that instead of there being an additive effect of the two poisons, one balances the other and protects in part from its action, so that the lethal dose of either is increased.

The ions of the inorganic salts, at the same time that they are in a loose type of union with the proteins, possess a freedom of movement which shows itself in their giving to the solution in which they exist in common with the colloidal proteins many of the more important physicochemical properties of a saline solution. For example, in the case of the blood-serum, the depression of freezing-point is almost the same as that of an equal amount of salts dissolved in distilled water, showing that here every ion in the solution has its full effect in producing osmotic pressure notwithstanding its adsorption by the serum proteins. Again, the electrical conductivity is practically the same as that of an isosmotic solution of the saline constituents alone in distilled water, showing that any adsorption which may be present does not interfere in the least with the movements or velocities of the ions in the electrical field. Yet there is other evidence that the salts of the serum are in union of some type with the proteins, and that the amount of salts in the serum as regulated by the kidney cells is dependent upon the combining power of the proteins.

One fact that gives a clear indication of this is the titration value for the serum in presence of one of the more stable-coloured indicators, such as methyl orange or "di-methyl." It has been pointed out earlier in this article that the proteins can act either as acids or bases, or, as it is termed, are *amphoteric* to indicators. Thus, blood-serum is *acid* to phenolphthaleïn, and must have *alkali* added to it to produce the pink colour denoting alkalinity; at the same time it is *alkaline* to methyl orange or di-methyl, and requires the addition of much *acid* before showing the acid colour of the indicator.

The actual reaction of the serum is almost that of exact neutrality in the sense of physical chemistry—that is to say, the concentrations of hydrogen ion and hydroxyl ion are about equal. Now although it is essential that the colour of an indicator for acid and alkali

should change before the ratio of the concentrations of the two
ions becomes a high one, no indicator used in practice actually
does change exactly at the chemical or exact neutral point, and
the turning-point is different for each one.   Hence it is that blood-
serum *appears* to be acid when tested by phenolphthaleïn, and
appears to be alkaline when tested by methyl orange, etc.   Not,
as is too often stated, because it is at the same time acid and
alkaline, for that is absurd, but that its actual position in reaction
lies very nearly at the neutral point, and just short of that slight
degree of alkalinity which shows the alkaline colour to phenolphthaleïn on the one hand, and just short of that degree of acidity
which gives the acid colour to methyl orange.   Now these two
points lie very close together, for if instead of the serum we take
distilled water and add the two indicators phenolphthaleïn and
methyl orange in traces to it, then a single drop of dilute alkali
will develop the alkaline colour of the phenolphthaleïn, and on
the other hand a single drop of dilute acid will show the acid colour
of the methyl orange.

In the case of the serum, however, the result is quite different,
for very considerable amounts of alkali must be added before it
turns alkaline to phenolphthaleïn, and proceeding in the opposite
direction still larger amounts of acid must be added before acidity
to methyl orange is realised   The reason for this is that the proteins, which can figure either as acid or base according to whether
there is excess of alkali or acid respectively in the solution, must first
be satisfied before the indicators are affected, and as the amount
of protein is large, so the amount of acid or alkali required before
it is neutralised and the acidity or alkalinity can commence rapidly
to run up and affect the coloured indicator, is very considerable.

This is a factor of great importance to the life of the cells, which
cannot bear any appreciable degree of either acidity or alkalinity,
and are protected from such variations by the very delicate regulation of the reaction by the amphoteric proteins.

The regulating action of the proteins upon the reaction of the
serum has been mentioned here, however, because it gives a strong
indication that the proteins are in union with the inorganic salts.
If a clear sample of serum be titrated with methyl orange or " di-
methyl " as an indicator, an alkalinity equivalent to the very high
figure of 0 17 to 0·18 normal is obtained.   This alkalinity is chiefly
due to proteins, for if the salts of the serum be separated off by

21

dialysis or incineration and titrated to the same indicator, the alkalinity now amounts to only 0·03 to 0·04 normal. Subtracting these amounts due to inorganic constituents from the higher figure, we obtain the result that the combining power of the serum proteins alone for acid is equivalent to about 0·14 normal.[1] Now the interesting point about this figure is that it coincides almost exactly with the *total* osmotic concentration of all the salts naturally occurring in the serum or plasma. The depression of freezing-point of mammalian sera is on the average equivalent to that of a 0·9 per cent. solution of sodium chloride, and the molecular weight of sodium chloride being 58, this corresponds to a 0·15 normal solution.

In addition to this direct evidence from the chemical side, there are certain physiological correspondences between amounts of protein and crystalloid in the blood which must be obeyed, or otherwise the excess of salt in the plasma is removed by the kidneys. This action comes into operation as soon as the plasma salts exceed the amounts which can be loosely held by the proteins.

The salts in cells are held more firmly adsorbed or combined than is the case in the plasma, as is shown by effects on the electrical conductivity and by the difficulty of dialysing the salts from the cells.

Thus it is found that although the osmotic concentration of the salts in the red blood-corpuscles is nearly the same as in the plasma, as shown by the depressions of freezing-points,[2] yet the electrical conductivity of the separated corpuscles is only one-fourteenth to one-seventeenth of that of the separated serum. Part of this difference is mechanical and due to the envelopes of the corpuscles rendering the conducting fluid non-homogeneous; but even after removing this factor by laking, the conductivity of the laked corpuscles still remains only at one-fifth to one-sixth of that of the serum. This difference is undoubtedly due to the attachment of the ions to the hæmoglobin interfering with the ionic velocities, for on dialysing against distilled water and then reducing the volume of the dialysate to such a degree as to represent the original concentration of the salts before dialysis, it is found that the conductivity of the free salts in the dialysate has

---

[1] The amount of this combining power of the protein may be better appreciated by some if it be stated as equivalent to about 0·51 per cent. of hydrochloric acid.   [2] *Vide infra.*

undergone a further increase above that which they possessed
when in union with the hæmoglobin, and now lies at about one-
half the value in the serum. Even dialysis, however, is unable
to detach the phosphates from the hæmoglobin, and the above
conductivity of one-half is chiefly due to chlorides detached in
the process of dialysis. It is only after incineration and making
up to original volume that the conductivities of corpuscles and
serum become practically equal.

The following table illustrates these interesting changes in
conductivity accompanying detachment of colloid and crystalloid
in two experiments on separated blood-corpuscles and serum.
The figures give specific conductivity multiplied by 10^5 to save
decimals

	Sample I		Sample II.	
Treatment to which subjected.	Serum.	Corpuscles.	Serum	Corpuscles
1. Fresh	1705	95	1519	109
2. Frozen solid and thawed (corpuscles laked) ..}	1602	310	1468	237
3 Dialysed and volume reduced to original ..}	1843	891	1623	754
4. Incinerated and ash made up to original volume ..}	1608	1677	1697	1655

That the phosphates are more firmly held than the chlorides,
so that the union persists even in presence of a very low concentration of phosphatic ions in the fluid, is shown by the following
analysis for chlorides and phosphates in the dialysates of corpuscles
and serum respectively, and in the two cases after incineration.
The figures also illustrate the very different distribution of chlorides
and phosphates in corpuscles and serum respectively.

	Serum Percentages		Corpuscle Percentages	
	Cl.	P_2O_5	Cl	P_2O_5
Dialysis .. .	0·3657	0·0197	0·1331	0 0329
Incineration ..	0·3373	0·0219	0·1704	0·1708

Even the chlorides are more strongly held in corpuscles than in
serum, the figure on incineration being considerably higher than
after dialysis, 0 1704 as against 0 1331, instead of being slightly
lower, due to volatilisation with organic matter, as in the case of
the serum, 0 3373 as against 0 3657. In the serum the phosphate
figures are almost equal by the two methods, but in the corpuscles
the evidence of union is clear, only 0 0329 per cent. dialyses out of

the 0·1708 shown to be present by incineration. These figures are completely confirmed by freezing-point determinations.

This experimental evidence is interesting as showing that the special affinities existing in each case between protein and ion demand very different pressures or concentrations to preserve the equilibrium.

We can now understand why so little phosphate is required in the Ringer's solution; the union of the phosphates is so strong that it is not possible to run the phosphate concentration down to such a level as rapidly to disintegrate the phosphatic ions of the cardiac tissue. The merest trace given off from the heart to the perfusing fluid suffices to stop further loss. The level for calcium and potassium, though low, is somewhat higher, and traces sufficient to preserve equilibrium must be added, or these ions break free from the cardiac cells, producing irregularity of function. Finally, the sodium and chlorine ions are but loosely held, and hence as much as 0·7 to 0·9 per cent. of sodium chloride must be present to preserve the equilibrium and normal conditions of physiological activity.

The facts as to the constitution of the colloidal material and its relationship with electrolytes and other crystalloids which have been given above, and the interpretation put upon those facts, are intended to demonstrate that the living cell is a peculiarly constructed energy machine or energy transformer, dependent for its activity upon a delicate labile equilibrium giving stability as a whole, and yet a weakness of union causing disruption and oxidation of parts, and so furnishing energy. The view put forward is intended as a reaction from that view which complacently regards all the work of the cell and peculiarity in its constitution as being due to the physical properties of inert membranes.

The attempt has been made to show that something is required more than membranes and osmotic pressure to explain the peculiar distribution of electrolytes in cell and nutrient medium, and, going farther, to give a basis for the understanding of the peculiar energy exchanges of cells. It has been sought to invoke the peculiar chemical constitution of protein and bioplasm, and the varying equilibria of these with the materials brought in from the nutrient media at varying pressures, giving rise to transient stages of association and dissociation, and an accompanying play of energy changes.

It is not intended in doing this, however, to suggest that membranes and variations in osmotic pressure play no part in the cell's work or in preserving the integrity of the cell, nor to depreciate work upon osmotic conditions in cell life Because there are other factors to be reckoned with, it does not follow that osmosis is to be neglected In fact a wider appreciation of the phenomena of union between the bioplasm and crystalloid constituents widens rather than narrows our conceptions of the cell as an osmotic centre, by allowing us to regard the cell as a chamber with varying osmotic properties, both of contents and wall, rather than, as heretofore, as a more- or less fixed solution, bounded by a membrane of fixed properties also, and resembling a semipermeable copper-ferrocyanide wall.

The rigorous conception of the cell as analogous in all respects to a fluid medium holding crystalloids simply in solution and bounded by a semipermeable wall is .most pernicious in biology, for there are no experimental facts to warrant such a view, but rather, as has been shown above, quite the reverse.

The whole chemical structure of the cell and that part of it which is physiologically active *is* the osmotic machine, and needs no membrane permeable or impermeable in order to exhibit the usual osmotic phenomenon of shrinking or swelling, leading finally to disruption In some cases membranes in the narrower sense of the word are demonstrable surrounding the cell mass, and in other cases which form the vast majority no such coarsely structural membranes exist; but in all cases the nature of the bioplasm is so differentiated chemically as to form a dividing surface readily permeable to the solvent, and this is all that is required, in addition to the varying unions or holding powers between the cell colloids and crystalloids, to establish an osmotic cell As an example of what is meant here we may instance the swelling of fibrin, connective tissue, and gelatine under the imbibition of water. Between gelatine and water there is no structural membrane with semipermeable pores, yet the gelatine takes in water in a truly osmotic fashion, and the pressure developed, if the swelling and uptake of water are resisted, is very high.

It is hence necessary to get our minds rid of the preconceived idea. derived from too closely drawn analogies with experimentally constructed osmotic cells, that the cell membrane is responsible for the osmotic behaviour of the whole cell

If instead of this we take the view, which is supported by experimental facts, that the bioplasm holds the crystalloids in loose union in the cell, so that they cannot for the time escape or diffuse out, and yet admits of a degree of molecular freedom to the crystalloids, so that they still attract water molecules by residual affinity, then we arrive at a conception which is capable of linking together the osmotic properties of the cell, not merely in a statical but in a dynamic way, and gives a basis for understanding the variations in osmotic effects which accompany cell activities from one phase to another.

With the view of an inert semipermeable membrane of fixed properties, not sharing the varying changes in chemical constitution associated with life, or in other words not possessing the properties of bioplasm outlined above, all that can be arrived at is a continual tendency in one direction to a fixed equilibrium.

The other view, that the osmotic properties are developed by the bioplasm itself in its varying unions with crystalloids, gives room for that up-and-down play of properties which is the outstanding characteristic of living matter.[1]

For example, a circulating hormone, a drug substance, or a nerve impulse arriving at a given set of cells in a tissue, may activate the cells by momentarily disrupting unions between bioplasm and crystalloids or the reverse, and so may cause an uptake or a giving out of water accompanied by certain crystalloids free in excess to or from the cell, or may alter water distribution in varying parts provoking muscular contraction or other form of protoplasmic movement.

Similarly molecular movements of radicles attached to the bioplasm may be induced, causing changes in molecular arrangement and synthesis of new bodies within the cell. Further, the osmotic pressures and concentrations of the crystalloids and other bodies so set free need obviously bear no immediate relationship to the concentration of these substances in the plasma outside the cell, and so the very varying concentrations of secretions may be understood in a way that cannot be realised on any basis of pure osmosis or filtration.

The experimental facts of cell life, both in regard to the taking

---

[1] It is interesting to note that serum proteins exactly at their neutral point show no osmotic pressure whatever, but addition of minute amounts either of acid or alkali at once gives rise to an osmotic pressure which up to certain limits increases with amount of acid or alkali added.

up and giving out water and substances in solution, furnish a clear demonstration that neither osmosis nor any other physical hypothesis which leaves out the peculiar and varying chemical constitution of bioplasm can yield an explanation of absorption, secretion, or excretion.

The whole of the experiments lend support to the view that the living cell exists in a periodically or phasically varying *osmotic equilibrium* with its surroundings, and not in a state of osmotic equality with them. The cell by its union with crystalloids preserves a distinct osmotic condition within its bounds different from that in the surrounding fluid media from which its nutrient materials are taken up. This. is particularly well seen when the medium without is subject to considerable and accidental variations. Even in those cases where the outer medium is practically constant, as in the extreme case, for example, of blood-corpuscle and plasma, although there appears to be an existence of osmotic equality within the cell and without, yet this is due to the peculiar conditions having induced a close coincidence of the two sets of osmotic phenomena, and the existence of an equilibrium and not an equality may be easily shown by suitably varying the conditions. So that even in these extreme cases what we have to do with is not really equality of osmotic pressures, but an equilibrium which happens to simulate equality from the presence of reducing conditions, the equality disappears as soon as these reducing conditions are disturbed

When the corpuscles of whipped blood are separated as completely as possible from the serum by means of the centrifuge, and the depressions of freezing-point of the corpuscles and of the serum separately determined, it is found that the freezing-point of the serum lies on the average at 0 02° to 0 03° C. lower than that of the corpuscles. This difference, small as it is, is constant in its occurrence, and corresponds to a difference in osmotic pressure of approximately 200 to 300 mms. of mercury. If the corpuscles after separation from the serum are thoroughly shaken up with saline solutions weaker and stronger than the serum, or as they are termed, hypo- and hyper-tonic solutions, it is always found, on again separating corpuscles and saline by means of the centrifuge, that the depression of the freezing-point of the saline is greater than that of the corpuscles, no matter whether the saline employed was hypotonic or hypertonic. The differences become in these cases much greater than the natural differences between corpuscles and serum. These results show that there is established, as the concentration of the saline is varied, an equilibrium for each strength of saline, but not an equality, there always being a negative osmotic difference within the corpuscle.

In other types of cell these differences in osmotic pressure within and without the cell become enormously greater. Thus, in plants, the root sap which carries up the electrolytes from the earth for the nutrition of the growing cells is exceedingly dilute, the depression of freezing-point being only about one-fifth part of that of the cell juice. Similarly, in the secretion of sweat and saliva the concentration of inorganic ions, as shown both by freezing-point methods and by direct chemical analyses, is only a small fraction of that of the plasma or lymph. In other cases, such as absorption by the intestinal cells and secretion by the kidney cells, the osmotic pressure on the side remote from the lymph may lie either above or below that on the lymph side, but nearly always differs widely from it. It has been shown that either distilled water or hypertonic salines can be taken up by the intact intestinal mucosa; and the Δ (i.e., freezing-point depression) of the urine may be many times greater than that of the plasma, or may after ingestion or intravenous injection of much water be a mere fraction of the Δ of the plasma.

Whether the tremendous pressure differences corresponding to these differences in Δ really exist within the cells must remain indeterminate so long as we possess no knowledge as to the degree to which the crystalloids of the secretion are adsorbed while the secretion is passing through the cell and is in contact with the bioplasm. By alternating or periodic dissociation and combination between colloid and crystalloid in the actively secreting (absorbing or excreting) cell, the pressures would appear and disappear alternately; and if by the action of the nerve-supply or any stimulating substance the bioplasm is thrown into any such rhythmic activity of adsorption and reseparation, there would follow an easy explanation of the passage of both water and crystalloid through cells, in any concentration. For the concentration would depend solely on the uptake of crystalloid by the cell colloid, before the next explosion, disrupting colloid and crystalloid, threw the crystalloid free in the cell and determined, by the osmotic pressure developed thereby in the cell, the flow of secretion.

It would appear that in nerve and muscle at the period of activity only, and in injured tissue (which is excited or active tissue), there exists in reality a detachment of potassium ions from the colloid which does not exist before or after the active period (Macdonald).

It has been already pointed out that for each constituent passing into union with the bioplasm there exists an optimum concentration or osmotic pressure of solution in the nutrient medium of the cell which alone is compatible with normal physiological activity; or rather it might better be put that there is a range of suitable concentrations with a minimum and maximum which must not be passed in either direction.

This point is particularly well illustrated in the case of the respiratory gases   For both oxygen and carbon dioxide there are well-marked limits of pressure which are required to be satisfied in order that the processes of respiration and oxidation in the tissues may proceed in a normal fashion.

Since the energy for all tissue activity is derived from the oxidation of organic bodies it is obvious that there must be a minimal pressure of oxygen below which life is impossible, but it is not so obvious that there is an upper limit of oxygen concentration at which life becomes equally impossible.   Yet it is found that when warm-blooded animals are exposed to a pressure of about 3 atmospheres of pure oxygen, death occurs in a few minutes after violent convulsions (Bert).   Short of this excessive pressure, exposure to over 1 atmosphere of pure oxygen for a longer period leads, as shown by Lorrain Smith and L. Hill, to a pneumonic condition of the lungs.

If pure oxygen at atmospheric pressure be breathed for a shorter time interval, the tissues become charged with oxygen at a higher pressure than normal, and Hill and Flack have shown that for a short period afterwards muscular work can be done at a more rapid rate in such forms of exercise as sprinting, hill-climbing, and working against resistance.   After exhaustive muscular exertion also the breathing of oxygen diminishes the dyspnœa and sense of fatigue

On proceeding in the direction of testing the effects of percentages of oxygen less than the atmospheric, it is found that the results obtained depend upon the type of mammal experimented with and upon the state of quiescence or activity of the animal.

As the percentage of oxygen decreases the will and energy to do work diminish, and at a partial pressure of about half that present in the atmosphere any attempt at muscular work has to be abandoned, and the mental processes also become most sluggish.

The earlier experiments on the absolute minimum amounts of oxygen required to support life in animals in a state of quiescence were vitiated by the simultaneous accumulation of carbon dioxide from the respiration of the animals.

When means are taken to exclude this source of error by absorbing the carbon dioxide with soda-lime as rapidly as it is formed, it is found that animals (rabbits) can be kept alive for as long as forty hours on a respiratory mixture containing as little as 5 to 6 per cent. of oxygen. With slightly less than 5 per cent. of oxygen death occurs very rapidly.

These results, considered together, show that there is a minimum concentration of oxygen necessary for sufficient oxidation to support life; that as the pressure rises the degree of combination or union between bioplasm and oxygen increases, quickening the oxidation processes in the tissues; that an optimum of activity exists somewhere above the normal amount present in atmospheric air; and that still higher up embarrassment occurs from too high pressure, causing firmer union between the oxygen and bioplasm.

A very parallel set of results are obtained in the case of carbon dioxide. Here it might be thought that since carbon dioxide is a waste product of the oxidation process, the best possible condition would be its complete removal; but it has been clearly shown by Haldane that a definite minimal percentage of carbon dioxide is required for the regulation of the respiratory exchange, and that when the percentage is reduced by artificial ventilation, the subject passes into apnœa or suspension of breathing until the amount is brought back towards normal in the lungs and tissues. The normal amount of carbon dioxide in the alveolar spaces lies between 4 and 5 per cent., and if it rises or falls but slightly from the normal corresponding changes take place in the respiratory rhythm and depth which tend to restore the balance once more.

It has further been shown by Henderson that excessive and prolonged ventilation of the lungs by artificial means leads by lowering of the carbon dioxide concentration to irregularity of the heart-beat, and finally, if pushed, to *delirium cordis* and death of the animal Short of this limit, stoppage of the positive ventilation has the effect of restoring the heart to regular rhythm

Passing in the opposite direction, and observing the effects of increasing amounts of carbon dioxide, administered in artificial mixtures containing as high, or higher, amounts of oxygen as are present in atmospheric air so as to avoid asphyxiation from deficiency of oxygen, it is found that carbon dioxide has directly poisonous effects upon the bioplasm. Thus, with 12 to 15 per cent of carbon dioxide and 20 to 25 per cent. of oxygen, it is found that animals become somnolent, and, as above stated, that the urine contains glucose, while with 20 to 25 per cent. of carbon dioxide, even in presence of excess of oxygen, death rapidly occurs.

The same effects are seen upon isolated tissues. Thus Waller has shown that the first effect of minimal traces of carbon dioxide is to increase the excitability of nerve, while larger doses diminish excitability, and finally all excitability disappears. Similar results are found in unicellular organisms and in ciliary movements.

All these results point to varying degrees of union and corresponding stability or instability of union between carbon dioxide and bioplasm

Exactly similar results are everywhere evident in the application of various drugs in therapeutics, in the action of the toxins of disease, and in the action of anæsthetics and antiseptics There is the same stimulating action seen, followed by paralysing action as the concentration is increased and the union between bioplasm and drug becomes more stable and complete.

One of the most striking results here is the adaptation between drug and different types of cell, due to molecular variations in the structure of the two reacting bodies causing them to possess higher affinities and unite at lower concentrations. For this reason one type of cell takes up a drug and robs the other cells of it, lowering the pressure in these other cells and the plasma, so that the particular type of cell becomes loaded up at a pressure which scarcely causes any uptake in other cells.

On such a basis it is easy to understand why all mercury salts produce the same specific action in syphilis, the result being due to the free mercury ion and not being affected by the anion of the salt used except in so far as this quantitatively alters the degree of ionisation, and hence the concentration of mercury ion. Similarly, the ferric ion in all iron salts stimulates the production of erythrocytes in anæmia. So, too, quinine, and the alkaloids generally, furnish a basic ion affecting specific cells of the organism in each case, or of pathogenic foreign organisms present in it, for which at different stages they possess special affinities.

The same specific action due to different detail in structure of bioplasm, which we see exemplified in the selective action of drugs in the multicellular organism, is seen, and from the same cause, in the action of different drugs upon different stages of the same parasitic organism.

For example, quinine only attacks the malarial parasite when it is breaking forth from the erythrocyte. Again, the drug atoxyl acts on the ordinary motile form of the trypanosome, but rapid recurrence shows that it does not destroy the latent bodies, while mercury is shown, by the prolongation in the period of recurrence which it causes when given after atoxyl, to attack the latent bodies, although it has no action whatever on the ordinary motile stage.

The closer and more detailed study of the conditions of the formation of these unstable unions between bioplasm and the dissolved substances of its natural and artificially varied environment must furnish the key to many of the intricate problems both of physiology and of practical medicine; and it may perhaps be added that these subjects, whether studied in the laboratory or by the bedside, form one organic whole, for the subject of study in both is the living cell in all its wealth of reaction to changes in its environment.

BIBLIOGRAPHY

MOORE Articles in *Recent Advances in Physiology* and *Further Advances in Physiology*. Edited by Dr. Leonard Hill, F R S. Edward Arnold, London, 1906.

MOORE *The Origin and Nature of Life.* Home University Library, vol. lxii., 1912. Williams and Norgate, London.

MOORE AND WEBSTER *Synthesis by Sunlight in Relationship to the Origin of Life.* Proceedings Royal Society, B, vol lxxxvii , 1913

MOORE *The Presence of Inorganic Iron Compounds in the Chloroplasts of the Green Cells of Plants. Ibid.*

MOORE *The Formation of Nitrites from Nitrates in Aqueous Solution by the Action of Sunlight Ibid.*

MOORE AND WEBSTER *The Action of Light Rays on Organic Compounds, and the Photo-synthesis of Organic from Inorganic Compounds Ibid* , B, vol. xc , 1917

MOORE AND WEBSTER· *Studies of Photo-synthesis in Fresh-Water Algæ, etc. Ibid* , B, vol. xci., 1920.

MOORE, WHITLEY, AND WEBSTER *Studies of Photo-synthesis in Marine Algæ Ibid* , B, vol. xcii , 1920.

CZAPEK *Biochemie der Pflanzen*

MOLISCH: *Die Pflanzen in ihren Beziehungen zum Eisen*   G. Fischer, Jena

JAMIESON *Reports Agricultural Research Association*   Aberdeen, 1905-1911.

MAMELI AND POLLACCI *Sull' Assimilazione dell' Azoto atmosferico nei Vegetali* Pavia, *Atti Ist. Bot* , 1911

HENRI *Lois générales de l'action des diastases*   A Hermann, Paris

HOBER *Physikalische Chemie der Zelle und Gewebe*   Hirzel, Leipzig

HAMBURGER *Osmotischer Druck und Ionenlehre*   Bergmann, Wiesbaden

BAYLISS *Principles of General Physiology*   Longmans, Green and Co , London

Monographs on Biochemistry   Edited by Plimmer and Hopkins   Longmans, Green·and Co , London

333

SUBJECT INDEX

335

CPSIA information can be obtained
at www.ICGtesting.com
Printed in the USA
LVHW081055260421
685527LV00018B/95